To Cameron,

Best Wishes for Christmas + the New Year.

1972.

The GUINNESS Book of
Animal
Facts and Feats

Endangered Wild Mammals

(Large species with an "estimated" world population of 10,000 or less)

Species	Legal Protection Status	Estimated Numbers	
		1872	1972
MARSUPIALS			
Tasmanian "wolf" (*Thylacine cynocephalus*)	Full	3,000	10–15
PRIMATES			
Orang utan (*Pongo pygmaeus*)	Nominal	40,000	5,000
CETACEANS			
Blue whale (*Balaenoptera musculus*)	Full	20,000	7,500
Greenland right whale (*Balaena mysticetus*)	Full	18,000	1,000
North Atlantic right whale (*Eubalaena glacialis*)	Full	600	50–100
North Pacific right whale (*Eubalaena sieboldii*)	Full	4,000	80–100
Southern right whale (*Eubalaena australis*)	Full	80,000	5,000
CARNIVORES			
Red wolf (*Canis rufus*)	Nominal	7,000	75–100
Polar bear (*Ursus maritumus*)	Part	40,000	8,000
Giant Panda (*Ailuropoda melanoleuca*)	Full	600	200
Caribbean monk seal (*Monachus tropicalis*)	None	800	15–20
Mediterranean monk seal (*Monachus monachus*)	Part	5,000	500
ODD-TOED UNGULATES			
Przewalski's horse (*Equus przewalskii*)	None	2,000	40–60
Mountain zebra (*Equus zebra*)	Full	500	75
Sumatran rhinoceros (*Diceros sumatrensis*)	Part	4,000	170
Savan rhinoceros (*Rhinoceros sondaicus*)	Full	1,000	28
Great Indian rhinoceros (*Rhinoceros unicornis*)	Full	10,000	740
EVEN-TOED UNGULATES			
Persian fallow deer (*Dama mesopotamica*)	Nominal	14,000	50–60
Addax (*Addax nasomaculatus*)	Nominal	20,000	5,000
Tamarau (*Anoa mindorensis*)	Full	2,000	80–100
Kouprey (*Bos sauveli*)	Nominal	30,000	200
Asiatic buffalo (*Bubalus bubalus*)	Nominal	50,000	2,000
Walia ibex (*Capra walie*)	Full	1,500	200
Black wildebeest (*Connochaetes gnou*)	Full	70,000	2,100
Hunter's hartebeest (*Damaliscus hunteris*)	Full	3,000	1,500
Arabian oryx (*Oryx leucoryx*)	Nominal	6,000	400–500
Nilgiri tahr (*Hemitragus hylocrius*)	Nominal	4,000	800

The GUINNESS Book of
Animal
Facts and Feats

by
Gerald L.Wood FZS

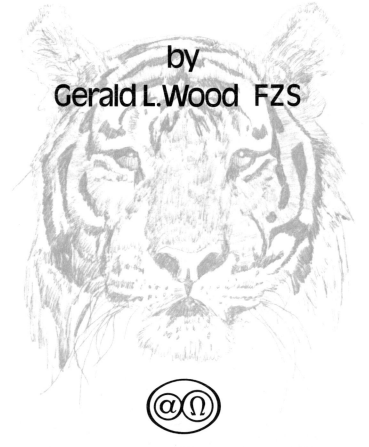

GUINNESS SUPERLATIVES LIMITED

2 CECIL COURT, LONDON ROAD, ENFIELD, MIDDLESEX

© 1972 Guinness Superlatives Limited

Published in Great Britain by
Guinness Superlatives Limited, 2 Cecil Court,
London Road, Enfield, Middlesex

SBN 900424 55 9

Set in Monophoto Baskerville Series 169,
printed and bound in Great Britain by
Jarrold and Sons Limited, Norwich

Contents

Acknowledgements

The subject of animals is so vast and complex that no single person could possibly write a book of this kind without utilising the work and researches of others to a very large extent. I am therefore immensely indebted to the many hundreds of men and women, some of them anonymous, who have contributed directly or indirectly to the text through their own zoological writings.

Similarly, this book could not have been written without the friendly co-operation of the Library of the Zoological Society of London, of which I am a Fellow, and I am especially grateful to the Librarian, Mr. Reginald Fish, and his two very able assistants Mr. John Owston and Miss Tinny Danos for generously placing at my disposal a mountain of books, journals and papers.

My special thanks also go to the many experts at the British Museum of Natural History, London who gave so liberally of their time and knowledge to answer my inquiries, and in particular to the late D. J. Clark of the Department of Zoology, who died suddenly while this book was still being written.

Acknowledgements are also due to Dr. Malcolm Clarke of the National Institute of Oceanography at Wormley, Surrey who read through the section of the manuscript dealing with cephalopods, as well as to Professor John L. Cloudsley-Thompson of Birkbeck College, University of London, who was suddenly hit by a barrage of awkward questions and came up with the answers in a remarkably short space of time.

Particular mention should also be made of the 180 or so correspondents listed at the back of this book who supplied me with much-needed information.

In addition, I would like to express my appreciation to Mr. Frank W. Lane, the well-known writer and naturalist, for his assistance and many helpful suggestions during the preparation of this book, and to my wife Susan for her enthusiastic support at all times.

Finally, I wish to thank Messrs. Angus and Robertson (Publishers) Ltd. for permission to include an extract from *Sharks and Rays of Australian Seas* by David G. Stead; also, the editor of the magazine *Animals* for allowing me to quote from the article "I saw a sea-monster" by J. D. Starkey; and the Marquis Cassar de Sain for permission to use his photographs of "Pronto", the heaviest bottle-nosed dolphin in captivity.

Introduction

In this book an attempt has been made to provide the answers to a host of questions connected with animal achievements—questions which the average reader cannot find by consulting generally available literature—and in the process expose many of the untruths and exaggerated statements that are synonymous with this fascinating subject.

Having had a more than average interest in zoology from a comparatively early age, particularly where extremes are concerned, I often used to pore over books at the local library for the answers to such vexing questions as the maximum length attained by the Great white shark, the longest period of time spent by an Edible dormouse in hibernation or the greatest altitude reached by a bird of prey like the Lammergeier, but it was invariably a fruitless task. There were plenty of publications in which the above-mentioned animals were discussed, sometimes at length, but none of them contained the *precise* information I was seeking. In the end I decided that the only solution to the problem was to write a book devoted entirely to animal superlatives myself; the result is this compilation.

Not surprisingly, the published facts regarding animal achievements are scattered through an incredible amount of literature printed in many languages and available only in large zoological libraries. In the course of my researches for this book I consulted over 2,000 volumes and something like 5,000 specialist journals and periodicals, and the sources of my information are listed in the extensive Bibliography at the back of this work, together with a list of the authorities with whom I corresponded personally. In addition, I have also quoted a number of anecdotes from popular sources to ensure that this record of animal achievement is not too statistical.

Although the basic theme of this book is animal facts and feats, and conservation is touched upon only lightly, it is imperative to mention here that the wildlife of this planet is presently decreasing at an alarming rate, and that many of the superlative creatures discussed in this work will have become extinct in the wild state by the end of this century—despite the splendid efforts of the international conservationists to save them.

The mass destruction of animal life by man began with the age of discovery. Since 1600 at least one per cent of our higher animals have become extinct, including the Quagga, Steller's sea cow, the Blauwbok, the Moa, the Great auk and the Passenger pigeon, and another three per cent are now on the danger list.

At the present time the most seriously threatened large species are the great baleen whales, and especially the Blue whale, the largest animal the world has ever known. This marine mammal is not recovering from over-exploitation because it has a long gestation period (i.e. eleven months) and normally gives birth to a single calf.

Before the invention of the harpoon gun in the middle of the nineteenth century there were probably 300,000 blue whales swimming the oceans of the world. By 1930 over-fishing had reduced this figure to about 100,000, and by 1938 to 60,000. In 1954 the total population was estimated at only 15,000, and by 1968 there were believed to be only between 650 and 1,950 blue whales left despite full protection. Fortunately this was an under-estimate and the world population is now thought to be in the region of 7,500, but even this figure is probably too low to ensure future survival.

Today the main threat to marine life is not so much man himself but his pollutants.

In November 1971 marine biologists at the Woods Hole Oceanographic Institute in Massachusetts, U.S.A. completed a twelve-month survey of the Atlantic Ocean, during which time they analysed hundreds of samples of plankton—the staple food of baleen whales—taken from an area stretching from the Antarctic to the Arctic and from the Americas to Africa and Europe.

They discovered that the plankton contained unexpectedly high levels of industrial pollutants known as P.C.B.s, which are closely related to the pesticide D.D.T.

The status of some land mammals is almost equally as precarious, and this is mainly due to the rapid expansion of urban civilisation since the beginning of this century.

Seriously threatened species include the Tiger, Snow leopard and Cheetah among the cat family, the Orang-utan and the Eastern gorilla among the primates, and the Giant panda.

In conclusion, in a book covering such a wide field it is only to be expected that a number of errors will occur despite the fact that every reasonable effort has been made to avoid them. The author will therefore greatly appreciate having mistakes or important omissions called to his attention by readers who feel qualified to do so.

SECTION I
Mammals
(class *Mammalia*)

A mammal is a warm-blooded, air-breathing vertebrate or backboned animal. It has a four-chambered heart and the body temperature is maintained by an insulating covering of hair or blubber. The brain is large and well developed. Young are usually born alive and are nourished on milk secreted from their mother's mammary glands.

The earliest known mammals were shrew-like creatures which lived about 190 million years ago, but practically nothing is known about their history. Their remains were first discovered at Thaba-ea-Litau, Lesotho, in 1966.

Living mammals are divided into (1) the primitive monotremes or egg-laying mammals; (2) the marsupials or mammals with pouches in which the embryonic young are nurtured soon after birth; and (3) the placentals whose young remain in the womb nourished by means of a placenta until they have reached a comparatively advanced stage of development.

These subclasses, in turn, are split up into 19 orders comprising 122 families and 4,230 species. Rodents account for 42 per cent (1,790 species) of this total, and bats for 23 per cent (981 species).

The largest and heaviest mammal in the world, and the largest animal ever recorded, is the Blue whale or Sibbald's rorqual (*Balaenoptera musculus*), which is also called the "Sulphur-bottom whale" because of the yellow film of microscopic plants (diatoms) often found on its underside.

Three races are recognised: the Northern blue whale (*B.m. musculus*) in the North Atlantic and North Pacific Oceans; the larger Southern blue whale (*B.m. intermedia*) in the Southern Hemisphere; and the Pygmy blue whale (*B.m. brevicauda*) in the southern Indian Ocean and Antarctic waters (Scheffer and Rice, 1963).

The average sizes of the three sub-species (both sexes) at physical maturity are listed in the following table:

Race	Male		Female	
	ft	tons	ft	tons
B.m. musculus	73	64	77	78
B.m. intermedia	79	85	86	109
B.m. brevicauda	67	54	72	67

Because of seasonal fluctuations in the thickness of the muscles and blubber, there are wide variations in the weights of individual blue whales at any given length.

For instance, in the captures of the Japanese whaling expeditions to the Antarctic in 1947/48 and 1948/49, Nishiwaki (1950) lists the following specimens:

The blue whale, the largest animal which has ever lived. This specimen measures 89 ft in length. ("Discovery" Committee, Colonial Office, London)

Sex	Length (ft)	Weight* (tons)
F	70	56·71
M	73	56·48
F	73	62·32
F	74	55·33
M	74	77·41
M	75	68·97
F	75	82·26
M	76	63·06
F	76	77·42
M	76	77·63
F	76	82·28
F	77	70·06
F	77	82·28
F	77	97·63
F	78	68·93
F	79	76·27
F	80	94·56
M	81	84·05
M	81	95·42
M	82	87·64
M	82	99·71
F	83	93·50
M	83	107·80
F	83	110·20
F	86	108·62
F	88	113·74
F	89	127·54

* Including blood and stomach contents.

The fattest blue whales were usually caught after the middle of January, although a few examples taken in December were just as heavy.

Some incredible lengths have been claimed for the blue whale in the past. For instance, a specimen with a length of 160 ft [sic] was reportedly washed ashore at Pondicherry, southern India, in 1757. Thompson (1856) says another one measuring 157 ft stranded in 15 ft of water at Spiddle, a small fishing village in County Killannin, Ireland, on 7th December 1843, but this figure must be considered a piece of Irish blarney unless, of course, it was a misprint for 57 ft. In December 1927 an insupportable length of 118 ft was reported for a blue whale caught off Victoria Land, Antarctica.

The largest accurately measured blue whale on record (length taken in a straight line from the point of the upper jaw to the notch in the tail) was a female caught near the South Shetlands (Falkland Islands Dependencies) in March 1926 which had a length of 33·27 m (109 ft 4·25 in). An enormous male measuring 32·64 m (107 ft 1 in) was also caught near the South Shetlands about the same time (Risting, 1928).

Seven other blue whales (all females) measuring in excess of 100 ft were also taken in the Southern Ocean between 1922 and 1925. The largest of these, measured at South Georgia by the Norwegian Tonsberg Whaling Company in 1924, had a length of 31·74 m (104 ft 2 in). Three of the others measured 31·40 m (103 ft), and the rest 31·08 m (101 ft 11 in).

The measurement from the point of the snout to the notch in the tail is known as the "total" length. The "over-all" length (projection of the lower jaw to the notch in the tail) is somewhat longer, but as the lower jaw is hardly ever in its natural position when the whale is lying on the flensing platform, this measurement is rarely taken. (One blue whale measured "over all" at Leigh Harbour, South Georgia, in *c.* November 1913, was 95 ft long, but the "total" length was 90 ft.)

Ivan Sanderson (1950) says the "record blue whale" measured 113·5 ft in length, but in a letter to the author dated 11th November 1970 he said: "It is more than possible that the measurement was taken over the curve of the back on a slipway. . . . ."

(A measurement taken along the curve of the body rather than in a straight line from the tip of the snout to the notch in the tail adds about another 6 per cent to the "total" length; this means that Sanderson's whale must have measured just over 106 ft.)

According to the *International Whaling Statistics* (Oslo) thirteen blue whales measuring 100 ft or more in length have been caught in the Southern Hemisphere since 1930. All of them were females, and their measurements were as follows: 100 ft, 100 ft, 101 ft (1930/31); 100 ft, 100 ft, 102 ft (1931/32); 100 ft, 100 ft (1932/33); 100 ft (1934/35); 101 ft (1946/47); 101 ft, 102 ft (1947/48); and 101 ft (1948/49). Most of these figures are probably reliable, but Mackintosh (1942) thinks that some of them may have been obtained by untrained whaling personnel. Even so, it is doubtful whether any of the measurements were much more than a foot or two out in the extreme.

Shortly after the First World War a female blue whale measuring 102 ft 4 in was brought into the shore station at Donkergat, Saldanha Bay, Cape Province, South Africa, and another one processed there at about the same time was longer than the 100 ft long flensing platform. Both whales were killed in Cape waters (Green, 1958).

The largest blue whales measured by members of the Discovery Committee's staff in the Southern Ocean between 1923 and 1926 measured 87 ft 5 in (male) and 93 ft 6 in (female) (Mackintosh, 1942).

Owing to the intensive exploitation of the Antarctic stock, very large individuals are now extremely rare. In 1947/48, for example, out of 6,908 blue whales caught, only one was over 100 ft in length, and the largest blue whale taken in the 1957/58 season measured 96 ft. Today, few if any Southern blue whales exceed 90 ft in length.

The largest accurately measured northern blue whale on record was a 98 ft specimen (probably female) which entered the Panama Canal from the Caribbean on 23rd January 1922. It swam up the canal towards the first locks at Gatun where, after threatening shipping, it was killed by machine-gun fire. The carcass was then towed by tugs to the Cristobal Docks, where unsuccessful efforts to raise it from the water were made with powerful 75 ton cranes. Its weight was estimated at 100 tons, but it was probably nearer 150 tons. The whale was towed out to sea and abandoned, but it later drifted ashore again at Nombre de Dios and, after being towed out once more, was bombed from the air by U.S. Army planes. Parts of the body subsequently came ashore at Santa Isabel, between Nombre de Dios and Cape San Blas, where the second and third cervical vertebrae were found by Mr. Mitchell Hedges, the English explorer and big-game fisherman, who later presented them to the British Museum of Natural History, London (Harmer, 1923).

Other reliable measurements over 90 ft include a 92 ft female killed by whalemen off Monterey, California, U.S.A. in 1862 (Scammon, 1874); a 96 ft female found floating dead in the North Sea in 1868 and towed into Vardo, north-eastern Norway (this measurement may have been in Norwegian feet, in which case the length would have been 98 ft 11 in) (Collett, 1886); a 92 ft female (with calf) stranded at Northmaven, in the Shetlands, in October 1860 (Turner, 1912); a 95 ft female killed in the North Atlantic by the American barque *Iceland* in *c.* 1870 (the weight of this specimen was calculated to be 294,000 lb or 131·2 tons) (Scammon, 1874); and a 92 ft female brought into the Balaena shore station, Hermitage Bay, Newfoundland, in May 1903 (Millais, 1906).

The largest male and female of thirty-six specimens measured by Cocks at the Norwegian shore stations in 1885 and 1886 were 85 ft and 87 ft 6·5 in respectively.

The largest blue whale in the 1919–29 American catches in the North Pacific was a female measuring 90 ft 3 in. The largest specimen in the Japanese catches (taken near Formosa) during the same period measured 27·4 m (88 ft 2·5 in), and the largest in the 1923–39 Russian catches near Kamchatka measured 26·5 m (88 ft 6 in) (Tomilin, 1957).

The largest accurately measured male blue whale recorded in the Northern Hemisphere was an 88 ft specimen killed near the Buneveneader station at Harris in the Outer Hebrides in 1904 which measured 38 ft in maximum girth (Millais, 1906).

In the early days of whaling lengths up to 120 ft were reported for blue whales taken in northern waters, but these figures are now considered unreliable.

Included in this category are: a 120 ft specimen cast ashore near Utrecht, Holland, in *c.* 1547; one measuring 101 ft which ran aground in the River Humber Estuary in September 1750 (Scoresby, 1823); a 105 ft long skeleton found near the mouth of the Columbia River, Oregon, U.S.A. on 8th January 1806 by Lewis and Clark during their expedition to the Pacific coast (the whale had been washed ashore a few days previously and the meat had been removed by the local Indians); one measuring 105 ft found dead in an inlet in the Davis Strait, Greenland, in *c.* 1815 (this whale was credited with a maximum girth of 38 ft, which suggests it was not much above average size) (Scoresby, 1823); a blue whale measuring 101 ft 8 in found floating dead in the North Sea between Belgium and England on 4th November 1827 and towed into Ostend (Dubar, 1828) (the skeleton of this specimen, now preserved in the Zoological Museum of the Academy of Sciences of the U.S.S.R. in Leningrad, measures 82 ft); a female measuring 102 ft found dead in Plymouth Sound on 27th September 1831 (Van Beneden & Gervais, 1889) (a more reasonable length of 79 ft has also been quoted for this specimen); a dead 117 ft blue whale driven ashore at Assateague Beach, near Snowhill, Maryland, U.S.A. in December 1833 (True, 1904); one measuring 98 ft 5 in stranded at Dunquerque (Dunkirk), northern France, in 1863 (Fischer, 1881); another example measuring 105 ft washed up on the island of Lewis, in the Outer Hebrides, in *c.* 1870 (the carcass was hacked to pieces for food and oil by the islanders before accurate measurements could be taken) (Figuier, 1892); a 102 ft 8 in female brought into a shore station on the Murman coast (European Russia) in 1883 (Guldberg, 1886); a 98 ft 5 in *male* beached at Oessant, northern France, in February 1893 (Beauregard, 1893); and a 102 ft *male* killed near Derejford, Iceland, in 1896 (Millais, 1906).

Nor can credence be given to reports of 30 m (98 ft 5 in) blue whales stranding on the coast of Bering Island (North Pacific) in 1742 (Berg, 1935) and 1929 (Barabash-Nikiforov, 1957).

In March 1965 a length of 32·99 m (108 ft 3 in) was claimed for a female captured by a Russian whaling fleet in the North Pacific and landed at Vladivostock, but subsequent inquiries (Louis, *in litt.* 6.10.65) revealed that the whale actually measured 27·3 m (89 ft).

In 1900 a blue whale measuring 90 ft ran aground in the River Thames at Gravesend. The carcass was towed to a factory on the Essex coast, just opposite Erith, where the blubber was rendered down.

Four blue whales have been stranded on British coasts since 1913. The last occurrence (about 60 ft) was at Wick, Caithness, Scotland, on 15th October 1923 (Harmer, 1925).

The Pygmy blue whale was not described until 1961. This race has a proportionately longer trunk than the northern and southern blue whales, and is correspondingly heavier (most of this extra weight is derived from its heavier internal organs). A 72 ft pygmy blue whale, for example, is about 4·5 tons heavier than a southern blue whale of the same length (Ichihara, 1961, 1966).

The largest accurately measured pygmy blue whale on record was a 24·1 m (79 ft) female captured by a Japanese whaling expedition in the Antarctic during the 1960/61 season. The male does not appear to exceed 21·6 m (70 ft 10 in).

The first piecemeal weighing of a blue whale took place at Balaena shore station, Hermitage Bay, Newfoundland in May 1903 under the supervision of Dr. F. A. Lucas, Director of the American Museum of Natural History in New York, N.Y., U.S.A. The 77 ft specimen scaled 63 tons, including blood, which accounted for 8 per cent of the total weight. The flesh weighed 40 tons, the blubber 8 tons, the blood, viscera and baleen 7 tons, and the bones 8 tons (Andrews, 1916).

A cast of this whale is in the U.S. National Museum, Washington, D.C., U.S.A.

Another blue whale, a gravid female, weighed piecemeal by Captain George Sorell (1928) at Stromness whaling station, South Georgia, on 8th November 1926, the day after it was killed, measured 27·18 m (89 ft 1·5 in) in length and weighed 122,040 kg (120·11 tons), including an estimated 8,000 kg (7·8 tons) for the blood. Height (lying on side) 3·10 m (10 ft 2 in); girth 13·90 m (45 ft 7·25 in); jawbone length 6·95 m (22 ft 9 in); flukes 5·90 m (19 ft 4·25 in); fins 3 m (9 ft 10 in). Weight: blubber 25,651 kg (25·19 tons); meat 56,444 kg (55·43 tons); bones 22,280 kg (21·4 tons); tongue 3,158 kg (3·05 tons); skull 4,508 kg (4·4 tons); jawbone 2,177 kg (2·09 tons); vertebrae 10,230 kg (10·04 tons); ribs 3,863 kg (3·43 tons); flukes 1,153 kg (1·13 tons); and fins 960 kg (0·94 tons).

This weight was exceeded on 27th January 1948 when Lieutenant-Colonel Walden C. Winston (1950) of the U.S. Army, General MacArthur's personal representative in charge of the First Fleet of the 1947/48 Japanese Antarctic Whaling Expedition, had an 89 ft female weighed piecemeal aboard the 10,000 ton factory ship *Hashidate Maru* in the Ross Sea.

This whale tipped the scales at 300,707 lb, or 134·2 tons, including an estimated 19,500 lb (8·7 tons) for the blood and stomach contents. Its measurements were as follows: maximum bodily girth 43 ft 6 in; jawbone length 22 ft 10 in; flukes 19 ft 10 in; fins 9 ft 6 in. Weight: blubber 19,970 kg (19·6 tons); meat 61,430 kg (60·3 tons); bones 18,590 kg (18·4 tons); tongue 3, 090 kg (3·03 tons); skull 4,610 kg (4·08 tons); jawbone 1,990 kg (1·9 tons); vertebrae 7,320 kg (7·1 tons); ribs 1,470 kg (1·44 tons); and fins 1,170 kg (1·14 tons).

It took eighty men three hours and forty-five minutes to flense, dismember and weigh this specimen, and the blubber, bones and meat were weighed on four platform scales, each capable of registering 200 lb. Twenty-five other men were working below in the processing section.

According to Lieutenant-Colonel Winston this whale was a "lean" specimen, and this is borne out by the small yield of blubber (i.e. 19·6 tons). He added: "Larger and heavier whales were caught by the expedition, but they were not officially weighed and recorded."

Two other blue whales weighed piecemeal by the Russians during the first cruise of the "Slava" whaling fleet in the Antarctic also scaled over 130 tons. One of them, a 27·6 m (90 ft 9 in) male caught on 20th March 1947, was stated to have weighed *190 tons*, but this figure must have been a misprint because the blubber, bones, flesh, tongue and internal organs, only added up to about 130 tons. The total weight of this animal was probably just over 140 tons. The other specimen, a 28·7 m (94 ft 2 in) female captured three days earlier, weighed 140 tons and yielded 32 tons of oil (Voronin, 1948).

A very corpulent 96·75 ft female brought into the shore station at Prince Olaf, South Georgia, in *c.* 1931 and processed by the Southern Whaling and Sealing Company, was calculated to have weighed 163·7 tons, inclusive of blood, judging by the number of cookers that were filled by the animal's blubber, meat and bones. The total weight of the whale was believed to have been 174 tons (Laurie, 1933).

Another female blue whale (no length given, but probably between 90 and 95 ft) killed in Walvis Bay, South-West Africa on 13th July 1924 and described as "very fat", yielded a record 305 barrels of oil weighing 50 tons (the yield from an average-sized southern blue whale is 80–100 barrels). Unfortunately, this enormous whale was not weighed piecemeal, but on the basis of its oil yield it must have weighed *a full 200 tons* (Risting, 1928).

On the principle that the weight should vary as the cube of the linear dimensions, a blue whale 50 ft long should weigh about 20 tons, and a 100 ft example about 160 tons.

Blue whales inhabit the colder seas and migrate to lower latitudes in winter for breeding. New-born calves measure 6·5 to 8·6 m (21 ft 3·5 in to 28 ft 6 in) in length and weigh up to 3,000 kg (2·95 tons). A calf's growth from a barely visible ovum weighing a fraction of a milligramme (0·000035 of an ounce) to a weight of about 26 tons in twenty-two and three-quarter months (made up of ten and three-quarter months gestation and the first twelve months of life) **is the most rapid growth in either the animal or the plant kingdoms**. This is equivalent to an increase of 30,000 millionfold.

During the 1947/48 whaling season R. W. Gawn (1948), a British scientist, carried out some speed tests on the blue whale in Antarctic waters. He found that it could maintain a speed of 20 knots (23 miles/h) for ten minutes when frightened, 14·5 knots (16·6 mile/h) for two hours, and keep ahead of a whaling ship travelling at 10 knots (11·5 mile/h) all day. He also calculated that a 90 ft blue whale would need to develop 520 hp to propel its smooth, rigid body along, or about 4 hp per ton of body weight. There is a record of a harpooned blue whale towing a catcher at 7 mile/h for several hours, although the ship's engines were working full speed astern. **This must be the ultimate in animal power**.

In 1930 there were an estimated 100,000 blue whales roaming the world's oceans, and in 1934 30,000 were caught in a single season in the Antarctic. By 1953, however, the stocks had been reduced to 15,000 through unrestricted slaughter, and in 1968 the total world population was estimated to be no more than 600–700 (500–600 in the Antarctic, and about 50–100 elsewhere) despite full protection.

Fortunately, this figure has since been found to be too low. In mid 1971 another survey put the number of blue whales in the Southern Hemisphere at 6,500 and increasing, with another 1,000 in the North Pacific and North Atlantic, and it now looks as though the species will survive in reasonable numbers under careful protection, if it isn't killed by industrial pollutants.

Studies of the growth period in the baleen plates of the blue whale (Tomlin, 1945; Ruud, 1950; Nishiwaki, 1950), and the counting of layers in the wax-like structure in the opening of the ear (Roe, 1967), indicate that both sexes reach physical maturity at the age of six years, and that the life-span is twenty-five to thirty years under natural conditions.

The greatest recorded depth to which a whale had dived, until quite recently was 620 fathoms (3,720 ft) by a 47 ft bull Sperm whale (*Physeter catodon*) found with its jaw entangled with a submarine telephone cable running between Santa Elana, Ecuador and Chorillos, Peru, on 14th October 1955 (the sperm whale probably became entangled in the cable as it skimmed along the bottom with open jaw in search of its natural prey, the giant squid). At this depth the whale withstood a pressure of 1,680 lb per square inch (Heezen, 1957).

It has since been discovered, however, that sperm whales can dive much deeper than this. On 25th August 1969 Dr. Malcolm Clarke (*in litt.* 14.9.71) of the National Institute of Oceanography, Wormley, Surrey, flew in an aircraft on spotter patrol for the Durban Whaling Company. During the flight he carried out some observations on two sperm whales in an effort to establish the durations of their dives. One of them remained below for fifty-three minutes, and the other for one hour and fifty-two minutes. Shortly afterwards both whales were caught by the whaling fleet, and inside the stomach of one of them were found two small sharks which must have been swallowed about an hour earlier. These were later identified as *Scymnodon* sp., which are found *only* on the sea-floor. At this point from land—93 miles—the depth of water is in excess of 1,746 fathoms (10,476 ft) for a radius of 30–40 miles. It therefore seems highly probable that the sperm whale can dive to a far greater depth than had hitherto been realised.

The fastest-swimming whale over short distances is probably the Sei whale (*Balaenoptera borealis*) which, when harpooned, "dashes off at a tremendous pace for perhaps a third of a mile or less" (Andrews, 1916). The same writer says this species can attain a speed of 30 knots (35 mile/h) on the surface during its initial rush.

During migration the Springbok (Antidorcas marsupialis) of South Africa travelled in the largest herds ever recorded. One "Trek-Bokke" observed moving between Prieska and Bittersprut, Cape Province in 1888 was estimated to contain 100,000,000 head.

The Pronghorn antelope (Antilocapra americana) of the western United States is the fastest of all land animals over a sustained distance. Specimens have been observed to travel at 55 mile/h for half a mile. (W. Miller/F. Lane.)

Recent observations of Fin whales (*Balaenoptera physalus*) in the Antarctic frightened by the echo-sounding Asdic apparatus of whale-catchers suggest that their top speed is also in the region of 30 knots (Slijper, 1961). Speeds up to 30 knots have also been quoted for the blue whale over short distances, but it is doubtful whether this species is as swift as the sei and fin whales. The normal cruising speed of all three species is 10–15 mile/h.

In 1960 Johannesen and Harder timed a large bull Killer whale (*Orcinus orca*) at 30 knots as it approached their ship. It then circled the vessel, which was travelling at 20·6 knots, for 20 minutes (Stenuit, 1969). Other observers (Maxwell, 1952; Blond, 1953) believe that this powerful marine predator can reach 40 mile/h for short bursts when chasing prey (despite its name, the killer whale is classified as a dolphin).

Speeds of 30–32 knots (35–37 mile/h) have been reported for Common dolphins (*Delphinus delphis*) riding the bow waves of destroyers (in bow-wave riding the dolphin attains its propulsive power from the moving vessel, while remaining almost motionless), but without this benefit the swimming speed is slower (maximum about 20–25 knots). Trained Leopard dolphins (*Steno rostratus*?) at Sea Life Park, in Hawaii, have been timed at 26 knots (29·9 mile/h), but they may be capable of even higher speeds.

Most dolphins are excellent jumpers. In 1962 a 500 lb Bottle-nosed dolphin (*Tursiops truncatus*) named "Pedro" reached a pole set 20 ft above the water at Marineland of Florida, St. Augustine, Florida, U.S.A. Specimens of the False killer whale (*Pseudorca crassidens*) at the Miami Seaquarium, Florida and the Sea Life Park, Hawaii have also been credited with perpendicular leaps of 20 ft.

During a big-game fishing expedition in the Virgin Islands, Zane Grey (1936) saw a young killer whale weighing about 2,000 lb shoot out of the water at tremendous speed and describe a wide arc. He estimated that the giant dolphin attained a height of 20 ft at the peak of its jump, and this is borne out by photographic evidence. Killer whales, of course, are noted for their spectacular leaping when attacking large whalebone whales.

In 1950 a blue whale was observed to jump clean out of the water— a staggering feat for a marine animal of this size—off Durban, South Africa and crash back into the sea with what must be the ultimate in "belly flops".

In September 1970 U.S. Navy scientists working in the Antarctic reported that the "voice" of the blue whale carries for 100 miles under water and hits the key of C. The sounds, which are probably a simple form of communication, occurred at regular 100 second intervals.

The largest marine mammal ever held in captivity was "Namu", a 6·5 m (21 ft 4 in) bull killer whale. This specimen was caught in a salmon-net in Fitzhugh Sound, British Columbia, Canada on 23rd June 1965 and sold to Edward I. Griffin, Director of the Seattle Public Aquarium, who had the 4 ton animal towed in a floating pen to a cove 15 miles from Seattle for public exhibition. Namu drowned on 9th July 1966 after getting entangled in the netting surrounding his pen while trying to escape.

In April 1968 a 20 ft long bull killer, four cows and two calves were netted in Pender Harbour, British Columbia, Canada.

The Piked whale (*Balaenoptera acutorostrata*) has also been kept in captivity in Japan. One specimen captured in 1957 reportedly measured over 20 ft in length, but further details are lacking.

The largest marine mammal held in captivity today is a 21 ft long Pacific grey whale (*Eschichtius gibbosus*) at the Sea Aquarium in Mission Bay, San Diego, California, U.S.A. which weighed an estimated 8,100 lb (3·61 tons) in June 1971 (Jones, 1971).

In September 1970 a bull killer named "Orky" at Marineland of the Pacific, California, U.S.A. measured 20 ft in length and weighed 6,200 lb (2·76 tons).

WHALES (maximum lengths and weights)

Species	Maximum length		Weight
	ft	in	tons
Blue whale (*Balaenoptera musculus*)	109	3·5	190*
Fin whale (*Balaenoptera physalus*)	90	0	97*
Sei whale (*Balaenoptera borealis*)	72	0	45*
Sperm whale (*Physeter catodon*)	67	10	72*
Greenland whale (*Balaena mysticetus*)	67	0	83*
Humpback whale (*Megaptera novaeangliae*)	65	0	64*
Right whale (*Balaena glacialis*)	60	0	71
Bryde's whale (*Balaenoptera edeni*)	59	0	31·5
Pacific grey whale (*Eschrichtius gibbosus*)	51	0	39
Berardius (*Berardius bairdi*)	41	0	16·5
Piked whale (*Balaenoptera acutorostrata*)	34	0	9

* Weight computed.

The largest living terrestrial animal is the African bush or savannah elephant (*Loxodonta africana africana*), which was formerly considered a full species. The average adult bull stands 10 ft 6 in at the shoulder and weighs 5·6 tons. The average adult cow is much smaller, standing 8 ft 6 in at the shoulder and weighing about 2·5 tons (most authorities give the weight of an adult cow as about 4 tons, but recent weighings in the field have shown that it is a lighter animal than had hitherto been realised).

At one time the bush elephant ranged over the entire African continent, but commercial exploitation, the expansion of cultivated land and the degeneration of grassy plains to desert, have greatly reduced its range over the past hundred years. Today its numbers (about 300,000) are largely concentrated in wildlife parks and game reserves in central, eastern and southern Africa.

"Wandle Robert", Britain's tallest horse posing with Christopher Greener, Britain's tallest man who stands 7 ft 5 in. A 6 ft rule is shown for comparison. (G. Wood.)

The Masai giraffe (Giraffa camelopardalis tippelskirchi) of Kenya and Uganda is the tallest living animal. Adult bulls have been measured up to 19 ft 3 in to the tips of the "horns". (F. Lane.)

"Orky", the largest killer whale living in captivity today. (Fox Photos.)

The largest accurately measured African bush elephant on record, and the largest recorded land animal of modern times, was an enormous bull shot by J. J. Fenykoevi, the Hungarian big-game hunter, 48 miles north-north-west of Macusso, Angola, on 13th November 1955. This bull was so huge that it required *sixteen heavy calibre bullets* from an 0·46 Rigby rifle before it finally succumbed. Lying on its side this mountain of flesh measured 13 ft 2 in in a projected line from the highest point of the shoulder to the base of the forefoot, which means that its standing height must have been about 12 ft 6 in (height measurements of wild elephants taken after death are about 5 per cent greater than the living height because the great weight tends to spread the body out laterally in all directions).

Other measurements included an over-all length of 33 ft 2 in (tip of extended trunk to tip of extended tail) and a maximum bodily girth of 19 ft 8 in. The weight was estimated at 24,000 lb (10·7 tons).

Tracks of this colossal elephant were first discovered by Jose Fenykoevi in 1964 while he was out hunting rhinoceros in the uninhabited and largely unexplored Cuando River region of Angola. The following year he organised a special expedition from his hunting-lodge at Humpata.

The skin of the "Fenykoevi Elephant" reportedly weighed more than

2 U.S. short tons (4,000 lb) and required a truckload of salt for preservation in the field. Fenykoevi says his crew of twenty-three native porters could not lift it between them. A week was needed to transport the skin (and bones) by truck through hundreds of miles of wilderness to the railhead at Silva Porto, 600 miles from the coast. Eight months later the remains arrived in Madrid in specially made zinc cases, and were put in the air-cooled cellar under Mr. Fenykoevi's home.

In September 1956 Mr. Fenykoevi flew to London for discussions with Rowland Ward Ltd., the famous Piccadilly taxidermists, to find out if they could stuff the elephant. He also asked the British Museum of Natural History, London, if they would be interested in putting the mounted

The fabulous "Fenykoevi Elephant", the largest recorded land animal of modern times. (Smithsonian Institution, Washington, D.C.)

elephant on exhibition. In the end, however, after talks with the Director of the U.S. National Museum in Washington, D.C., U.S.A., it was decided that the elephant would go to that institution. "They are the only people who can spare the space this elephant deserves and must have," said Mr. Fenykoevi.

In a letter to the author dated 21st October 1966, Mr. Charles O. Handley, jun., Curator of Mammals at the U.S. National Museum, wrote:

"The mammalogists on our staff reviewed the first reports of the size of this elephant with considerable scepticism, but their doubts were dispelled when the specimen itself and a full set of photographs and measurements, made immediately after it was killed, arrived in Washington.

"Mr. J. J. Fenykoevi, who shot the elephant and measured it personally, is himself an engineer with a lifetime of experience in dealing with precise dimensions. He was well aware of the importance of these measurements as scientific data and as a guide for the taxidermists. Knowing that measurements of this enormous animal might be questioned, he took the precaution of obtaining affidavits from witnesses, sworn to before the local Portuguese authorities in Angola. For these reasons, we feel that more confidence can be placed in Mr. Fenykoevi's measurements than in those of the average big-game hunter.

"The shoulder height of 13 ft 2 in was obtained by measuring the elephant lying on its side as it fell when it was shot. Mr. Fenykoevi has shown films of this process, including the position and reading of the measuring-tape, and we do not see how it could have been carried out more accurately under the conditions existing at that time and place."

Only the limb bones, skull and tusks of this monstrous elephant were sent to the U.S. National Museum with the skin, so it was not possible to assemble and take measurements of the skeleton.

The elephant, as it now stands in the Museum rotunda supported by a relatively light wooden armature, measures 13 ft 2 in from the level of the shoulder to the floor in a straight drop (taxidermists who set up elephant specimens soak the hide for a long time in water in order to soften and make it pliable enough to work with; consequently, there would have been little difficulty in giving the "Fenykoevi Elephant" the shoulder height reported for it in the field).

Another outsized African bush elephant known as "Zhulamati" ("Taller than the Trees") may have equalled the "Fenykoevi Elephant" in size. Experienced game-rangers in Rhodesia familiar with this animal said he stood "well over 12 ft at the shoulder", and one of his giant tusks was so long that it trailed along the ground.

According to the Shangaan tribesmen of south-eastern Rhodesia, a notorious ivory-poacher and hunter named Bvekenya Barnard, with 300 elephants to his credit—or discredit—tried to track down this massive bull in 1929. Eventually he spotted the huge pachyderm and inflicted a slight shoulder wound, but the great beast then disappeared into the bush. A few days later Barnard had the elephant in his sights again, but he was reportedly so overwhelmed by the animal's extraordinary size that he hung up his guns, vowing never to hunt again. Some hunters, however, assert that this just does not fit the Barnard character (*Rhodesia Herald*, 26th November 1970).

From that day onwards, the story goes, hunters and game-rangers alike swore never to shoot this lord of the bush, even if he wandered into a tsetse-fly control corridor where animals are automatically shot on sight. Over the years there were unconfirmed sightings of him in Portuguese East Africa and South Africa as well as Rhodesia, and he appeared to be domiciled in an area where all three countries are close to each other (King, *in litt.* 2.12.66).

In 1959 Mr. B. J. Olivier, a roads overseer who has worked in the Lowveld for many years, spotted Zhulamati near Chipinga Pools in south-eastern Rhodesia, and there were several other sightings of this elephant right up to January 1965. After that, the enormous bull dropped from sight until 1967 when he was killed in mysterious circumstances in the Gonare Zhou area of Nuanetsi, south-eastern Rhodesia by a high-ranking South African policeman on safari in the area.

According to the *Rhodesia Herald* (2nd December 1970) the whole trip was hushed up by officialdom (two *game-rangers* were present at the killing), but so far the Rhodesian Government has remained silent on the issue.

In August 1950 P. K. van der Byl shot another huge tusker in the Cuando River region which measured 12 ft 6·5 inches in the prone position (standing height about 11 ft 11 in) and had an over-all length of 29 ft 11·5 in (Rowland Ward, 1962).

Other African bush elephants for whom shoulder heights of 12 ft or more between pegs have been claimed include: a 12 ft bull shot by William Cornwallis Harris (1839) in South Africa in 1836, and another one killed there in *c.* 1849 by William Cotton Oswell which measured 12 ft 2 in; an enormous bull shot by the Duke of Edinburgh (Prince

Alfred, second son of Queen Victoria) in the Knysna Forest, South Africa, in 1875 which reputedly measured 13 ft at the shoulder and 32 ft over-all (the girth of this animal was given as 28 ft, but this must be a misprint for 18 ft) (Bisset, 1875); and a bull shot by A. Haig on the Blue Nile (Sudan) which was estimated by him (on the basis of the circumference of the elephant's forefoot) to have measured "over 13 ft at the shoulder" (the ears of this specimen were enormous, measuring 6 ft 5·5 in in vertical diameter and 4 ft 1·5 in in transverse diameter, and probably constitute a *record* in themselves) (Lydekker, 1907).

Another bull shot by Edouard Foa (1899), the famous French explorer, in the part of the Belgian Congo adjoining Tanganyika in *c.* November 1897, reportedly measured 12 ft 2·5 in between pegs.

Two bulls shot by Major P. J. Pretorius (1947), the famous South African hunter, in Knysna Reserve, South Africa, in *c.* 1920 were credited with shoulder heights of 12 ft 8 in and 13 ft respectively in the Press (Major Pretorius himself said one of them measured 12 ft 6 in at the shoulder and was 22 ft 6 in over-all), but these measurements were grossly exaggerated. According to official museum records in Cape Town, where the larger of the two animals was stuffed and put on display, the shoulder height was only 9 ft 4 in.

A large tusker shot by Sir William Gowers, Governor of Uganda from 1925 to 1932, was stated to have measured 12 ft at the shoulder, and another bull reputedly measuring 3·8 m (12 ft 5·5 in) was shot near Fada N'gourma, French West Africa (Bigourden & Prunier, 1927). In 1929 a mighty bull said to have measured 12 ft at the shoulder was found dead on the Nile bank just below the Murchison Falls, apparently from old age (Pitman, 1953), and the famous "Mohammed" or "Ghost Elephant" of Marsabit Mountain Reserve in Kenya was credited with the same shoulder measurement between pegs at the time of its demise in 1960.

A number of other African bush elephants measuring between 11 and 12 ft at the shoulder between pegs have also been reported. Probably the most famous example was the 11 ft 6·5 in bull shot by Major P. H. G. Powell-Cotton near Wadelai, on the Upper Nile, Uganda, in 1906 (the set-up forelimb or humerus in the Quex Park Museum, Birchington, Kent, is equal to a skeletal height of 10 ft 9·25 in) (Rowland Ward, 1907).

Messrs. E. S. Grogan and A. H. Sharp (1900) shot another bull measuring 11 ft 6 in (circumference of forefoot 63 in) in Toro, East Central Africa, in *c.* 1898, and Mr. Grogan killed another large tusker in the same locality which measured 11 ft 2 in (circumference of forefoot 60 in).

Arthur Neumann (1898), probably the greatest of all elephant-hunters and a very reliable observer, shot two tuskers in East Africa measuring 11 ft 3 in, and Colonel James J. Harrison killed another large bull in Mozambique which measured 11 ft 1 in (Rowland Ward, 1935). Another specimen shot by H. Weld-Blundell in Abyssinia (Ethiopa) before 1907 measured 11 ft 8·5 in (Rowland Ward, 1907).

Denis Lyell (1924) says he shot an exceptionally large bull in north-eastern Rhodesia in *c.* 1904 which he estimated measured 11 ft 9 in at the shoulder, but the animal fell awkwardly against a good-sized tree and he found it impossible to measure its height properly.

In 1905 T. Alexander Barns (1922) shot a large tusker measuring 11 ft 4 in at the shoulder near Fort Manning, in Nyasaland. It had an over-all length of 28 ft 6 in and a maximum bodily girth of 17 ft 4·5 in. This specimen was later mounted and put on display in the British Museum of Natural History, London.

Abel Chapman (1908), the famous American big-game hunter, shot an 11 ft 3 in tusker at Lake Solai, Kenya, on 23rd February 1906, and the same height was reported for a bull shot by Major Powell-Cotton in the Lado Enclave, Sudan, in December 1904 (now mounted in the Royal Scottish Museum, Edinburgh).

A large tusker collected by Carl K. Akeley (1912), the American naturalist, in the Budongo Forest, east of Lake Albert, north Uganda, in 1909 for the African Hall in the American Museum of Natural History in New York, N.Y., U.S.A. measured 11 ft 4 in (the mounted specimen measures 10 ft 8 in at the shoulder). His wife Mary shot a rogue bull in Uganda which measured 11 ft 3 in, and he killed another bull near Mount Kenya which measured 11 ft 2 in (now on display in the Field Museum of Natural History in Chicago, Illinois, U.S.A.).

During his expedition to the Ituri Forest region of the Congo on behalf of the Belgian Government in 1912–14, Dr. Cuthbert Christy (1924) shot a large tusker measuring 3·4 m (11 ft 1 in) at the shoulder. Another big tusker shot by Mary Hastings Bradley (1927) at Katiabu in the Congo measured 11 ft 2·5 in.

The Bulawayo Museum has a mounted bull measuring 11 ft 7 in at the shoulder and 28 ft 5 in overall. It was shot in southern Rhodesia in June 1960 (Rowland Ward, 1962).

The shoulder height of an adult African bush elephant corresponds roughly to the width across the expanded ears or six times the forefoot diameter.

The largest African bush elephant ever held in captivity was probably the famous "Jumbo", who was acquired by the London Zoological Gardens on 26th June 1865 from the Jardin des Plantes in Paris in exchange for an Indian rhinoceros (the elephant had been caught originally south of Lake Chad in the French Sudan, although another source claims he was captured by some Arabs on the banks of the Settite River in Ethiopia). Jumbo was then two years old and measured 5 ft 6 in at the shoulder and 9 ft 6 in in maximum bodily girth. His height progressed as follows:

Age in years	Height ft	in	Age in years	Height ft	in
3	6	5	10	8	11
4	7	1	11	9	3
5	7	9	12	9	7
6	7	10·5	13	9	8
7	7	10·5	14	10	3
8	8	1	15	10	6·5
9	8	8·5	16	10	9

Jumbo was an unusually docile animal, and soon became a zoo favourite, carrying thousands of children in a howdah fitted to his back. However, he gradually became less reliable as he neared maturity, and by 1881 only his keeper, Matthew Scott, could approach him.

In January 1882, after two days of private negotiations with the London Zoological Society, Jumbo was sold to Phineas T. Barnum, the famous American showman, for £2,000. At that time the elephant allegedly stood 11 ft at the shoulder and could reach an object 26 ft from the ground with his trunk. His weight was given as 6·5 tons (Bartlett, 1898).

All England wept at this "dastardly deed", and there was a storm of protest throughout the country. Even Queen Victoria demanded that the contract be declared null and void. But it was to no avail. On 9th March 1882 the Chancery Division of the High Court of Justice ruled that the sale was "proper and valid", and a few days later Jumbo was crated (with difficulty) and hauled by a team of heavy draught-horses to the chartered British freighter *Assyrian Monarch* lying at anchor in the Thames. The Atlantic crossing took fifteen days, and on 9th April the elephant arrived safely in New York to a tumultuous welcome.

Jumbo achieved great fame with the Barnum and Bailey Circus until he was struck down and killed by a railway engine at St. Thomas, Ontario, Canada, on the night of 15th September 1885.

The famous "Jumbo", probably the largest elephant ever held in captivity. When this picture was taken he measured 10 ft 9 in at the shoulder. (Picture Post Library.)

The tragic accident occurred as the grey colossus and a baby elephant named "Tom Thumb" were being led by Matthew Scott across an unused spur-line of the Grand Trunk Railway to their private car after they had finished their circus performance. The track disappeared round a large bend a few hundred yards away. Suddenly, an unscheduled freight train rounded the bend of the supposedly disused branch-line and Jumbo, completely bewildered by the noise and glaring headlights of the train, was hit by the full weight of the engine as his keeper leapt to safety.

The force of the impact was so great that the locomotive and two cars were derailed, and the driver killed. Jumbo's massive head was crushed between the box car and the next flat car, and he died within seconds (Wallace, 1960; Mathieson, 1963).

In a lawsuit that followed between the railroad and the circus a settlement was reached out of court, Barnum receiving $10,000 in cash and full use of that railroad for one year free of charge for the transportation of the circus. The showman claimed that the death of Jumbo meant at least $100,000 in lost gate, which, surprising for him, was probably an understatement (in the first six weeks of his stay in America Jumbo grossed $336,000 for his owners).

The true standing height of Jumbo will never be known for certain because Barnum refused to allow anyone to measure his prize exhibit.

According to him the elephant measured 11 ft 7 in in March 1883 and 12 ft shortly before his death, but both these figures were exaggerated for commercial reasons.

Professor Henry Ward of Ward's Natural Science Establishment in Rochester, N.Y., who was asked by Barnum to mount Jumbo for exhibition purposes, said the elephant measured 11 ft 4 in at the shoulder between pegs (maximum bodily girth 16 ft 4 in), which suggests that the animal must have stood about 10 ft 9 inches in life. But even this measurement is incorrect. In 1883 Robert Gillfort, a pole-jumper with the Barnum and Bailey Circus, attempted to find out the true height of Jumbo by casually standing his pole alongside the elephant and carefully noting the height on the wood that corresponded with the beast's highest point at the shoulder (Hornaday, 1911). The measurement came out at 10 ft 9 in, which means that Jumbo, who was still growing at the rate of an inch or so a year, must have stood a *full* 11 ft at the shoulder at the time of his death. This is interesting, because according to Osborn (1942) the skeleton of Jumbo in the American Museum of Natural History in New York (presented by Barnum in 1889) has a mounted shoulder height of 10 ft 5.25 in. This, he says, is equivalent to a height in the flesh of 11 ft 1.75 in.

After touring North America for two years the model of Jumbo was dismantled and the 1,538 lb hide reconstructed, stuffed and sent to the Barnum Museum at Tufts College in Medford, Massachusetts, where it is still on display today (the mounted animal stands 12 ft at the shoulder and measures 18 ft round the body).

Another African bush elephant named "Jino" received at the London Zoological Gardens on 8th July 1882 was reputed to have been 2 in taller than Jumbo (one report gives his height as 12 ft), but although he was described as an elephant "tall of stature", he never reached the impressive dimensions attained by Jumbo. At the time of his purchase for £300 from Carl Hagenbeck, the German animal-dealer, he stood 4 ft at the shoulder and weighed 788 lb, and on 8th October 1883 he was 4 ft 11 in and 1,460 lb. His last recorded height was 9 ft 7 in. On 4th March 1903 Jingo was sold to Mr. F. Bostock, the circus-proprietor, for £200, but the following month he died from sea-sickness while *en route* to the United States, and his body was dumped overboard (Flower, 1931). According to Lloyd's shipping paper of 27th April 1903, the S.S. *Colorado*, on her arrival in New York on 24th April 1903, reported that on 7th April, in latitude 45.26 longitude 36.45, she sighted the body of the elephant Jingo floating on the surface.

Jumbo's closest rival for size among captive bush elephants was a bull named "Khartoum", who was captured in the Mataschie area, Upper Atbara, Sudan by Captain (later Major) Stanley Flower, then Director of the Giza Zoological Gardens. A few months later the elephant was purchased by the New York Zoological Society through Carl Hagenbeck (Crandall, 1964).

Khartoum arrived at Bronx Zoo on 25th June 1907 when he was estimated to be four years old. In March 1929 he stood 10 ft 7.5 in at the shoulder (Blair, 1929), and on 30th December 1930 he was 10 ft 8.5 in (Osborn, 1942). On 23rd October 1931 he suddenly collapsed and died, death being attributed to heart failure (Noback, 1932). His posthumous weight was given as a very light 10,399 lb (4.64 tons) and his shoulder height between pegs as 10 ft 10 in, but there appears to be some discrepancy here because an elephant with a standing height of 10 ft 8.5 in would normally be expected to measure about 11 ft 3 in between uprights. In August 1970 a posthumous shoulder height of 3.70 m (12 ft 1.5 in) and a weight of 6,250 kg (6·13 tons) were reported for a bull African elephant named "Tembo" at the Zoologisk Have, Copenhagen, Denmark but the author has not yet been able to confirm these figures.

The largest adult cow bush elephant to be accurately measured between pegs was probably a specimen shot on 25th March 1964 in Murchison Falls National Park, Uganda, during "cropping" operations. It measured 2·93 m (9 ft 7·25 in) at the shoulder and scaled 2,942 kg (2·90 tons). Another cow measuring 2·83 m (9 ft 3·5 in) and weighing 2,375 kg (2·53 tons) was shot in the same park three weeks later (Laws *et al.*, 1966).

The largest of the thirty-one cows killed in Kenya/Uganda in *c.* 1965 during cropping operations measured 2·84 m (9 ft 3·8 in) at the shoulder and scaled 2,620 kg (2·57 tons). Another example measured 2·82 m (9 ft 3·1 in) and weighed 2,438 kg (2·37 tons), and a third 2·8 m (9 ft 2·2 in) and 2,920 kg (2·86 tons). The heaviest of these three elephants had a girth of 3·66 m (12 ft 1 in), and 5 per cent of the body weight covered blood and fluid losses.

According to Dr. Sylvia Sikes (1971) the record cow measured 3 m (9 ft 10 in) at the shoulder, but unfortunately she does not give any other details. The same authority also puts the *probable* maximum shoulder height for cows at 3·5 m (11 ft 5·75 in), but as this measurement is exceptional even for bulls this figure should be treated with caution.

The largest cow bush elephant ever held in captivity was probably a specimen named "Sudana". She was captured on the south-eastern slopes of Mount Kilimanjaro in Tanganyika on 6th May 1929 when aged two and arrived at Bronx Zoo, New York, on 9th November 1931. In 1947 she measured 8 ft 7 in at the shoulder, and recorded the same height on 15th September 1958. She was destroyed on 11th August 1962 after being rendered immobile by arthritis (Crandall, 1964).

This size was matched by the famous "Dicksie" of the London Zoological Gardens (received October 1945 from Kenya) who measured 8 ft 7 in in July 1965 when aged twenty-five. She died on 6th September 1967 from heart failure after falling into the moat surrounding her enclosure.

Another cow called "Alice", purchased by the London Zoological Society as a mate for Jumbo on 9th September 1865 and later shipped to the United States, reputedly measured "a few inches over 9 ft" in 1886, but this claim has not yet been substantiated. She died in the fire at P. T. Barnum's winter quarters at Bridgeport, Connecticut on 20th November 1887.

The African forest elephant (*Loxodonta africana cyclotis*), which is found in the rain forests of Guinea, French Equatorial Africa and the Congo, is a shorter animal than the bush elephant, although it is stockier and proportionately heavier.

The average adult bull measures 2·35 m (7 ft 8·5 in) at the shoulder and weighs about 2·5 tons, and the average adult cow 2·10 m (6 ft 10·5 in) and 1·75 tons.

The greatest standing height at the shoulder recorded for a forest elephant is 3 m (9 ft 10 in) for a bull measured at Api by Commandant Pierre Offermann (1953) while Director of the Belgian Congo army-run elephant training centre. This centre was at Api from 1900 until 1926, and then at Gongala-na-Bodia.

In *c.* 1913 Dr. Cuthbert Christy (1924) shot a large tusker in the

Belgian Congo which measured 2·96 m (9 ft 8·5 in) at the shoulder between pegs.

The greatest standing height at the shoulder recorded for a cow forest elephant is 2·50 m (8 ft 2·4 in) for a specimen measured at Api (Offermann, 1953).

A 2·85 m (9 ft 4·2 in) bull shot at the Api station in 1906 and immediately cut up and weighed was found to total about 6,000 kg (5·89 tons), which is slightly more than the average weight of a bull bush elephant measuring 10 ft 6 in at the shoulder.

The trunk accounted for 117 kg (257·4 lb); liver 74 kg (163·8 lb); heart 21 kg (46·22 lb); fat 106 kg (233·2 lb); brain 5 kg (11 lb); muscles 2,766 kg (6,085 lb); entrails 300 kg (660 lb); ears 84 kg (184·8 lb); skin 542 kg (1,292 lb); and the skeleton 1,600 kg (3,520 lb). The weight of the blood and stomach contents was estimated at 340 kg (748 lb).

The largest forest elephant ever held in captivity was a cow named "Doruma" received at Bronx Zoo, New York, in October 1946 from the training centre at Gongala-na-Bodia as a gift from the Belgian Congo Government (Bridges, 1946). She was born in 1938 and was measured at 1·65 m (5 ft 4·19 in) shortly before leaving for the United States. On 27th June 1963 her height was recorded as 7 ft 8·5 in (Crandall, 1964), and in October 1969 she measured 7 ft 9 in. She died in the spring of 1970, when her weight was estimated to be 7,000 lb (3·12 tons) (Conway, *in litt.* 8.12.70).

Another cow named "Josephine" received at Philadelphia Zoological Gardens, Pennsylvania, U.S.A. on 4th April 1925 measured 7 ft 8 in shortly before her death on 12th March 1943. Her posthumous weight was given as a more reasonable 4,000 lb (Ulmer, 1953).

The status of the African pygmy elephant (*Loxodonta africana pumilio*) which is found in the swampy forests of Gabon and the Congo, is still uncertain, but although this animal has been credited with sub-specific rank (Noack, 1906; Hornaday, 1923), the modern consensus of opinion is that pygmy elephants (maximum shoulder height 6 ft 8 in) are a race of undersized forest elephants living in an unfavourable environment.

The greatest true weight recorded for an elephant is 14,641 lb (6·53 tons) for a huge bull shot by Captain Hewlett (with Dr. George Crile) near Ngaruka, Tanganyika, on 26th December 1935 (Benedict and Lee, 1938; Crile, 1941).

The body was cut up into 176 parcels and weighed piecemeal on scales capable of registering 600 lb. The skin—except that of the four legs from the knees down and the tail—weighed 2,005 lb, the stomach and intestines (with contents) 2,034 lb, the muscles and fat 4,365 lb, the liver 235 lb, the heart 57·5 lb and the kidneys 40 lb.

Because there was considerable loss of blood and body fluids due to evaporation and spillage into the gravel and sand of the dried river-course where the animal fell, Dr. Crile, an American endocrinologist, allowed 10 per cent of the total weight for seepage, but it is fairly reasonable to assume that this elephant must have weighed nearly 7 tons when alive.

The shoulder height of this colossus was not recorded, but as the front foot measured 60 inches in circumference it must have stood about 11 ft in life.

Another large tusker killed in Kenya in *c.* 1965 measured 3·46 m (11 ft 4·2 in) at the shoulder between pegs and weighed 6,071 kg (5·9 tons) excluding blood.

Four bulls (shoulder heights not recorded) weighed piecemeal in the eastern province of Northern Rhodesia in *c.* 1960 during cropping operations weighed 6,004 kg (5·93 tons); 5,174 kg (5·08 tons); 5,148 kg (5·05 tons) and 4,380 kg (4·4 tons) respectively (Robertson-Bullock, 1962).

In 1965 a relationship between dressed hind-leg weight and "live body weight" was demonstrated for twenty-six bush elephants (thirteen bulls and thirteen cows) killed in the Murchison Falls National Park during cropping operations by Uganda National Parks rangers; and another twelve elephants (six bulls and six cows) were killed in Kenya's Tsavo National Park the following year to check the accuracy of the earlier findings.

According to Laws et al. (1967) the hind-leg weights of the thirty-eight elephants collected varied between 5·3 and 6·3 per cent of the total live weight and could be used to predict live weight more accurately than by carefully weighing the animal in pieces with considerable blood and fluid losses.

In the Murchison Falls experiment the greatest weight recorded for a dressed hind-leg was 308·4 kg (678·5 lb) for a bull which weighed 5,002 kg (4·9 tons), while in Tsavo National Park the maximum weight was 294 kg (648·8 lb) for a 5,000 kg (4·9 ton) bull.

On the basis of these findings, the dressed hind-leg weight of the "Fenykoevi Elephant" must have been between 1,272 and 1,512 lb, although this poundage is not borne out in photographs.

The greatest true weight recorded for a cow bush elephant in the field is 3,232 kg (3·18 tons) for a specimen killed in Murchison Falls National Park on 16th January 1964. The shoulder height of this animal was 8 ft 6 in (Law et al., 1967). Another cow (shoulder height 8 ft 10 in) killed in the same park fifteen days previously weighed 3,133 kg (3·08 tons)

The greatest true weight recorded for a cow bush elephant in captivity is 9,670 lb (4·31 tons) for Sudana (see page 28) who, owing to her infirmity, was rather obese.

One of the most awesome sights in nature is a drunken bush elephant. This sorry state of affairs often occurs when an elephant gorges itself on the ripe fruit of the Marula tree (Schlerocarya cafra) and the Borassus palm and then drinks gallons of water. The fruit rapidly ferments in the animal's huge stomach, and within a few hours a 5·5-ton drunk is staggering through the undergrowth. Colonel T. Owen (1960) quotes the case of an acquaintance of his in Uganda who rather foolishly pitched his tent under a clump of Borassus palms at ripening-time and was rudely awakened in the early hours of the morning by a small herd of drunken elephants "tripping" over his guy-ropes. Owen himself says he has seen more than one elephant leaning against a palm tree "like a reveller against a lamp-post".

In 1934 a sober Uganda Game Department official reported seeing a large herd of drunken elephants near Kampala. They had eaten over-ripe fruit from Borassus palms and were staggering into trees and each other.

Unfortunately, elephants, like their human counterparts, suffer from hangovers, and they are often bad-tempered and liverish after the event. Sometimes they charge through the park or reserve and rangers have great difficulty in diverting them away from African villages and game camps. After the fruit season ends a few elephants turn rogue and have to be shot.

Several races of the Asiatic elephant (Elephas maximus) have been described (Deraniyagala, 1955 lists eight), but only four are generally recognised. They are: E.m. indicus of India, Burma, Thailand, Indochina and Borneo, where it is thought to have been introduced a few hundred years ago; *E.m. maximus* and *E.m. ceylanicus* of Ceylon; and *E.m. sumatranus* of Sumatra (Chasen, 1940; Morrison-Scott, 1951).

The average adult bull Indian elephant (*E.m. indicus*) stands 9 ft at the shoulder and weighs 4·5 tons, and the average adult cow 7 ft 6 in and 2·5 tons.

The two races of Ceylon elephant (*E.m. maximus* and *E.m. ceylanicus*) average rather larger and heavier than the typical race from the Indian mainland, while *E.m. sumatranus* is slightly smaller.

The shoulder heights attained by the Asiatic elephant have been greatly exaggerated in the past. This is mainly due to the fact that measurements were often taken by throwing a tape over the shoulders of the animal. The ends were then taken down to the outside of each front foot and half the subsequent length taken as the elephant's height.

Benedict (1936) says an 8 ft cow elephant measured by this method recorded a height of 8 ft 10 in, while a 10 ft bull came out at 11 ft 4 in. Other mahouts (elephant-drivers) used to measure their charges from the ground to the crown of the head and then claim the result as the elephant's shoulder height.

Twice the circumference of an Asiatic elephant's forefoot when resting on the ground and enlarged by pressure gives approximately its height at the shoulder (up to 6 per cent error), but this rule does not always apply in the case of young growing animals. The formula for the African bush elephant is twice the circumference of the forefoot plus 10 per cent.

The largest recorded Asiatic elephant to be accurately measured between pegs was a bull (*E.m. maximus*) shot by Mr. W. H. Varian at Chalampia Madua, in the North Coast Province of Ceylon, in 1882. The following measurements were taken immediately after death: height at arch of back 11 ft 9 in; at the shoulder 11 ft 1 in; length from tip of extended trunk to tip of extended tail 26 ft; girth of body at thickest part 22 ft 4 in; estimated weight about 8 tons (Osborn, 1942).

Another bull tusker shot by Mr. W. M. Smith at Bilkandi, Bengal, India on 19th January 1870 reportedly measured 12 ft at the shoulder between pegs (Lydekker, 1894), but this figure was exaggerated. In a letter to the author dated 15th March 1971 Dr. A. P. Kapur, Director of the Zoological Survey of India, said that this elephant, now on display in the Indian Museum, Calcutta, has a mounted shoulder height of 10 ft 9·92 in and measures 11 ft 2·25 in at the arch of the back.

Holder (1886) gives details of another bull shot in a gorge in the Himalayas about 1,000 miles from Calcutta in 1865 which he says measured 11 ft 2 in between pegs and had a forefoot circumference of 39 in, but this latter figure must be a misprint. The skeleton of this animal is supposed to be preserved in the Museum of the Medical College at the University of Chicago, Illinois, U.S.A., but the author has not yet been able to confirm this.

On 2nd June 1950 Reuters announced that a Mr. H. Mant had shot an elephant (*E.m. maximus*) in a Ceylon swamp with a forefoot circumference of 73·5 in. Normally this would be equal to a shoulder height of 12 ft 3 in, but Deraniyagala (1955) says swamp-dwelling elephants often have disproportionately large feet because of the nature of their habitat.

Other Asiatic elephants for whom shoulder heights between pegs of 10 ft or more have been reliably recorded include: an enormous tusker shot by Sir Victor Brooke in the Billiga-rungun Hills, Bengal, in 1863 which measured 11 ft; one measuring 10 ft 4 in shot by Colonel F. Pollock in the neighbourhood of Twinge, Assam, in November 1895 (Pollock & Thom,

1900); another 10 ft 4 in bull shot by J. N. Clough in the Kyaikto District, Lower Burma, in 1896; a rogue bull measuring 10 ft 4 in shot in the Ramnagar Division, United Provinces, in 1914, and another one measuring 10 ft 4·5 in shot in Haldwani District, Uttar Pradesh, about the same time; a 10 ft 5 in tusker shot by E. H. Peacock (1933) in the Upper Chindwin, Burma, in February 1917, and another bull measuring 10 ft 2 in shot by A. J. Jones in Bhamo District, Burma, on 8th October 1917; a 10 ft 6 in tusker shot by E. L. Walker in the swamps of Tamankaduwa, Ceylon, in 1919; a 10 ft bull shot by Major Brook Purdon in Burma in 1925; a tusker shot by D. R. Wadia of Bombay on the Gamdamanayaka-noor Zamindaries in the Madrua District, southern India, on 15th April 1928 which measured 10 ft 2 in; and the notorious "Cradle Tusker" shot by Lieutenant-Colonel E. G. Phythian-Ides in the Areipalaiyam, Mysore, in January 1932 which measured 10 ft 6 in.

In December 1937 a tuskless bull measuring 10 ft 8 in was shot by a game ranger employed on elephant control in the Bhama District, Burma.

Turning to more recent records Patrick Stracey (1963), a former Chief Conservator of Forests in Assam, gives details of four bulls measuring in excess of 10 ft 9 in. One of them shot by L. Mackrell at Bismuri, in the Goalpara Division of Assam, measured 10 ft 11 in. Another huge tusker shot by the Maharajah of Mysore in the Mysore jungle during the Second World War was 11 ft, and the same measurement was reported for a bull shot by Lalji, Kumar of Gauripur, in the Garo Hills in 1945 (the height of this elephant could not be taken because it fell in an awkward position, but its forefoot measured 66 inches in circumference). The fourth bull, a rogue tusker measuring 11 ft, was shot by the Maharajah of Talcher in Khenkanal, Orissa, in 1953.

Dr. D. Pieters of Java shot two large bulls in Sumatra in 1932 which measured 10 ft 5·5 in and 10 ft 1·5 in respectively.

The largest Asiatic elephant ever held in captivity was the Maharajah of Nepal's famous tusker "Hari Prasad", which measured 10 ft 9 in at the shoulder in 1957 (Stracey, 1963). Another large tusker owned by the Rajah of Nahan-Sirmour in the Punjab measured 10 ft 7·5 inches in c. 1870.

Wolff (1750), in his account of the Ceylon elephant, says he saw a huge bull near Jaffna which was 12 ft 1 in tall, but this measurement was taken to the crown of the raised head. The shoulder height was 10 ft 6 in.

A tusker owned by Asaph-ul-Daulon, Vizier of Loudh, and described by J. Corse (1799), a former Superintendent of the East India Company at Tiperah, east Bengal, measured 22 ft 10·5 in foot to foot over the shoulder and 12 ft 2 in to the crown of the raised head. Corse, who probably saw more elephants than any other European of his time, says that before he saw this specimen he had never seen another Asiatic elephant over 10 ft at the shoulder. He did hear of one owned by the Nabob of Dacca which allegedly stood "14 ft [sic]" at the shoulder, but when he investigated the claim he found that the animal measured exactly 10 ft.

Sanderson (1879) offered a reward of a brand-new rifle to anyone who could produce an Asiatic bull elephant measuring 10 ft or more at the shoulder, but the largest he saw measured 9 ft 10 in. The largest bull seen by Evans (1910) also measured 9 ft 10 in. Of 150 adult bull elephants measured in Bengal in 1923 only a few attained 9 ft 6 in, and not one of them measured 10 ft (Osborn, 1936).

"Jung Pasha", also known as "Jung Pershad", a bull presented to the London Zoological Society by the Prince of Wales (later Edward VII) on 17th May 1876, was stated to have been nearly as big as Jumbo. At the time of his death on 8th March 1896 aged twenty-five and a half years he was reportedly over 10 ft at the shoulder, but the last recorded measurement for this animal was 9 ft 10 in (Flower, 1931). A fighting elephant owned by the King of Nepal in the 1870s was also credited with a height of over 10 ft, and another big tusker named "Debraj" in the same stable was said to have measured 10 ft 4·5 in (Maharajah of Cooch Behar, 1908).

According to Stracey a magnificent tusker named "Jung Bahudur" belonging to the Rajah of Gauripur stood 10 ft 4·5 in at the shoulder shortly before the outbreak of the Second World War, and another big tusker owned by the Maharajah of Gwalier measured 10 ft 5 in.

The famous tusker "Chandrasekharan" belonging to the Maharajah of Travancore measured 10 ft at the shoulder in 1913, and shortly after his death on 10th August 1940 the Trivandrum Museum taxidermist reported that his height between pegs was 10 ft 7 in (Flower, 1947).

The largest Asiatic elephant ever held in a zoo was the well-known "Bolivar", who was presented to the King of Italy by the Maharajah of Oudh in 1871. The animal was then three years old and stood 5 ft high. When King Victor Emmanuel died on 9th January 1878 the elephant was sold to Carl Hagenbeck, who in turn sold it to Adam Forepaugh, the American circus-owner, in 1881 (Flower, 1931). Forepaugh presented the bull to Philadelphia Zoological Gardens, Pennsylvania, U.S.A., on 1st January 1889. He was then 9 ft at the shoulder. On 3rd June 1890 he weighed 8,800 lb (3·9 tons) (Conklin, 1890).

"Ziggy", the largest Asiatic elephant living in captivity today. (Chicago Brookfield Zoological Park, Illinois, U.S.A.)

Shortly before his death on 31st July 1908 aged about forty years Bolivar measured 10 ft at the shoulder and weighed 12,000 lb (5·35 tons) (Benedict, 1936). His skeleton was later mounted and put on display in the entrance hall of the Academy of Natural Sciences in Philadelphia.

Another Asiatic bull named "Ziegfeld" (born 1917) of Chicago Brookfield Zoological Park, Illinois, U.S.A. is nearly as large. He was purchased by Florenz Ziegfeld from John Ringling in 1920 as a birthday-present for his six-year-old daughter, and was sent to the famous showman's estate on Long Island in a taxi.

Before long, however, Ziggy (or "Herman" as he was then known) developed a craving for cakes and buns, and he became so greedy that within a year Ziegfeld was forced to sell him back to Ringling.

Ziggy was acquired by the Chicago Brookfield Zoological Society in the summer of 1936 after reportedly killing a circus musician at the San Diego Exposition, but this story has not yet been fully authenticated. On 26th April 1941 he suddenly turned upon his keeper, George "Slim" Lewis, and threw him to the ground, where he tried to gore him. Lewis managed to scramble to safety, but as a precaution the zoo authorities decided to restrict Ziggy to his stall permanently rather than risk possible injury to visitors or keepers. In 1963 the elephant reportedly measured 10 ft 3 in at the shoulder and weighed an estimated 12,000 lb (5·35 tons). On 12th July 1966, however, the temperamental bull was cautiously measured by an engineering firm who reported that the elephant measured 9 ft 8 in at the shoulder and 10 ft 1·5 in to the crown of the head in the normal position. On 23rd September 1970 Ziggy was let out of his stall for the first time for twenty-nine years, and it is planned eventually to put him in a new outdoor enclosure with a pool (Crowcroft, *in litt.* 4.12.70).

The American circus elephant "Tusko", prominent in the 1920s and 1930s, was credited with a shoulder height of 10 ft 2 in and a weight of just over 14,000 lb (6·25 tons), but the author has not yet been able to confirm these figures.

Another large tusker named "Chunie", exhibited from 1814 to 1826 at the Royal Menagerie at Exeter Change, London, and a great favourite with the English public, reputedly measured "upwards of 10 ft high" and "5 tons weight" (the skull and a tusk of this elephant are preserved in the Museum of the Royal College of Surgeons, London), but these figures were probably a showman's exaggeration. In March 1826 Chunie was "barbarously murdered" by soldiers and private citizens with rifles after Mr. Cross, the owner of the menagerie, had declared the animal mad. Thirty-one years later one of the elephant's executioners described what happened to Francis T. Buckland (1865), the famous naturalist, in the following words:

"I was at the gunmaker's, Stevens of Holborn, when Mr. Herring of the New-road came in to borrow rifles and beg Mr. Stevens to return with him to the 'Change to shoot the elephant. Mr. Stevens was a man in years and full of gout, and I knew directly what would happen; he pointed to me as one for his substitute, and in a very few minutes I had selected the rifles, cast balls, Etc., and we were on the way to the Exeter 'Change. We arrived there and found the greatest confusion; beasts and birds most uproarious, set on by witnessing the struggle to keep in order the ungovernable elephant. . . . I was supposed in that day a steady rifle shot, and with Mr. Herring, in my conceit and ignorance, intended to kill the poor brute with our first fire. Dr. Brooks had tried the poisons, and by his directions we fired into a crease rather below the blade-bone. I expected to see him fall; instead of which he made a sharp hissing noise, and struck heavily at us with his trunk and tried to make after us, and would but for the formidable double-edge spear-blades of the keepers. These spears were ten feet long at least, wielded from a spiked end below, and the trunk wounded itself in endeavours to seize the double-edged blades.

"It was most fortunate the poor beast stood our fires so long afterwards, for, had he fallen suddenly, and struggled in death, his struggles would have brought him from out of his cage or den, and if he had fallen from the strong flooring built under for the support of his great weight, my belief is, through the whole flooring we should have all gone together, lions and men, tigers and birds. He struggled much to come after us, and we were compelled to reload in the passage, and after firing about six shots more the soldiers came from Somerset House; they had but three cartridges each man, and I forget now how they were allowed to come off duty. He bore the presence of the soldiers much better than ours, and I for a time was compelled to load the muskets for the men; they had not the least notion of a flash: they ran the powder into the musket-barrels in most uncertain quantities, and I was compelled to unload and reload for them, or we should have had some much worse accident. The murderous assault was at length closing, and I entered with a loaded gun, taking the last shot as the noble brute seated himself on his haunches; he then folded his forelegs under him, adjusted his trunk, and ceased to live, the only peaceful one among us cruel wretches; and the only excuse I can now find for the cruel slaughter is that it was commenced and must be finished. Poor brute! It was a necessary though cruel act; he was ungovernable in a frail tenement."

According to Buckland an autopsy revealed that the elephant had been suffering from raging toothache.

"Big Charlie", owned by Butlin's Ltd., allegedly stood 10 ft 6 in at the shoulder and weighed 7·5 tons in 1957 when he was twenty-five years old, but these figures were commercial exaggerations. He actually measured 9 ft 7 in at the shoulder and weighed about 5 tons.

In 1932 a large bull named "Harry" (born 1880) at Berlin Zoological Gardens was credited with a shoulder height of 3·15 m (10 ft 4 in) and a weight of 7,500 kg (7·3 tons), but the author has not been able to substantiate these figures because the records of this animal were destroyed by Allied bombing during the Second World War (Klos, *in litt.* 23.11.70).

The greatest true weight recorded for an Asiatic elephant is 6,198 kg (6·1 tons) for a 3·1 m (10 ft 2 in) bull at the Elephant Stables in Mysore in 1953.

The largest Asiatic cow elephant ever held in captivity was a Nepalese specimen named "Suffa Calli", who was presented to the London Zoological Society by the Prince of Wales (later Edward VII) on 17th May 1876. At the time of her death on 2nd December 1917 aged about fifty-one years she measured 9 ft 1 in at the shoulder (Flower, 1931).

This size was closely matched by another cow named "Mandjula", received at Zürich Zoological Gardens in 1929 when she was an estimated twenty years. She measured 2·75 m (9 ft 0·25 in) shortly before her death on 6th December 1966 (Hediger, *in litt.* 29.8.67).

In 1953 a height of 2·75 m (9 ft 0·25 in) was also reported for the tallest cow in the Elephant Stables at Mysore.

Other Asiatic cow elephants for whom heights in excess of 8 ft have been reliably reported included an unnamed specimen received at Frankfurt Zoological Gardens in 1863 when she was believed to be about fourteen years old. She was said to have been brought from India when about seven years old, and to have spent another seven years in various menageries in Europe. In 1863 she measured 6 ft 11·5 in, and in 1864 7 ft 2·5 in. In May 1883 she was 8 ft 6·25 in and weighed 6,200 lb (2·7 tons). She died in November 1893 aged thirty-seven or possibly forty-four years. Another cow named "Barbar", received at Chester Zoological Gardens from Whipsnade Zoological Park in 1933 when aged one, measured 8 ft 4 inches in November 1970. Her companion "Sheba", received at Chester Zoo in February 1965 when aged eight to nine years, stands 8 ft 3 in.

The fine Asiatic cow "Burma" (born 1937) of Philadelphia Zoological Gardens, Pennsylvania, U.S.A. measured 8 ft 1 inch in June 1953. She arrived at the zoo on 12th June 1939 from Rangoon, Burma, when she stood 3 ft 9 in and weighed 700 lb (Crandall, 1964). At the time of her death in 1961 from severe arthritis she measured 8 ft 2 in (Ulmer, *in litt.* 30.12.70).

In 1922 a height of 8 ft 1·875 in was reported by Milroy for a twenty-seven-year-old cow named "Hyte" in Darrang District, Burma.

Sanderson (1879) says the two largest cows in the collection at Dacca in 1876 measured 8 ft 5 in and 8 ft 3 in respectively, but the largest of the 140 cows captured by him was exactly 8 ft.

The largest of the sixty-two American circus and zoo adult cow elephants measured by Francis Benedict (1936) stood 8 ft 4 in at the shoulder. This was a thirty-eight-year-old specimen named "Trilbie" owned by Al. G. Barnes Circus. Four others measured 8 ft 3 in, two 8 ft 2 in, two 8 ft 1 in and three 8 ft.

The greatest true weight recorded for an Asiatic cow elephant is 9,180 lb (4·09 tons) for a 7 ft 10 in example named "Big Modoc" owned by the Ringling Brothers—Barnum and Bailey Circus (Benedict, 1936). Trilbie, already mentioned, scaled 9,000 lb, and two other cows in the same circus weighed 9,098 lb and 9,053 lb respectively.

"Zebi", an Asiatic cow elephant received at Clifton Zoological Gardens, Bristol, on 4th November 1868 when about eight years old, reputedly stood 10 ft at the shoulder and weighed about 5 tons at the time of her death in January 1910 aged about forty-nine years, but the author has not been able to substantiate these figures. Photographic evidence, however, indicates that Zebi was an extremely large example of her sex (Flower, 1931; Greed, *in litt.* 15.12.70).

The large cow Mandjula (see page 35) was credited with an estimated weight of 4·5 tons at the time of her death, but this figure was based on an estimate.

Clarke (1969) estimates that between 200 and 500 people are killed by elephants in Africa annually, and Carrington (1955) puts the annual death-toll in India at about the fifty mark. Circus and zoo elephants, which are 90 per cent Asiatic, probably account for another ten deaths annually.

In 1952 a one-tusked rogue elephant killed twenty-seven people in East Pakistan before it was shot, and Clarke says one highly trained work elephant in India killed eighteen men and still managed to avoid execution because it was considered too valuable an animal to be destroyed. The same writer also says a rogue elephant in northern Zululand once killed twelve natives in quick succession during a temporary bout of insanity.

The largest wild mammal found in the British Isles is the Exmoor pony. Stallions measure up to 51 in at the shoulder and weigh about 700 lb.

The tallest living animal is the Giraffe (*Giraffa camelopardalis*), which is now found only in the dry savannah and semi-desert areas of Africa south of the Sahara.

Nine races are generally recognised, although up to thirteen have been described. They are: the Nubian giraffe (*G.c. camelopardalis*) of the eastern Sudan and Ethiopia; the Nigerian giraffe (*G.c. peralta*); the Congo giraffe (*G.c. congoensis*); the Baringo giraffe (*G.c. rothschildi*) of north-western Kenya and south-eastern Uganda; the Reticulated giraffe (*G.c.*

The long-furred Siberian tiger (Leo tigris altaica) is the largest member of the cat family. Adult males average about 10 ft 4 inches in total length and weigh about 585 lb. (F. Lane.)

The Kodiak bear (Ursus arctos middendorfii) of Alaska is the largest living terrestrial carnivore. The average adult male stands 9 ft in height on his hind-legs and weighs about 1,200 lb. (G. Laycock/B. Coleman Ltd.)

The giraffe is the tallest living animal. This mounted specimen measures 18 ft 11·5 in to the tips of the "horns". (American Museum of Natural History, New York.)

reticulata) of northern Kenya and southern Ethiopia; the Masai giraffe (*G.c. tipperskirchi*) of Kenya and Uganda; Thornicroft's giraffe (*G.c. thornicrofti*) of northern Rhodesia; the Angolan giraffe (*G.c. angolensis*) of Angola and South-West Africa; and the Southern giraffe (*G.c. capensis*) of South-West Africa.

Of these, the five tallest are the Masai, Southern, Baringo, Angolan and Thornicroft sub-species. The average adult bull stands 16–17 ft in height (tip of forehoof to tip of "false" horn with neck erect) and weighs about 2,376 lb (1·15 tons).

The cows are smaller than the bulls, and are always lighter in build. They average about 14·5 ft in height and weigh about 1,240 lb.

The greatest reliable height recorded for a giraffe between pegs is 19 ft 3 in (standing height about 19 ft) for a Masai bull shot by Caswell in Kenya (Shortridge, 1934). It was thus 4·75 ft taller than a London double-decker bus. This animal was not weighed piecemeal, but it must have scaled nearly 2 tons. Less credible heights of up to 23 ft have been claimed.

Another bull of the same race shot by Holwood measured 19 ft (Shortridge, 1934).

Other reliable heights over 17 ft between pegs include a Masai bull shot by ex-President Theodore Roosevelt (1915) near Ulu, central Kenya, which measured 17 ft 2 in (length of head and body 13 ft 4 in); two Southern bulls measuring 18 ft 7 in and 17 ft 6 in respectively shot by F. Vaughan Kirby (1896) in south-east Africa; a Baringo bull shot by the Duc d'Orléans which measured 17 ft 6 in, and another bull of the same race shot by Major P. H. G. Powell-Cotton (1904) on the Uasin Gishu Plateau in western Kenya which taped 17 ft 3 in (shoulder height 10 ft 11 in); a Masai or Baringo bull shot by Hall in Kenya which taped 18 ft 6 in; a Baringo bull measuring 17 ft 3 in (length of head and body 12 ft 10 in, tail 2 ft 10 in) shot by Kermit Roosevelt near Lake Baringo, Kenya; an Angolan bull shot by Edouard Foa (1897) in Barotseland, which taped 17 ft 3·5 in; a Southern bull (mounted) killed in Ngamiland which measured 5·32 m (17 ft 5·5 in), and another bull of the same race shot by Cornwallis Harris which measured 18 ft (shoulder height 12 ft); an Angolan bull measuring 17 ft (shoulder height 9 ft 8 in) shot by F. C. Selous in west Matabeleland; a Masai bull shot by Lady Hindlip in Kenya which measured 17 ft 3 in (Ward, 1907); a Southern bull measuring 18 ft 11·5 in shot by Henry Bryden, and another one taping 17 ft 6 in shot in the Kaokoveld and estimated to weigh between 1·5 and 2 tons (now mounted in the Kaffrarian Museum, Cape Province) (Shortridge, 1934); and a Masai bull shot by Colonel R. Meinertzhagen in Kenya which measured 17 ft 8 in *to the base of the horns* (the length of the horns varies from 6 to 9 inches in adult bulls).

The greatest reliable height recorded for a cow giraffe between pegs is 16 ft 10 in for an example of the Southern race shot by Henry R. Bryden in the desert country near the Botletli River, Ngamiland, in *c.* 1889.

The tallest giraffe ever held in captivity was a massive Masai bull named "George" who arrived at Chester Zoological Gardens on 8th January 1959 from Kenya when he was an estimated eighteen months old. In 1968 his head almost reached the roof of the 20 ft high Giraffe House. George was very fond of licking the telephone wires which ran past his enclosure, and he caused many a short-circuit before the trouble was traced to him. He died on 22nd July 1969 (Mottershead, *in litt.* 24.11.70).

A Baringo bull named "Peter", received at Whipsnade Zoological Park in June 1934 from Kenya reportedly stood 18 ft, but the last height recorded for him was 17 ft 6 in (Manton, *in litt.* 30.10.70). Another Baringo bull named "George", received at London Zoological Gardens on 27th May 1935 measured 17 ft. He died from pneumonia on 3rd January 1950 (Davie, *in litt.* 25.10.70).

In September 1958 a height of 17 ft 5 in was reported for a Reticulated bull called "Socrates" at Cheyenne Mountain Zoological Park, Colorado Springs, Colorado, U.S.A., but in a letter to the author dated 3rd December 1970 Michael J. Crotty, the General Curator, wrote: "Our bull giraffe Socrates was probably just under 17 ft in height. He was never exactly measured, but an estimate was made by counting the tile blocks in

*The Edible dormouse (*Glis glis*) of southern England and central Europe spends more time in hibernation than any other living mammal. (A. Fatras.)*

*The Pipistrelle or Common bat (*Pipistrellus pipistrellus*) is the smallest bat found in Britain. Mature specimens have a wing-span of 8–9 in and weigh up to a quarter of an ounce. (G. Kinns.)*

his stall, and measuring the distance from the floor to approximately where the tips of his horns reached. . . . He was probably the tallest giraffe ever imported, but not necessarily the tallest ever in captivity."

The tallest cow giraffe ever held in captivity was probably a specimen named "Rosie", a member of the Baringo race, who arrived at Whipsnade Zoological Park from Kenya with the bull Peter (see page 39). She stood approximately 17 ft (Manton, *in litt.* 30.10.70).

The first giraffe ever seen in England was a six-month-old cow of the Nubian race presented to George IV by Mohammed Ali, Pasha of Egypt, in 1826. The 9 ft 2 in tall animal arrived in London in August 1827, accompanied by two Arab keepers and an interpreter, and was taken to Windsor where "the King hastened to inspect his extraordinary acquisition and was greatly pleased with the care which had been taken to bring it to his presence in fine order" (Spinage, 1968).

The giraffe lived at Windsor for two years two months and grew another 18 in before its death in October 1829.

Giraffes grow at a tremendous rate in the first few days of life. A calf born to the Baringo cow Rosie at Whipsnade Zoological Park on Boxing Day 1937 measured 5 ft 2 in tall shortly after birth and was 6 ft 3 in a day later, which means *it was growing at a rate of just over half an inch an hour.*

The largest privately owned herd of giraffes on record is that belonging to Alexander Douglas, who lives alone on his 18,000 acre farm near Eldoret, Kenya. He acquired about 120 of these animals in 1954 when the Government was shooting off all the giraffes in the district because of the damage they were doing to the grazing.

A few albino giraffes have been recorded. Rowland Ward Ltd. of London possess a mounted white giraffe from Tanganyika, and others have been seen in Kenya. Totally black specimens are even rarer. Spinage says there was one living in the Murchison Falls National Park, Uganda, at one time.

The smallest living mammal is Savi's white-toothed Pygmy shrew (*Suncus etruscus*), also called the "Etruscan shrew", which is found along the coasts of the northern Mediterranean and southwards to Cape Province, South Africa (Rode, 1938; Morrison-Scott, 1947).

Not much is known about this tiny species, and most of the published information has come from studies of owl pellets in which this animal's teeth, fur and bones have been found.

Mature specimens have a head and body length of 36–52 mm (1·32–2·04 in), a tail length of 24–29 mm (0·94–1·14 in) and weigh between 1·5 and 2·5 g (between 0·052 and 0·09 oz) (Van den Brink, 1955).

Some idea of this creature's diminutive size can be gauged by the fact that it can travel through tunnels left by large earth-worms!

Its nearest rival for tininess is the very rare Least shrew (*Sorex minutissimus*) which has been recorded twice in Finland; and also in the Valdai Hills and the Province of Moscow in the U.S.S.R. (Siivonen, 1956).

Mature specimens have a head and body length of 35–55 mm (1·37–2·08 in), a tail length of 21–32 mm (0·82–1·2 in) and weigh between 1·5 and 4 g (between 0·052 and 0·141 oz).

Another strong contender is the North American pygmy shrew (*Microsorex hoyi*). Mature specimens have a head and body length of

58–78 mm (2·28–3·07 in), a tail length of 27·31 mm (1·06–1·22 in) and weigh between 2·2 and 3·8 g (between 0·078 and 0·134 oz) (Walker *et al.*, 1964).

The smallest land mammal found in the British Isles is the European pygmy shrew (*Sorex minutus*). Mature specimens have a head and body length of 43–64 mm (1·69–2·51 in), a tail length of 31–46 mm (1·22–1·81 in) and weigh between 2·4 and 6·1 g (between 0·084 and 0·213 oz) (Crowcroft, 1954; Shillito, 1960).

The smallest totally marine mammal is the Sea otter (*Enhydra lutris*). Two races are recognised: the Northern sea otter (*E.l. lutris*) and the Southern sea otter (*E.l. nereis*), but the distinction between them rests entirely on minor cranial differences (Merriam, 1904), and the validity of *E.l. nereis* has been questioned by two authorities recently (Scheffer & Wilke, 1950). Adult specimens of both races measure 120–156 cm (47·24–61·5 in) in total length and weigh 25–38·5 kg (55–81·4 lb), although males are a bit larger and heavier than females.

At one time the sea otter was found in abundance along both shores of the North Pacific, its range extending from northern Japan, the Kurils and the Kamchatka Peninsula to the west coast of North America via the Commander (Kommandorskiye) and Aleutian chains, and then southwards to the coast of Lower California. In the early nineteenth century, however, it was ruthlessly exploited by hunters for its valuable fur, and by the beginning of this century the Sea otter had been virtually exterminated. Finally, in 1910 the U.S. Government introduced a law forbidding its capture in American waters, and the following year other interested Governments (for example Russia, Britain and Japan) banned the taking of sea otters in international waters under the Fur Seal Treaty.

At that time the total world population was probably less than 500 animals. But despite the protective measures the numbers of sea otter still decreased, and by 1926 it was believed that the animal was extinct. Then, in 1936 the U.S. Government heard reports that some still survived in the Aleutians. A naval boat was sent to investigate, and a small colony was found on Amchitka Island. Two years later, in 1938, another small colony numbering ninety-four animals was discovered off the coast of Monterey, California (Fisher, 1939). Today there are probably more than 20,000 sea otters in the Aleutian Islands (Coolidge, 1959), 27,000–47,000 on the Alaskan coast (Lensink, 1960), about 1,000 between Point Lobos and the Santa Barbara Islands, California, and a few dozen others off the coasts of Oregon and Washington (Harris, 1968).

On 6th November 1971 an estimated 300 to 800 sea otters were killed following the detonation of a U.S. underground nuclear device on Amchitka. The animals were either buried by rock falls along the coast or were swept out to sea by the storm created by the explosion.

The rare Marine otter (*Lutra felina*), also called the "Chingungo", which ranges along the entire coast of Chile south to Tierra del Fuego, and northwards to the coast of northern Peru, is considerably smaller than the sea otter, but it is not strictly marine because it ascends freshwater rivers in search of prawns on which it feeds.

An adult male taken at the southern end of Chiloe Island, 30 miles west of the Chilean mainland, by a Field Museum of Natural History (Chicago) expedition in 1923 measured 91 cm (35·82 in) in total length and weighed only 9 lb (Osgood, 1943).

The smallest marine mammal found in British waters is the Common porpoise (*Phocaena phocaena*). Adult males measure 5·5 7 ft in length and weigh 170–300 lb, and adult females 5·25–6 ft and 130–200 lb.

The smallest freshwater mammal is the European water shrew (*Neomys fodiens*), which has a head and body length of 72–96 mm (2·83–3·77 in), a tail length of 47–77 mm (1·85–3·05 in) and weighs 10–23 g (van der Brink, 1967).

The rarest mammal in the world is probably the Pygmy possum (*Burramys parva*) which, until quite recently, was known only from 20,000-year-old fossil material from the Wombeyan Caves in New South Wales, Australia and from the remains of allegedly prehistoric owl pellets found in caves in eastern Victoria. On 19th August 1966, however, a single male was caught in a ski club hut on Mount Hotham, in the Victorian Alps, 130 miles north-east of Melbourne, Victoria. This unique specimen was taken to the Fisheries and Wildlife Department of Victoria in Melbourne for study, where it was still alive in 1968 (Fitter, 1968). In March 1970 three more specimens were discovered in Kosciusko Park, New South Wales.

The pygmy possum which, until quite recently, was known only from 20,000-year-old fossil material. (Fisheries and Wildlife Department, Melbourne, Victoria, Australia.)

Leadbeater's possum (*Gymobelideus leadbeateri*), a nocturnal animal first discovered (two specimens) along the Bass River, South Gippsland, Victoria, Australia in 1867 (M'Coy, 1867) and thought to have become extinct in *c.* 1931 (Brazenor, 1932), was rediscovered in April 1961 when H. E. Wilkinson of the National Museum of Victoria saw a single specimen in a dense eucalyptus forest in the Cumberland Valley, 50 miles north-east of Melbourne. Four others were later collected in the same area. Today there is a small thriving colony in the Tommy's Ben District in the Central Highlands of Victoria (Fisher *et al.*, 1969).

The Congo water civet (*Osbornictis piscivora*) is known from only two specimens, and has never been captured alive (Walker *et al.*, 1968)

The rarest placental mammal in the world is the Javan rhinoceros (*Rhinoceros sondaicus*), also known as the "Smaller one-horned rhinoceros", which was formerly found throughout South-East Asia, but was ruthlessly exploited by Man because of the widespread belief that its horn was a powerful aphrodisiac in powdered form.

In mid 1970 the population was reportedly reduced to a single herd of twenty-eight animals in the Udjung-Kulon (Oedjoeng Kuelon) Reserve of 117 square miles at the tip of western Java, Indonesia, where it is now strictly protected, but there may also be a few left in the Tenasserim area on the Thai-Burmese border where it was once particularly abundant.

The Javan rhinoceros is found in tall grass and reed-beds in swampy areas, although it has been found at an altitude of 10,000 ft on the narrow rims of active volcanoes. It is so rarely seen that field-workers have to rely on tracks for estimating numbers.

The Udjung-Kulon Reserve was created in 1921 by the Netherlands Indies Government, and its administration has been continued by the Indonesian Government (Harper, 1945; Sody, 1959; Talbot, 1959; Guggisberg, 1966).

The Javan rhinoceros's closest "rival" for the title of rarest placental mammal is probably the "hairy" two-horned Sumatran rhinoceros (*Didermocerus sumatrensis*), the smallest of the world's living rhinoceroses. Like *R. sondaicus*, the Sumatran rhinoceros was once distributed over a wide area of South-East Asia, but it was also mercilessly persecuted because of the belief in the value of its horn.

The Sumatran rhinoceros, one of the rarest placental mammals in the world. (Zoological Society of London.)

Today, small and isolated populations of the Sumatran rhinoceros still exist in dense forests, usually near streams, in Burma, Thailand, Malaya, Sumatra and Sabah, and the total population is now estimated at between 100 and 170 animals. The rhinoceros population in Sumatra itself is now about sixty specimens, some of which live in the Loser Reserve in northern Sumatra and the South Sumatran Nature Reserve (Simon, 1969).

D. sumatrensis is now legally protected over the greater part of its range and may be hunted only with a special licence, but the animal still falls occasionally to poachers.

The rarest terrestrial mammal found in Britain is the Pine marten (*Martes martes*), which is found in the Highlands of Scotland, particularly in Coille na Glas, Leitire, Ross and Cromarty, and thinly distributed in North Wales and the

The pine marten, Britain's rarest land mammal. (Francis Pitt.)

Scottish Border country. This species was formerly very abundant, but later on it was heavily persecuted for its rich pelt. The last one to be killed near London was shot in Epping Forest in 1883, but two more have been killed in southern England since the Second World War. The largest specimens measure up to 34 in from nose to tip of tail (tail 6–9 in) and weigh up to 4 lb 6 oz (Hurrell *et al.*, 1965).

The Polecat (*Mustela putorius*), which was almost exterminated by the beginning of this century, is now recovering, although it is mainly restricted to Wales, Devon, Cornwall and the Lake District (Taylor, 1952, Condry, 1954).

The rarest marine mammals are the three species which have only been recorded once. These are: Hose's Sarawak dolphin (*Lagenodelphis hosei*), which is known only from the type specimen collected at the mouth of the Lutong River, Barama, Borneo, in 1895 in an advanced state of decomposition (the skull of this dolphin is preserved in the British Museum of Natural History, London) (Fraser, 1956); the New Zealand beaked whale (*Tasmacetus shepherdi*) which is known only from the type specimen cast up on Ohawe Beach, New Zealand (the skeleton is preserved in the Wanganui Museum) (Oliver, 1937); and Longman's beaked whale (*Mesoplodon pacificus*) which is known only from a skull discovered on a Queensland beach in 1926 (Longman, 1926).

The fastest animal on earth over short distances (i.e. up to 600 yd) is the Cheetah or Hunting leopard (*Acinonyx jubatus*) with a probable maximum speed of 60–63 mile/h over suitably level ground. Speeds of 71, 84 and even 90 mile/h have been claimed for this animal, but these figures must be considered exaggerated.

According to Schaller (1968) 89 per cent of cheetah kills in the Serengeti National Park between June 1966 and November 1967 consisted of Thomson's gazelles (*Gazella thomsonii*) which has a top speed of 50 mile/h. But 56 per cent of these were sub-adult. He also found that nearly 50 per cent of cheetah pursuits after adult Thomson's gazelles ended in failure.

The cheetah lives on the open plains and semi-arid savannahs of East Africa, Iran, Turkmenia and Afghanistan. It was also found in India until quite recently, but it became extinct in the wild state in that country

The cheetah, the fastest mammal on earth over a short distance, in full stride. (Frank Lane.)

in the early 1950s (the cheetahs used by Indian princes today for the hunt are imported from Kenya).

In September 1937 eight cheetahs brought to England from Kenya by Mr. K. C. Gandar Dower, the well-known animal-collector and writer, were matched singly against greyhounds in a series of practice races on the oval dog-track at Harringay, London. Unfortunately, cheetahs will never run flat-out under domestic conditions, and this was subsequently proved in the trials.

The fastest times were put up by a female cheetah named "Helen", who recorded an average speed of 43·4 mile/h (cf. 43·26 mile/h for the fastest racehorse) over three 345 yd runs, compared to 36·9 mile/h for the fastest greyhound. The trials also revealed that a cheetah could give a greyhound a 20 yd start over this distance and still win comfortably.

It was interesting to note that in the races between the two animals the greyhound was the more difficult to manage and the worst tempered. If the dog caught the electric hare the cheetah left him alone. If the cheetah caught the hare, however, the dog would sometimes show fight. When this happened the cheetah would soundly cuff the dog and force it to retreat.

A few months earlier, at Romford Stadium, Essex, it had been discovered that when two cheetahs were raced against each other and one of them forged ahead, the other would stop and refuse to finish the course.

In 1960 Milton Hildebrand of the Department of Zoology at the University of California, Los Angeles, carried out some studies on the locomotion of the cheetah by timing and photographing a specimen as it ran after a piece of meat attached to a cord pulled at speed by a special mechanism (an adapted bicycle wheel and crank).

The cheetah was a female named "Ocala", who was used in an animal show at Ocala, Florida, and trained to run in a 65 yd long enclosure for rewards of meat.

The speed was determined for each of nine runs. The slowest speed was 27·7 mile/h, the fastest 37·5 mile/h, and the average 33 mile/h.

"Unfortunately," said Hildebrand, "the cheetah never extended itself over any of the runs, and probably regard the exercise as a game."

In an earlier study (1959), based on a film sequence of a running cheetah in the wild obtained from Walt Disney Productions, the same researcher calculated the top speed of the animal at 56 mile/h. At this velocity, which took 3 seconds to reach from a standing start, the cheetah completed one stride in 0·28 second, and each stride covered a distance of 23 ft.

Colonel Richard Meinertzhagen (1957) says a cheetah in Kenya reached 51 mile/h "when pressed by a car on a road over 200 yards".

The fastest of all land animals over a sustained distance is the Pronghorn antelope (*Antilocapra americana*) of the western United States.

In Oregon the speed of the pronghorn has been measured on several occasions because this antelope delights in racing cars which pass close to it.

On 10th October 1941 Mr. Don Robins of the United States Grazing Service paced four bucks for 4 miles near the Tudor Ranch in Malheur County. The antelope had already run about 200 yd before they came level with the car, and they travelled at a speed of 35 mile/h for another 4 miles, outdistancing the car which was travelling at 30 mile/h. This was probably their cruising speed, because they showed no evidence of tiring (Einarsen, 1948).

Another small group of pronghorns which raced parallel with a car on a road near Rincon, New Mexico, in 1918 averaged 30 mile/h for 7 miles (Carr, 1927).

It is only when hard pressed that the pronghorn attains really high speeds.

"On August 14, 1939," writes A. S. Einarsen, "I was with a group that paced many Pronghorns on the dried bed of Spanish Lake, in Lake County, Oregon. This lake-bed was as hard as adobe. It was a clear, breezy day, ideal to stir the racing instincts of the pronghorns, and as we rolled along the lake edge we had many challenges. Small groups here and there raced beside the car, until five, led by a magnificent buck, ran parallel to us, pressing toward the shore from the feeding area in the lake centre while we drove on a straight course. As they closed in from the right the buck took a lead of about 50 feet and Meyers [Field Observer of the Research Unit at the School of Agriculture, Oregon State College] increased speed to keep even with the animal. Dean Schoenfeld [also of the School of Agriculture] watched the speedometer, Meyers drove the car and I photographed the moving animals.

"The buck was now about 20 feet away and kept abreast of the car at 50 miles an hour. He gradually increased his gait, and with a tremendous burst of speed flattened out so that he appeared as lean and low as a greyhound. Then he turned toward us at about a 45 degree angle and disappeared in front of the car, to reappear on our left. He had gained enough to cross our course as the speedometer registered 61 m.p.h. After the buck passed us he quickly slackened his pace, and when he reached a rounded knoll about 600 feet away he stood snorting, in graceful silhouette, against the sky as though enjoying the satisfaction of beating us in a fair race. No sprinter could have posed in victory with a greater show of gratification. His action was typical and indicated no fright, or he would have continued to run until out of sight."

If the car speedometer was accurate, then this particular pronghorn must have been travelling at a speed of about 65 mile/h as it crossed in front of the car, which means it rivals the Cheetah for the title of "fastest animal on earth".

Other specimens have been observed to travel at 42 mile/h for 1 mile and 55 mile/h for half a mile.

During the Third Asiatic Expedition mounted by the American Museum of Natural History in 1922–23, Dr. Roy Chapman Andrews (1924), leader of the party, described how a herd of Mongolian gazelles (*Procapra guttorosa*) made a semicircle in front of his car which was moving in a straight line across the Gobi Desert at a rate of 40 mile/h. He estimated their speed at "not less than 55 or even 60 m.p.h.".

On another occasion Dr. Andrews said he timed by car speedometer a small group of Mongolian gazelles at 60 mile/h for 2 miles across the Gobi Desert before a punctured tyre ended the chase.

"They ran so fast that we could not see their legs, any more than you can see the blades of an electric fan. We found they would leg it at 60 m.p.h. for about two miles, and then slow down to 40 or 50. We chased an antelope one day for 20 minutes at an average rate of 40 m.p.h., and then he quit because he was so darned surprised that anything on earth could keep up with him. When we reached him he was squatting flat on the sand waiting, not winded a particle."

The 60 mile/h rate quoted by Dr. Andrews must be treated with reserve, however, because the car had a reported top speed of only 40 mile/h.

The Springbok (*Antidorcas marsupialis*) and Thomson's gazelle (*Gazella thomsonii*) of the grasslands and open plains of Africa, and the Blackbuck (*Antilope cervicapra*) of the open plains of West Pakistan and India, are also exceptionally fast and can probably reach 50 mile/h over short distances when hard pressed. Their normal cruising speed, however, is about 30 mile/h.

The handsome blackbuck of India, one of the fastest of all land animals. (Press Association.)

The fastest wild mammal found in the British Isles is probably the Roe deer (*Capreolus capreolus*), which can cruise at 25–30 mile/h for more than 20 miles, with occasional bursts of up to 40 mile/h. On 19th October 1970 a frightened runaway

Red deer (*Cervus elephus*) registered a speed of 42 mile/h on a police radar trap as it ran through a street in Stalybridge, Cheshire.

The slowest-moving mammal is the Ai or Three-toed sloth (*Bradypus tridactylus*) of tropical America which moves over the ground at a rate of 6 to 8 ft a minute (0·07–0·10 mile/h). In the trees, however, it can increase this speed to 120 ft a minute (1·4 mile/h) (Beebe, 1926).

MAMMALIAN SPEED TABLE

Common Name	Maximum running speed mile/h
Cheetah (*Acinonyx jubatus*)	63
Pronghorn antelope (*Antilocapra americana*)	61+
Mongolian gazelle (*Procapra guttorosa*)	55
Springbok (*Antidorcas marsupialis*)	52
Thomson's gazelle (*Gazella thomsonii*)	50
Grant's gazelle (*Gazella granti*)	47
Red deer (*Cervus elephus*)	42
Black-tailed deer (*Odocoileus columbianus*)	40·5
Mountain zebra (*Equus zebra*)	40
California jack rabbit (*Lepus californicus*)	40
Cape hartebeest (*Alcelaphus caama*)	40
Blue wildebeest (*Gorgon taurinus*)	37
Guanaco (*Lama huanacos*)	30
Mongolian wolf (*Canis* sp.)	36
Coyote (*Canis latrans*)	35
Indian jackal (*Canis aureus*)	35
European rabbit (*Oryctolagus cuniculus*)	35
Cape buffalo (*Syncerus caffer*)	35
Roan antelope (*Hippotragus equinus*)	35
Bison (*Bison bison*)	32
Giraffe (*Giraffa camelopardalis*)	32
Reindeer (*Rangifer tarandus*)	32
Indian wild ass (*Equus hemionus*)	32
Snowshoe hare (*Lepus americanus*)	31
Black bear (*Ursus americanus*)	30
Wart-hog (*Phachochoerus aethiopicus*)	30
Black rhinoceros (*Diceros bicornis*)	28
Common wolf (*Canis lupus*)	28
Grey fox (*Urocyon cinereoargentus*)	26
African elephant (*Loxodonta africana*)	24·5
Arabian camel (*Camelus dromedarius*)	20
Rocky mountain goat (*Oreamnos americanus*)	20
Kouprey (*Bos sauveli*)	18
Asiatic elephant (*Elephas maximus*)	16
Banteng (*Bibos banteng*)	11
Malayan tapir (*Tapirus indicus*)	10
Rat (*Rattus* sp.)	6
Common mole (*Talpa europaea*)	2·5
Three-toed sloth (*Bradypus tridactylus*)	0·1

Sources: Andrews, 1924; Howell, 1944; Lane, 1955; Bourlière, 1955; Foran, 1958; Breland, 1963.

The longest-lived mammal, excluding Man (*Homo sapiens*) is the Killer whale (*Orcinus orca*), which has a world-wide distribution. A bull with distinctive physical characteristics known as "Old Tom" was seen every winter from 1843 to 1930 in Twofold Bay, Eden, New South Wales, Australia and must have been over ninety years old at the time of his death.

The co-operation that existed between the killer whale packs and the early Twofold Bay whaling-men is unique in the annals of whaling. Every year, for the best part of a century, the killer whales, led by Old Tom (formerly known as "Stranger"), turned up in the bay, which they used as a forward base to prowl the adjacent ocean in search of the whalebone whales that migrated up and down the coast during the winter months.

If the whalemen were in close proximity when a large whale came within reasonable distance of the coast, the killers (some forty-five in number) would work with the boats, snapping at the whale like a pack of hungry wolves and trying to force it into the shallow bay. If the whalemen were not around, however, the main group of the killer force would round up their victim, while another detachment dashed into the bay and slapped their flukes on the surface with a resounding smack until the crews came out in their boats. Then, often at night, the submarine pack would lead the boats out to where the other killers were harassing the whale.

When they attacked a large whale the Twofold Bay killers worked with remarkable military precision. First of all four of them would separate from the main group, and while two of them seized the great tail in their massive jaws in an attempt to stop the whale thrashing about and slow it down, the others would station themselves under the head of their victim, thereby preventing it from sounding.

The rest of the killers would then swim alongside the leviathan and, at regular intervals, hurl themselves out of the water to land with a vicious thud across the sensitive blowhole of their victim. They were quickly thrown off again, but the action continued until the whale's breathing became laboured. This was the signal for the boatmen to move in close and push their lances home.

When the whale was dead, the killers would seize the carcass and drag it down to the bottom where they feasted on the tongue and lips. This was their reward for helping the whalemen. In twenty to twenty-eight hours the body would float to the surface, distended by the gases of putrefaction, and would then be towed to the trying works for processing.

Most of the whales killed in and around Twofold Bay were Rights or Humpbacks, but a few Fin whales were also taken, and on one occasion (1910) a 97 ft Blue whale was killed, with hand harpoon and lance, by Archer Davidson, leader of one of the boats, after it had been driven into the bay by Old Tom and his pirate band. The tail flukes of this whale measured 20 ft across, and its jaw bone was 23 ft 4 in long. *To date this has proved to be the ultimate in "fishing stories".*

Mead (1962) says many of the Twofold Bay killers were given names by the whalers and were easily recognised by sundry physical peculiarities. There was "Hooky" with the bent dorsal fin; "Jackson" with a long scar from an accidental lance thrust; "Typie" with the jagged serrated dorsal fin; "Charlie", the cow killer with the short dorsal fin and, of course, Old Tom, who had a distinctive broad green-white band encircling his body and an unusually shaped dorsal fin.

Old Tom was the best-known individual, and most of the stories refer to him. For instance, one of his favourite tricks was to seize the harpoon line between the whale and the boat and hang on to it, apparently for the thrill of being dragged forcibly through the water. The habit was deliberate, and sometimes the 4-ton killer would hang on for twenty to thirty minutes at a time, much to the whalers' annoyance.

The killers started to disappear in the Twofold Bay area during the First World War when the Norwegians were using their whaling ships off the coast of Queensland. The Norwegians weren't over-keen on the killers because they attacked their whales and sometimes pulled them under and cut their harpoon lines. At sea that means a lost whale. They didn't need the assistance of the killers, so they destroyed them.

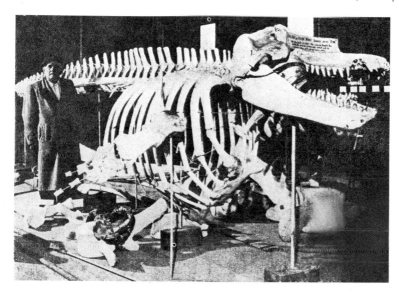

The skeleton of "Old Tom", leader of a pack of killer whales which frequented the coast of New South Wales, Australia for more than seventy years.

Once the killers were gone the whalebone whales stopped coming into Twofold Bay, and the whaling industry there packed up in 1922.

In 1928 only two killer whales, Old Tom and Hooky, turned up in the bay, and the following year Old Tom was on his own.

On 16th September 1930 Old Tom was sighted in the bay he loved so much again, but this time he appeared to be in a bad way, and the next day his carcass was found drifting just outside Snug Cove. No injuries were visible, and the killer had apparently died from some internal complaint or senile decay.

Drawings and measurements of the body were made (length 22 ft, dorsal fin 5 ft 5 in, pectoral fins 4 ft 6 in by 2 ft 10 in); then the blubber and meat was hacked away and the bones removed and cleaned up. Today the complete skeleton is mounted in the Eden Museum, which also contains relics of the Twofold Bay whaling industry.

The top jaw of Old Tom's skull is missing several teeth and some of the bone is missing, and this has been attributed to the killer's bad habit of swinging on the harpoon line. A well-known dental surgeon who examined the skull, however, said the damage was caused by a severe abscess at some time or other (Fripp, *in litt.* 9.9.60).

Shortly after Old Tom's death his faithful lieutenant Hooky turned up in Twofold Bay herding a Humpback whale and her calf. A scratch boat crew was hastily mustered and, after an exciting fight in which Hooky more than played his part, both whales were killed. From that day onwards, however, the killer whale was never seen again.

A large bull Sperm whale (*Physeter catadon*) captured in the North Pacific by a Japanese whaling expedition in 1961 was believed to have been sixty-five years old based on a count of dental annuli (Nishiwaki, *in litt.* 23.11.68).

The longest-lived land mammal, excluding Man, is the Asiatic elephant (*Elephas maximus*).

The greatest age that has been verified with reasonable certainty is an estimated sixty-nine years in the case of a cow named "Jessie", who arrived at Taronga Park Zoo in Sydney, New South Wales, Australia in 1882 as a gift from the King of Siam (now Thailand). She was destroyed on 26th September 1939 after developing abscesses on the soles of her feet which eventually made walking impossible (Le Souef, quoted by Flower, 1947). The exact age of Jessie on arrival in Australia was not recorded, but it was generally believed that she was about twelve years old. Patton (1940), however, thinks that she was about twenty, in which case she would have been about seventy-seven at the time of her death.

Like their heights and weights, exaggerated statements have been made about the ages attained by elephants, and stories of individuals living 100, 150 and even 200 years have been published. These extreme claims, however, were largely based on the huge size of the elephant, for it was argued that the larger an animal was the longer it could live.

Take, for instance, the case of the "Napoleon elephant". The Emperor was presented with the animal in Egypt in *c.* 1798 and brought it back to Paris with him. Later, he presented it to his father-in-law Francis, Emperor of Austria, who in turn sent the pachyderm to the Imperial Menagerie at Schönbrunn, Vienna. Here it turned dangerous, and eventually the beast was passed on to Budapest Zoological Gardens where it was said to be still living in 1930 at the age of about 150 years.

Fortunately, Major Stanley S. Flower, famous for his research on the longevity of animals, investigated this case thoroughly and discovered that the animal referred to was at the most "only about 40".

Apparently "Siam", as the elephant was known, arrived at the Imperial Menagerie at Schönbrunn on 11th November 1897 when a five-year-old calf, and was moved from Vienna to the Budapest Zoological Gardens in 1900 (Flower, 1948).

A pair of Asiatic elephants did in fact arrive at Schönbrunn in 1799, but the bull died in September 1810 aged approximately seventeen years, and the cow in July 1845 aged about fifty-three years (Fitzinger, 1863, quoted by Flower).

In 1932 a Berlin newspaper reported that a pair of Asiatic elephants belonging to the Zirkus Conrado were both eighty years old, but subsequent inquiries by Flower revealed that the bull was twenty-eight and the cow thirty years old.

An Asiatic cow elephant named "Babe" presented to the National Zoological Park, Washington, D.C. on 16th May 1934 by Ringling Brothers–Barnum and Bailey Circus after spending fifty-one years with them, was reputedly ninety-seven years old, but Flower believed her age was "slightly over 54 years" at the time of her death on 12th August 1937.

In 1940 Mr. Daniel Harkins, Curator of the Franklin Park Zoo, Boston, Massachusetts, U.S.A., stated that an Asiatic cow elephant named "Waddy" living there was the "oldest living captive elephant in the world". The cow was purchased by the zoo in 1914 after reputedly performing for twenty-five years on the stages of the world, and in 1940 her age was believed to be seventy-four years. She was "sunken at the temples, and arthritic in her right foreleg" and not expected to live much longer. After exhaustive inquiries, however, Flower said that her known age was fifty to fifty-one years.

Jessie's closest rival for age was probably the fine Asiatic tusker "Chandrasekharan" (see page 33), who died on 10th August 1940 aged sixty-seven years. He was handed over from the Travancore Forest Department to the Royal Stables on 15th August 1883 when aged about ten years. His mounted skeleton is now in the Trivandrum Museum (Pillai, 1941).

Sir Henry MacNaughten, in a letter to *The Times* on 4th May 1938, said that of the 1,700 elephants then working in Burma for the famous Bombay Burmah Trading Company, 1·4 per cent (= 24) were classified as over sixty-five years, 8·4 per cent between fifty-five and sixty-five years, and 90·2 per cent under fifty-five years. These figures were based upon records that had been carefully kept for over fifty years.

Further information on the longevity of elephants is given by R. D. Richmond (1933), Chief Conservator of Forests, Madras, who published a list of the 78 elephants over twenty years of age then working for the Madras Forest Department. There was 1 elephant over sixty, 7 over fifty, 16 over forty, 38 over thirty and 16 over twenty. The oldest elephant, a cow named "Peri", was stated to be sixty-seven, but this figure must have been a misprint because her age was estimated at fifteen years when she was captured in 1889.

Elephants living in captivity will always live longer than those in the wild state provided they have proper attention with regard to diet, exercise and bodily comforts, yet most of them die before the age of fifty. A wild elephant's age is determined by the persistence of its last molar teeth, which generally wear out about the fifty to fifty-fifth year and precipitate death by starvation because it is unable to masticate its food.

The greatest reliable age reported for an African bush elephant is an estimated fifty-five years for a cow shot in Murchison Falls National Park, Uganda, on 13th December 1963. The age was based on a count of seasonal and annual growth layers on the roots of the teeth. This is exceptional, however, because studies carried out by Laws *et al.* (1967) on 325 elephants that had died of natural causes in Uganda's two national parks in 1963–64 indicated that the average life-expectancy was "less than 15 years".

The magnificent tusker "Ahmed" of Marsabit National Park, Kenya, was reputedly sixty years old in 1970, but this age is largely based on hearsay.

The greatest reliable age reported for a bush elephant in captivity is "over 41 years" for a cow named "Jumbina" received at the National Zoological Park in Washington, D.C., U.S.A. on 8th August 1913. She died there on 30th June 1952 after living in the zoo for 38 years 10 months 22 days. Her age on arrival was about three years (Mann, 1953).

Another cow named "Karjoj" caught on the Blue Nile at the beginning of May 1905 and received at Giza Zoological Gardens on 10th July 1905 was thirty-nine to forty years old at the time of her death from tuberculosis on 11th February 1944 (Flower, 1948).

The greatest reliable age reported for a forest elephant is forty-three years for a cow named "Colonie" at the Gangala-na-Bodio training centre in the Congo, who was still alive in 1959. Another cow at the same centre named "Bakela" was forty at the time of her death (Bourlière & Verschuren, 1960).

MAXIMUM LONGEVITIES IN TERRESTRIAL MAMMALS
(excluding Domestic Animals)

Species	Age in years
Asiatic elephant (*Elephas maximus*)	69
African elephant (*Loxodonta africana*)	55
Hippopotamus (*Hippopotamus amphibius*)	54
Chimpanzee (*Pan troglodytes*)	51 †
Short-beaked spiny anteater (*Tachyglossus aculeatus*)	49
Indian rhinoceros (*Rhinoceros unicornis*)	47
European brown bear (*Ursus arctos*)	47
Mandrill (*Mandrillus sphinx*)	46
Lowland gorilla (*Gorilla g. gorilla*)	40 †
Chapman's zebra (*Equus burchelli antiquorum*)	40
Brown capuchin (*Cebus paraguayanus*)	37
Orang-utan (*Pongo pygmaeus*)	34
Bison (*Bison bison*)	33
Gibbon (*Hylobates hoolock*)	32 †
Asiatic two-horned rhinoceros (*Rhinoceros sumatrensis*)	32
Malayan tapir (*Tapirus indicus*)	30
African lion (*Leo leo*)	29
Giraffe (*Giraffa camelopardalis*)	28
Two-humped Camel (*Camelus bactriarus*)	27
African buffalo (*Syncerus caffer*)	26
Black lemur (*Lemur macaco*)	25
Ratel (*Mellivora capensis*)	24
Two-toed sloth (*Choloepus didactylus*)	23
Tiger (*Leo tigris*)	22
Llama (*Llama peruana*)	21
Common porcupine (*Hystrix cristata*)	20
Common wombat (*Vombatus hirsutus*)	19
Sumatran porcupine (*Hystrix longicauda*)	18
Sambar (*Rusa unicolor*)	17
Red kangaroo (*Macropus rufa*)	16
Indian otter (*Amblonyx cinerea*)	15
Red fox (*Vulpes vulpes*)	14
Grey kangaroo (*Macropus major*)	13
Common marmoset (*Callithrix jacchus*)	12
American marten (*Martes americana*)	11
Golden marmoset (*Leontocebus rosalia*)	10
Capybara (*Hydrochoerus hydrochoeris*)	9
Grey squirrel (*Sciurus carolinensis*)	8
Native cat (*Dasyurus quoll*)	7
Coypu (*Myocastor coypus*)	6
Algerian hedgehog (*Erinaceus algirus*)	5
Lesser Egyptian gerbil (*Gerbillus gerbillus*)	4
Black rat (*Rattus rattus*)	3
Common hamster (*Cricetus cricetus*)	2
Pygmy shrew (*Sorex minutus*)	1

Sources: Flower, 1931; Comfort, 1964; Jones, 1968.
† Still alive.

The shortest-lived mammals are True shrews (family Soricidae). Some species have a life-span of less than two years, including the Common shrew (*Sorex araneus*) of Europe and Asia which usually dies before it is one year old (Crowcroft, 1956).

The highest living mammal is probably the Yak (*Poephagus grunniens*), the wild ox of Tibet, which has occasionally been found at an altitude of 20,000 feet in the Himalayas. Its closest rival is probably the Tibetan pika (*Ochotona thibetana*), which lives up to the 18,000 ft mark

In May 1954 two members of the *Daily Mail Abominable Snowman Expedition* to the Himalayas saw what appeared to be a Red bear (*Ursus arctos isabellinus*) at an altitude of 18,000 ft on the Reipimu glacier and later found a fresh set of footprints. The Blue bear (*U.s. pruinosus*) of Tibet and western China is also found at high altitudes. Most of the sightings and discovery of tracks of the so-called yeti can be attributed to these two animals.

The largest herds ever recorded were those of the Springbok (*Antidorcas marsupialis*), also called the "Springbuck", during migration across the high open plains of the western regions of southern Africa in the nineteenth century. These great *trekbokkens*, as the Boers called them, occurred at irregular intervals when overcrowding became acute and food- and water-supplies dwindled. The gazelles would join up to form a herd of almost inconceivable magnitude, and then set off across the desert tracts and veld in search of fresh pastures. They moved in such densely packed masses that any unfortunate animals met on the way were either trampled to death or forced along with them, and the country was left completely devastated in their wake. Hardly any of the springbok survived the migrations. Most of them died from starvation, drowning (attempting to cross the Orange River) or disease; others fell to predators (including Man) or died from drinking salt water if they reached the sea.

Sometimes it would take days for the living wave of animals to pass a given point. In 1849, for instance, John Fraser (later Sir John Fraser) saw a *trekbokken* that took three days to pass through the settlement of Beaufort West, Cape Province.

Between 1887 and 1896 there were four great springbok treks in the Prieska District of the Karoo in Cape Province. In 1888 T. B. Davie, a local citizen, and Dr. Gibbons, a naturalist, tried to estimate the number of Springbok moving in a trek near Nels Poortje.

"In the morning as soon as it was daylight we were out," says Davie (1921), "and there we were sure enough in a veritable sea of antelopes. The Doctor saw at once, upon being rallied as to counting them, that it was impossible, but he made a guess after this fashion. Seeking a kraal [a fold for stock], a good large one, he asked how many sheep could stand in it, and Mr. Danth replied 1,500. 'Well,' said the Doctor, 'if 1,500 can stand there, then about 10,000 can stand on an acre, and I can see in front of me 10,000 acres covered with "boks"; that means at least 100,000,000; then what about the miles upon miles around on all sides as far as the eye can reach covered with them?' He gave it up. We left Nels Poortje after breakfast and rode for 4½ hours right straight through them, they never giving more road than was required for us to pass. . . ."

According to an eyewitness account of the last great migration in July 1896 the enormous herd covered an area of 2,170 square miles (138 miles long and 15 miles wide) as it advanced towards Karree Kloof near the Orange River (Cronwright-Schreiner, 1925).

These great periodic movements are now a thing of the past. The migrations were so ruinous to crops and livestock that the farmers began destroying the springbok in great numbers, and this extermination, combined with outbreaks of rinderpest, reduced the populations drastically. Today springbok are found in reasonable abundance only in the Kalahari Desert (especially around Etosha Pan) and parts of South-West Africa, and their numbers no longer threaten to disturb the delicate balance of nature.

With the possible exception of one or two other African game animals, the only other land mammal known to travel in herds numbering more than a million strong was the Bison or North American buffalo (*Bison bison*) during migration in the nineteenth century.

The largest bison herd ever recorded was the "southern herd" observed moving between Fort Zarah and Fort Larned in Arkansas, U.S.A. in May 1871. According to Colonel Richard Irving Dodge (1887), who passed through the herd in a light wagon, the buffalo were moving on a front 25 miles wide and 50 miles deep, and were "as thick as they could graze".

On the basis of these figures Dr. William T. Hornaday (1887), Director of the New York Zoological Society, calculated that the herd must have contained 12,000,000 head. He added, however: "But, judging from the general principles governing such migrations, it is almost certain that the moving mass advanced in the shape of a wedge, which make it necessary to deduct about two-thirds from the grand total, which would leave 4,000,000 as our estimate of the actual number of buffaloes in this great herd, which I believe is more likely to be below the truth than above it."

Dr. Hornaday's calculations were based on the buffalo averaging ten head per acre of ground in a wedge covering 625 square miles or 400,000 acres, but there could just as easily have been fifteen head to the acre, making a grand total of 6,000,000 (another observer once counted 228 buffalo feeding in one acre, but this is exceptional).

In 1873 a party of hunters reportedly took seven days to pass through a herd moving between Medicine Hat, Alberta, Canada, and the Red Deer Forest on the South Saskatchewan River (Allen, 1876).

Voorhees (1920) says another herd observed moving between the North and South Platte in Nebraska in August 1859 was over 200 miles deep.

According to Garretson (1938) General Philip H. Sheridan and a member of his Staff, Major Henry Inman, once tried to estimate the number of buffalo in a herd encountered by them between Fort Dodge and Fort Supply in Oklahoma in 1866. The buffalo were moving north on a 100 mile wide front, but the depth of the herd was not known. Their first estimate was 10,000,000,000, but this figure was so astronomical that they tried again and came up with 1,000,000,000. Even then they weren't satisfied with the result, and in the end decided that the herd contained over 100,000,000 animals. This figure, of course, is still impossibly high, and it is interesting to note that in January the previous year Major Inman was quoted as saying that there were 15,000,000 buffalo in the whole of the United States! (Roe, 1951).

In 1830 there were an estimated 40,000,000 buffalo roaming the plains of North America from Canada to Texas. By 1870, however, the total had been reduced to 14,000,000 through indiscriminate slaughter, and five years later to approximately 1,000,000. Finally, in 1894, there were less than a thousand buffalo left alive in the whole of North America.

Lacking any motive to kill more buffalo than could be used, the Indians never took more than a few hundred thousand animals a year with their bows and arrows and lures; consequently there was no noticeable thinning of the ranks, even after the introduction of horses by the Spanish *conquistadores*.

However, the coming of the white man to the New World in large numbers changed all this. He was a killer of the first order, and it wasn't long before he saw in the buffalo a commercially valuable animal. As he expanded westwards the great plains became littered with the bones of slaughtered bison.

The poor bison learned nothing from these orgies of killing. Stupid, sluggish, inoffensive creatures, they were easy targets for the hordes of commercial hunters that invaded the lush plains armed with heavy, long-range rifles.

Probably the greatest single contribution to the downfall of the bison was the construction of the transcontinental Union Pacific railroad, which was completed in 1869.

Up to that time the bison had occupied one large and continuous tract of land, but now the railroad cut this area in half and, at the same time, divided the animals into two groups known as the "southern" and "northern" herds. The southern herd, the larger of the two, was centred in Kansas, Oklahoma and Texas.

The vast army of men employed on building the railroad were provided with "buffalo" meat and Colonel William F. Cody, better known as "Buffalo Bill" was the first individual to supply it to the railroad pioneers. He and his cowboys fed the railroad for a year and a half, and in that time he *personally* supplied the commissariat with 4,280 bison.

The wholesale slaughter of the bison reached its peak between 1872 and 1874 when the settlers—and the Indians, who by then had been given modern shooting weapons—killed over 3,500,000 head in the southern herd, and by 1878 the herd had ceased to exist as a body.

The virtual extinction of the southern herd was followed by heavy exploitation of the northern herd, but the massacre did not really begin in earnest until 1880 when the Northern Pacific Railroad extended its line from Bismarck, Montana, into buffalo country; by 1891 the herd had been reduced to a small remnant numbering about 300 animals which had wandered into the inaccessible region near Great Slave Lake, northern Canada. These were Wood bison (*B.b. athabascae*), which are larger and darker than the typical race of the plains.

The depletion of the great herds was so startling that sportsmen and naturalists alike suddenly awoke to the danger. In 1893 protective legislation was introduced in Canada, and the following year the U.S. Congress rushed a law through making it illegal to kill bison in that country. At that time, says Seton (1927), there were probably no more than 800 specimens left in the world.

Finally, in 1905, the American Bison Society was founded which subsequently established suitable reservations for what had once been one of the most abundant game animals the world has ever known.

Today the bison is strictly protected. There are now over 30,000 of these noble monarchs divided up equally between the big national parks and zoological gardens of the United States and Canada, plus a small number in foreign zoos.

The longest of all mammalian gestation periods is that of the Asiatic elephant (*Elephas maximus*) with an average of 608 days or just over 20 months. Burne (1943) gives a record of a cow named "Mai Mai", captured in the Mongpan Forest, Southern Shan States, Burma, who gave birth to a bull calf after a gestation period of 760 days—more than two and a half times that of a human. Another cow named "Mai Myat" in the same stable gave birth to a bull calf after a gestation period of 743 days. Asiatic elephants usually have their first calf at between the ages of 16 and 20 years, and the captive specimens average seven pregnancies during their lifetime (this figure may be higher in the wild state) (Hundley, 1922). The gestation period of the African bush elephant is reported to be 549 days for a female calf, and 668 days for a bull calf (Mitchell, 1931), but these figures have been questioned.

The elephants' closest rival for duration of gestation is the White or Square-lipped rhinoceros (*Diceros simus*) with 548 to 578 days, followed by the Black rhinoceros (*Diceros bicornis*) with 485 to 550 days, and the Indian rhinoceros (*Rhinoceros unicornis*) with 484 to 548 days (Ali, 1927). The Hippopotamus (*Hippopotamus amphibius*), rather surprisingly, has a gestation period of only 210 to 255 days (Kerbert, 1922).

The shortest of all mammalian gestation periods is probably that of the American opossum (*Didelphis marsupialis*), also called the "Virginian opossum", which is normally twelve to thirteen days but may be as short as eight days (Reynolds, 1952). This species is born in a very immature state, and the young are immediately transferred to the ventral pouch, where they remain for ten weeks until embryonic development is completed. The gestation periods of the rare Water opossum or Yapok (*Chironectes minimus*) of central and northern South America (average twelve to thirteen days), and the Eastern native cat (*Dasyurus viverrinus*) of Australia (average twelve days) may also be as short as eight days (Walker *et al.*, 1964).

The shortest of all mammalian gestation periods in which the young are fully developed at birth is probably that of the Golden hamster (*Mesocricetus auratus*) of Syria with an average of fifteen to sixteen days. Gestations as low as thirteen days have been reported for both the Common shrew (*Sorex araneus*) and the House mouse (*Mus musculus*), but the average periods are sixteen and seventeen days respectively (Burton, 1962).

The highest recorded number of young born to a wild mammal at a single birth is thirty-two (not all of which survived) in the case of the Common tenrec (*Centetes ecaudatus*) found in Madagascar and the Comoro Islands. The average litter size is thirteen to fourteen.

In March 1961 a litter of thirty-two was also reported for a House mouse (*Mus musculus*) at the Roswell Park Memorial Institute in Buffalo, N.Y., U.S.A. (average litter size thirteen to twenty-one).

The only other mammals to produce litter sizes in excess of twenty are the Brown rat (*Rattus norvegicus*) with a maximum of twenty-three (average litter size five to eight), and the Golden hamster (*Mesocricetus auratus*) with a maximum of twenty-two (average litter size fifteen to seventeen).

The common tenrec, producer of the largest litters among mammals. (Central Photographic Agency.)

The greatest number of litters produced by a mammal in a single year is seventeen (average litter size four to nine) by the North American meadow mouse (*Microtus pennsylvanicus*) (Burton, 1965). This animal is also the most prolific breeder in the mammalian world.

The fastest-developing mammal in the world is the Streaked tenrec (*Hemicentetes semispinous*) of Madagascar. It is weaned after only five days, and females are capable of breeding three to four weeks after birth.

The heaviest mammalian brain is that of the Sperm whale (*Physeter catadon*), also called the "Cachalot". During the Japanese whaling expedition to the Antarctic in 1949/50, Dr. Tokuzo Kojima (1951) of the Brain Institute, University of Tokyo, weighed the brains of sixteen adult bulls brought aboard the factory ship *Nissin Maru No. 1*. The heaviest example, taken from a 49-footer, weighed 9·2 kg (20·24 lb), and the lightest 6·4 kg (14·08 lb) (the latter brain was removed from a very old individual for measuring). The average weight was 7·8 kg (17·16 lb). This brain weight may be matched by that of the adult bull Killer whale (*Orcinus orca*), but further information is needed.

The heaviest fin whale brain on record according to Slijper (1962) weighed 8·3 kg (18·36 lb), and he says the brain of a 90 ft long blue whale weighed 6·9 kg (15·38 lb).

The heaviest weight recorded for an elephant brain is 16·5 lb for a 4,355 lb Asiatic elephant (Gilchrist, 1851).

The heaviest brain of any mammal in relation to body weight is probably that of the Common marmoset (*Callithrix jacchus*), which accounts for one-eighteenth of the total weight of the animal (cf. the brain of man which is in the ratio of 1 : 45).

The mammal that spends the longest time in hibernation is the Edible dormouse (*Glis glis*). The period of hibernation usually lasts between five and six months

(October to April), but there is a record of an English specimen sleeping for six months and twenty-three days without interruption. The Common hedgehog (*Erinaceus europaeus*) may also spend six months in hibernation, but it is not a continuous sleep.

In some parts of its northern range the Grizzly bear (*Ursus arctos horribilis*) has been known to remain in its winter den for as long as seven months (McCracken, 1957), but it is not a true hibernation because the bear always remains in full possession of its senses.

The largest living terrestrial carnivore is the Kodiak bear (*Ursus arctos middendorfii*), which is found on Kodiak Island and adjacent Afognak and Shuyak islands in the Gulf of Alaska, U.S.A. The average adult male has a nose to tail length of 8 ft (tail about 4 in), stands 52 in at the shoulder and weighs between 1,050 and 1,175 lb. Females are about one-third smaller.

The greatest weight recorded for a Kodiak bear in the wild is 1,656 lb for a male shot at English Bay, Kodiak Island, in 1894 by Mr. J. C. Tolman, later Customs officer on Wrangel Island. The bear was killed by a single shot in the head from a Winchester rifle. The *stretched* skin (pegged to the side of a cabin on a frame and then weighted down with rocks at the bottom edge) measured 13 ft 6 in from the tip of the nose to the root of the tail, and the hind-foot was 18 in long (Phillips-Woolley, 1894).

The largest Kodiak bear ever held in captivity was a male at Cheyenne Mountain Zoological Park, Colorado Springs, Colorado, U.S.A., which scaled 1,670 lb at the time of its death on 22nd September 1955 (Crandall, 1964). Unfortunately, nothing is known about the physical condition of this animal, but it was probably "cage fat". The bear arrived at the zoo as a cub direct from Kodiak Island on 29th June 1940.

According to Couturier (1954) a weight of 1,200 kg (2,640 lb) was recorded for a Kodiak bear at Berlin Zoological Gardens in 1937, but this figure is incorrect. In a letter to the author dated 13th January 1968 Dr. Heinz-Georg Klos, the zoo's Scientific Director, said the bear, which was killed in an air raid in 1943, scaled about 550 kg (1,210 lb).

In June 1953 a male Kodiak bear weighing 1,400 lb drowned in his pool at Taronga Park Zoo, Sydney, New South Wales, Australia after being knocked unconscious by a brick thrown by a vandal.

The largest Kodiak bear ever held captive in a British zoo was a male (one of twins) named "Pick" born at Whipsnade Zoological Park on 29th January 1954. At the time of his death in October 1963 he weighed 1,148 lb. He could reach meat suspended 10 ft 3 in from the ground (Tong, *in litt.* 27.3.65).

Thomas Henry (1958) has described a giant variety of Kamchatka bear (*U.a. piscator*) from the southern part of the peninsula which he says exceeds even the Kodiak bear in size, but this claim is not supported by Russian findings. Baturin, who shot a great number of bears in Kamchatka, says his largest specimen weighed 40 poods (1,441 lb), and another male killed by him on 19th April 1917 in the Zheltaya River Estuary measured 244 cm (8 ft) nose to root of tail. Baikov quotes a maximum weight of 425 kg (935 lb) for males (Ognev, 1931).

The Peninsula giant bear (*U.a. gyas*) of the Alaska Peninsula and other parts of the country has also been credited with the title of "largest living land carnivore" by some authorities, but this race of brown bear

A peninsula giant bear weighing an estimated 1,700 lb shot in Alaska in May 1948. (Robert C. Reeve.)

is slightly smaller on the average than the kodiak bear. Adult males measure about 7·75 ft nose to tail and weigh about 1,100 lb. On 28th May 1948 Robert C. Reeve of Anchorage shot an enormous specimen near Cold Bay which measured 10 ft nose to tail (the skin weighed 193·5 lb). Its weight was *estimated* at 1,600 to 1,700 lb. Reeves said that the bear had just come out of hibernation and carried little or no fat, and he believed that the animal would have weighed about 1,850 lb at the end of the summer (Couturier, 1954).

Another bear shot in Clearwater Gap, about 60 miles south-west of Rocky Mountain House, Alberta, Canada, in November 1949 had a nose to tail length of over 9 ft and weighed an *estimated* 1,600 lb.

The big brown bear shot by Harold McCracken (1957) near Frosty Peak at the western end of the Alaska Peninsula in November 1916 was also credited with a weight of 1,600 lb. The skin of this animal measured 11 ft 4 in from nose to tail and 10 ft 6 in across the outstretched front paws.

In 1904 Lieutenant-Colonel N. Armstrong of Preston, Ontario, killed a bear while out hunting in the Yukon west of the Mackenzie River which had a skin length of 10 ft 4 in and weighed an *estimated* 1,800 lb. Another huge example shot by Arthur Johnson at Herendeen Bay, Alaska Peninsula, in May 1948 measured 9 ft nose to tail and weighed an *estimated* 1,500 lb (now on display in the Museum of the University of Alaska). On 2nd June 1918 Robert H. Rockwell of Brooklyn Museum, New York, shot a very dark male on the Alaska Peninsula which measured 48 in at the shoulder, 67 in round the chest and 10 ft 6 in nose to tail (skin). Its weight was estimated at 1,500 lb, but judging from its girth measurement this figure was too high. Another male shot by Dr. J. Wylie Anderson on Unimak Island in June 1909 reportedly weighed 1,320 lb, but Rowland Ward (1928) gives the weight of this specimen as 1,460 lb and says its skin measured 11 ft in length.

The largest Peninsula giant bear ever held in captivity was probably a male captured on 24th May 1901 near Douglas Settlement, at the western entrance to Cook Inlet on the Alaska Peninsula and sent to the National Zoological Park, Washington, D.C. where it was received on 9th January 1902.

Its weight progressed as follows: 15th January 1903 450 lb; 18th January 1904 625 lb; 28th January 1905 770 lb; 28th February 1906 890 lb; 11th March 1907 970 lb; 21st March 1908 1,050 lb; 5th March 1909 960 lb; 20th January 1911 1,160 lb; 13th December 1911 1,090 lb. Seton (1919) says the bear was heaviest about 1st December 1910 when it scaled an estimated 1,200 lb, but unfortunately it could not be weighed at that time.

The drastic loss of weight during 1909 followed a corn-removing operation on 15th June 1908 which immobilised the animal for some time. According to Seton the diet of this bear was very carefully regulated, and at no time during its twelve-year stay at the zoo was it over-fat.

Weights in excess of 1,000 lb have also been reliably reported for the Grizzly bear (*U.a. horribilis*), although the average adult male weighs about 600 lb and stands about 42 in at the shoulder. One huge male killed in the Okanogan Forest Reserve, Washington, U.S.A. in early August 1924 weighed "over 1,100 pound". It was a notorious cattle-killer, and over a period of three years took nearly fifty head of cattle and more than 150 sheep (*Annual Report of the Department of Agriculture*, 1924). Another grizzly killed in Idaho in the nineteenth century was sold to a butcher in Spokane who claimed that he paid for 1,173 lb of bear meat. This figure was placed on the carcass as it hung in front of his shop (Wright, 1909).

In May 1920 archer Arthur Young of San Francisco killed a monstrous grizzly in the Yellowstone National Park, Wyoming, with a single arrow through the heart. Later, Dr. Saxton Pope, who accompanied Young on the trip, wrote: "As we dismembered him, we weighed the parts. The veins were absolutely dry of blood, and without this substance which represents a loss of nearly ten per cent of his weight he was 916 lb. There was hardly an inch of fat on his back. At the end of the summer this adipose layer would be nearly 6 inches thick. He would then have weighed over 1,400 lb."

Much less reliable is a claim by another hunter named Johnny Zantus that he shot one "grey bear" near Fort Tejon, Kern County, California in 1857–58 which weighed 2,000 lb and was the largest bear ever killed in those parts (Grinnel *et al.*, 1937). Another grizzly killed in the same area in June 1875 reportedly weighed 1,600 lb, but once again this figure was based on an estimate.

Merriam (1918) says an old male grizzly of huge size killed at the head of Trabuco Canyon, California, in January 1901 had an *estimated* weight of 1,400 lb.

Hendrick (1946) mentions a "mammoth grizzly" taken in what is now El Dorado County, California, in the last century which produced no less than 1,100 lb of meat and earned the hunter $1,375. Another grizzly killed in the hills near Matilija Canyon, Ventura County, California, in September 1882 allegedly scaled 1,500 lb and required the efforts of two strong horses to drag it away, but the true weight was believed to have been nearer the 1,000 lb mark. Newmark (1926) give a record of a grizzly which tipped the scales at 2,350 lb [*sic*], but this poundage is much too extreme to be acceptable.

A 9 ft long grizzly killed by the Lewis and Clark Expedition in Montana in 1805 was estimated to weigh 1,000 lb (Ord, 1894), but this figure was probably an *understatement* judging by the measurements quoted for this beast.

Although the largest brown bears are now found in Alaska, it has been claimed by some authorities (Lydekker, 1901; Hittell, 1926) that those which formerly inhabited the high peaks of the Sierra Nevada Range were in fact the biggest of all, weights of 1,700 and 1,800 lb being regularly recorded.

While these poundages must be considered excessive, it is interesting to note that Rowland Ward list a Nevada grizzly of 1,536 lb in their 1907 edition. The bear, shot by W. F. Sheard in 1881, was stated to have measured 11 ft 6 in in length (skin) and 10 ft 2 in across the outstretched front paws.

The largest grizzly bear ever held in captivity was a male which lived for eighteen years in Lincoln Park Menagerie, Chicago, Illinois, U.S.A. Shields (1899) says the bear "was fed to suffocation by the thousands of visitors, and in his later years grew so fat that he could not walk, could only crawl around." His weight was variously estimated at 1,800 to 2,200 lb, but he actually scaled 1,153 lb at the time of his death. His nose to tail length was given as 7 ft 8·5 in, and his shoulder height as 41·75 in.

Another male grizzly known as "Monarch" caught in a log trap by some Mexicans on Mount Gleason in the San Gabriel Mountains of Los Angeles County, California, in October 1889, was also about the same size. He was billed as "the largest grizzly in captivity" and credited with weights up to 1,600 lb, but when he was shot in May 1911 because of advanced senility he tipped the scales at 1,127 lb. This bear was later *over-stuffed* and put on display in the Museum of the California Academy of Sciences in Los Angeles (Grinnel *et al.*, 1957).

"Grizzly Adams", alias James Capen Adams, an enterprising hunter and animal-collector who toured the country with his menagerie, claimed that his grizzly bear "Sampson" (trapped in the Sierra Nevada Range in the winter of 1854–55) was "the largest specimen of the Grizzly species perhaps that ever was taken alive". He said the bear had been weighed on a hay scale and tipped the beam at 1,510 lb (Hittell, 1926), but this was a showman's exaggeration. Dr. Hornaday, Director of the New York Zoological Society, who saw the animal, estimated its weight at 800 lb.

Merriam (1918) lists seven full species and fifteen sub-species of brown and grizzly bears in North America, but these identifications are largely based on differences in size and colours of pelts. The modern view is that they are all races of a single species—*Ursus arctos*.

Weights in excess of 30 poods (1,080 lb) have also been reported for the Manchurian or Ussurian bear (*U.a. mandchuricus*), but further information is lacking. The average weight of an adult male is 12–20 poods (430–720 lb), and the average length 214 cm (7 ft 0·5 in) (Przhevalskii, 1870).

The greatest reliable weight recorded for a European brown bear *(U.a. arctos)* is 480 kg (1,056 lb) for a 243 cm (8 ft) long male shot in the Oural District, northern Russia (Kazeeff, 1878). The average adult male weighs 450–550 lb and measures 6 ft in length.

The Polar bear (*Ursus maritimus*), which is found in the Arctic regions of North America, Europe and Asia, is a more streamlined animal than the brown bears. It has a proportionately longer body, a longer neck and a less massive skull.

The average adult male measures 7·75 ft nose to tail (tail 3–8 in), stands 48 in at the shoulder and weighs 850–900 lb (adult females are one-third smaller), but much larger individuals have been recorded.

Captain George F. Lyon (1825), for instance, describes how members of his crew killed a large polar bear at the entrance to Hudson Strait, North-West Territories, Canada, in July 1821 which measured 8 ft 7 in in length, 7 ft 11 in in maximum girth and 4 ft 9 in at the shoulder. "On lifting him in, we were astonished to find that his weight exceeded 1,600 pounds."

James Lamont (1876) says he shot a huge male in Deeve Bay, Spitsbergen. "He was so large and heavy that we had to fix the ice-anchor, and drag him up with block and tackle as if he had been a walrus. This was an enormous old male bear and measured upwards of 8 feet in length, almost as much in circumference, and 4½ feet at the shoulder. . . . He was in very high condition, and produced nearly 400 pounds of fat; his skin weighed upwards of 100 pound and the entire carcase of the animal cannot have been less than 1,600 pounds."

The Jackson-Harmsworth Expedition to the Arctic shot several bears. One old male killed at Cape Flora, Franz Josef Land, on 7th October 1894 measured 8 ft 1 inch in length and 7 ft in girth, and another male measuring "over 8 feet in length" was shot at Beel Island on 20th March 1895 (Jackson, 1899). Unfortunately, no weights were quoted for these two bears, but they both probably exceeded 1,300 lb.

Rowland Ward (1907) list a large male killed by W. Livingstone Learmouth in Baffin Bay which measured 9 ft 5 inches in length (skin) and 4 ft 6 in at the shoulder, but the bear was not weighed.

Robert A. Bartlett (1939), the American hunter and explorer, says he killed a monstrous bear while travelling from Wrangell Island across Long Strait to the Siberian shore in 1914. "The Eskimo who was with me, and I, turned him face down on his belly. He measured about 12 feet in length and must have weighed a ton [U.S. short ton of 2,000 lb]."

These figures, however, must be considered exaggerated because two men could not possibly turn a 2,000 lb bear over by themselves.

According to Perry (1966), the French-Canadian explorer and hunter André Tremblay shot a monstrous bear near Cape York, northern Baffin Island, in the early part of this century which measured 11 ft in length, 4 ft 6 in at the shoulder and weighed an estimated 1,800 lb. The local Eskimoes told him it was the largest bear they had ever seen. Perry also mentions a polar bear killed on Franz Josef Land by members of the Russian research station there in the winter of 1931 which measured 12 ft 4 inches in length and scaled between 1,300 and 1,550 lb, but the length quoted for this bear must have been a skin measurement.

In October 1957 three Eskimo hunters returning to Point Barrow, northern Alaska, claimed they had seen a polar bear over "30 ft long [sic]" roaming the ice-shelf along the Arctic Sea coast. A few months later Tom Bolock, an American big-game hunter, shot a giant bear which could have been the same animal as it was making a beeline for Siberia. The bear measured just over 10 ft in length, and its weight was conservatively *estimated* at 1,800 lb.

Another specimen measuring 10 ft in length and weighing 1,498 lb was shot by Robert E. Petersen in the same area in July 1965.

In 1960 Arthur Dubs of Medford, Oregon, U.S.A. shot a polar bear at the polar entrance to Kotzebue Sound, north-west Alaska, which was stated to have weighed 2,210 lb before skinning, but this figure needs confirming. In April 1962 the 11 ft 1·5 in tall mounted specimen was put on display at the Seattle World Fair, but judging from photographic

The controversial polar bear shot in Kotzebue Sound, Alaska in 1960 which allegedly weighed 2,210 lb before skinning.

evidence this bear has been made to stand about a foot taller than it would have done in life.

In *Records of North American Big Game* (1952), the official book of the Boone and Crockett Club, the compilers state: "Contary to public belief, no known bear exceeds 8 feet 10 inches in a standing position."

That it is possible for polar bear bears to exceed 2,000 lb, however, has been confirmed by Ognev, who says that some of the old males killed on Spitsbergen have scaled as much as 60 poods (2,160 lb), but even a weight of 1,600 lb must be considered extraordinary.

The largest polar bear ever held in captivity was probably a male which lived in Bronx Zoo, New York, for fourteen years. At the time of its death in 1960 this bear weighed 1,030 lb (Crandall, 1964).

On 21st February 1936 a posthumous weight of 1,160 lb was reported for a male hybrid between a male Polar bear and a female Kodiak bear at the National Zoological Park, Washington, D.C., U.S.A. (Davis, 1950).

At a meeting of the American Institute of Biological Sciences in New York in October 1965 Dr. Martin Schein, Professor of Zoology at Pennsylvania State University, told members that the polar bear was appearing to be evolving into a mammal of the sea like the whale.

He said he had noted, among other things, that it does not kick with its hind-legs while swimming like most land mammals, but uses them as a rudder the way a whale uses its tail.

Dr. Schein added, however, that evolution was a slow process, and that it would take millions of years for the polar bear to become a sea animal similar to the whale, walrus and dolphin (Myler, United Press International).

The largest land carnivore found in Britain is the Badger *(Meles meles)*, which is widely distributed. The average adult male measures 3 ft in total length (including 4 in tail) and weighs 27 lb (Neal, 1964), but there are several records over 50 lb, including one of 66 lb.

The badger, Britain's largest land carnivore. (R. A. Harris and K. R. Duff—F. Lane.)

The largest toothed mammal ever recorded is the Sperm whale *(Physeter catodon)*, which has a world-wide distribution. The average adult bull measures 47 ft in length and weighs 33 tons, and the average adult female 33 ft and 9·5 tons.

The largest accurately measured sperm whale on record was a 20·7 m (67 ft 11 in) bull captured near the Kurile Islands in the north-west Pacific by a Russian whaling fleet during the summer of 1950 (*International Whaling Statistics*, 1950/51). The whale was not weighed, but it must have scaled about 78 tons. Another bull measuring 20·43 m (67 ft) was taken in Japanese waters in 1946, and one captured near the Faroes by the Norwegians in 1964 measured 19·8 m (65 ft).

In the early days of whaling lengths up to 84 ft and estimated weights up to 100 tons were reported for bull sperm whales killed in the South Seas (Beale, 1839), but as no whales approaching anywhere near this size have been measured by qualified biologists these figures must be considered unreliable.

There is, however, an interesting record of a very large sperm whale captured off the Galapagos Islands (600 miles off Ecuador) by the British barque *Adam* in 1817 which yielded 100 barrels of oil (the average yield is 50–55 barrels). A tooth from this whale measured 9·5 inches in length, 9 inches in circumference and weighed 3 lb (Lydekker, 1894).

According to Roberts (1951) a sperm whale measuring 75 ft in length was killed in Algoa Bay, on the south-east coast of Cape Province, South Africa, on 15th May 1897. It yielded 3,000 gal of oil, 4,000 gal of spermaceti and 4 lb of ambergris, and the skeleton was presented to the Port Elizabeth Museum.

In a letter to the author dated 17th June 1966, however, Dr. G. McLachlan, Director of Port Elizabeth Museum, said the skeleton (now dismantled) had originally been erected in a 63 ft long hall and measured 58 ft. This means that the bull must have had a length in the flesh of about 63 ft which, although not a record, is still very impressive.

On the 25th June 1903 a length of 68 ft was reported for a bull killed 60 miles west of Shetland Island and landed at the Norrona whaling station (Millais, 1906), but the measurement was believed to have been taken over the curve of the body instead of in a straight line.

The bull sperm whale with an alleged length of 71 ft caught off the Aleutian Islands in 1921. (Provincial Archives, Victoria, B.C., Canada.)

In 1921 a length of 71 ft was reported for a sperm whale caught off the Aleutian coast and towed to the Akutan whaling station in Alaska (Young, *in litt.* 29.4.65), but this measurement is not borne out in photographs.

In September 1931 Reuters reported that a 70 ft sperm whale found dead on the beach near Dusky Sound, at the south-west tip of South Island, New Zealand, yielded nearly a quarter of a ton of ambergris, but the author was told by J. Moreland, a cetologist at the Dominion Museum, Wellington (*in litt.* 15.3.68) that the Museum had no record of this whale, and that he personally doubted the report.

In November 1948 it was announced in the *Norwegian Whaling Gazette* (Sandefjord) that a 90 ft sperm whale had recently been captured off the north-west coast of Vancouver Island, British Columbia, Canada, and brought into the whaling station at Nanaimo. In April 1949, however, the *Gazette* carried an amendment by Gordon C. Pike, a biologist working at the station, who said that the largest sperm whale brought into Nanaimo that season had measured 56 ft (Budker, 1958).

Eleven sperm whales have been stranded on British coasts since 1913. The largest, a 61 ft 5 in bull, was washed ashore at Birchington, Kent, on 18th October 1914 (Harmer, 1927). Another bull measuring 60 ft stranded at North Roe, Shetland, on 30th May 1958.

In 1667 a 70 ft long sperm whale was cast up at Youghal, County Tipperary, Ireland after a storm, and another bull measuring 71 ft stranded at Ballyshannon, County Donegal, Ireland in August 1691 (Thompson, 1856). Both these measurements, however, were taken over the curve of the body.

The largest accurately measured cow sperm whale on record was a 12·2 m (40 ft 9 in) specimen caught in the Southern Ocean in 1940/41 (*International Whaling Statistics*, 1940/41). Another cow measured by Robert Clarke (1956) at the whaling station on Horta in the Azores was exactly 40 ft, and the same length has been recorded for a specimen caught off Kamchatka (Tomilin, 1936).

There are records of cow sperm whales measuring 50, 57 and even 60 ft, but these were all wrongly sexed bulls.

The smallest living toothed mammal is the Least weasel (*Mustela rixosa*), also called the "Dwarf weasel", which is circumpolar in distribution. Four races are recognised (Hall, 1951), the smallest of which is *M.r. pygmaea* of Siberia. Mature specimens have a head and body length of 158–184 mm (6·22–7·24 in), a tail length of 19–23 mm (0·74–0·90 in) and weigh between 35 and 70 g (between 1·25 and 2·5 oz).

The least weasel probably packs more nervous energy into its tiny body than any other living mammal.

Nelson (1930) writes: "Once when camping in spring among scattered snowbanks on the coast of the Bering Sea, I had an excellent opportunity to witness their almost incredible quickness. Early in the morning one suddenly appeared on the margin of a snowbank within a few feet. After craning its neck one way and the other as though to get a better view of me, it vanished, only to reappear so abruptly on a snowbank three or four yards away that it was almost impossible to follow it with the eye . . . certainly no other mammal can have such flashlike powers of movement."

In Europe this family is represented by the larger Common weasel (*Mustela nivalis*), although a pygmy form has been found in Finland and

The least weasel, the smallest living carnivore. (Ernest P. Walker.)

eastern Europe which rivals the least weasel for diminutiveness. This latter animal has a head and body length of 130–195 mm (5·11–7·67 in) and a tail length of 28·52 mm (1·10–2·04 in) (Van den Brink, 1967).

The largest member of the cat family is the long-furred Siberian tiger (*Leo tigris altaica*), also called the "Amur" or "Manchurian" tiger. Adult males average 10 ft 4 inches in length (nose to tip of extended tail), stand 39–42 in at the shoulder and weigh about 585 lb. Adult females are four-fifths this size.

The maximum size attained by this northern race of tiger is still a matter of some dispute, but if we are to believe the records of the old Russian hunters, some of the tigers killed before the advent of "over-shooting" were very much larger than those that exist today.

A group of Siberian tigers keeping cool at Carl Hagenbeck's Tierpark, Hamburg. (Associated Press.)

Yankovsky (quoted by Perry, 1964), for instance, says he killed one with the aid of dogs which measured 13 ft, while Barclay (1915) mentions another tiger killed near Vladivostock which had a length of 13 ft 5 in. Both these measurements, however, were taken "over the curves" or sportsman fashion, which means that the tape was stretched round the curves of the body—from the nose following a line between the ears and along the spine.

The *correct* way to measure a tiger is to lay the animal on its back and take a reading between pegs placed at the point of the nose and the tip of the extended tail, the result being some 10–12 per cent less than the "over the curves" measurement. If Yankovsky had used this method on his largest tiger it would have pegged about 12 ft, but even this measurement is difficult to believe.

According to Baikov (1936) the man-eating tiger known as "Great Van" which he shot in the Khailin-khe Forest, south-eastern Manchuria, measured nearly 4 m (13 ft 1·5 in) over the curves, but a published photograph showed a tiger of quite ordinary dimensions.

Another tiger shot by the same hunter in Kirin Province, central Manchuria, measured 11 ft 9·75 in over the curves and weighed 560 lb.

There is also the question of skin measurements. Rowland Ward (1928) list five Mongolian (=Siberian) dressed skins measuring 13 ft 6 in, 12 ft 4 in, 12 ft, 12 ft and 11 ft 3·5 in respectively. Cavendish (1894) speaks of a 14 ft 6 in skin from Korea (the range of the Siberian tiger includes Korea), and Burton (1928) says he saw skins of "immense size" at the Nijni Novgorod Fair in 1893. Such measurements, however, are quite valueless and bear no relationship to the true length of the tiger (the skin of a 10 ft long tiger can be *stretched* to 13 or 14 ft).

The tiger's length is also governed by its tail measurement. On an average this appendage is less than half the length of the head and body, but measurements up to 4 ft have been recorded.

Richard Perry (1964) says all the Russian hunters, including Yankovsky and Baikov, claimed that there were *two* races of tiger, one large and one "small", living in Manchuria, which would account for the wide variation in reported sizes. But although the larger-race Manchurian tigers outweigh their heaviest Indian counterparts, Perry believes there is not much to choose between them as regards total length.

Very little information has been published on the weights attained by large Siberian tigers. Filipek (1934) quotes a weight of 350 kg (770 lb) for a specimen killed near the Amur River, and Baikov (1938) says he shot a tiger in Manchuria which tipped the scales at 325 kg (715 lb). A weight of 320 kg (704 lb) has also been reported for another tiger killed in central Manchuria (Novikov, 1962).

During his visit to India in 1955, the Russian Premier, Nikita Khrushchev, presented an adult pair of tigers captured in Ussuria (eastern Manchuria) to the Governor of West Bengal. Perry says the male was estimated to measure 10 ft 6 inches in length and weigh 700 lb, and his mate 10 ft and 630 lb in 1964, but although the lengths quoted for these two specimens are probably correct (photographic evidence) their weights must be considered over-estimated.

Not surprisingly, lengths in excess of 12 ft have also been reported for the Indian tiger (*Leo tigris*). Buffon (1778) speaks of one that measured 15 ft, and Blythe (1856) says another enormous tiger presented to the Nawob of Arcot measured 18 ft in length!

Another tiger killed on Cozzimbazar Island, West Bengal, reportedly measured "13 feet and a few inches from the tip of his nose to the end of his tail" (Williams, 1807), and General W. Rice (1857) says the largest tigers shot by him and his friends in Rajputana and central India between 1850 and 1854 measured 12 ft 7·5 in, 12 ft 6·75 in and 12 ft 2 in respectively.

All these measurements, however, were (1) exaggerated; (2) taken from stretched skins; or (3) based on faulty tape readings.

Colonel F. T. Pollock (1903) says he shot a heavy, loose-skinned tiger in southern India which measured 10 ft 1 in between pegs when shot and yielded a 13 ft 4 in long dried skin, and there is another record of an Indian tiger 1 in shorter yielding a 14 ft skin when pegged out and dried.

It was also a common practice, says Perry, for shakaris to carry with them special steel measures on which every inch had been reduced by one-sixth. This meant that every 10 ft tiger measured out at 12 ft and guaranteed them a good monetary reward from a grateful sportsman.

Sir John Prescott Hewett (1938), who had records of 250 tigers shot in India (mostly in the swampy Terai), says the largest specimen was a 10 ft 5·5 in male shot at Naini Tal, United Provinces, in 1893. Only seven of the others measured over 10 ft.

The average adult male Indian tiger measures 9 ft 3 inches in total length, stands 36–38 in at the shoulder and weighs about 420 lb. Adult tigresses are 6–12 in shorter in length and about 100 lb lighter.

The longest accurately measured tiger on record was a 10 ft 7 in male (tail 3 ft 7 in) shot by Colonel Evans Gordon at Ramshai Hab, in the Duars, Bengal. It measured 40 in at the shoulder and weighed 491 lb (Rowland Ward, 1907). Another male measuring 10 ft 6·75 in was shot at Bhandai Pari, Central Provinces, by V. A. Herbert (Rowland Ward, 1907).

According to Rowland Ward (1935) Lord Hardinge shot a tiger in Gwalior which measured 11 ft 5·5 inches in overall length (tail 3 ft 9 in), but this measurement was taken over the curve of the body. Another tiger shot in Gwalior by Lord Reading was credited with an overall length of 11 ft 5 in (tail 3 ft 7 in) but this was also a curve measurement.

The heaviest Indian tiger on record was a huge male shot by E. A. Smythies (1942) in Nepal which weighed 705 lb. Another tiger (length 9 ft 11·5 in) killed by Captain M. D. Goring-Jones in Central Provinces scaled 700 lb (Rowland Ward, 1910).

Other reliable records over 600 lb include a 645 lb tiger (length 10 ft 6 in) shot by E. H. Morbey in Kumaon, United Provinces (Rowland Ward, 1928), and one weighing 608 lb (length 10 ft 2 in) shot by the Kumar of Bikaner in Gwalior (Rowland Ward, 1928).

Another tiger shot by the Maharajah of Cooch Behar (1908) at Haldibari on 4th March 1886 measured 10 ft 1·5 inches in length and weighed "close on 600 pounds", and Brander (1923) says he shot a huge tiger (length 9 ft 11 in) in Central Provinces which was "about 600 pounds in weight" (a rough estimate of this animal's poundage was obtained by balancing it against a number of men).

All of these exceptionally heavy tigers were confirmed cattle-killers and consequently very fat.

Leveson (1877) says some cattle-killers have turned the scales at 800 lb, but this must be considered an exaggerated claim.

In March 1932 *The Times of India* announced that Colonel G. F. Waugh of the U.S. Army (retired) had shot a tiger in southern India measuring 11 ft in length (tail 43 in) and weighing 700 lb, but the author has not yet been able to confirm these figures.

Although the African lion (*Leo leo*) is smaller than the Siberian tiger, it rivals the Indian tiger for size. The average adult male measures 9 ft in length, stands 36–38 in at the shoulder and weighs 400–410 lb. Adult females are one-fifth smaller.

The longest accurately measured African lion on record was a 10 ft 11 in black-maned giant shot by G. Prud'homme in Uganda (Rowland Ward, 1969). Another lion shot by J. K. Roberts in the Sudan also measured 10 ft 11 in (Rowland Ward, 1969). These measurements are rather surprising, because the lion is a shorter-bodied animal than the tiger.

Edouard Foa (1899) says he shot a lion on the Zambezi which measured 11 ft 8·75 in, and Wells (1933) quotes a length of 12 ft 6 in for another lion killed on the Klaserie River in northern Transvaal, but these were skin measurements.

Jules Gerard (1856) claims he shot several lions in Algeria measuring "17 feet [sic]", but he must have been measuring the animals in pairs to obtain this length!

Very few lions exceed a weight of 500 lb in the natural state. Colonel Richard Meinertzhagen (1938) shot a 9 ft 4 in male in Kenya which weighed 506 lb, and another male (9 ft 10·5 in) killed in the same country by Rear-Admiral R. A. J. Montgomerie tipped the scales at 516 lb (Rowland Ward, 1928). Roberts (1951) gives a record of a 9 ft 10 in lion shot in the Sabi District, Transvaal, which scaled 553 lb, and a weight of 583 lb was reported for a lion shot in the Orange River Colony in 1865. Another lion shot by White (1912) was stated to have measured 9 ft 11 inches in length and weighed just under 600 lb. Gerard speaks of killing lions weighing up to 300 kg (660 lb) in Algeria, but this statement is as reliable as the one about 17-footers.

In May 1964 a posthumous weight of 600 lb was recorded for a giant lion named "Castor", who was leader of a large pride in the Etosha Game Park, South-West Africa, for more than ten years, He was killed by a game warden after being found lying ill on the veld surrounded by a circle of jackals and hyenas.

The heaviest wild African lion on record was a specimen shot just outside Hectorspruit in the eastern Transvaal in 1936 which scaled 690 lb. This weight was so extreme that it was checked by several people before being officially accepted (Campbell, 1937).

Less reliable is the claim made by Martin Johnson (1929), the American big-game hunter and explorer, that he once shot a lion weighing over 750 lb.

The largest lion ever held in captivity, and the heaviest "Big Cat" on record, is a 10 ft 6 in black-maned giant named "Simba", who weighed a staggering 826 lb in July 1970. Other statistics include a 52 in neck, an 83 in chest and a shoulder height of 44 in.

Simba's owner, professional wild-animal trainer Adrian Nyoka, caught the lion as a six-month-old cub on the Serengeti Plains in Kenya in 1959 after he had accidentally become separated from his mother.

Up to the age of three Simba grew along normal lines. Then suddenly, for some unknown reason, he started growing at an alarming rate. At four and a half years he tipped the scales at 500 lb, which is the weight of a large lion, and at six years he was 620 lb. Two years later he weighed in at 704 lb, and by 1969 his weight had increased to 756 lb.

The world's heaviest ever "big cat", the 826 lb lion "Simba". (G. L. Wood.)

His daily diet consists of 20 lb of meat and a gallon of milk.

Another outsized lion known as "Louis the Great" was credited with a weight of 800 lb at the time of his death, but this American circus animal was extremely obese and was used only for exhibition purposes.

Clyde Beatty (1964), the famous American animal-trainer, says he worked with a number of lions weighing over 550 lb, including a magnificent specimen named "Caesar" who reputedly scaled 650 lb.

In January 1966 a weight of "1,000 lb [*sic*]" was reported for a giant maneless lion living within the grounds of the Imperial Hotel at Piet Retief, Natal, South Africa, but further information is lacking.

In 1953 a weight of 750 lb was recorded for an eighteen-year-old male liger (a lion-tigress hybrid) living in Bloemfontein Zoological Gardens, South Africa (Crandall, 1964).

Another male liger owned by Carl Hagenbeck reportedly weighed as much as his two parents put together.

The protected Asiatic or Indian lion (*Leo leo persica*), which is now confined to the Gir Forest in the south-western part of the Kathiawar Peninsula in western India and the Chandraprabha Sanctuary in Uttar Pradesh, United Provinces (Fitter, 1968) is about the same size as its African cousin, although it is a little stockier in build. One male shot by Lord Lamington measured 10 ft 4 inches in length (Rowland Ward, 1928), and an 8 ft 9·5 in male shot by Captain Smeel weighed 490 lb excluding entrails (Sterndale, 1884).

The smallest member of the cat family (Felidae) is the Rusty-spotted cat (*Felis rubiginosa*). Two races are recognised: *F.r. rubiginosa* of southern India and *F.r. phillipsi* of Ceylon. The average adult male has a head and body length of 16–18 in, a tail length of 9–10 in and weighs about 3 lb, while adult females are slightly smaller.

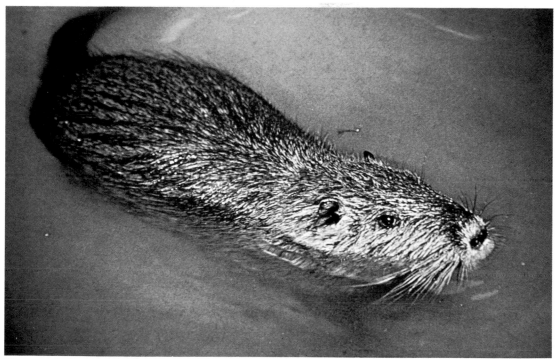

*The largest rodent found in Britain is the Coypu (*Myocastor coypus*), also known as the Nutria, which was introduced from Argentina in 1929 by East Anglian fur breeders. Weights up to 40 lb have been reported for captive males. (G. Kinns.)*

*The smallest totally marine mammal is the Sea otter (*Enhydra lutris*) of the North Pacific. Adult specimens measure up to 5 ft in total length with a maximum weight of 80 lb. (S. McCutcheon/F. Lane.)*

FELIDAE (Maximum weights)*	Male Maximum recorded weight (lb)
Tiger (*Leo tigris*)	770
Lion (*Leo leo*)	690
Jaguar (*Leo onca*)	350
Snow leopard (*Leo uncia*)	286
Puma (*Leo concolor*)	276†
Leopard (*Leo pardus*)	233
Cheetah (*Acinonyx jubatus*)	143
Northern lynx (*Felis lynx*)	70
Bobcat (*Felis rufa*)	69
Clouded leopard (*Felix nebulosa*)	51
Serval (*Felis serval*)	40
Caracal (*Felis caracal*)	40
Ocelot (*Felis pardalis*)	35
Margay (*Felis wiedi*)	34
Little spotted cat (*Felis tigrina*)	31
Fishing cat (*Felis viverrina*)	30
Golden cat (*Felis temmincki*)	29
European wild cat (*Felis silvestris*)	22
Jaguarundi (*Felis yagouarundi*)	21
Andean cat (*Felis jacobita*)	20
Jungle cat (*Felis chaus*)	18
African golden cat (*Felis aurata*)	17
Geoffroy's cat (*Felis geoffroyi*)	15
African wild cat (*Felis libyca*)	14
Sand cat (*Felis margarita*)	11
Chinese desert cat (*Felis bieti*)	10
Bornean red cat (*Felis badia*)	10
Black-footed cat (*Felis nigrepes*)	9
Leopard cat (*Felis bengalensis*)	8·5
Marbled cat (*Felis marmorata*)	8
Kodkod (*Felis guigna*)	8
Pallas's cat (*Felis manul*)	7·5
Pampas cat (*Felis colocolo*)	7
Flat-headed cat (*Felis planiceps*)	5·6
Rusty-spotted cat (*Felis rubiginosa*)	3·5

* Wild specimens
† Excluding the intestines

The rarest large member of the cat family is the Javan tiger (*Leo tigris mondaica*). Up to the early 1930s this tiger was still fairly abundant, but in the years that followed excessive killing by Man virtually wiped out the population. By 1955 there were only an estimated twenty to twenty-five tigers left in Java, of which ten to twelve were in the Udjung Kulon Reserve at the western tip of the island (Talbot, 1959). Today there may be a dozen tigers left in Java, plus another ten in foreign zoos.

    The Bali tiger (*L.t. balica*), which is similar in appearance to the Javan tiger but smaller, was also fairly common at the turn of this century, but indiscriminate hunting eradicated the population even faster than that of the Javan tiger. The last specimen killed in the wild was shot at Sumbar Kima, West Bali, on 27th September 1937. The Bali tiger probably became extinct in 1952, but Simon & Geroudet (1970) say it may still survive in one or both of the National Parks at the western end of the island.

Despite legal protection there are now only an estimated 100 to 110 Siberian tigers left in the Soviet Far East today, and about 90 of these live in the Khabarovsk and Primorye territories (Abramov, 1969). There may also be another 40–50 in Korea, and a further 30 in north China (Simon, 1968). There is still a heavy demand for the magnificent coat of this tiger, and in addition the Chinese believe that the bones, blood, heart and even flesh of this animal have medicinal properties.

In 1955 there were 290 lions in the Gir Forest, but by 1968 the number had dropped to 177. Unfortunately, the lions prey on the cattle in surrounding villages, and in recent years the cattle-owners have been retaliating by putting out poisoned bait in the forest.

The greatest reliable age reported for a "Big Cat" in captivity is about twenty-nine years for a lion named "Nero" at Cologne Zoological Gardens, Germany. He died in May 1907 or May 1908 (Flower, 1931).

Another lion called "Pluto" at Dublin Zoo died on 14th July 1914 aged 25 years and 18 days (Flower, 1931).

Lions rarely live longer than twenty years in the wild state, the expectation of life usually being twelve to fourteen years (Guggisberg, 1961).

According to Russian estimates the Siberian tiger lives up to fifty years, but this figure is not supported by zoo records. A Siberian tigress which died in Cologne Zoological Gardens in October 1930 from "extreme senile debility" was only nineteen years old. Perry puts the maximum life potential in the wild state at about twenty-five years, but he says few tigers live longer than fifteen years.

The greatest reliable age recorded for a tiger in captivity is twenty-two years one month and four days for a female Sumatran-Bengal cross named "Sandra" who died at Racine Zoological Park, Wisconsin, U.S.A. on 17th June 1968. At the time of her death she weighed only 138 lb compared to 530 lb in her prime (Christensen, *in litt.* 17.6.68). The previous record-holder was a tiger named "Slome" who died in Rotterdam Zoological Gardens, in the Netherlands, on 5th January 1966 aged twenty-one.

A question that has intrigued a great number of people, zoologists and laymen alike, for centuries about lions and tigers, is: **Who would be the winner in a hypothetical combat between these two great cats in the open if both animals were in prime condition and of equal size?**

At one time both these cats roamed extensively in southern Asia, and there were probably frequent clashes, but today their different distributions no longer make this possible, although Perry says an African lion released from an enclosure in Gwalior was almost certainly killed by a tiger or tigers (the lions in Gir Forest are more than a hundred miles from the nearest tiger territory, so the two animals never make contact).

The general consensus of opinion is that the tiger is a better fighter than the lion, and this is partly borne out by the records of the ancient Roman arena where lion versus tiger fights were often staged for the gratification of the crowds. In most of these combats the tiger emerged the winner.

Certainly the striped cat is a faster-moving, more powerful and agile

*The Giant panda (*Ailuropoda melanoleuca*), found in eastern Tibet and south-western China, is the most valuable land mammal in the world. (G. Kinns.)*

animal than the lion, and has a superior fighting technique.

Dr. Osmond Breland (1963), Professor of Zoology at the University of Texas, says that in one staged fight between the two animals, which ended with the lion being quickly routed, the tiger balanced itself on its hind-legs and struck with both front paws like a trained boxer. This gave it a tremendous advantage over its opponent which used only one front paw at a time.

In another lion versus tiger fight the tiger gripped the lion with both forepaws, rolled it over on its back and then began tearing indiscriminately with both teeth and hind-claws, making no particular effort to reach its rival's mane-protected throat. The lion had no answer to this form of attack and was quickly killed.

The late Alex Kerr (1957), the famous wild-cat trainer of Bertram Mills Circus, was another tiger-supporter. "The tiger is more determined and tenacious", he says, "and, providing that other lions do not gang up to help their mate, he will usually prove the stronger."

Unfortunately, lions and tigers have a different code of battle. A lion is a group animal and will help a companion in a fight, but a tiger will calmly sit and watch while a member of his own kind is being torn to pieces by lions.

On 7th January 1957 eight lions killed a pair of tigers in a night battle at Frankfurt Zoological Gardens, Germany, after the door between their adjoining enclosures had been left unlocked.

Not everyone believes that the tiger is a better fighter, though. The late Clyde Beatty (1965), for instance, was a strong lion-supporter and based his opinion on forty years of close observance of the two animals.

"I can cite a few instances of male tigers whipping male lions, but I can't think of one such case where the tiger didn't have a distinct advantage. I also recall a case where a tiger had a marked advantage and lost the fight. . . . The lion seems to have no fear of the tiger. Seated next to a tiger, the lion is composed. The tiger, on the other hand, is usually nervous and apprehensive. . . . The tiger does not seem to have the lion's capacity for calm analysis and appraisal. This puts him at a disadvantage in a fight with a lion."

Beatty mentions one tough lion named "Sultan the First" who once took on every tiger in his act and defeated them one after another.

"It was an amazing performance since my entire entourage consisted of big, young, powerful animals. So these were not pushovers that Sultan defeated. This remarkable lion, feinting like a clever boxer and making his opponents miss, would then send the off-balance enemy sprawling across the arena with a tremendous clout."

It should be pointed out here that lions settle down in captivity much better than do their striped cousins, and this gives them an important psychological advantage in a fight.

In June 1949 a circus at New Bedford, Massachusetts, U.S.A. lost its tiger after a battle with a lion.

The following month a large Bengal tiger named "Tim" was killed by a lion named "Nero" at Perth Zoological Gardens, Western Australia. The tiger was in a cage adjoining the lion and a lioness named "Bessie". The lioness forced up the steel slide dividing the cage and Tim, curious, put his head through. Nero, the zoo's biggest lion, promptly bit him in the throat, and in three minutes the tiger was dead.

In February 1951 a lion fought and killed a tiger as 3,000 children looked on at the opening performance of a circus at Detroit, Illinois, U.S.A., and another tiger was killed by a lion at Madras Zoological

Gardens in September the same year after being transferred to the lion's cage while its own quarters were being cleaned.

On the other side of the coin, Francis Buckland (1865) says a *tigress* in a menagerie at Birmingham seized a lion by the throat and killed it in a few minutes, while Proske (1957) describes a fight to the death between a circus lion and tiger, which the latter won after crushing the lion's neck.

On 19th November 1945 visitors to the Zoological Gardens at Bangalore, southern India, witnessed a fight between a tiger and a lioness which ended in the death of the lioness.

Another fight to the death between a tiger and a lioness took place in Chamrajendra Zoological Gardens, Mysore City, southern India, in January 1946. The lioness wandered into an adjoining cage occupied by a large tiger after a keeper had accidentally left the door open. The tiger at once attacked the lioness which was very quickly killed.

In 1951 a tiger killed a lioness during a circus performance in Milan, Italy.

In the last three mentioned fights the tiger had a distinct weight advantage, so they cannot be considered fair contests.

An African lion, of course, would stand virtually no chance against a huge Siberian tiger in a straight fight, but it could easily handle the much smaller Sumatran and Javan tigers.

Alfred Court (1954), another famous wild-animal trainer, had three enormous Siberian tigers at one time but he was afraid to put them in a mixed group with lions and other animals for fear there would be a massacre. Instead, he used them in a tiger act with four Bengal tigers, but even then he said he was always terrified they would attack their smaller relatives.

The only true man-eaters of the cat family are the lion, tiger and leopard which, between them, probably account for close on 1,000 deaths annually. The individual man-eating record is held by a notorious tigress known as the "Champawat man-eater", who operated first in Nepal and then in Kumaon. She killed 438 people in eight years before being shot by Jim Corbett in 1911.

In January 1966 a man-eating tiger said to have killed and eaten 500 people in six years was shot at Ramgiri Udaygiri by Mrs. Alida Sverdsten of Idaho, U.S.A., but Clarke (1969) says this figure was grossly exaggerated.

The infamous man-eating leopard of Panar accounted for 400 victims before it was shot by Corbett in 1910.

Man-eating lions prefer to do their killing in prides rather than singly, but there is a record from Malawi of a lion which killed and ate fourteen people in one month (Clark, 1969). Another lion which had reportedly killed forty people in the Kasama District of northern Rhodesia was shot in October 1943.

The largest of the thirty-two known species of pinniped is the Southern elephant seal (*Mirounga leonina*), which is circumpolar in distribution and is found on most of the subantarctic islands. Adult bulls average 16·5 ft in total length (tip of inflated snout to the extremities of the outstretched tail flippers); 12 ft in maximum bodily girth and weigh about 5,000 lb (2·18 tons). Adult cows are much smaller, averaging 9–10 ft in total length, 6 ft in maximum bodily girth and weighing about 1,000 lb.

The largest accurately measured southern elephant seal on record was probably a bull killed in Possession Bay, South Georgia, on 28th February 1913 and examined by Dr. Robert C. Murphy (1914) of the American Museum of Natural History, New York, N.Y., U.S.A. It measured 21 ft 4 in after flensing (original length about 22·5 ft) and must have weighed in the region of 4 tons. The maximum bodily girth of this animal was not taken, but it was probably about 18 ft.

According to Dr. Murphy the fattest bull he saw on South Georgia was a specimen measuring 18 ft 4 inches in length. "It was so round and distended that it had the appearance of being pneumatic and inflated under pressure. Seven men could barely turn its body over with the aid of ropes and hand holes in the blubber, even after half the blubber had been removed and a trench had been scooped under one side of its carcase."

Another exceptionally large bull shot by Mr. Herbert Mansel 45 miles west of the Falkland Islands in 1879 measured just over 21 ft in length and "must have weighed several tons". The skeleton of this specimen is preserved in the Museum of the Royal College of Surgeons in London (Flower, 1881).

On 29th May 1789 a bull measuring 21 ft in length and nearly as much in maximum bodily girth was shot on the Island of Amsterdam in the southern Indian Ocean (Moore, 1791), but this measurement may have been taken along the curve of the back instead of in a straight line.

According to Ring (1923) the beachmasters on Kerguelen Island, also in the southern Indian Ocean, measure up to 21 ft in length and "tower up to 10 feet in height".

Of 226 elephant seals shot on South Georgia and examined by Dr. R. M. Laws (1953), the largest bull measured 18 ft 1 inch in length, but this measurement was taken over the curve of the back. Another bull measuring in excess of 20 ft was observed, but it was not killed.

There are old records of bulls measuring 25, 30 and even 33 ft, but these figures must be considered exaggerated. For instance, Peron (1817) says he saw elephant seals on Kerguelen Island measuring 8–10 m in length (26·25–32·75 ft), and Wood (1898) quotes lengths up to 30 ft and maximum bodily girths of 15–18 ft for this species (the latter figures are much too low for a seal of this supposed length). Lydekker (1894), too, says that a length of 30 ft was far from improbable, and Morrell (1832) claims that he saw bulls measuring more than 25 ft in length.

According to Hamilton (1949) a 13 ft 4 in bull weighed in pieces by Messrs. Christian Saluesen and Company at Leigh Harbour, South Georgia, tipped the scales at 4,357 lb (1·94 tons). The skin weighed 254 lb, the blubber 1,469 lb, the heart 92 lb, the head 114 lb and the blood (estimated) 218 lb. "It was a medium-sized bull," says Hamilton, "and in the absence of further data it is reasonable to believe that a large bull may weigh anything up to four or five tons."

In 1924 a large southern sea elephant hauled up on the beach at Simonstown, South Africa, and caused a great deal of panic among the local population before it was shot. It measured 16 ft in length and weighed just over 2 tons.

The largest accurately measured cow southern sea elephant on record was an 11 ft 5 in long specimen obtained by Harris in the Falkland Islands in 1909. The weight of this animal was not recorded, but it probably scaled about 1,700 lb.

Another cow shot on South Georgia in c. 1952 measured 11 ft 6 in, but the length was taken along the curve of the back (Laws, 1953).

Most of the cows measured by Dr. Murphy on South Georgia were under 8 ft 6 in.

The much rarer Northern elephant seal (*Mirounga angustirostris*), now restricted to the islands off the coast of Mexico and southern California, is slightly smaller than *M. leonina*, but its proboscis is much larger. Adult bulls average 14 ft in length, with a maximum of 17 ft, but in former times before they were commercially exploited, the northern beachmasters grew much larger. Adult cows, on the other hand, are about the same size as their southern counterparts.

The largest accurately measured northern elephant seal on record was a 22 ft bull seen by Captain Charles M. Scammon (1870). Another bull taken at Santa Barbara Island by the brig *Mary Helen* in 1852 measured 18 ft in length and yielded 210 gal of oil.

On 20th September 1929 a large bull was towed into San Diego Harbour after being killed by swordfish fishermen about 40 miles off Point Loma, California. It measured 15 ft 7 inches in length and weighed an estimated 5,000 lb (2·23 tons).

In January 1940 another bull elephant seal was washed up dead on a beach at Kasaan, Prince of Wales Island, Alaska, U.S.A., the furthest north this species has been recorded. This one measured 14 ft in length and weighed an estimated 4,000 lb (1·74 tons).

The largest accurately measured cow of the northern race on record was probably an 11 ft specimen collected by Townsend (1912) on Santa Barbara Island, California. Another one measuring 11 ft 5 in was reportedly killed in the same area in *c.* 1909 (Scheffer, 1958), but further details are lacking.

The largest elephant seal ever held in captivity was a bull of the southern race named "Goliath" (one of several of that name) received at Carl Hagenbeck's Tierpark, Hamburg-Stellingen, Germany in 1928 from South Georgia, who measured 20·5 ft in length and weighed over 3 tons at the time of his death in 1930

"Magog", the largest captive elephant seal in Britain. (Press Association.)

(Hagenbeck *in litt.* 20.5.71). This magnificent animal died from severe lacerations after a sadistic member of the public had thrown the jagged neck of a broken beer-bottle into his open jaws (Hediger, 1969).

In 1968 a length of 20 ft and a weight of 4 tons were reported for another southern bull named "Roland" at Berlin Zoological Gardens (received 1962), but Dr. Heinz-Georg Klos tells me (*in litt.* 18.9.70) this seal measured approximately 5 m (16 ft 5 in) and weighed 1,540 kg (3,338 lb) at the time of his death in 1969. In 1966 the same animal weighed 4,850 lb (2·16 tons), and his mate "Bollie" 1,562 lb.

Another bull also named "Roland" received at Berlin Zoological Gardens on 10th March 1930 from Carl Hagenbeck's Tierpark was stated to have measured 18 ft at the time of his death on 26th December 1935 (Heck, 1936), but the author has not been able to confirm this length because most of the zoo records were destroyed during the Second World War.

The most famous captive elephant seal was the original "Goliath", who arrived at Carl Hagenbeck's Tierpark in February 1926 from South Georgia. He was then 15 ft long and weighed 3,360 lb (1·5 tons). In 1928 he was sold to the Ringling Brothers Circus in the United States when he measured 16 ft 6 in and weighed 4,821 lb (2·15 tons) (Steinmetz, 1954), and toured the country with the show for several years. In the winter of 1933–34 he was exhibited at the Philadelphia Zoological Gardens, Pennsylvania, by which time he measured 17 ft in length and weighed an estimated 6,000 lb (2·69 tons). He was later sold by Ringling Brothers, but further information is lacking.

In 1970 a posthumous weight of 6,287 lb (excluding blood) was recorded for a southern bull called "Spot" at Edinburgh Zoological Gardens. This specimen measured 14 ft 8 inches in length and had a maximum bodily girth of 14 ft 3 in! As the blood usually accounts for about 8 per cent of the total body weight in seals, Spot must have scaled about 6,800 lb (3·03 tons) when alive.

"Tristan", the southern bull at Wilhelma Zoo, Stuttgart, weighed 5,680 lb in 1968. He arrived there on 24th May 1958 from Tristan da Cunha when three to four years old.

In November 1971 an unconfirmed weight of 3 tons was reported for a bull of the southern race named "Jonah" at Fujisawa Oceanarium, Japan.

The larger of the two elephant seals held in British zoos at the present time is the southern bull "Magog" at Flamingo Park Zoo, Yorkshire, who measures 16 ft in length and weighs an estimated 2·5 tons.

The largest northern elephant seal ever held in captivity was a bull received at San Diego Zoological Gardens, California, U.S.A. in 1929 which measured 16·5 ft in length and weighed "nearly five thousand pounds" (Benchley, 1930).

The elephant seal has the longest intestinal tract of any known mammal, although the reasons for this are not really clear. One 15 ft 9 in southern bull had a gut measuring 662 ft or forty-one and a half times its own body length (cf. 30 ft for a human and 80 ft for a horse) (King, 1964).

The elephant seal also has the most supple spine in the mammalian kingdom. This fact is often demonstrated by zoo-keepers to amuse visitors. A fish is placed on the animal's back near its hind-flippers, and the great creature then bends over backwards to seize its reward.

An elephant seal demonstrating the remarkable flexibility of its spine. (Carl Hagenbeck's Tierpark, Hamburg.)

The largest pinniped among British fauna is the Grey seal (*Halichoerus grypus*), also called the "Atlantic seal", which is found mainly on the western coasts of Britain. Adult bulls average 8 ft in length and weigh about 500 lb, and adult cows 6·5 ft and 350 lb (lactating cows can be 100 lb heavier).

According to Hickling (1962) one of the largest grey seals killed by Blacket on the Farne Islands in *c.* 1772 measured 9 ft in length, 7·5 ft in maximum bodily girth and weighed 658 lb. Edmondston (1837) says the largest bull collected by him on Shetland Island measured 8 ft in length and weighed 672 lb, but as the maximum bodily girth of this animal was only 6 ft this poundage must be considered suspect. The largest of the twenty-seven adult bulls measured by Millais (1904) was 9 ft 6 in. He also mentions another bull shot by Sir Reginald Cathcart on South Uist, in the Outer Hebrides, which scaled 700 lb. Lengths up to 12 and even 13 ft have been claimed, but these figures should be treated with caution. Adult cows have been reliably measured up to 7 ft 7 in and 550 lb.

The smallest pinniped is the Baikal seal (*Pusa sibirica*) of Lake Baikal, a large freshwater lake in southern Siberia, U.S.S.R. Adult specimens average 4 ft 6 in from nose to tail and weigh about 140 lb (King, 1964).

The Ringed seal (*Pusa hispida*), found on the circumpolar Arctic coasts, is not much larger. Adult animals measure 4 ft 6 in to 4 ft 10 inches in length and weigh 170–200 lb.

Some species of seal are among the swiftest mammals in the sea.

The highest swimming speed recorded for a pinniped is 25 mile/h for a Californian sea lion (*Zalophus californianus*) (McGinitie, 1949). This speed may be matched by the Leopard seal (*Hydrurga leptonyx*) of the subantarctic islands which chases and frequently catches the swift penguin (maximum speed about 23 mile/h).

The deepest-diving pinniped is the Weddell seal (*Laptonychotes weddelli*), the world's most southerly mammal, which is found along the Antarctic mainland and neighbouring

islands. Adult bulls regularly descend to 900–1,000 ft in search of food like fish, squids and crustaceans, and dives can last from twenty minutes to an hour or more.

In March 1966 a large bull with a depth-gauge attached to it recorded a dive of 600 m (1,968·5 ft) in McMurdo Sound and remained below for forty-three minutes and twenty seconds. This seal withstood a pressure of 875 lb per square inch of body (Kooyman, 1969). Some examples have been observed to swim under the ice for 19 miles, utilising the layers of air trapped under the ice.

Ray (1966) says the Weddell seal survives these tremendous dives by constricting surface blood-vessels to a minimum to ensure a steady supply of blood to the heart and brain, and that it also tolerates large amounts of carbon dioxide in the blood.

According to King, all seals spend a certain amount of time lazing in the sun during the spring and summer months in order that their bodies may be re-oxygenated before the start of a new dive in search of food.

The Harp seal (*Pagophilus groenlandicus*), also called the "Greenland seal", may also dive deeper than 1,000 ft, but this figure has not yet been confirmed (one specimen was caught in a net dropped to a depth of 600 ft).

The greatest reliable age reported for a pinniped is "at least 43 years" for a Ringed seal (*Pusa hispida*) collected on the south-west coast of Baffin Island, in the eastern Canadian Arctic, in 1954. The age of this animal was based on the growth layers in the roots of the canines (McLaren, 1962).

The greatest reliable age reported for a pinniped in captivity is forty-one to forty-two years for a bull grey seal called "Jacob". He was captured in the Baltic Sea and arrived at Skansen Zoological Gardens, Stockholm, Sweden, on 28th October 1901 when he was an estimated two years of age. He died there on 30th January 1942 (Matheson, 1950).

"*Jacob*", *the oldest grey seal on record. (Nordiska Museet and Stansen, Stockholm.)*

There is also a record of a Californian sea lion living in Bremerhaven Zoo, Germany, for thirty years (Ehlers, 1957).

A cow ringed seal received at Skansen Zoological Gardens in the autumn of 1914 lived there for fifteen years, dying in April 1929 shortly after giving birth to a hybrid pup (Crandall, 1964).

The life potential of elephant seals in the wild state is unknown, but for captive specimens the record is held by a cow called "Nixe" who died in Stellingen in 1940 aged about sixteen years (Steinmetz, 1954).

The rarest of all pinnipeds is the Caribbean or West Indian monk seal (*Monachus tropicalis*). At one time this animal was the basis of a profitable seal fishery in both the Caribbean and the Gulf of Mexico, but it was so persistently slaughtered for its oil and skin, that by the end of the nineteenth century the seal was virtually extinct.

On 14th June 1909 an adult bull and two yearlings were received at New York Aquarium (Townsend, 1909). In March 1911 one of the young seals was still living, but Crandall says "no further information concerning it is now available".

In January 1911 some fishermen visited the Triangle Keys, a group of islets to the west of Yucatan, and killed about 200 seals (Allen, 1942), and on 15th March 1922 one was killed near Key West, Florida, U.S.A. (Townsend, 1923). In 1949 two specimens were reportedly seen in the waters south of Kingston, Jamaica, and another one was sighted in the same area in 1952. In 1962 a Caribbean monk seal was seen on the beach at Isla Mujueres off the Yucatan Peninsula, Mexico (Fisher *et al.*, 1969). Some Monk seals may still survive in the remoter areas of the Caribbean, but the total population must be very small.

Of sub-species, the Japanese sea lion (*Zalophus californianus japonicus*), formerly widespread in the Japanese archipelago, probably became extinct in the early 1950s.

The Juan Fernandez fur seal (*Arctocephalus p. philippii*), which was believed to have become extinct at the turn of this century, was rediscovered on the Juan Fernandez Islands, some 400 miles west of Chile, in November 1968. Today there are an estimated thirty seals on Más á Tierra, and the population on Más Afuera is probably larger (Simon & Geroudet, 1970).

The only flying mammals are bats, of which there are about 1,000 living species. They are found throughout the world with the exception of the polar regions.

The largest known bat is probably the Kalong (*Pteropus niger*), a fruit bat found in Indonesia. It has a wing-span of up to 170 cm (5 ft 7 in), a head and body length of about 40 cm (15·75 in) and weighs up to 900 g (31·7 oz) (Walker *et al.*, 1968).

The largest flying mammal is the kalong, a fruit bat found in Indonesia, which may have a wing-span of over 5 ft. (American Museum of Natural History, New York.)

According to Petersen (1964) a specimen of *P. neohibernicus* from New Guinea preserved in the American Museum of Natural History in New York has a head and body length of 455 mm (17·91 in) and a wing-span of 1,650 mm (5 ft 4·9 in), and he thinks that some unmeasured specimens may have a wing-span of 6 ft.

A wing-span of more than 5 ft has also been reported for *P. giganteus* (= *P. medius*) of India, and *P. vampyrus* of Malaysia and Indonesia, and Nelson (1962) says some of the large Colonial fruit bats (*Pteropus* sp.) found in Australia weigh up to 2 lb.

Fruit bats have a remarkable sense of smell, and Moehres and Kulzer (quoted by Nelson, 1962) say Rousette fruit bats (*Rousettus amplexicaudatus*) can smell 100 mg (0·003 oz) of banana extract from a distance of 3 to 4 m (9·84 to 13·12 ft).

The largest native British bat is the Noctule or Great bat (*Nyctalus noctula*). Mature specimens have a wing-span of 353–387 mm (13·89–15·23 in), a head and body length of 69–82 mm (2·71–3·2 in) and weigh up to 40 g (1·4 oz) (Blackmore, 1964).

The largest bat found in Britain is the very rare Large mouse-eared bat (*Myotis myotis*). Mature specimens have a wing-span of 355–450 mm (13·97–17·71 in), a head and body length of 68–80 mm (2·67–3·1 in) and weigh up to 45 g (1·58 oz) (Blackmore, 1964).

The smallest known bat is the rare Tiny pipistrelle (*Pipistrellus nanulus*), found in West Africa. Mature specimens have a wing-span of about 152 mm (6 in), a head and body length of 38 mm (1·5 in) and weigh about 2·5 g (0·88 oz), which means it rivals the Etruscan pygmy shrew (*Suncus etruscus*) for the title of "smallest living mammal".

The smallest native British bat is the Pipistrelle (*Pipistrellus pipistrellus*). Mature specimens have a wing-span of 200–230 mm (7·87–9·05 in), a head and body length of 45–52 mm (1·65–2·04 in) and weigh between 5·5 and 7·5 g (between 0·193 and 0·264 oz) (Lovett, 1961).

The rarest species of bats are those known only from the type specimen. They include: the American leaf-nosed bat (*Corvira bidens*) (collected in northern Ecuador in 1914); the New Guinean big-eared bat (*Pharotis imogene*) (collected from south-eastern New Guinea); the Painted bat (*Anamygdon solomonis*) (collected from Roviana Island in the Solomon Group in 1928); the Fruit bat (*Haplonycteris fischeri*) (collected on Mount Halcon, Mindoro, Philippine Islands, in 1937); the Fruit bat (*Neopteryx frosti*) (collected at Tamalanti, West Celebes in 1938 or 1939); the Horseshoe bat (*Rhinomegalophus paradoxolophus*) (collected near Chapain, in the Province of Lao-Kay, Tonkin, Indochina); and the Old World leaf-eared bat (*Paracoelops megalotis*) (collected at Vinh, Annam, Indochina in 1945). (Walker *et al.*, 1968.)

The rarest native British bat, and the rarest native mammal, is Bechstein's bat (*Myotis bechsteini*), which is confined to a small area in southern England, with the New Forest as the main centre of population.

Up to 1886 there was only one English record of this species (New Forest before 1837), but that year a small colony was discovered in a woodpecker's hole near Burley, Hants. Ten years later an adult male was shot near Battle, Sussex, and in 1901 one was found asleep in a chalk-tunnel on the Berkshire side of the river at Henley-on-Thames. Two more specimens were shot at Newport, Isle of Wight, in 1909, and there have been about half a dozen records since.

The rarest bat found in Britain is the large Mouse-eared bat (*Myotis myotis*). The first specimen (a male) to be positively identified was taken alive at Girton in Cambridge-shire in 1888 and is now preserved in the Museum of Zoology at Cambridge University. On 18th February 1956 another specimen was found dead in a tunnel on the Isle of Purbeck, where several more were found sub-sequently (Blackmore, 1956), but the tunnel was destroyed in 1966. In December 1969 a small colony of mouse-eared bats was discovered by naturalists in an old disused underground passage in Sussex. Soon afterwards the 9 acres of land surrounding the spot were purchased by the National Trust and iron doors fitted with grilles put up at each end of the underground passage to protect the occupants during their six-month hibernation (a mouse-eared bat skin is worth £10 to a collector).

The Parti-coloured bat (*Vespertilio murinus*) of eastern Europe has only been recorded three times in Britain, but unlike *Myotis myotis* which *may* be resident, this species is considered a rare vagrant.

In January 1965 about fifteen specimens of the Grey long-eared bat (*Plecotus austriacus*) were discovered in the roof of the Nature Conservancy's Research Station at Furzebrook, Dorset, by Mr. R. E. Stebbings, an assistant at the station. Up to then this species, which is found all over Europe, had only been recorded once in Britain (Hampshire 1875).

The greatest reliable age reported for a bat under natural conditions is "at least 24 years" for a female Little brown bat (*Myotis lucifugus*) found on 30th April 1960 in a cave on Mount Aeolis, East Dorset, Vermont, U.S.A. It had been banded at a summer colony in Mashpee, Massachusetts on 22nd June 1937. Another banded specimen found in the same cave on 27th December 1964 was also twenty-four years old.

The greatest reliable age reported for a British bat under natural conditions is "at least 16½ years" for a banded Greater horseshoe bat (*Rhinolophus ferrumequinum*) recovered in Devon in 1964 (Hooper & Hooper, 1964).

The greatest reliable age reported for a captive bat is 19 years and 9 months for a Rousette fruit bat (*Rousettus leachii*) at Giza Zoological Gardens, Cairo, Egypt. An Indian fruit bat (*Pteropus giganteus*) lived in London Zoological Gardens for 17 years and 2 months (Flower, 1931). The smaller bats rarely live long in captivity.

In January 1952 workmen demolishing a wall in Indianapolis, Indiana, U.S.A. reportedly found a bat (species not identified) sealed inside which later flew off. The wall had been built in 1937.

The highest measured flying speed recorded for a bat is 32 mile/h for a Free-tailed or Guano bat (*Tadarida mexicana*) in New Mexico which flew 31 miles in fifty-eight minutes. This speed is closely matched by the Noctule bat (*Nyctalus noctula*) and the Long-winged bat (*Miniopterus schreibersi*), both of which have been timed at 31 mile/h.

Bats fly considerable distances during migration. A Noctule bat (*Nyctalus noctula*) ringed near Dresden, Germany, was recovered in Lithuania over 475 miles, and others have been recaptured nearly 300 miles from the spot where they were ringed. The Northern bat (*Eptesicus nilsonii*) of Scandinavia has been recovered as far south as southern Germany, which means it must have flown nearly 700 miles.

Bats have the most highly developed sense of hearing of any known mammal, and Petersen says that some varieties like the vampire bats (Desmodontidae) and the fruit bats (Pteropodidae) can hear frequencies as high as 150,000 c/s (150 kc/s). The average adult human ear, by comparison, can hear 15,000 c/s (15 kc/s), although young people and those with exceptional hearing can hear frequencies up to 20,000 c/s (20 kc/s).

Another remarkable thing about bats is the enormous amount of food they can eat at one sitting. One of the most prodigious feeders is the Short-nosed fruit bat (*Cynopterus sphinx*) of South-East Asia. One specimen weighing 1 oz was observed to eat 2 oz of ripe banana in three hours!

(The only other mammals capable of eating their own body weight in food at a single meal are shrews, and Pearsons (1955) cites a record of a male *Sorex cinereus* weighing 3·6 g (0·126 oz) which ate 93 g (3·26 oz) of food in eight days!)

The most dangerous of all bats are the vampires (Desmondontidae) of tropical and subtropical America, which are responsible for transmitting rabies and foot-and-mouth disease.

These bats feed only on the fresh blood of mammals, and their method of feeding is to hover, like humming-birds, over the sleeping prey and inflict a quick razor-like bite so as to draw blood, frequently without causing the animal to wake. The tongue is very long, so that the bats are able to lap the blood while on the wing, but sometimes they alight and crawl over the flanks of the animals they have scarified by means of the clawed thumbs on their wings. The saliva is similar to that of leeches, which delays the clotting of blood and allows the nightmarish creatures to obtain full meals from the tiny wounds they have made.

Sometimes the bats gorge themselves with blood to such an extent that they look like furry balls, and Eisentraut (1936) says one specimen fed on the blood of a domestic goat for ten minutes was so bloated that it could not fly.

When these animals attack sleeping humans they usually go for the toes, sometimes creeping under the bedclothes. During a collecting expedition to Brazil in 1927 on behalf of the New York Zoological Society Dr. William Beebe carried out some experiments to determine the puncturing properties of the vampire. He crept up on his companions in their sleep and attempted to puncture their toes with the finest needles he could find without waking them.

In every case they woke immediately, yet each of these men was robbed of quantities of blood by vampires without being aware at the time of the attack. Dr. Beebe believed that the bat actually lulls its victims into a gentle slumber by the vibratory action of its wings.

In May 1961 the U.S. Army in Washington, D.C. revealed that during the Second World War a plan was devised to turn millions of bats into living incendiary bombs and release them over enemy territory.

The man behind the "bat bomb" was Dr. Lytle Adams, a well-known Pennsylvanian dental surgeon, who studied bats as a hobby. In January 1942 he drafted a detailed plan for attaching tiny explosives to the bodies of captured bats and sent it to the White House.

President Roosevelt was enthusiastic about the scheme, and soon afterwards an official order went out for a mass recruiting drive by the army. The first bats to be enlisted for the operation were taken from the Ney Caves in Texas where there was a bat colony (Tadarida) numbering about 30,000,000 animals.

"In 1943 the Chemical Warfare Service began to design an incendiary bomb weighing less than one ounce for attachment to bats," the Army report said.

"The finished product was an oblong case of nitro cellulose packed with thickened kerosene, equipped with a delayed action igniter. It was made in two sizes—the larger burning for six minutes, and the smaller for four minutes.

"The bomb was attached to the loose skin on the bat's chest by a surgical clip and a piece of string."

The plan after that was to pack the bats into special containers which would be dropped by parachute over Germany or Japan and open automatically at 1,000 ft.

The released bats would then fly into the eaves of buildings in the target area where they would gnaw away at the string round their bodies, releasing the bombs. Those that didn't carry out this task would have to pay with their lives.

On paper and in early tests it looked a good idea.

But the U.S. Army and Dr. Adams hadn't reckoned on the ravenous appetites of the bats, and rather than divert whole armies of troops to insect-hunting the military scientists decided instead to put the bats into forced hibernation until they were needed. So the animals were cooled artificially until they fell asleep.

Here again the idea was better on paper than in practice. Once asleep the bats were slow to wake up again. Some never did.

"Those that were taken aloft proved unco-operative in the early stages," the Army report went on. "Many flew away when the container opened, and others dropped like stones to the ground."

Sometimes there were more positive—if less gratifying—results. On one occasion a bat bomb got loose on a U.S. airfield and succeeded in burning down a large hangar and setting fire to a general's car.

Incidents such as this apparently cooled the enthusiasm of the Army experimenters, and in the end they passed the whole project over to the Marines who are more accustomed to unorthodox warfare. The Marines were more successful (in one trial a mock village was burned down), and reported that the first bat bombs would be ready for use in mid 1945.

But by then the war had ended . . .

The largest living Primate is the Eastern lowland gorilla (*Gorilla gorilla graueri*), which inhabits the lowlands of the eastern part of the Upper Congo (Zaire) and south-western Uganda. An average adult bull stands 5 ft 8 in tall (the total length from crown to heel in the lying position), has a chest circumference of 58–60 in and weighs 360–400 lb. The average adult female stands about 4 ft 7 in and weighs 170–210 lb.

The two other races of gorilla, the Mountain gorilla (*G.g. beringei*), which is found on the Virunga Mountains, a volcanic range in the eastern Congo and south-western Uganda, and the Western gorilla (*G.g. gorilla*), which lives in the lowland rain forests of the Congo (now the Republic of the Congo), the Cameroons and the west coast of Africa, are both generally slightly shorter in stature than the eastern lowland gorilla and not quite so bulky. It is interesting to note, however, that most of the record-sized gorillas have been of the mountain race.

If we are to believe the stories of some of the early gorilla-hunters a number of really colossal bulls have been killed in the past, but these claims were either grossly exaggerated or the measurements taken in such a way as to considerably enhance the true size of the animal.

For instance, one western gorilla killed in the eastern Cameroons (now part of the Federal Republic of Cameroon) allegedly measured 7 ft 6·5 inches in height, 3 ft 7 in across the shoulders and weighed 770 lb, but Willoughby (1950) says a photograph published in the French journal *La Nature* on 29th July 1905 showed a gorilla of quite ordinary size.

Another bull of the same race shot by M. Villars-Darasse in the Forest of Bambio, Haute-Lobaze, in *c.* February 1920 was stated to have measured 9 ft 4 in [*sic*], but once again photographic evidence showed a gorilla of just average proportions.

In the first example the hunter probably obtained his height measurement by running the tape over the contours of the body instead of in a straight line, and in the second the measurement must have been taken from the tip of the uplifted arms to the end of the longest toe with the foot bent downwards. Either (or both) of these methods were favoured by gorilla-hunters in the past who were anxious to make the total length as great as possible.

The *correct* way to measure a gorilla in the field is to take the distance from the crown of the head (excluding the elongated crest or pad) to the base of the heel as in humans.

In December 1930 an Italian scientific expedition which had been granted a special permit to explore the Virunga Mountains reportedly shot a 213 cm (7 ft) bull in the Albert National Park. Other measurements included a chest circumference of 185 cm (72·8 in) and an arm-span of 309 cm (10 ft 1·6 in), and the weight of this monster was given as 325 kg (716·5 lb).

If the arm-span measurement quoted for this animal was reliable then it must have stood at least 6 ft 9 in tall in life (the arm-span of an adult bull gorilla is normally 50 per cent greater than the standing height), but as no photographic evidence has ever been produced to substantiate these figures—or, for that matter, the embalmed body or skeleton—it must be assumed the dimensions of this gorilla were exaggerated.

Paul Belloni du Chaillu (1861), the French-American explorer and father of gorilla hunters, said adult bull gorillas ranged in height from 5 ft 2 in to 6 ft 2 in. The largest of the nine specimens collected by him in Gabon, Equatorial Africa, between 1856 and 1859 measured 5 ft 8 in.

According to Bourgoin (1955) the *record gorilla* was a bull of the mountain race shot in the Angumu Forest, in the eastern Congo, in March 1948 which measured 196 cm (6 ft 5·1 in) in height and 166 cm (61 in) round the chest, but as the arm-span of this specimen was only 249 cm (8 ft 2 in), the stature could not have been much above 5 ft 7 in.

The largest accurately measured gorilla on record was probably a bull of the mountain race shot by T. Alexander Barns (1923), a competent observer, in the eastern Congo which measured 6 ft 2 in from the crown of the head to the heel.

In 1900 Henry Paschen, the German animal-trader, shot an Eastern lowland gorilla near Yaounde, in the Cameroons, which he said measured 207 cm (6 ft 9·5 in) in length, but the measurement was taken from the crown of the head to the tip of the extended middle toe (the mounted specimen in the Rothschild Museum, Tring, Herts., has a standing height of 5 ft 7 in).

A mountain gorilla shot by Commander Attilio Gatti (1936) in Tshibinda Forest, near Lake Kivu (Republic of the Congo) in 1930 for the Museum of the Royal University, Florence, Italy, was credited with a height of 6 ft 9 in from crown to heel and 8 ft 9 in from the ground to the top of the uplifted arms, but both measurements were taken from the end of the longest toe with the foot bent downwards.

Another bull of the mountain race known as "N'gagui" shot in the Kivu region allegedly stood 184 cm (6 ft 0·5 in) and weighed 200 kg (440 lb) (Gromier, 1952), but as the arm-span was only 258 cm (8 ft 5·5 in) the height measurement must have been taken from the crown of the head to the tip of the extended toe.

The greatest reliable weight recorded for a gorilla in the field is 482 lb for the large mountain bull shot by Commander Gatti in the Tshibinda Forest in 1930 (see page 89). Another bull of the same race shot by Henry Raven (1931) of the Columbia University–American Museum of Natural History Expedition, west of Lake Kivu in July 1929, measured 5 ft 10 inches in height, 58·5 in round the chest, and weighed 460 lb.

In the winter of 1934 the George Vanderbilt African Expedition collected a huge old bull of the eastern lowland race which had been killed by natives in the neighbourhood of Aboghi in the Sanga River area, French Equatorial Africa. This gorilla measured exactly 6 ft in height and boasted a chest circumference of 55 in (Coolidge, 1937). Unfortunately, this specimen was not weighed, but it must have scaled nearly 500 lb.

Another large bull killed on Mount Sabini by Edmund Heller's American expedition in 1925 measured 5 ft 11·5 inches in height and was estimated to weigh over 500 lb, and Ben Burbridge (1928) shot a gorilla on Mount Kikeno in the Kivu area which measured 5 ft 11·75 in and was extremely bulky.

Fred Merfield (1956) says he shot an eastern lowland gorilla at Ambam in the French Cameroons which stood just over 6 ft tall and was estimated to weigh "between forty-one and forty-two stone" (between 574 and 588 lb), but this poundage must be considered excessive (the skin of this gorilla is preserved in the Science Museum at the University of Texas).

A large eastern lowland gorilla killed in Rio Muni, Spanish Guinea, West Africa by a hunter named Skulina for the Prague Museum, Czechoslovakia, reportedly weighed 600 lb, but the actual figure was just over 400 lb.

Very few adult female gorillas have been measured in the field and information is correspondingly scanty. In 1924 the following measurements were reported for a large female of the mountain race killed in open country (very unusual) on the Uganda–Congo border:

Arm-span 7 ft 9·5 in; crown of head to crutch when in sitting position 4 ft 2 in; hip to heel 2 ft 8 in.

Other measurements included a neck of 26·25 in; a forearm of 16 in; a thigh of 28·75 in; a chest of 64 in (post-mortem inflation); a hand length of 9·75 in and a foot length of 11·75 in.

This specimen was stated to have stood 6 ft 10 in tall in life (Pitman, 1931), but its true height was probably nearer 5 ft 2 in.

Gromier says a female eastern lowland gorilla killed in the Cameroons stood 5 ft 6·25 inches in height with an arm-span of 7 ft 8·75 in.

The largest female (*G.g. gorilla*) in a series of sixty skeletons examined by Schultz (1931) measured about 4 ft 9·25 inches in life.

A female mountain gorilla collected by the Swedish Expedition to Central Africa north of Lake Kivu in 1921 weighed 214·5 lb (Gyldenstople, 1928), and Grzimek (1957) quotes a weight of 159·5 lb for a female eastern lowland gorilla.

The heaviest gorilla ever held in captivity was a bull of the mountain race called "Mbongo" who died in San Diego Zoological Gardens, California, U.S.A. on 15th March 1942. During an attempt to weigh him shortly before his death Benchley (1942) says the platform scales "fluctuated from 645 pounds to nearly 670". Mbongo's posthumous weight was given as 631 lb, but there was some loss due to desiccation (Mckennery *et al.*, 1944). His posthumous measurements were: height 5 ft 7·5 in (Hooton, 1947, says he was 6 ft 5 in tall!); chest 69 in; waist 72 in; wrist 14·375 in; thigh 27·25 in; and calf 15·375 in.

Mbongo and another mountain gorilla called "Ngagi" arrived at San Diego Zoological Gardens on 5th October 1931. They had been captured the previous year by Martin and Osa Johnson in the Alumbongo Mountains in the Kivu region of the Congo (the Republic of the Congo). At the time of their arrival they were between four and five years of age, and their combined weight was 269 lb. Mbongo was about six months younger than Ngagi, and his weight was estimated at 125 lb.

Throughout their life in captivity Ngagi was always the dominant animal, although when the gorillas did actually fight Mbongo always proved the fiercer and more clever of the two. In February 1940 Mbongo overtook his big companion in weight for the first time, tipping the scales at 517 lb, compared to Ngagi's 468 lb, but this was only because the latter animal had been unwell for six months and had lost considerable weight (in September 1939 Ngagi weighed 501 lb). On 23rd April the same year they were weighed again and scaled 592 lb and 525 lb respectively. But whereas Mbongo was "round and paunchy with an enormously fat abdomen", Ngagi was "broad of shoulder and very trim and slender of waist and hips" (Benchley, 1940). Fifteen days later Mbongo tipped the scales at 602 lb, and Ngagi 539 lb.

Ngagi weighed 639 lb just before his death on 12th January 1944 (Anon, 1944).

In 1958 a posthumous weight of 776 lb was reported for a large western gorilla named "Phil" at St. Louis Zoological Park, Missouri, U.S.A., but this poundage was wrongly recorded.

In a letter to the author dated 25th July 1966, R. Marlin Perkins, Director of the zoo, wrote: "Since coming to the St. Louis Zoo four years ago, I have made inquiries of the staff about the weight of Phil the Gorilla. They assure me that the animal was placed in a truck, taken to a public scale, weighed, returned to the Zoo for autopsy, and that the figure of 776 pounds is the weight of the Gorilla. I, too, find this very difficult to believe. I was not in St. Louis at the time and had no part in the weighing of the animal. I had been at the Zoo a short time before Phil's death, however, and had seen him alive. Because of this, and because of my knowledge of Bushman at Lincoln Park Zoo in Chicago and Mbongo at the San Diego Zoo (whom I saw also a few months before death), I still find it difficult to accept 776 pounds for Phil. It must be remembered that Phil had been ill for several months and had lost considerable weight. The keepers tell me that he ate practically nothing for a period of ten days to two weeks prior to death."

Phil's posthumous measurements were given as: height 5 ft 11 in; chest 72·25 in; waist 64 in; neck 36 in; and wrist 15 in, and as the weight can be closely calculated where the height and maximum girth are known, this animal must have scaled about 615 lb when alive.

The western gorilla "Bobby" of Berlin Zoological Gardens (received 30th March 1928) was another exceptionally heavy bull. He weighed 242 kg (532·4 lb) at the age of ten and a half years (Koch, 1937), and 262·5 kg (577·5 lb) at the time of his death on 1st August 1935 (Heck, 1936).

His posthumous measurements were: height 5 ft 7·75 in; chest 65·75 in; waist 63 in; upper arm 22·75 in; circumference of shoulders 60 in.

The famous "Bushman" of Lincoln Park Zoological Gardens, Chicago, Illinois, U.S.A. (received 18th August 1930) weighed 550 lb in November 1949 (Steiner *et al.*, 1955), 565 lb in April 1950 and 542 lb at the time of his death on 1st January 1951 (this animal was credited with a height of 6 ft 2 in, but he actually stood just under 6 ft).

Another western gorilla called "Gargantua", owned by Ringling Brothers Circus, was billed as standing 6 ft 6 inches in height and weighing 750 lb, but both these figures owed much to commercial exaggeration. Gargantua was acquired by the American authoress Mrs. Gertrude Lintz in 1931 when he was aged one year, and she kept the gorilla for six years before selling him to the circus for $10,000. According to Riess (1949) Gargantua weighed 550 lb at the time of his death on 22nd September 1949 aged seventeen years. His posthumous measurements were: height 5 ft 6·5 in; chest 67 in; upper arm 24 in.

In 1953 Ringling Brothers Circus claimed a weight of 650 lb for another western gorilla called "Toto", who came to the circus via Mrs. Maria Hoyt of Havana, Cuba, in 1941, but this poundage was also exaggerated. Riess (1949) says this animal weighed 438 lb in 1947 when aged fourteen years. In 1956 Mrs. Hoyt repurchased Toto, and he remained with her until his death in 1968.

"Congo", the largest gorilla ever held in a British zoo. (Associated Press.)

The largest gorilla ever held captive in a British zoo was the western bull "Congo" of Bristol Zoological Gardens. He arrived there on 30th August 1954 and weighed 476 lb in February 1966. At the time of his death in December 1968 he scaled an estimated 550 lb (the scales in his cage only registered up to 500 lb) (Greed, *in litt.* 15.12.70).

Another western bull called "Alfred", who arrived at Bristol Zoological Gardens on 5th September 1930 when aged two years, weighed

*The Three-toed sloth (*Bradypus tridactylus*) of Central and tropical South America, the slowest-moving land mammal.*

*Britain's rarest land mammal, the Pine marten (*Martes martes*), which is now confined to the highlands of Scotland, North Wales and possibly the Lake District.*

476–490 lb in his prime. During the Second World War this very popular gorilla developed a fear of aeroplanes and when there was a heavy blitz on Bristol he used to take shelter in his den and cover himself with straw. A low-flying aircraft is supposed to have caused his death on 9th March 1948 from a heart attack. His stuffed body is now on permanent display in the Bristol Museum.

The heaviest gorilla living in captivity today anywhere in the world is believed to be the western bull "Samson" of Milwaukee Zoological Park, Wisconsin, U.S.A., whose weight fluctuates between 585 and 605 lb.

Another western bull called "Casey" living at Como Zoo, St. Paul's, Minnesota, U.S.A. (received 14th May 1959) has scaled as much as 576 lb, but his best weight is about 545 lb. This latter gorilla, named after Casey Stengle, the American baseball-player because he has a wicked side-arm throw with a rock and has been known to hit visitors on occasion, was loaned to the Henry Doorly Zoo in Omaha, Nebraska, in 1970 for "family purposes". He was shipped there by anaesthetising him, strapping him to a litter and then placing him in a small aircraft uncaged but attended by a veterinarian. This was the *first* time this technique had ever been used on an adult gorilla (Fletcher, *in litt.* 14.4.71).

The heaviest gorilla held captive in a British zoo today is the famous western bull "Guy" of London Zoological Gardens, who was born in the French Cameroons in *c*. May 1946 and arrived at the zoo on 5th November 1947. In February 1966 he scaled 468 lb, and in July 1967 he was 488·5 lb. His weight now fluctuates between 370·5 lb and 390 lb. Guy is rather short for an adult western gorilla, standing only 5 ft 3·5 in tall, but his estimated chest measurement of 72 in is one of the largest on record.

The heaviest female gorilla on record was a very obese specimen of the western race called "Susie" who lived in Cincinnati Zoological Gardens, Ohio, U.S.A. from 20th June 1931 to 29th October 1949. In 1940 she weighed 305 lb (Stephan, 1940), and at the time of her death an astonishing 458 lb.

With the exception of the giraffe and bats, the gorilla and the other anthropoid (man-like) apes are the only mammals that do not swim naturally, although they can probably be taught. Under natural conditions the gorilla fears water, and Schaller says that one small group refused to escape across a stream 2 to 3 ft deep and 20 ft wide when they were being pursued by natives with spears.

On 13th May 1951 a 448 lb western bull called "Makoko" fell into the 6 ft deep water-filled moat surrounding his enclosure at Bronx Zoo, New York, and sank immediately. According to Crandall (1951) the gorilla made no effort to save himself and was completely submerged when a keeper who had dived in reached him. By this time, however, the gorilla had been under water for over five minutes, and all attempts at resuscitation failed.

Although the ferocity of the gorilla has been greatly exaggerated, most of the stories about its incredible strength are true.

On one occasion an explorer watched a group of gorillas upending large boulders in their search for grubs. They were casually flipping them over with one hand as though they were hollow, and some of the gorillas were only half-grown. After the group had moved on the man decided to test the weight of one of these boulders and found that it took him all his strength *just to raise it a few inches off the ground with both hands!*

Du Berrie says he once saw a gorilla push on all fours against an 18 ft high tree as thick as a man's thigh and bring it crashing to the ground.

There are also reliable reports of gorillas bending rifle barrels in half and killing leopards by snapping their necks.

One of the guides on the Carl Akeley African Expedition of 1921 told the American collector that a few weeks previously a native had been killed by a mountain gorilla after stepping out suddenly from a thicket into an open space where a family of them were resting. When some of the missing man's companions found his body a few hours later the head and neck and one arm had been torn completely from the trunk.

According to another story the famous "Gargantua" (see page 92) of Ringling Brothers Circus was once given a rope with fifteen large men holding on the other end and succeeded in pulling them up to his cage with one hand! Such a feat, however, would be impossible *even* for a gorilla, and leads one to suspect that the circus-workers had been told beforehand to put up only token resistance in order to exaggerate the ape's strength. In other words, it was a good publicity stunt.

Dr. William T. Hornaday (quoted by Lane, 1955), believed that an adult bull gorilla was as strong as three powerful men, and this is probably about as accurate an estimate as we are ever likely to get of this animal's strength.

In one strength experiment carried out by Yerkes (1927) on "Congo", a five-year-old female gorilla, which involved the pulling of a rope attached to a spring-balance in an effort to obtain food, the 128 lb subject pulled 240 lb working with both hands and feet braced, but she was only half trying. Yerkes concluded from this that the arm strength of the young gorilla was two to three times greater than that of a human of comparative size.

In 1924 "Boma", a 165 lb male Chimpanzee (*Pan troglodytes*) at Bronx Zoo, New York, recorded a right-handed pull of 847 lb on a dynamometer, while a man of comparative weight recorded a pull of 210 lb. From these results Bauman (1926) deduced that the chimpanzee was 4·4 times stronger than the well-developed young college football-player. He did add, however, that an adult female chimpanzee called "Suzette" (estimated weight 135 lb) registered a right-handed pull of 1,260 lb while in a rage, and another of 905 lb when she was quite calm and collected.

Finch (1943), on the other hand, who carried out similar strength experiments with eight chimpanzees from the Yale Laboratory of Primate Biology and four humans of varying weights, found that there was "no great absolute strength discrepancy between the human and chimpanzee males", and that the males of both species were stronger than the female chimpanzees. The best pull registered by a male chimpanzee was 487 lb (body weight 107 lb), and the best pull by a human subject 525 lb (body weight 190 lb) which, says Finch, strongly indicated that the male chimpanzee pound for pound is relatively stronger than the human male.

The smallest known primate is the Lesser mouse lemur (*Microcebus murinus*) of Madagascar. Adult specimens have a head and body length of 125–150 mm (4.9–5.9 in) and a tail of about the same length. The weight varies from 45 to 85 g (from 1·58 to 2·99 oz) (Hill, 1953).

In the dry season this species falls into a torpor known as "aestivation" because it has a less efficient temperature-regulating mechanism than most mammals, and during this period it lives on the fat stored in its rump and tail.

This animal also has the fastest development of any primate, being fully mature at seven to eight months.

*The largest living member of the monkey family is the Mandrill (*Mandrillus sphinx*) of equatorial West Africa. Adult males have a head and body length of up to 38 in and sometimes exceed 100 lb in weight. (H. Eisenbeiss/F. Lane.)*

The male chimpanzee "Heine", the oldest primate on record. (Lincoln Park Zoological Gardens, Chicago, Illinois, U.S.A.)

The greatest reliable age recorded for a primate (excluding man) is fifty-plus years for a male chimpanzee called "Heine" at Lincoln Park Zoological Gardens, Chicago, Illinois, U.S.A. He arrived there on 10th June 1924 when aged about three years (Fisher, *in litt.* 18.6.71)

Another chimpanzee received at Moscow Zoo in 1924 was reportedly still alive in the autumn of 1966, but Jones (1968) says he has not yet been able to confirm this.

The *potential* life-span of this species has been estimated at sixty years (Riopelle, 1963).

The greatest reliable age recorded for a chimpanzee in a British zoo is twenty-six-plus years for a male specimen named "Mickie" at London Zoological Gardens who died on 7th June 1924 (Flower, 1931).

The longest-lived gorilla on record is the forty-one-year-old western bull "Massa", who arrived in New York on 16th September 1931 from West Africa. His owner, Mrs. Gertrude Lintz, sold him to Philadelphia Zoological Gardens, Pennsylvania, U.S.A. on 30th December 1935 where he has remained ever since.

Another western bull called "Bamboo" received at the same zoo on 5th August 1927, died on 21st January 1961 aged thirty-four years (Crandall, 1964).

A female western gorilla called "Solange" received at the Jardin des Plantes, Paris, on 20th September 1931, died on 20th December 1954 after 23 years 3 months in captivity (Crandall, 1964).

The greatest reliable age recorded for a gorilla in a British zoo is twenty-five-plus years for "Guy" of London Zoological Gardens (see page 94), who was still alive in December 1971.

According to Schaller (1963) the maximum age reached by gorillas under natural conditions is about thirty years.

The largest member of the monkey family is the Mandrill (*Mandrillus sphinx*) of Equatorial West Africa. Adult males have an average head and body length of 24–30 in and weigh 55–70 lb. Females are about 25 per cent smaller.

The greatest reliable weight recorded for a mandrill is 54 kg (119 lb) for a specimen which measured 36 inches in length (without tail), but unconfirmed weights up to 130 lb have been reported.

    This size is closely matched by the Chacma baboon (*Papio ursinus*) of South Africa, and the Anubis baboon (*P. anubis*) of tropical Africa, both of which have been weighed up to 90 lb and reach 40 inches in length (without tail) (Dorst & Dandelot, 1970).

The smallest known monkey is the Pygmy marmoset (*Cebuella pygmaea*) of Ecuador, northern Peru and western Brazil. Mature specimens have a maximum total length of 304 mm (12 in), half of which is tail, and weigh from 49 to 80 g (from 1·7 to 2·81 oz) (Walker *et al.*, 1968).

The rarest monkey is the Hairy-eared mouse lemur (*Cheirogaleus trichotis*) of Madagascar which, until fairly recently, was known only from the type specimen (Gunther, 1875) and two skins. In 1966, however, a live example was found on the east coast near Mananara (Fisher *et al.*, 1969).

The greatest reliable age recorded for a monkey is "about forty-six years" for a big male mandrill called "George", who was deposited at London Zoological Gardens on 30th November 1906 by the Hon. Walter Rothschild (later Lord Rothschild) and died on 14th March 1916. Lord Rothschild purchased this specimen in Paris for £124, and he told Major Stanley Flower (1931) that he was "practically certain" that it was the same mandrill as one that had been imported into Europe in 1869.

    Flower also gives a record of a Chacma baboon living for forty-five years.

The most intelligent of sub-human primates is the chimpanzee. At one time, however, it was thought by morphologists and students of animal behaviour that the gorilla was superior to the chimpanzee intellectually, but African natives familiar with both animals have always taken the opposite view. "If you throw a spear at the njina [gorilla]," say the natives, "he will spring out of its way; but if you throw one at the nchigo [chimpanzee] he will catch it in his hand and throw it back at you." (Reade, quoted by Yerkes, 1929.)

    The chimpanzee is also one of the very few animals that uses tools, and the stick has been described as the "universal instrument" of this species. In the forest the stick is used to extract termites or honey from nests, and in captivity to reach objects which are beyond the reach of its arms.

    According to Reynolds (1967) chimpanzees at the 6571st Aeromedical Laboratory in New Mexico have been taught to play noughts and crosses electronically, the winner getting a reward of food.

    In September 1971 it was reported that "Washoe", the most advanced of another group of chimpanzees being taught to communicate by signs at Norman, Oklahoma, U.S.A. knew 200 words and could construct simple sentences.

The most intelligent monkeys are baboons. Probably the most famous example was a male Chacma baboon called "Jack", who used to work the railway signals at Uitenhage Station, about 200 miles north of Port Elizabeth, Cape Colony, South Africa.

"Jack", the male chacma baboon who worked the railway signals at Uitenhage Station, South Africa.

According to the story a railwayman named Wylde lost both his legs below the calf as the result of an accident on the Port Elizabeth main line in 1877 and was later given a job as a signalman at Uitenhage Station. In order to make the journey between his wooden shack and the signal-box, a distance of some 150 yd, he constructed a trolley by means of which he propelled himself along the track with the aid of a pole. One day he saw Jack for sale in the local market and purchased him as a pet. The baboon soon became extremely devoted to his master, and during the next few months Wylde trained him to fetch water, sweep out the shack and even to hand a special key to passing engine-drivers who used it to adjust certain "points" further up the line. When Jack heard an engine approaching he would rush to the signal-box and take down the key from a peg on the wall. The signalman also taught the baboon to push him on his trolley to the signal-box where the animal would sit and watch his master pulling the levers with great interest.

Soon Jack learned to operate the signals for the Graaf Reinet and Port Elizabeth trains by himself while Wylde sat on the trolley ready to correct any mistakes that were made. Eventually, however, the baboon became so proficient at his job that he was able to carry out the whole operation by himself while his master remained in the shack. He was never known to make a mistake.

The amazing partnership lasted for over nine years until Jack died from tuberculosis in 1890.

At the time of writing, another Chacma baboon called "Jock" is working as a signalman on a branch-line near Pretoria, South Africa. Unlike Jack, however, this baboon is paid 1s. 6d. a day and gets a bottle of beer every Saturday night!

There is also a record of a Chacma baboon being used to herd sheep on a South African farm with astonishing success.

In Australia there is a Rhesus monkey (*Macaca mulatta*) called "Johnnie" who drives a tractor!

This remarkable animal is owned by Mr. Lindsay Schmidt, who runs a sheep-farm at Balmoral some 220 miles west of Melbourne, Victoria.

Says Mr. Schmidt: "Johnnie is almost human. He was a pet to start with, then he started to follow me about the farm. Now he can open and shut paddock gates and, at shearing time, he picks burrs out of the wool. I couldn't keep him away from the tractor, which is now virtually his special job about the place. He'll never press the tractor starter button if it's in gear. He makes sure it's in neutral, then presses the button and springs smartly into the driving seat to take the wheel."

Johnnie then steers a straight or curved path according to the commands of his master, who stands at the rear of an attached truck and throws out fodder for the grazing animals.

When lunch-time comes the pair sit down in the shade of the tractor and enjoy separate lunch-bags consisting of sandwiches, fruit and soft drinks. When the meal is over the monkey carefully puts his litter back into the bag (humans please note).

Johnnie has proved to be so valuable that Mr. Schmidt has been given a tax deduction of £40 a year by the Australian Government for his services.

The least intelligent of the subhuman primates are the lemurs (family Lemuridae), which are confined to Madagascar and the Comoro Islands. In some tests they have been found to be inferior to dogs and even pigeons in intelligence.

The largest rodent in the world is the Capybara (*Hydrochoerus hydrochaeris*), also called the "Carpincho" or "Water hog", which is found in tropical South America. Mature specimens have a head and body length of 3·25–4·5 ft and weigh up to 150 lb. A smaller species (*H. isthmius*) found in Panama scales about 60 lb (Walker *et al.*, 1968).

The capybara of tropical South America is the world's largest rodent. ("Evening News", London.)

The largest rodent found in Britain is *now* the Coypu (*Myocastor coypus*), also known as the "Nutria", which was introduced from Argentina by East Anglian fur-breeders. In 1937 four escaped from a nutria-farm near Ipswich, Suffolk. One was killed almost immediately, but the other three founded a dynasty of wild specimens (the coypu breeds three times a year and produces six to ten young in a litter). When the Second World War broke out coypus from thirty-seven of the fifty-one fur-farms in East Anglia also managed to escape, and they soon became established in Norfolk and parts of Suffolk. They then began attacking crops and threatening drainage systems by burrowing in banks, and the farmers quickly declared war on them. In the three-year period 1962–65 alone 136,000 coypus were killed. In December 1969 the farmers in East Anglia reported that they had finally got the wild coypu under control.

Adult males measure 30–36 inches in length (including short tail) and average 11–12 lb in weight, but much larger specimens have been recorded. On 5th December 1951 a coypu measuring 3 ft 6 inches in total length and weighing 18 lb was killed in a dike by three boys at Ditchingham, Suffolk, and another specimen measuring 3 ft 4 inches in total length and weighing 17·25 lb was killed by a car as it ran across the road near Ludham Bridge between Yarmouth and Norwich in October 1953.

In January 1960 a coypu measuring 3 ft 2 inches in total length and weighing 20 lb was shot at Horsford, Norfolk, and a weight of 28 lb was reported for another specimen caught in Suffolk in 1962.

In captivity weights up to 40 lb have been reported for cage-fat animals.

Coypus are good swimmers and can remain submerged for long periods of time. One large male chased by dogs in Norfolk remained under water for twenty minutes.

The smallest known rodent is probably the Old World harvest mouse (*Microymys minutus*), of which the British form measures up to 13·5 cm (5·3 in) in length, including tail, and weighs between 4·2 and 10·2 g (between 0·15 and 0·36 oz). It is thus about half the size of the Common house mouse (*Mus musculus*).

In June 1965 it was announced that an even smaller rodent had been discovered in the Asian part of the U.S.S.R. (probably a more diminutive form of *M. minutus*), but further information is lacking.

The rarest rodent in the world is believed to be the James Island rice rat (*Oryzomys swarthi*), also called "Swarth's rice rat". Four specimens were collected on this island (Galapagos Group) by J. S. Hunter for the California Academy of Sciences in 1906 (Orr, 1938), and it was not heard of again until January 1966 when the skull of a recently dead animal was found (Fitter, 1968).

The greatest reliable age recorded for a rodent is twenty-two years for an Indian crested porcupine (*Hystrix indica*) which died in Trivandrum Zoological Gardens, south-western India, in 1942 (Simon, 1943).

Flower gives a record of a Common porcupine (*H. cristata*) which died at London Zoological Gardens on 9th January 1886 after spending 20 years 4 months 14 days in captivity.

The only other rodent of comparable age is the American beaver (*Castor canadensis*). Flower says a female living at Stellingen in September 1923 was "at least nineteen years of age".

The largest of all known insectivores is the Moon rat (*Echinosorex gymnurus*), also known as "Raffles gymnure", which is found in Burma, Thailand, Malaysia, Sumatra and Borneo. Mature specimens have a head and body length of 265–445 mm (10.43–17.52 in), a tail measuring 200–210 mm (7.87–8.26 in) and weigh up to 1,400 g (3.08 lb) (Walker *et al.*, 1968).

The Common tenrec (*Tenrec ecaudatus*) of Madagascar and the near-by Comoro Islands has a head and body length of 265–390 mm (10.43–15.36 in).

The moon rat or gymnura of South-East Asia, the largest of all insectivores. (Zoological Society of London.)

The largest insectivore found in Britain is the Common hedgehog (*Erinaceus europaeus*). Mature specimens have a head and body length of 245–310 mm (9.64–12.2 in), a tail measuring 20–35 mm (0.7–1.37 in) and usually weigh 450–1,200 g (15.4 oz–42.24 oz) (van den Brink, 1967), but Burton (1969) quotes a record of a male which weighed 1,400 g (49.28 oz).

The smallest known insectivore is the Etruscan pygmy shrew (see Smallest living mammal).

The greatest reliable age recorded for an insectivore is six and a half years for a Haitian solenodon (*Solenodon paradoxus*) which died in Leipzig Zoological Gardens, Germany, in 1950 (Mohr, 1951).

Crandall (1964) gives a record of 5 years 11 months 4 days for a male Philippine tree shrew (*Urogale everetti*) which died in Bronx Zoo, New York, on 13th June 1953.

The rarest insectivore is the Tenrec *Dasogale fontoynonti*, which is known only from the type specimen collected in eastern Madagascar (preserved in the Paris Museum of Natural History). The Ceylon shrew (*Podihik kura*) is known only from two specimens collected near Madirigiriya, in the North-Central Province of Ceylon, and the African forest shrew (*Praesorex goliath*) from three specimens collected in the Cameroons, West Africa (Walker *et al.*, 1968).

The largest of all antelopes is the rare Derby eland (*Taurotragus derbianus*), also called the "Giant eland", of West and north-central Africa. Several races have been described, all about the same size, but some of these are of doubtful

The common eland of East and South Africa, which rivals the Lord Derby eland for the title of "largest living antelope". (Central Photographic Agency.)

validity. Adult bulls average 5 ft 8 in at the shoulder and scale about 1,500 lb, but shoulder heights up to 5 ft 10 in and estimated weights up to 2,000 lb have been reported.

The Common eland (*T. oryx*) of East and South Africa has the same shoulder height of up to 5 ft 10 in, but is not quite so massively built (the average weight of adult bulls is 1,300–1,400 lb). There is one record, however, of a 5 ft 5 in bull shot in Nyasaland (now Malawi) which weighed 2,078 lb, and two other bulls shot in Kenya both scaled 1,969 lb (Meinertzhagen, 1938).

Adult females of both species rarely exceed 5 ft at the shoulder and 1,000 lb in weight.

Elands can be domesticated. The Astaniya-Nova Zoo in the Ukraine, U.S.S.R., has a free-grazing herd of about forty animals, and twenty-two have been trained for milking since 1948 (Treus & Lobanov, 1971). Elands have also been imported into Texas, U.S.A. where there are now a small number of established herds (Laycock, 1966).

During the mating season, however, mature bull elands are extremely dangerous animals and there are at least two records of zoo keepers being seriously injured by the 2 ft long horns of this massive antelope.

On 21st June 1971 the Head Ranger at the Duke of Bedford's Woburn Abbey "Wild Animal Kingdom" was gored to death by an enraged bull eland (*T. oryx*) while locking up the animal's compound. The man was rushed to a local hospital but died from a massive haemorrhage shortly after being admitted.

The royal antelope, the smallest living antelope. (General Photographic Agency.)

The smallest antelope is the Royal antelope (*Neotragus pygmaeus*), which lives in the dense forests of West Africa from Sierra Leone to Gabon. Mature specimens (both sexes) measure 10–12 in at the shoulder and weigh only 7–8 lb, which is the size of a large Brown hare (*Lepus europaeus*).

The slender Swayne's dik-dik (*Madoqua swaynei*) of Somalia, East Africa, weighs only 5–6 lb when adult, but this species stands about 13 in at the shoulder. Phillips's dik-dik (*M. phillipsi*) of the same country also stands 13 in at the shoulder, but Rowland Ward (1969) gives its weight as 8 lb. Drake-Brockman (1930) says some adult examples of *M. swaynei* and *M. phillipsi* tip the scales at no more than 4–5·5 lb, but these weights need confirming.

According to Lydekker (1911) dik-diks are so small that "two or three may be killed at one shot".

The rarest antelope is probably Jentink's duiker (*Cephalopus jentinki*), also known as the "Black-headed duiker", which is thinly scattered in the deep forests of Liberia, Senegal and the Ivory Coast. Very little is known of its numbers—or habits for that matter—but the total population may be anything from a few dozen to possibly a few hundred (Fitter, 1968).

The greatest reliable age recorded for an antelope is 20 years 1 month 22 days for a female White-bearded gnu (*Connochaetes taurinus albojubatus*) which died in Philadelphia Zoological Gardens, Pennsylvania, U.S.A. on 27th July 1928 (Flower, 1931). Another specimen reportedly lived for twenty years in the Chicago Zoological Park, Illinois, U.S.A. (Robb, 1960). Crandall cites a record of a female Brindled gnu (*C. taurinus*) received at Bronx Zoo, New York, on 2nd September 1920 which was sold on 26th August 1940 after spending 19 years 11 months 22 days in captivity.

Flower says he was shown a female Nilgais (*Boselaphus tragocamelus*) at Antwerp Zoological Gardens, Belgium, on 26th September 1929 which he was told had been living there since 1908, but as this species is known to have a moderate life-span (i.e. eight to twelve years) this statement must be considered suspect.

The fastest antelope is the Pronghorn antelope (see Fastest Mammal).

The largest deer is the Alaskan moose (*Alces A. gigas*), which is found in the eastern Yukon, Alaska, U.S.A. and British Columbia, Canada. Adult bulls stand about 6 ft at the shoulder on the average and weigh between 1,100 and 1,200 lb, but one specimen standing 7 ft 8 in at the shoulder and weighing an estimated 1,800 lb was shot on the Yukon River by Dall de Weese in September 1897 (Anon, 1898). Unconfirmed measurements up to 8·5 ft at the shoulder and estimated weights up to 2,600 lb have been claimed. Cows are about five-sixths the size of bulls.

Lockhard (1895), speaking of the Alaskan moose, says: "Those down at Peel River and the Yukon are much larger than up this way [Great Slave Lake]. There I have known two cases of extraordinary moose having been killed; the meat alone of each of them weighing about 1,000 pounds."

These weights imply a live weight of 1,700 or 1,800 lb, but Seton (1927) says the weight of the meat was guessed. The same writer also points out that the standing height of an Alaskan moose may be 8–10 in less than the same measurement taken between pegs (see the African bush elephant).

Several attempts have been made to domesticate the moose (four races are recognised) and use it as a draught-animal in North America, but they have not been very successful. The moose doesn't mind pulling heavy loads, but every time it sees water it invariably swerves from its chosen path and wallows in the aquatic depths, much to the discomfort of the cart-driver!

Mature bulls can be formidable adversaries, and there is a record of an Alaskan moose attacking a car and killing the driver (Caras, 1964).

Britain's largest wild mammal: the Scottish red deer.

The largest deer found in Britain is the Red deer (*Cervus elephus*). A full-grown stag stands about 3 ft 8 in at the shoulder and weighs 230–250 lb; hinds are about two-thirds this size.

The heaviest wild red deer on record was probably a stag killed in Glenmore Deer-forest, Inverness, Scotland in 1877 which weighed 462 lb. Another stag killed on the Isle of Islay in the Inner Hebrides in 1940 may have been even heavier. It weighed 456 lb "clean" without the liver, which would have accounted for another 6–8 lb (Whitehead, 1964). In 1831 a stag weighing 525 lb was reported from Scotland, but further information is lacking.

The heaviest park red deer on record was a huge stag killed at Woburn, Bedfordshire, in 1836 which weighed 476 lb (height at shoulder 4 ft 6 in). Another stag weighing 472 lb 7 oz was killed in Warnham Court Park, Sussex, on 7th September 1926, and one weighing 472 lb was killed in the same park in 1952 (Whitehead, 1964).

The smallest deer, and the smallest known ruminant, is the Lesser Malayan chevrotain or "Mouse deer" (*Tragulus javinicus*) of south-eastern Asia, including Sumatra, Borneo and Java (more than fifty forms of Tragulus are recognised). Adult specimens measure 8–10 in at the shoulder and weigh 6–7 lb.

> This animal has been credited with extraordinary cunning and intelligence by the natives of south-eastern Asia, which probably explains why it has rarely been photographed in the wild!

The rarest deer is Fea's muntjac (*Muntiacus feae*), which is known only from two specimens collected on the borders of Tennasserim, Lower Burma, and Thailand (Tate, 1947).

> The Black muntjac (*M. crinifrons*) is known only from three specimens collected in the State of Chekiang, south-eastern China (Allen, 1938–40).

The greatest reliable age recorded for a deer is 26 years 6 months 2 days for a Red deer (*Cervus elephus*), which died in the National Zoological Park, Washington, D.C., U.S.A. on 24th March 1941 (Jones, 1958, quoted by Crandall). A female Malayan sambar (*Cervus unicolor equinus*) died in Bronx Zoo, New York, on 11th December 1955 aged 26 years 5 months 6 days (Crandall, 1964).

The longest recorded elephant tusks are a pair from the eastern Congo (Zaire). They were originally owned by King Menelek of Abyssinia (Ethiopia), who later presented them to a "European political officer". They were eventually put up for sale in London and were purchased by Rowland Ward Ltd., the famous Piccadilly taxidermists, who presented them in 1907 to the National Collection of Heads and Horns kept by the New York Zoological Society in Bronx Park, New York City, N.Y., U.S.A. The right tusk measures 11 ft 5·5 in along the outside curve and the left 11 ft. Their combined weight is 293 lb, but they probably weighed about 305 lb when fresh. Another huge pair of tusks measuring 11 ft 1·25 in and 10 ft 0·5 in respectively, with a combined weight of 244·5 lb, were collected by T. Christensen in Kenya in February 1959 (Rowland Ward, 1969).

> The right tusk of a bull elephant is nearly always slightly longer and heavier than the left because the animal prefers to dig and root about with its left tusk. In the case of the Christensen elephant, however, the difference is rather pronounced.

> A single tusk of 11 ft 6 in has been reported, but further details are lacking.

> Less reliable is a claim by Hartenfels that he saw a tusk exceeding 14 ft in length in a merchant's shop in Venice (Sanderson, 1963), unless of course it came from an extinct mammoth.

> R. G. Cummings (1850) speaks of a tusk which measured "21 ft 9 in [*sic*]", but this figure must represent the combined length of a pair.

The *16 ft plus tusk of an imperial mammoth unearthed near Post, Gorza County, Texas, U.S.A. in 1933 which is now preserved in the American Museum of Natural History. (American Museum of Natural History.)*

The heaviest recorded elephant tusks. (Photo-Reportage Ltd.)

A giant bull tusker in Gwalior, central India who could not lie down before his tusks were trimmed. (F. D. Fayrer.)

The longest recorded Asiatic elephant tusks are a pair in the Royal Siamese Museum, Bangkok, which measure 9 ft 10·5 in and 9 ft respectively (Rowland Ward, 1928).

The largest elephant tusks on record. (New York Zoological Society.)

The heaviest recorded tusks are a pair in the British Natural History Museum, London, which were collected from an aged bull shot by an Arab with a muzzle-loading gun at the foot of Mount Kilimanjaro, Kenya, in 1897. They were first sold in Zanzibar (now part of Tanzania) in 1898 to an American company, who in turn sent them to London for auction in 1901. The heavier of the two tusks was acquired by the Trustees of the British Museum of Natural History, London, and the other by a cutlery firm in Sheffield which deposited the specimen in its private museum. This second tusk was purchased by the Trustees of the British Museum of Natural History, London in July 1933. The tusks were measured in 1955, when the first was found to be 10 ft 2·5 in long, weighing 226·5 lb, and the other 10 ft 5·5 in, weighing 214 lb, giving a combined weight of 440·5 lb. According to Blunt (1933), however, the tusks weighed 236 and 225 lb respectively when they were fresh, giving a combined weight of 461 lb, although he doubted whether they were both from the same elephant (the longest tusk of a pair is generally the heaviest).

Another huge pair collected by Major P. H. G. Powell-Cotton from an average-sized bull shot near Lake Albert on the Uganda–Congo border in 1905 and now preserved in the Powell-Cotton Museum at Quex Park, Kent, measure 9 ft and 8 ft 11 in respectively and have a combined weight of 372 lb.

Captain C. R. S. Pitman (1953) gives details of a pair of tusks collected in Bunyoro, Northern Province, Nigeria, in c. 1921 which totalled 355·75 lb, and another pair collected from an elephant shot in western Kigezi, in south-western Uganda, in 1944 totalled 328 lb.

According to Hallett (1967) the tusks of the famous "Mohammed" of Marsabit Mountain Reserve in northern Kenya were so long and heavy that the elephant couldn't raise his head properly, and the poor creature had to walk in a backward direction to avoid getting them stuck in the ground. In 1950 game wardens estimated that there was 10 ft of tusk outside each gum and put their combined weight at 400 lb (Stockley, 1953). When Mohammed died of "old age" in 1960, however, the tusks were found to total just over 250 lb, the longest measuring 10 ft 9 inches in length and scaling 141 lb (Bere, 1966).

Another aged bull elephant called "Ahmed" living in the same reserve is stated to have the longest and heaviest tusks in the world. Game circles believe they may top 200 lb each and measure 9 ft in length. In November 1970 Ahmed was accorded complete protection by the Kenya Government.

The heaviest recorded Asiatic elephant tusks are a pair collected from a bull killed in the western Terai jungle, northern India and later presented to King George V which have a combined weight of 321 lb (Rowland Ward, 1928).

Another elephant shot by Colonel F. S. Gillespie in southern India carried tusks weighing 91 lb and 90·5 lb respectively (Morris, 1940).

The heaviest single tusk on record was a specimen weighing 117 kg (257·4 lb) collected in Dahomey, West Africa. It was put on display at the Paris Exposition of 1900. Kolokner says a tusk weighing 350 lb was sold in Amsterdam during the last century, but this must have come from an extinct mammoth.

Owing to selective shooting for sport and ivory very few big tusks are now left in Africa, and anything over 70 lb is now considered exceptional.

The heaviest single tusk of an Asiatic elephant on record was the larger of the pair presented to King George V (see above). It weighs 161 lb.

The longest recorded cow elephant tusks are a pair collected from an elephant shot by Paul J. Rainey near Mount Marsabit, northern Kenya, which measure 5 ft 10 in and 5 ft 7 in respectively (Roosevelt & Heller, 1915).

Cow tusks rarely exceed 15–20 lb in weight (some cows never grow tusks at all), but they are more valuable than those of boars because of their closer grain.

The heaviest recorded cow tusks are a pair taken from an elephant shot by Peter Pearson, the well-known Uganda game ranger, on the north-eastern shore of Lake Albert in 1923 which have a combined weight of 108 lb (Pitman, 1953). The tusks are now preserved in the British Museum of Natural History, London.

In 1945 an African killed a four-tusked elephant in the Rutshuru region, south-western Uganda. Each tusk weighed about 32 lb (Pitman, 1953). Another four-tusked elephant was shot by a native near Kasongo, in the Belgian Congo (now Zaire) in September 1947. This time the tusks weighed 55 lb, making a total of 220 lb.

Chapman mentions an elephant with five small tusks on one side and four on the other, and Colyer (1931) says he shot a rogue elephant with a multiple tusk composed of seven small tusks. A seven-tusk growth from a single socket has also been reported for an elephant shot in Uganda.

Most of these small and useless tusks are the result of bullet damage to the main tusk. An abscess follows, and a number of tusks sprout from the injured socket.

The longest narwhal tusk on record is one measuring 9 ft 4·5 in with a maximum circumference of 7·5 in. Another tusk measuring 8 ft 7 in weighs 15 lb (Rowland Ward, 1907).

The largest recorded walrus tusk measures 37·5 inches in length, 10·5 inches in maximum circumference and weighs 10 lb 13 oz. Perry (1967) says there is an old Russian record of a pair of Pacific walrus tusks weighing 35 lb, but further information is lacking.

The horns of Watussi cattle are among the longest grown by any animal.

The longest record animal horn is one measuring 81·25 in on the outside curve, with a maximum circumference of 18·25 in, found on a specimen of domestic Ankole cattle (*Bos taurus*) near Lake Ngami, Botswana (formerly Bechuanaland) (Rowland Ward, 1907). There is also a record of a single horn from an Indian buffalo (*Bos bubalis*) measuring 77·375 in on the outside curve (Rowland Ward, 1907). Horn-spans up to 12 ft have been reported for Texan longhorn cattle.

The longest horns grown by any wild animal are those of the Pamir argali (*Ovis poli*), also called "Marco Polo's argali", a wild sheep found in the mountains of Soviet Central Asia. One of these has been measured at 75 in along the front curve, with a maximum circumference of 16 in (Rowland Ward, 1907). The horns of the females are much smaller.

*The anterior horn of the
black rhinoceros has been
measured up to 53·5 inches
in length. This specimen
measures over 30 in. (J. van
Coevering—F. Lane.)*

The longest recorded anterior horn of a rhinoceros is one of 62·25 in found on a female southern race White rhinoceros (*Ceratotherium simum simum*) shot by Colonel W. Gordon Cumming (1850) in South Africa. The anterior horn measured 22·25 in. Hans Schilling, the German explorer, says he saw another anterior horn which measured 81 in, but this length has never been confirmed.

The world's finest stag head is the 23-pointer in the Maritzburg Collection, Germany. The outside span is 75·5 in, the longest antler 47·5 in and the weight 41·5 lb.

The greatest number of points recorded is 62 (33 × 29) for a stag shot in 1696 by Frederick III (1657–1713), the Elector of Brandenburg, later King Frederick I of Prussia.

The record head for a British red deer is a 47-pointer (longest antler 33·5 in) weighing 17 lb 10 oz shed in Great Warnham Park, Sussex, in 1892 (Whitehead, 1964). The record for a semi-feral stag is a 20-pointer (longest antler 45·375 in) for a specimen found dead in Endsleigh Wood, near Tavistock, Devon in December 1950. The antlers were not weighed because they were still attached to the skull, but Whitehead says they probably scale about 19 lb.

The heaviest antlers are those grown by the Alaskan moose. A bull shot by Bruce Hodson near Lake Iliamna, about 200 miles south-west of Anchorage in 1967 had a rack weighing just over 90 lb. Unconfirmed weights up to 100 lb have been reported.

The highest mammalian blood temperature is that of the Domestic goat (*Capra hircus*) with an average of 39·9 °C (103·8 °F), and a normal range of from 38·7 to 40·7 °C (101·7 to 105·3 °F) (Dukes, 1947).

The lowest mammalian blood temperature is that of the Spiny anteater (*Tachyglossus aculeatus*), a monotreme found in Australia and New Guinea, with a normal range of 22·2 to 24·4 °C (72 to 87 °F). The blood temperature of the Golden hamster (*Mesocricetus auratus*) sometimes falls as low as 3·5 °C (38·3 °F) during hibernation, and an extreme figure of 1·4 °C (29·6 °F) has been reported for a myotis bat during a deep sleep.

The highest-priced animal pelts are those of the Sea otter (*Enhydra lutris*), also known as the "Kamchatka beaver", which fetched up to $2,700 (then £675) before their fifty-five-year-long protection started in 1912 (see page 42). The protection ended in 1967, and at the first legal auction of sea otter pelts at Seattle, Washington, U.S.A. on 31st January 1968 Neiman-Marcus, the famous Dallas department stores, paid $9,200 (then £3,832) for four pelts from Alaska. On 30th January 1969 a New York company paid $1,100 (£457) for an exceptionally fine pelt from Alaska, and 500 others put up for sale at the same auction fetched on an average $256 (£106) from bidders representing top fashion-houses in the United States, Canada and Europe.

On 26th February 1969 forty selected pelts of the mink-sable crossbreed "Kojah" from the Piampiano Fur Ranch, Zion, Illinois, U.S.A. realised $2,700 (£1,125) in New York City. In May 1970 a Kojah coat costing $125,000 (£52,083) was sold by Neiman-Marcus to Welsh actor Richard Burton, who wanted it as a present for his wife, actress Elizabeth Taylor.

In April 1966 Neiman-Marcus sold a blackwillow mink coat for $75,000 (£21,000). The pelts for this coat were purchased at an auction at the Hudson Bay Company for $1,100 (then £308) apiece (Stanley Marcus, *in litt.* 14.6.67).

The heaviest piece of ambergris on record was a 1,003 lb lump recovered from a Sperm whale (*Physeter catadon*) taken in Australian waters on 3rd December 1912 by a Norwegian whaling fleet (Matthews *et al.*, 1968). It was later sold in London for £23,000.

Another piece of ambergris weighing exactly 1,000 lb was taken from a sperm whale killed off the coast of New Zealand (Tonnessen, 1962), and a lump weighing 975 lb was formerly owned by the Dutch East India Company (Van Beneden and Gervais, 1880).

In April 1953 a lump of ambergris weighing 926 lb was removed from a sperm whale processed aboard the British factory ship *Southern Harvester* in the Antarctic Ocean (Clarke, 1954).

Weights in excess of 1 ton have also been reported. On 14th December 1946, for instance, the American cargo ship *Richard K. Call* arrived at Buenos Aires, Argentina, from Las Palmas, Canary Islands, with a lump of ambergris reportedly weighing 2 tons which the crew had picked up at sea 200 miles off the Uruguayan coast. Local "experts" put its value at "£250,000 [*sic*]".

Another lump even larger was stated to have been found by the crew of the Brazilian coaster *Araxa* in December 1947 while on a coal run from southern Brazil to Rio de Janeiro. According to one newspaper report the ambergris weighed "10 tons [*sic*]" and had been ejected by a sperm whale "probably weighing 80 tons".

Needless to say, nothing more was heard of these two "prizes".

Ambergris, literally "grey amber" and looking like mottled soap, is a morbid fatty concretion found in the intestines or stomachs of sperm whales which hardens on exposure to the air. The substance is formed as the result of irritations set up by the indigestible horny beaks of the multitudes of squid the whale feeds on. Ambergris is usually found floating on the surface of the sea and rarely inside the whale. When dried it is light and inflammable and yields an odour faintly resembling that of honey. On being melted by heat it evaporates slowly, leaving no trace behind.

Ambergris was once a very valuable raw material of the perfume industry because of its peculiar property of fixing and holding the fragrance of flowers in fine colognes and other perfumery preparations, but the development of synthetic substitutes has now reduced the market price considerably. Until quite recently it was believed that ambergris was an abnormal product found only in sickly and emaciated sperm whales, but Gilmore (quoted by Caldwell *et al.*, 1966) believes that this substance may serve as "a communicatory function via the gustatory senses".

The largest of all marsupials is the Red kangaroo (*Macropus rufia*) of southern and eastern Australia. Adult males or "boomers" stand 6–7 ft tall, weigh 150–175 lb and measure up to 8 ft 11 inches in a straight line from the nose to the tip of the extended tail (unconfirmed lengths up to 11 ft have been reported for specimens measured over the curve of the body).

The Great grey kangaroo (*Macropus giganteus*) of eastern Australia and Tasmania, although slightly smaller, sometimes rivals *M. rufus* for size, and there is one authentic record of a boomer measuring 8 ft 8 in from nose to tail (9 ft 7 in along the curve of the body) and weighing 200 lb. The skin of this specimen is preserved in the Australian Museum, Sydney, New South Wales (Lydekker, 1893–96). Adult females are about half the size of males.

Kangaroos roam in "mobs", and the leader is known as "the old man". It is his task to keep the ambitious young bucks in order, and he often does so with vicious upper cuts and straight lefts worthy of Joe Frazier.

Boxing thus comes naturally to kangaroos because their method of fighting with one another or with an enemy is to stand upright and use their strong tail (it weighs up to 20 lb) to support the weight of the body. They are thus able to use their arms and legs as weapons.

The kangaroo, however, is most deadly when it has its back up against a tree or rock. It is then able to strike with the nails of its two great toes, and many an incautious hound has been disembowelled by these weapons when it moved in too close.

In December 1934 a "boxing" kangaroo called "Aussie" was presented to the Zoological Society of London. For nine years this animal had been a "professional" boxer, but he had been forced to retire from the ring because of arthritis in his tail. All kinds of remedies had been tried, but none were successful. The kangaroo was all right in himself, but when he stood up to box and leaned too far back on his tail the pain was excruciating.

Another boxing kangaroo called "Joey the Thug" escaped from Adelaide Zoological Gardens, South Australia, on 11th November 1948 and promptly "floored" a reckless police constable who tried to intercept him. He was recaptured after three hours of freedom.

In July 1957 a circus kangaroo called "Katie" inadvertently sat too close to a tiger's cage at feeding-time in Memphis, Tennessee, U.S.A. and lost 18 in of her tail as a result. Her trainer quickly wrapped the "stump" in bandages and rigged a sling round the kangaroo's neck to keep her tail from hitting the ground. She made a full recovery.

Kangaroos are excellent swimmers. One old boomer chased by dogs into the sea off the coast of Western Australia was last seen swimming strongly about a mile offshore where it probably fell victim to sharks.

In December 1931 a remarkable fight between an old kangaroo and a giant Wedge-tailed eagle (*Aquila audax*) was witnessed by a man returning from a shooting trip near Molong, New South Wales. He noticed an eagle flying low and making swift dives at the marsupial. Almost exhausted,

A boxing kangaroo. (Topical Press Agency.)

the kangaroo was making desperately for a dam about 200 yd away.

Eventually, the kangaroo reached its objective and entered the water up to its shoulders. The eagle swooped again, but this time the kangaroo, with a lightning movement, caught the bird in its arms and held it under water until it was dead.

Refreshed by the cold water, the kangaroo bounded away into the bush as the hunter approached, but the body of the eagle was recovered. The span of its wings was stated to have been 9 ft 2 in, but this measurement was probably exaggerated (see page 142).

Both the red kangaroo and the great grey kangaroo can bound across open country at speeds up to 35 mile/h over short distances (i.e. 300 yd), and leaps of 25 ft are quite common.

The red kangaroo has been credited with leaps measuring up to 42 ft in length. (Australian News and Information Bureau.)

The longest recorded leap was reported in January 1951 when, in the course of a chase, a female red kangaroo made a series of bounds which included one of 42 ft. There is also a record of a great grey kangaroo jumping nearly 13·5 m (44 ft 8·5 in) on the flat (Walker *et al.*, 1968).

The high-jumping ability of these two species is equally as impressive. Normally they do not jump much higher than 5 ft, but 9 ft fences have been cleared on occasion, and one kangaroo chased by dogs cleared a pile of timber 10 ft 6 in high.

On 27th April 1927 a race was staged between a racehorse and a kangaroo in Sydney, in which the horse was badly beaten. The kangaroo's bounds, some of which measured as much as 33 ft, enabled it to draw away from the racehorse, although the rider was a well-known jockey.

The smallest marsupial is the very rare Kimberley planigale (*Planigale subtilissima*), which is found only in the Kimberley District of Western Australia. Adult males have a head and body length of 44·5 mm (1·75 in) and a 50 mm (2 in) tail, and the weight is about 4 g (0·141 oz). Females are smaller than males.

*The Tasmanian "tiger",
the largest and the rarest of
the carnivorous marsupials.
(British Museum of
Natural History, London.)*

The rarest marsupial is probably the little-known Thylacine (*Thylacinus cynocephalus*), also known as the "Tasmanian wolf" or "Tasmanian tiger", the largest of the carnivorous marsupials, which is now confined to the remoter parts of southwestern Tasmania.

The last thylacine held in captivity was caught in a trapper's snare in the Florentine Valley a few miles west of Mountain Field Park in 1933, and was exhibited at Hobart Zoo for a few months before it died.

On 2nd January 1957 it was reported that one had been kept in sight for two minutes and photographed by a helicopter pilot, Captain J. Ferguson, on Birthday Bay Beach, 35 miles south-west of Queen's town, Tasmania. Experts who examined the photograph, however, declared that the animal was a dog, although this seems a bit improbable.

The thylacine is now fully protected by law, but in 1961 a young male was accidentally killed at Sandy Cape on the west coast. In December 1966 the traces of a lair in which a female and pups had been living were found by zoologists in the boiler of a wrecked ship near Mawbanna on the west coast. On 3rd November 1969 the tracks of a thylacine were positively identified in the Cradle Mountain National Park, and other definite sightings have been made since in the Cardigan River area of the northwest coast and the Tooms Lake region (Fisher *et al.*, 1969).

A hundred years ago the thylacine was fairly common in Tasmania. Its prey then was the kangaroo and the wallaby, but as man invaded the primitive forests and steadily exterminated much of the indigenous wildlife, the thylacine was forced to seek alternative prey. It developed a taste for sheep and poultry, and this soon brought it into sharp conflict with the farmers, who began a relentless war of extermination.

In 1888 a Government bounty was brought in, and official statistics show that between this year and 1914, 2,268 thylacines were killed, although the total figure was probably much higher. One Tasmanian and his brother killed twenty-four of these animals in one day and were paid £1 per head bounty money (Boswell, quoted by Harper, 1945). On top of this, in 1910, the thylacine population was decimated by an outbreak of disease, possibly distemper (Simon & Geroudet, 1970).

Apart from its unique colouring (tawny grey with sixteen to nineteen blackish brown bands extending a cross the rump and back) this animal is also remarkable for the unusually wide gape of its jaws, and some of the earlier observers say it would often rise on its hind-legs and bound along like a kangaroo when it was being chased.

According to Harman (1949) "at least a dozen" thylacines have been exhibited at London Zoological Gardens. The last specimen died on 9th August 1931.

The Kimberley planigale (see page 114) is known from only two specimens, but Fitter (1968) thinks that this creature may eventually prove to be reasonably common in this unworked area.

The longest sirenian is the Florida manatee (*T. Trichechus manatus*), which was formerly widely distributed along the coasts of the Gulf of Mexico, the West Indies and the north-eastern part of South America.

Some of the early explorers in British Guiana reported seeing immense manatees measuring 18–20 ft, but these lengths were exaggerated. Adult males average 8–10 ft in length and weigh 400–500 lb. Females are slightly smaller. The longest manatee on record was one caught off the coast of Texas, U.S.A. in *c.* 1910 which measured 15 ft 3 inches in length and weighed 1,310 lb.

The heaviest sirenian is the Dugong (*Dugong dugong*), which ranges from the coastal waters of the Mozambique northwards along the East African coast to the Red Sea and thence along the coasts of the Indian Ocean to New Guinea, northern Australia and the Solomons and New Caledonia in the Pacific. Adult males average 8 ft in length and weigh about 620 lb, and adult females 9 ft and 830 lb.

In October 1958 a male dugong captured alive off Malindi, 70 miles north of Mombasa, Kenya, measured 10 ft in length and weighed 1,000 lb. According to Mani (1960) the largest dugong on record was a female measuring 13 ft 4 inches in length and weighing a ton landed by fishermen at Bedi Bunder off the Saurashtra coast, Indian Union, on the 30th July 1959. Another specimen captured in the Red Sea reportedly measured 5·8 m (19 ft 4·33 in), but as this sirenian was a *male* this length must be considered suspect. Storer (1963) says an Australian dugong measuring 12 ft in length and weighing more than a ton hauled itself out of the sea at Punta Arenas, Chile in 1942 and dragged its great bulk through the streets of the city. It then attempted to make its way back towards the sea but was shot by policemen in the mistaken belief that they were dealing with a sea monster. Later, however, a published photograph showed that the animal was *a southern elephant seal!*

The smallest (and rarest) sirenian is the freshwater Amazonian or Southern manatee (*Trichechus inunguis*), which is found only in the Amazon and Orinoco drainage areas of north-eastern South America. Adults measure up to 2·5 m (8 ft 2 in) in length and weigh up to 140 kg (308 lb). The little-known West African manatee (*T. senegalensis*) is also seriously threatened through over-hunting for meat.

Manatees reportedly live for more than fifty years in the wild, but captive specimens seldom live longer than eight years.

A pair of Amazonian manatees received at Carl Hagenbeck's Tierpark in 1912 were still alive after twelve and a half years in captivity (Crandall, 1964). Herrera mentions a tame manatee that was kept by the Cacique Carametex in a pond for twenty-six years (Allen, 1942), but this record was partly based on hearsay.

Two dugongs received at Mandapam Camp, India, in October and December 1959 were still alive in June 1966 (Jones, 1967).

The most valuable of all zoo exhibits – and the most expensive to feed – is the Killer whale (*Orcinus orca*). In 1971 Flamingo Park Zoo's 17 ft long bull "Cuddles" was insured for £30,000.

The most valuable zoo exhibit among land animals is the Giant panda (*Ailuropoda melanoleuca*). In 1968 London Zoological Garden's female specimen "Chi-Chi" was valued at £12,000, but she is probably worth £20,000 today.

Parque Zoologico de Barcelona's white western gorilla "Capito de Nieve" ("Little Snowflake") may be equally valuable, although no figures have been quoted. This *unique* specimen – he has been described as an *albino* although he has *blue* eyes – was found clinging to his dead mother, who was normal in colour, in a tiny jungle clearing in Rio Mundi, Spanish Equatorial Guinea, on 1st October 1966. He was then estimated to be two years old (Riopelle, 1968).

The heaviest of the sixty or so breeds of horse (*Equus caballus*) are the heavy draught-breeds, all of which evolved from the Great Horse of Europe.

The heaviest horse ever recorded was a 19½-hand (6 ft 6 in) pure-bred Belgian stallion named "Brooklyn Supreme" (foaled 12th April 1928), owned by Ralph Fogleman of Callender, Iowa, U.S.A., who weighed 3,200 lb (1·42 tons) shortly before his death on 6th September 1948 aged twenty. Other statistics included a maximum bodily girth of 10 ft 2 in and a 40 in neck, and 30 in of iron were needed to make one shoe (Fogleman, *in litt.* 30.4.66). This horse was so powerful that one previous owner was afraid to team him up with any of the other draught-horses on his farm in case he worked them to death.

Another Belgian stallion owned by the Ringling Brothers–Barnum and Bailey Circus and later sold to Jack Shelly of Butte, Montana, was credited with a weight of 3,151 lb (1·40 tons) in 1947, but this poundage has not yet been substantiated.

In 1926 an unconfirmed weight of 3,000 lb (1·33 tons) was reported for a percheron stallion named "Thunderation" living in Chicago, Illinois, U S A

The heaviest horse living in Britain today is "Saltmarsh Silver Crest" (foaled 1955), an 18¼-hand (6 ft 1 in) champion percheron stallion owned by George E. Sneath of Money Bridge near Pinchbeck, Lincolnshire. He weighed 2,660 lb (1·18 tons) in 1961, and 2,772 lb (1·23 tons) in 1967 (maximum bodily girth 8 ft 4 in). His grandson "Pinchbeck Union Crest" (foaled 1964) stands 18 hands (6 ft 0 in) and weighs 2,576 lb (1·15 tons).

In 1942 a weight of 2,579 lb (1·15 tons) was also recorded for the champion Suffolk stallion "Monarch" at the Ipswich Stallion Show. This horse stood 17·5 hands (5 ft 10 in) and measured 8 ft 4 inches in maximum bodily girth. In a letter to the author dated 5th January 1967 Mr. W. J. Woods, Acting Secretary of the Suffolk Horse Society, said: "I feel sure we have had Stallions weighing round about 24 to 25 cwt. [2,688 to 2,800 lb]."

A weight of 2,632 lb (1·17 tons) has been quoted for a six-year-old shire gelding.

The greatest weight ever recorded for a draught-mare of any breed was probably for the shire mare "Erfyl Lady Grey", London Show Champion 1924–26, who scaled 2,502 lb (1·11 tons) at her last show. She stood 17·5 hands (5 ft 10 in) and measured 9 ft in maximum bodily girth.

The eight-horse team of Suffolk geldings owned and exhibited by Mr. W. C. Saunders of Billingford Hall, Diss, Norfolk, at the 1966 Peterborough Show, each weighed over 1 ton.

Nowadays most breeders of heavy draught-horses aim for animals that are not unduly over-bulky, because they tend to lose the quality of their breeding by being too large.

"Dr. Le Gear", the tallest horse on record. (Marvin Studios, Washington, Mo., U.S.A.)

The tallest horse ever recorded was "Dr. Le Gear", a seal-brown dapple percheron gelding standing 21 hands (7 ft) and weighing 2,995 lb (1·33 tons). Foaled in 1902 this horse, which measured 16 ft from nose to tail, died in St. Louis, Missouri, U.S.A. in 1919.

Robert Jarvis (*in litt.* 6.1.67), Secretary of the Clydesdale Horse Society, says a Clydesdale shipped to the United States some years ago also stood 21 hands.

"The horse was so tall that great difficulty was experienced in getting him into his stall between decks. On this occasion the animal had to be coaxed with a handful of hay held low at ground level so that he would lower his head to get him under the beams supporting the top deck. This was the biggest horse I ever saw, but he was never weighed to my knowledge."

In 1951 a measurement of 21·25 hands (7 ft 1 in) was reported for a three-year-old Clydesdale gelding named "Big Jim", owned by Mr. Lyall M. Anderson of West Broomley, Montrose, Scotland, but this height is not supported by photographic evidence which shows a horse standing about 19 hands (6 ft 4 in).

A shire gelding from Herefordshire standing 19 hands was exhibited at the Shire Horse Society's Show at the Royal Agricultural Hall, Islington, London on 22nd February 1938.

(In 1902 a freak 21 hand *donkey* named "Dinah", owned by Mr. E. H. Bostock, was exhibited at the Glasgow Hippodrome.)

The tallest horse living in Britain today is "Wandle Robert", a shire gelding owned by Young & Company's Brewery Ltd., Wandsworth, London. He stands 18·5 hands (6 ft 2 in) and weighs 2,360 lb (1·04 tons).

The smallest breed of horse is the Falabella of Argentina. Adult specimens range from under 3 hands (12 in) to 10 hands (40 in) at the shoulder and weigh up to 150 lb. It is claimed that these miniature horses originated from a herd which got trapped in a canyon by a landslide. For generations they were unable to escape and had only cactus to eat—and they gradually decreased in size. In the end their plight was discovered by Julio Falabella, owner of the 2,500 acre El Peludo Ranch, who had the animals brought out of the canyon by crane. At the present time he owns about 800 of these horses, which sell from £70 to £450 depending on their size, colour and shape. The smaller the horse the higher the price.

On 2nd August 1970 a Falabella mare named "Little Girl", who stands 6·4 hands (25·5 in) gave birth to a female foal measuring 3·4 hands (13·5 in) and weighing 6·6 lb at Froso Djurpark, Froso-Ostersund, Sweden. The sire "Little Boy", stands 6·9 hands (27·5 in) (Netterstrom, 1970).

There are several authentic records of horses living over forty years. Edmund Crisp (1860) mentions a Suffolk mare that foaled at the age of forty-two, and Smyth (1937) gives a record of a forty-six-year-old brood mare which foaled for the thirty-fourth time at the age of forty-two. An Orkney mare died at Fintray, Aberdeenshire, Scotland in 1936 aged forty-five years.

The greatest reliable age recorded for a horse is fifty-two years for a 17 hands (5 ft 8 in) light draught-horse named "Monty", owned by Mrs. Marjorie Cooper, of Albury, New South Wales, Australia, who died on 25th January 1970. He was foaled in Wodonga, New South Wales, in 1917. The jaws of this horse are now preserved in the School of Veterinary Science at Melbourne University.

In February 1960 an ex Italian Army horse named "Topolino", foaled in Libya on 24th February 1909, died in Brescia, Italy, aged about fifty-one years.

On 3rd November 1969 a mare named "Nellie" died of a heart attack on a farm near Danville, Missouri, U.S.A. reputedly aged fifty-three years, but this claim has not yet been fully substantiated.

The celebrated "Old Billy", an English barge horse believed to be a cross between a Cleveland and Eastern blood, died in Manchester on 29th November 1922 allegedly aged sixty-two years, but this record lacks authentic documentation (Flower, 1931).

The longest recorded mane was one of 13 ft reported for a percheron measured in Dee, Scotland, in 1891. Another horse (breed not identified) named "Linus" living in Oregon, U.S.A. was also credited with a 13 ft mane in 1901.

The longest tail on record was one of 18 ft reported in 1905 for a horse named "Maud" owned by George O. Zillgitt of Inglewood, California, U.S.A. Linus (see above) had a 17 ft tail.

All heavy draught-breeds are renowned for their great strength and pulling power. In the time of Queen Elizabeth I, Hollmshead (1587) wrote: "Our cart or plough horses (for we use them indifferently) are commonlie so strong that fifty foot of timber, forty bushels of salt or four quarters of wheat is considered a normal load."

In the eighteenth century hauling tests for big wagers were regularly held in England. Horses would often have to pull carts full of sand with the wheels partly sunk in the ground and wood blocks placed in front of them to make the test more difficult. According to Lady Wentworth (1946) "these fearful weights could not be moved till the horses went down on their knees, a cruel test, which must have ruptured many".

The greatest load ever pulled by a pair of draught horses.

The heaviest load hauled by a pair of draught-horses (probably shires) was fifty logs comprising 36,055 board-feet of timber (=53·8 tons) on a "sledge litter" across snow at the Nester Estate, Ewen, Ontonagon County, Michigan, U.S.A. in 1893.

On 25th February 1924 two shires named "Ulverston" and "Humber", owned by the Liverpool Corporation, pulled with ease for 50 yd on a surface of granite setts in the ring at the Agricultural Hall a load of metal weighing 18·5 tons. On another occasion the same pair hauled a 20 ton load of cotton, plus the 2 tons of the lorry, for 50 yd over the granite setts in Liverpool.

On 24th September 1935 two percheron stallions named "Rock" and "Tom", owned by George H. Statler Farms, Piqua, Ohio, U.S.A., pulled a load of 3,900 lb (1·73 tons) a distance of 37·5 ft at Hillsdale, Michigan. The load was placed on a specially built wagon with four dual pneumatic-tyred wheels, chains over the tyres and all wheels locked. The pull exerted by these two horses was stated to have been equivalent to hauling 22·4 tons on a wagon for twenty consecutive starts on granite block pavement (Imhof, *in litt.* 27.10.66)..

The largest of all ponies is probably the Fjord pony of Norway, which measures up to 14 hands (4 ft 8 in) and reaches a weight of 1,100 lb.

The largest pony found in Britain is the Exmoor pony (see page 36).

The smallest pony found in Britain is the Shetland pony which measures 8–10 hands (32–40 in) and weighs 275–385 lb (Clausen & Ipsen, 1970).

In March 1969 a measurement of 3½ hands (14 in) was reported for a "miniature" Shetland pony named "Midnight" owned by Miss Susan Perry of Worths Circus, Melbourne, Victoria, Australia.

Ponies are generally longer-lived than horses on the average. Lord Rothschild told Flower (21st October 1919) that he had an authentic record of a pony living for fifty-four years in France, and there is an unconfirmed claim of fifty-eight years for a Shetland pony (*The Times*, 3rd May 1944). In July 1970 a Welsh pony living on a farm near Pebbles Bay, Gower Peninsula, South Wales, was reported to be sixty-six years old (Cooper, *in litt.* 24.7.70), but this claim lacks proper documentation.

Of heavyweight cattle, the heaviest on record was a Hereford-Shorthorn named "Old Ben", owned by Mike and John Murphy of Miami, Indiana, U.S.A. When this animal died at the age of eight in February 1910 he had attained a length of 16 ft 2 in from nose to tip of tail, a maximum bodily girth of 13 ft 8 in, a height of 6 ft 4 in at the forequarters and a weight of 4,720 lb (2·1 tons). The stuffed and mounted steer is displayed in Highland Park Museum, Kokomo, Indiana, as proof to all who would otherwise have said "there ain't no such animal".

A Holstein-Friesian bull named "Mac", owned by Mr. J. D. Avery of Massachusetts, U.S.A., weighed 4,628 lb (2·06 tons) at slaughter (nose to tail length 15 ft 11 in).

The British record is held by "The Bradwell Ox", owned by William Spurgin of Bradwell, Essex, which weighed 4,480 lb (2 tons) in 1830 and had a nose to tail length of 15 ft.

The Hereford-Friesian bull "Big Bill Campbell", owned by Major C. H. Still of Hall Farm, Northamptonshire, weighed 3,920 lb (1·75 tons) at his peak in 1954, but by 1956 his weight had dropped to 3,640 lb (1·62 tons). This animal stood over 6 ft at the forequarters and measured 12 ft 6 in from nose to tail. He was destroyed on 13th June 1958.

The famous "Durham Ox" scaled 3,808 lb (1·69 tons) in 1807 when it was ten years old.

The highest recorded birthweight for a calf is 225 lb from a British Friesian cow at Rockhouse Farm, Bishopston, Swansea, Glamorganshire, in 1961.

In 1955 a heifer measuring only 29·5 in at the shoulder was exhibited at the Royal American Show.

On 25 April 1964 it was reported that a cow named "Lyubik" had given birth to seven calves at Mogilev, U.S.S.R. A case of five live calves at one birth was reported in 1928 by T. G. Yarwood of Manchester, Lancashire.

The lifetime prolificacy record is thirty in the case of a cross-bred cow owned by G. Page of Warren Farm, Wilmington, Sussex, which died in November 1957 aged thirty-two. A cross-Hereford calved in 1916 and owned by A. J. Thomas of West Hook Farm, Marloes, Pembrokeshire, Wales, produced her thirtieth calf in May 1955 and died in May 1956 aged forty.

A painting of the 1,410 lb pig bred by Joseph Lawton of Astbury, Cheshire.

The largest pig ever recorded was one bred by Joseph Lawton of Astbury, Cheshire. In 1774 it stood 4 ft 8·5 in at the shoulder, measured 9 ft 8 inches in length and weighed 1,410 lb.

The highest weight recorded for a piglet at weaning (eight weeks) is 81 lb for a boar, one of nine piglets farrowed on 6th July 1962 by the Landrace gilt "Manorport Ballerina 53rd", alias "Mary", and sired by a Large White named "Johnny" at Kettle Lane Farm, West Ashton, Trowbridge, Wiltshire.

The highest recorded number of piglets in one litter is thirty-four, thrown on 25th–26th June 1961 by a sow owned by Aksel Egedee of Denmark. **This is the greatest number of young born to a mammal at a single birth.** In February 1955 a Wessex sow owned by Mrs. E. C. Goodwin of Paul's Farm, Leigh, near Tonbridge, Kent, also had a litter of thirty-four, but thirty of these were stillborn. A litter of thirty-two piglets (twenty-six live born) was thrown in February 1971 by a British saddleback owned by Mr. R. Spencer of Toddington, Gloucestershire. In September 1934 a Large White sow, owned by Mr. H. S. Pedlingham, died after having farrowed 385 piglets in 22 litters in 10 years 10 months.

The highest recorded birthweight for a lamb in Britain is 26 lb in the case of a lamb delivered on 9th February 1967 by Alan F. Baldry from a ewe belonging to J. L. H. Arkwright of Winkleigh, Devonshire. A case of eight lambs at a birth was reported by D. T. Jones of Priory Farm, Monmouthshire, in June 1956, but none lived.

The heaviest breed of domestic dog (*Canis familiaris*) is the St. Bernard. The heaviest one on record was "Schwarzwald Hof Duke", also known as "Duke", owned by Dr. A. M. Bruner of Oconomowoc, Wisconsin, U.S.A. He was whelped on 8th October 1964 and weighed 295 lb (21 stone 1 lb) on 2nd May 1969, dying three months later aged 4 years 10 months. This dog measured 32·5 in at the shoulder (40·5 in to the crown of the head) and 55 in round the chest (Bruner, *in litt.* 8.8.69).

"Schwarzwald Hof Duke", the heaviest St. Bernard dog on record. (Dr. A. M. Bruner, Oconomowoc, Wisconsin, U.S.A.)

The heaviest St. Bernard ever recorded in Britain was probably one named "Brandy", owned by Miss Gwendoline L. White of Chinnor, Oxfordshire. He weighed 18 stone 7 lb (259 lb) on 11th February 1966, dying twenty-three days later aged six and a half years. "Westernisles Ross", also known as "Lindwall", owned by Miss Jean F. Rankin of Glasgow, Scotland, weighed 18 stone 4 lb (256 lb) on 28th April 1966 (Rankin, *in litt.* 30.4.66), and *may* have attained 19 stone (266 lb) by the time of his death on 17th August 1967 aged five (Rankin, *in litt.* 19.8.67).

The Old English mastiff "Montmorency of Hollesley", the heaviest dog ever recorded in Britain. (G. L. Wood.)

"Montmorency of Hollesley", also known as "Monty", an Old English mastiff owned by Mr. Randolph Simon of Wilmington, Sussex, was also of comparable size. He was whelped on 1st May 1962 and weighed 18 stone 7 lb in July 1969. In April 1970 his weight was estimated at 19 stone, at which time he measured 56 in round the chest and 33 in round the neck. He was put to sleep in April 1971 aged 8 years 11 months.

The heaviest dog living in Britain today is believed to be a St. Bernard named "Shandy", owned by Mr. Charles Langley of Southery, Norfolk and whelped on 30th May 1966, who weighed 18 stone 1 lb (253 lb) in November 1971.

In December 1971 an unconfirmed weight of 18 stone was reported for another St. Bernard named "Scott" who was deposited at the R.S.P.C.A. animal shelter at Radcliffe-on-Trent, Nottinghamshire because his owners found him too expensive to feed.

The only other breed of dog which has been known to exceed 16 stone (224 lb) is the Great Dane. In January 1959 a weight of 16 stone 1 lb was reported for an example named "Zazon of Clarendon", owned by Mr. Ernest Booth of Romiley, Cheshire. Another Great Dane named "Simon" (see below) weighed 16 stone 5 lb on 14th October 1971.

The tallest breed of dog is the Irish wolfhound. The extreme recorded example was "Broadbridge Michael", whelped in 1926, owned by Mrs. Mary Beynon of Sutton-at-Hone, Kent. He stood 39·5 in at the age of two years.

According to Dalziel (1889) a German boarhound (the forerunner of the modern Great Dane) exhibited at the International Dog Show in Hamburg in 1887 measured 40·5 in, but this height was believed to have been taken to the crown of the head.

The tallest dog now living in Britain is "Moderator of Merrowlea", also known as "Simon", a four-year-old Great Dane owned by Mr. Terry Hoggarth of North Wingfield, near Chesterfield, Derbyshire, who stands 38·5 in at the shoulder. Another four-year-old Great Dane named "Marron of Merrowlea" of the same strain, owned by Mr. Gordon Jeffrey of Banstead, Surrey, stands 38 in, but is nowhere near as bulky.

The smallest breed of dog is the Chihuahua from Mexico. New-born pups average 3·5–4·5 oz and weigh 2–4 lb when fully grown, but some "miniature" specimens weigh only 16 oz.

The smallest British breed is the Yorkshire terrier, one of which named "Cody Queen of Dudley" was reported in July 1968 to have weighed only 20 oz at sixteen months. Another example was stated to have weighed only 4 oz (height at shoulder 2·5 in), but it was later discovered that this dog was only a two-week-old puppy.

In January 1971 a full-grown white toy poodle named "Giles", owned by Mrs. Sylvia Wyse of Bucknall, Staffordshire, stood 4·5 in at the shoulder and weighed 13 oz. His father, "Samson", the previous breed record-holder for diminutiveness, stands 5 in at the shoulder and weighs 16 oz.

Authentic records of dogs living over twenty years are extremely rare, but even thirty-four years has been accepted by one authority (Lankester, 1870). Even more surprising is the fact that large breeds are shorter-lived than small (see page 52). St. Bernards and mastiffs, for instance, have a maximum life-span of about ten years, while Yorkshire terriers and King Charles spaniels may live fifteen years (Flower, 1931).

The greatest reliable age recorded for a dog is 27 years 3 months for a black Labrador gun-dog named "Adjutant", who was whelped on 14th August 1936 and died on 20th November 1963 in the care of his lifetime owner, James Hawkes, a gamekeeper at the Revesby Estate, near Boston, Lincolnshire. Less reliable is a claim of twenty-eight years for an Irish terrier which died in 1951. On 18th December 1937 the death of a collie aged twenty-seven years was

The black Labrador gun-dog "Adjutant", the oldest dog on record. ("Lincolnshire Standard".)

reported by its owner, Mrs. Cole of Clerkenwell, London, and in 1960 the same age was reported for a pekinese owned by Miss Winter of Hounslow, Middlesex. Both these records, however, have not yet been fully substantiated. On 20th April 1956 a cross-bred terrier named "Toss" died at Studfold Farm, Horten-in-Ribblesdale, Yorkshire, aged twenty-three. In July 1960 the death was reported of a twenty-one-year-old Dandie Dinmont named "Obie", owned by Mrs. Miller of Portlaw, County Waterford, Ireland.

The fastest breed of untrained dog—and the oldest at about 5,000 years—is the Saluki, also called the "Arabian gazelle hound" or "Persian greyhound". Speeds up to 43 mile/h have been claimed, but tests in the Netherlands have shown that it is not as fast as the present-day greyhound which has attained a measured speed of 41·25 mile/h over 345 yd on a track. It is generally conceded, however, that the saluki has more stamina than the greyhound and can easily outstrip it over 1,000 yd.

The Afghan hound, which is often mistaken for the saluki, has a maximum speed of 27–30 mile/h.

At the end of the eighteenth century a number of racehorses and foxhounds were raced against each other over the Beacon Course on Newmarket Heath. The course was 4 miles 1 furlong 132 yd in length. The winning hound took eight minutes and a few seconds, and of the sixty

The saluki, the fastest breed of domestic dog. (C. M. Cooke & Son.)

horses that started only twelve were able to run in with the hounds. The speed of the winning hound was worked out at 31 mile/h.

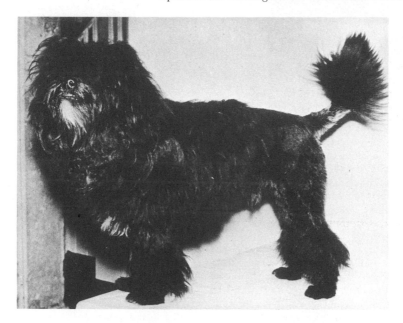

The lowchen or little lion dog, the rarest breed of dog. (R. V. McMillan.)

The rarest breed of dog is the Lowchen ("Little Lion"), which has been described as the missing link between the poodle and the Maltese terrier, or the early toy dogs Teneriffe and Bolognese.

    This dog was the drawing-room pet of the nobility of Spain and Italy during the Renaissance, and a number of them are included in paintings of that and later periods. Goya was particularly fond of them, and a lowchen is featured in his full-length portrait of the Duchess of Alba, painted in 1795.

The precise origin of this "living antique" is not known, but it probably evolved in Spain or Portugal during the fifteenth century. From there the breed spread to France, Italy, Germany and Belgium.

The lowchen started to get scarce during the nineteenth century, and the breed declined so rapidly that shortly before the First World War there were probably fewer than a dozen examples left. The dog was saved from extinction only by the intervention of a Belgian woman and a German veterinary surgeon, who between them set about re-establishing the breed.

In October 1971 the total number of lowchens in the world was fifty-two, forty-five of which were in Britain, five in Germany and two in Majorca (the latter pair were discovered by the author in Cala Rajada in July 1970).

The Chinese crested dog (now extinct in China) is also extremely rare. In October 1971 the world population was estimated at fifty-five to sixty, of which total twenty-two were in Britain.

The largest litter of puppies on record is one of twenty-three thrown on 11th February 1945 by "Lena", a foxhound bitch owned by Commander W. N. Ely of Ambler, Pennsylvania, U.S.A. On 9th February 1895 a St. Bernard bitch named "Lady Millard", owned by a Mr. Thorpe of Northwold, Norfolk, produced a litter of twenty-one. In February 1958 a one-year-old Irish setter gave birth to eighteen puppies at El Cajon, California, U.S.A., and a litter of eighteen has also been reported for a Bassett bitch named "Muffet", owned by Mr. Keith Keen of Kensal Rise, London. On 23rd October 1963 a two-and-a-half-year-old bull mastiff named "Delia", owned by Mrs. Lucy Scheerboom of Southend, Essex, gave birth to seventeen puppies, five of which died.

The greatest sire of all time was the champion greyhound "Low Pressure", nicknamed "Timmy", whelped in September 1957 and owned by Mrs. Bruna Amhurst of Regent's Park, London. From December 1961 to his death on 27th November 1969 he fathered 2,414 registered puppies, with at least 600 others unregistered.

On 28th August 1970 a three-year-old Basset hound named "Hamlet", owned by Keith Keen (see above), fathered his 944th puppy.

The most valuable dog on record was the champion pekinese "Caversham Ku-Ku of Yam", owned by Miss Mary de Pledge, of Bracknell, Berkshire. In January 1956 she turned down an offer of £10,500 from an American breeder for this animal. In 1968 Mrs. Eilish Banks of Newbury Park, Essex, turned down an offer of £5,250 from a Japanese breeder for her international champion Chihuahua bitch "Cluneen Red Velvet".

In September 1945 Mrs. G. M. Jewell of Chew Stoke, near Bristol, turned down an offer of £2,500 from an American breeder for her three-year-old champion Great Dane "Hyperion of Ladymead".

The highest price ever paid for a dog is £2,000 by Mrs. A. H. Kempton in December 1929 for the champion greyhound "Mick the Miller" (whelped in Ireland in June 1926 and died 1939). In 1947 a figure of £2,000 was also quoted for a champion English bulldog sold to an American breeder, but further details are lacking. Other breeds of dogs which have fetched over £1,000 include: the Sealyham (£1,100); the Scottish terrier (£1,150); the smooth-haired fox terrier (£1,200); the chow (£1,500); and the wire-haired fox terrier (£1,600).

The richest dog in the world is an Alsatian named "Viking Baron von Heppeplatz", who was left a block of houses worth £130,000 in the will of his master, Mr. George Ritt, who died in Munich, West Germany in August 1971. Income from the dog's property goes to the Munich Animal Protection Society after the dog's needs have been met.

The greatest altitude attained by an animal is 1,050 miles by the Samoyed husky bitch fired as a passenger in *Sputnik II* on 3rd November 1957. The dog was variously named "Kudryavka" (feminine form of "Curly"), "Limonchik" (diminutive of lemon); "Malyshka", "Zhuckha", or by the breed name "Laika".

The canine "high jump" record is held by the British police alsatian "Mikeve", who scaled a 9 ft 6 in high wall off a springboard in a test at Moray Lodge, Kensington, London, in 1934. In 1897 a greyhound-lurcher cross named "Boy", described as the "champion dog jumper of the world", allegedly cleared a 12 ft high hurdle off a springboard at a performance in Hull, but the true height of the hurdle was nearer 7 ft 6 in. According to Schwabaches (1958) the world canine high jump record is held by an alsatian named "Crumstone Wanko" at 16.5 ft, but this figure must be considered exaggerated. There is also an unconfirmed record of a 140 lb Bouvier scaling a 16 ft high wall.

The greatest load ever shifted by a dog was 3,260 lb pulled by "Nelson", a 168 lb Newfoundland, for a distance of 15 ft in a test at Bothell, Washington, U.S.A. on 10th October 1970. The previous record had been held by "Charlie", a husky owned by Larry Clendenon, who pulled a freighting sledge weighing 3,142 lb. (1·40 tons) for a distance of 50 ft in a test at Anchor Point, Alaska, U.S.A. on the 11th February 1961.

In July 1971 Mr. Howard Baron of Big Bear City, California, U.S.A. announced that his 160 lb Alaskan malamute "Lobo", whom he describes as the strongest dog in the world, would attempt to pull 5,000 lb (2·23 tons) when the snows came.

In U.S. Army tests at the Chinook Kennels, Wonalancet, New Hampshire, a seventy-three-dog team led by the Siberian husky "Waka" pulled a 10 ton Army truck, but Lobo (see above) has also been credited with pulling the same tonnage (i.e. a truck and trailer) by himself for a distance of 20 ft!

The Newfoundland dog "Nelson", new holder of the title "Strongest Dog in the World". (Chuck Lee, Seattle, Washington, U.S.A.)

The impressive horns of the Mouflon (Ovis musimon) a species of wild sheep found in Sardinia and Corsica, which have been measured up to 38·5 in on the front curve. (F. Lane.)

The Southern elephant seal (Mirounga leonina) of the sub-Antarctic islands is the largest living pinniped. Adult bulls may weigh more than 2·5 tons.

The greatest ratter of all time was Mr. James Searle's bull terrier bitch "Jenny Lind", who killed 500 rats in 1 hour 30 minutes at The Beehive, Old Crosshall Street, Liverpool on 12th July 1853. Another bull terrier named "Jacko", owned by Mr. Jemmy Shaw, was credited with killing 1,000 rats in 1 hour 40 minutes, but the feat was performed over a period of ten weeks in batches of 100 at a time. The last 100 were accounted for in 5 minutes 28 seconds in London on 1st May 1862 (the first batch took 10 minutes 55 seconds).

The highest canine blood temperatures, not surprisingly, are found in hairless dogs. That of the Chinese crested dog (see page 127) is 40·5 °C (105 °F),while that of the Xoloiseuinti of Mexico is 40 °C (104 °F).

The greatest tracking feat on record was performed by a Doberman named "Sauer", trained by Detective-Sergeant Herbert Kruger. In 1925 he tracked a stock-thief 100 miles across the Great Karroo, South Africa, by scent alone.

In January 1969 a German alsatian bitch was reported to have followed her master 745 miles from Brindisi to Milan, Italy, in four months. The owner had left her behind when he went on a visit. An alsatian's sense of smell is one million times better than man's (Droscher, 1969).

The most successful bloodhound of all time was one named "Old Boston", who tracked down more than 100 criminals in the United States during a career lasting nine years.

Although half-blind, this dog was gifted with an uncanny sense of smell. He was also noted for his sour disposition and tolerated no interference when he was at work.

If his keeper was slow on the trail, the veteran would turn upon him with impatience.

On one man-hunt through rugged, mountain country the old dog broke away on his own and was gone all night. The following morning he limped into camp thoroughly morose.

Later the story came out. The criminal he had been tracking was captured later in the day after spending a night in a tree.

Old Boston had forced him up it, the man said, and stayed guard all night, but when the search-party failed to turn up the dog grew disgusted and gave it up as a bad job.

His most notable achievement was tracking down Floyd Hamilton of the "Public Enemy" Hamiltons after losing the scent twice.

Old Boston died in McAlester, Oklahoma in March 1939.

Bloodhounds don't always "get their man" though. Their most notable failure was in 1889 when they were used by Sir Charles Warren, Commissioner of the Metropolitan Police, as an experiment in an effort to catch Jack the Ripper. Sir Charles proved then that bloodhounds could follow a scent over grass but were thwarted by pavements and city streets.

The Jack the Ripper murders, however, stopped immediately it became known that the police were using bloodhounds, and police authorities maintain that as a crime deterrent bloodhounds have more than proved their worth in the past.

The heaviest domestic cat (*Felis catus*) on record is probably a female tabby named "Gigi" (born 1959), owned by Miss Ann Clark of Carlisle, Cumberland. The weight of this cat normally fluctuates between 37 and 40 lb, but in April 1970 she weighed 42 lb and had a maximum bodily girth of 37 in. In July 1950 a weight of 40 lb was reported for a "tiger and white" tom named "Clauz" living in San Francisco, California, U.S.A. He was then eight years old

The 42 lb female tabby "Gigi", the heaviest cat of all time. (Border Press, Carlisle.)

and had a maximum bodily girth of 36 in. Another outsized cat named "Roger" living in Accrington, Lancashire, was credited with a weight of 38 lb in January 1968, but further information is lacking. The average adult weighs 11 lb.

Cats are longer-lived animals than dogs, and there are a number of authentic records over twenty years. Mellen (1940), for instance, found sixteen in North America, including two thirty-one-year-olds. Dr. Alex Comfort (1956) mentions a gelt male that was still alive at twenty-eight and he says "at least" ten other authentic cases over twenty have been recorded in England in recent years.

The oldest cat ever recorded was probably the tabby "Puss" owned by Mrs. T. Holway of Clayhidon, Devon, who celebrated his thirty-sixth birthday on 28th November 1939. A more recent and better-documented case was that of the female tabby "Ma", owned by Mrs. Alice St. George Moore of Drewsteignton, Devon. She was put to sleep on 5th November 1957 aged thirty-four.

The 34-year-old female tabby "Ma", one of the oldest cats on record.

According to the American Feline Society a cat living in Hazleton, Pennsylvania, celebrated its thirty-seventh birthday on 1st November 1958, but subsequent inquiries by the Society revealed that this figure was probably exaggerated or there were two or more cats involved!

In October 1959 a black tom named "General" of the Beehive Inn, Osbournby, Sleaford, Lincolnshire, died aged twenty-eight and a half. Another tom named "Twink", owned by Miss K. Partridge of Sharnbrook, Bedfordshire, died in June 1969 aged twenty-eight. Three months later a black tom named "Black Boy", owned by Mrs. Gwendoline Dewsnap, of Fleetwood, Lancashire died aged twenty-nine. On 17th April 1971 a cat named "Chummy", owned by Mr. A. T. Hislop of Clapham Park, London, died aged twenty-seven.

The oldest cat living in Britain today is believed to be a ginger tom named "Sandy" (born 7th June 1943), owned by Mrs. Elsie Emmett of Isleworth, Middlesex, who is twenty-eight. "Flip", a black and white female Manx owned by Mrs. Rosemary Morley of Brighton, Sussex, celebrated her twenty-seventh birthday in November 1971 (a female tabby named "Buncle" also owned by Mrs. Morley died on 13th February 1971 aged 26 years 2 months).

*The largest marsupial in the world is the Red kangaroo (*Marcropus rufas*) of Australia. Adult males stand 6–7 ft tall and weigh up to 200 lb. (G. Pizzey/B. Coleman Ltd.)*

*The Alaskan moose (*Alces a. gigas*), the largest of all living deer. Adult bulls measure up to 7 ft 8 in at the shoulder and may weigh nearly a ton. (W. Miller/F. Lane.)*

The largest litter ever recorded was one of thirteen kittens born on 13th April 1969 to "Boccaccio Blue Danielle", a one-year-old blue-pointed Siamese cat owned by Mrs. Helen J. Coward of Klemzig, South Australia. On 30th April 1971 a litter of thirteen (eleven stillborn) was also reported for a nine-month-old black cat named "Spur", owned by Mrs. Grace Sutherland of Walthamstow, London.

In July 1970 a litter of nineteen kittens (four incompletely formed) was reportedly born by Caesarean section to "Tarawood Antigone", a brown Burmese owned by Mrs. Valerie Gane of Church Westcote, Kingham, Oxfordshire (*Fur and Feather*, 20th May 1971), but this claim has not yet been fully substantiated. The litter was stated to have been the result of a mismating with a half Siamese.

A seventeen-year-old cat named "Dusty" living in Bonham, Texas, U.S.A. gave birth to her 420th kitten on 12th June 1952.

Domestic cats are surprisingly hardy creatures and can survive for long periods without food and water. The endurance record is probably held by a two-and-a-half-year-old tabby named "Thumper", owned by Mrs. Reg Buckett of Westminster, London, who was rescued from a lift-shaft on 29th March 1964 after being trapped for fifty-two days.

The richest cats on record were two fifteen-year-olds named "Hellcat" and "Brownie", owned by Dr. William Grier of San Diego, California, U.S.A. who left his entire estate of $415,000 (£172,916) to them. When the cats died in 1965 the money went to the George Washington University in Washington, D.C.

The most valuable cat in the world is the champion copper-eyed white Persian tom "Coylum Marcus", owned by Miss Elspeth Sellar of Grafham, Surrey. In 1967 she turned down an offer of 2,000 guineas (£2,100) for him from an American breeder.

On 7th March 1965 a tom cat named "Pussycat", owned by Miss Ann Walker of Maida Vale, London, slipped and fell 120 ft from the balcony of his mistress's eleventh-storey flat. The cat landed unhurt on all four paws, but he was so shocked by the experience that he refused to eat any food for several days afterwards.

Although dogs normally have a better sense of direction than cats there are a number of authentic cases of cats walking more than 100 miles back to their old homes when their owner has moved.

The champion white Persian tom "Coylum Marcus", the most valuable cat in the world. (R. V. McMillan.)

The greatest distance covered by a cat under these circumstances is 950 miles for a ginger tom named "Rusty", who followed his owner from Boston, Massachusetts, U.S.A. to Chicago, Illinois in 1949. It took him eighty-three days to complete the journey.

The British record is held by a three-year-old tabby named "McCavity", who in 1960 walked 500 miles to his old home at Kea, near Truro, Cornwall, from Cumbernauld, near Glasgow, Scotland in *three weeks!* The cat was so exhausted after his marathon journey that he was unable even to lap milk, and he died the following morning.

The greatest mouser on record was a tabby named "Mickey", owned by Shepherd & Sons Ltd. of Burscough, Lancashire, who killed more than 22,000 mice during his twenty-three years with the firm. He died in November 1968.

The greatest ratter on record was probably a five-month-old tabby kitten named "Peter" living at Stonehouse railway station, Gloucestershire, who killed 400 rats during a four-week period in June–July 1938. Many of the kitten's victims were almost as large as himself.

The greatest age at which a cat has survived a minor operation is 27 years 1 month 3 days in the case of "Flip", the female Manx owned by Mrs. Rosemary Morley of Brighton (see page 131). On the 9th November 1971 this cat had her front right foot and part of the forearm amputated after a bony tumour had developed and was successfully fitted with an aluminium splint.

The largest cat population is that of the U.S.A. with 28,000,000.

Of Britain's cat population of 6,000,000, an estimated 100,000 are "employed" by the Civil Service.

The largest breed of domestic rabbit is the Flemish giant (*Oryctolagus cuniculus*), which has an average toe to toe length of 36 in when fully extended and weighs 12–14 lb. The heaviest recorded specimen was a male named "Floppy" who weighed 25 lb shortly before his death in June 1963 aged eight. In May 1971 a weight of 25 lb was also reported for a four-year-old Norfolk Star named "Chewer", owned by Mr. Edward Williams of Attleborough, Norfolk.

The greatest reliable age recorded for a domestic rabbit is eighteen years for a doe which was still alive (Flower, quoted by Comfort, 1964). A buck rabbit named "Blackie", owned by Mrs. H. H. Chivers of Brixham, Devon, died on 13th March 1971 aged 16 years 3 months.

The most prolific domestic breed is the Norfolk Star. Females produce nine to ten litters a year, each containing about ten young (cf. five litters and three to seven young for the wild rabbit).

The champion sire among domestic rabbits is Chewer (see above) who has fathered more than 12,000 offspring.

The largest ears of any rabbit belong to the Lop of which there are several varieties. Spans up to 28 in ear tip to ear tip have been reliably reported, and the width may be as much as 7 in (Clausen & Ipsen, 1970).

SECTION II

Birds

(class *Aves*)

A bird is a warm-blooded, air-breathing bipedal vertebrate covered with feathers and having the forelimbs modified into wings which are sometimes rudimentary and useless for flight. The brain is well developed, and the jaws are covered with horny sheaths forming a beak. Young are produced from eggs. Other features include a four-chambered heart and an essentially high constant body temperature because flight requires a tremendous output of energy over a long period.

The earliest known birds were the magpie-sized Archaeopteryx and Archaeornis, which lived about 140,000,000 years ago. Unlike modern birds, however, they had well-developed teeth in their jaws and a long jointed bony tail like a lizard's, but their wings bore characteristic feathers. Their remains were first discovered in Bavaria, West Germany, in 1861.

The class Aves was originally divided into two subclasses, the Ratitae (running birds) and the Carinatae (flying birds); but now it is split up into 27 orders of equal status comprising 154 families and about 8,650 species. One of these orders, Passerines (perching birds) contains about 5,100 species or nearly 60 per cent of the total number.

The largest living bird is the North African ostrich (*Struthio camelus camelus*), which is found in reduced numbers south of the Atlas Mountains from Upper Senegal and Niger across to the Sudan and central Ethiopia. Adult cock examples of this ratite or flightless bird stand about 8 ft tall (height at back 4 ft 6 in) on the average and weigh 265–280 lb, but heights up to 9 ft and weights up to 345 lb have been reliably recorded. Adult hens are smaller, standing about 7 ft tall and weighing 200–220 lb.

The Southern ostrich (*S.c. australis*), which is now found only in the wilder parts of South Africa south of the Zambezi and Cunene Rivers, is slightly smaller. Adult cocks are 7–8 ft tall and scale 220–250 lb, but larger specimens have been reported. William A. Hooper, owner of Highgate Ostrich Farm in the Oudtshoorn District, Cape Province, South Africa tells the author (*in litt.* 18.8.71) that abbatoir birds measuring a few inches over 8 ft and weighing 320 lb have been recorded.

This race of ostrich was formerly very abundant in the open and savannah veld of southern Africa, but its numbers were drastically reduced when ostrich plumes became the fashion rage. Fortunately, ostrich-farming, which was started in 1868 by Arthur Douglas, an English immigrant to South Africa, resulted in large stocks of domesticated birds being established, and instead of the birds being slaughtered as had previously been the custom the feathers were obtained by a revolutionary method of periodical clippings. During the period 1904–8 more than £1,000,000 worth of feathers were exported each year, and between 1909 and 1913 over £2,000,000.

After that the market for feathers declined rapidly, and by 1920 the once enormous and valuable export trade had disappeared.

Later, various royal personages tried temporary revivals. In 1938, for instance, the Duchess of Kent was seen in public wearing ostrich feathers, but apart from a small flutter of interest the fashion was not followed up again.

It was soon after this that the industrial value of ostrich skins came to light. South African farmers found that properly treated ostrich skins could be manufactured into attractive bags, shoes, suitcases, etc., and within a year a new industry came into existence. In 1953 alone 10,000 ostriches were killed in the Oudtshoorn District for their skins and meat, which is dried and sold for food as "biltong" in South Africa, and today there are some 36,000 ostriches distributed over approximately 200 farms.

As a result of introduction there is also a small population of southern ostriches living in South Australia at the present time.

Ostriches are fast runners and can travel at 28–30 mile/h for fifteen or twenty minutes without showing undue signs of fatigue, but Stevenson-Hamilton (1947) says their habit of running in wide circles "deprives them of much of the advantage derived from their speed".

In discussing the speed of the ostrich, Sir Frederick J. Jackson (1938) writes: "The pace of the bird is difficult to estimate, but a test may convey a fair idea, and the following note on a game drive I once had may serve.

"The object of the drive was a bull eland that had proved quite unapproachable. Besides the eland there were about 150 buffaloes, several hundred zebras, and 70 or so Coke's hartebeests, all of which, together with one of the troops of 13 ostriches . . . passed within two hundred yards, when the ostriches attempted to break back, but turned again on the beaters firing a couple of shots. These shots frightened everything into full gallop; but the ostriches, in spite of having lost so much ground and being so far behind in their futile attempt to break back, overtook and shot ahead of the hartebeests, which had, in their turn, far outpaced everything else. At its own distance, whatever that may be, it is very doubtful whether there is an animal living, not even excepting the cheetah, that could beat an ostrich going at top speed."

The suggestion that an ostrich could outsprint a cheetah is, of course, quite unacceptable, but the fact that a small group could overtake a herd of Coke's hartebeest travelling flat out (i.e. 37–38 mile/h) would indicate that this bird is capable of a speed of 45 mile/h when frightened.

In 1907 a famous racing ostrich named "Black Diamond" sprinted half a mile in 1 minute 3 seconds (28·5 mile/h) at Greenville, Ohio, U.S.A., setting an American record which has never been beaten, but this bird was carrying a jockey . . . and he wasn't frightened.

During the mating season the cock ostrich is one of the most dangerous animals on earth and its war-dance has to be seen to be believed. It stamps its feet, waves its neck in erratic circles and generally works itself up into a furious rage before charging at the object of its wrath, which it then proceeds to kick with its long, powerfully clawed legs.

An unarmed man's only defence against an ostrich attack is to lie down flat on the ground where the vicious kick can do no harm, but even in that position he will still receive several painful pecks.

Martin (1891), describing life on a South African ostrich-farm and the aggressiveness of some of the cock ostriches, writes: "Another gentleman had a theory that any creature, however savage, could be subdued—'quelled' as he said—by the human eye. One day he tried to quell one of his own ostriches; with the result that he was presently found by T—— in a very pitiable predicament, lying flat on the ground while the subject of his experiment jumped up and down on him, occasionally varying the treatment by sitting on him."

According to Grzimek (1970) one angry cock ostrich at Hanover Zoological Gardens bent a 0·5 in thick iron bar at right angles with a single kick. Another cock at Frankfurt Zoological Gardens ripped the clothes off an unsuspecting keeper's back with a well-placed kick and half threw him through a wire fence at the same time. There is also a record of an introduced ostrich kicking a young camel to death on a ranch near Nuevo Laredo, Mexico (Laycock, 1966).

Ostriches regularly swallow stones or quartz-pebbles to aid digestion, and if they can't find suitable ones in captivity they will happily gulp down an amazing variety of articles as substitutes. Heck (1929) cites the case of a Masai ostrich (*S.c. massaicus*) which died in Berlin Zoological Gardens after swallowing half a horseshoe and a coffee-spoon thrown into its enclosure by an ignorant visitor, and an ostrich at Halle Zoological Gardens, Germany, died from severe stomach injuries after gulping down a modelling tool made of nickel-steel (Schmidt-Hoesndorf, 1930). In the stomach of another specimen which died suddenly in London Zoological Gardens several years ago were found a 3 ft long piece of rope, a spool of film, an alarm-clock key, a cycle valve, a pencil, a comb, three gloves, a handkerchief, glove-fasteners, pieces of a gold necklace, two collar-studs, a Belgian franc, two farthings and four halfpennies.

Ostriches are also partial to padlocks, and a cock bird named "Ossie" died in Chester Zoological Gardens on 12th February 1953 after swallowing two of them.

On 27th January 1967 officials at Newcastle winter zoo called in soldiers of the Royal Engineers with a mine-detector because they suspected that "Tony", their one-year-old ostrich, or his mate "Sylvia" had swallowed a padlock. After an hour of tests, however, both birds were given a clean bill of health.

In October 1971 the Director of the Parc Zoologique du Terte Rouge at La Fleche, Western France refused to kill his southern ostrich in order to recover a 4,000-franc (£330) gold watch studded with diamonds which the bird had swallowed. He told the owner that she would have to wait until the animal died of natural causes.

The most dangerous objects swallowed by ostriches are coins because they wear so thin in the bird's stomach that they become razor-sharp and eventually cause its death.

An eleven-month-old ostrich which died on a farm in the Oudtshoorn District in April 1962 was found to have swallowed 484 cent and half-cent coins weighing 8 lb 3 oz.

Many years ago a hunter shot a wild ostrich near Walvis Bay, South-West Africa and found several diamonds in the bird's gizzard. This immediately started a diamond-rush in the district, but no more gems were found.

The growth of the ostrich is amazingly rapid. The average chick grows at the rate of 12 in a month during the first five months of life, and by the time it is six months old it is nearly as tall as an adult bird.

Although the ostrich is not a particularly bright bird, it is not nearly so stupid as tradition would have us believe. The classic story that it will bury its head in the sand when frightened in the belief that it cannot be seen is based on the manner in which it sits on its nest. By laying its long neck flat on the ground the ostrich looks just like another hillock on the bare scrub-covered veld and is overlooked by its natural enemies. It is also interesting to note that the dull brown hen sits on the eggs during the day-time when her feathers are practically indistinguishable from the sandy earth, while the black cock bird sits during the hours of darkness.

Further evidence that ostriches are reasonably intelligent animals comes from South-West Africa where they have been trained to herd sheep! Two specimens owned by a farmer near Leonardsville take the flock out by themselves each morning and spend the day fussing over their charges in the grazing area. When evening comes the great birds bring the sheep back home and peck at any that wander.

The ostrich has the largest eye of any terrestrial animal. In cock birds the optic has a diameter of 2 in and is larger than the brain.

The heaviest flying bird or carinate is the Kori bustard or Paauw (*Otis kori*) of East and South Africa. Very little weight data has been published for this species, but adult cock birds average about 28 lb. Hens are smaller and much lighter in weight.

One of the heaviest birds on record was one shot by H. T. Glynn, a well-known sportsman, in South Africa which weighed exactly 40 lb. The head and neck of this specimen were presented to the British Museum of Natural History, London (Bryden, 1936).

Frederick C. Selous (1890) says he shot a paauw on the Botletli River, Ngamiland, South Africa which was enormously fat. "Unfortunately, I had no scales with which to weigh it; but I do not think it could have been less than 40 pounds before it was cleaned. The fat on its back was nearly an inch thick."

Another huge bird shot by William Baldwin (1894) in the western Transvaal was "the fattest and largest I have ever seen" and he estimated its weight at 54 lb. This figure is probably too high, but if the weight *was accurate* then the aerodynamic problems presented by this enormous poundage would have made it most improbable that this bird could have flown, despite an 8 ft 4 in wing-span.

During the summer months the Kori bustard feeds greedily on the rich sweet gum running from the acacia bushes and puts on tremendous poundage as a result.

On one occasion, says Bryden an old friend of his and a companion were stalking a paauw in the vicinity of a rocky hill.

"It rose seven yards away, and both sportsmen fired their rifles. One of the bullets told, and the great bird, towering above the kopje, fell headlong. So fat was the bustard that when it struck the rocks it burst literally into pieces, and, to the chagrin of the gunners, they found, on reaching the spot, nothing worth carrying away."

In 1959 a scientific expedition from the Durban Museum to South-West Africa shot a Kori bustard weighing 35 lb which kept them in meat for nearly a week (Clancy, *in litt.* 8.2.65).

The Great bustard (*Otis tarda*) of western Europe, North Africa and central Asia is another exceptionally heavy bird. The average adult cock weighs about 26 lb, but Baturin (1935) says one huge specimen shot in the U.S.S.R. tipped the scales at 21 kg (46·2 lb). The hen bird has a maximum weight of only 13 lb (Hvass, 1961).

According to Bertin (1967) the Australian bustard (*Ardeotis australis*) is the heaviest flying bird, but the maximum weight recorded for this species is 32 lb.

The Mute swan (*Cygnus olor*), which is resident in Britain, has an average weight of 28 lb but may exceed 40 lb, and there is a record from Poland of a cob weighing 22·5 kg (49·5 lb) (Zanden, 1935).

Weights in excess of 30 lb have also been reliably reported for the rare Trumpeter swan (*C.c. buccinator*) of North America, the White pelican (*Pelecanus onocrotalus*) of Europe, Equatorial Africa and northern India, and the very rare Manchurian crane (*Grus japonensis*) of north-eastern Asia.

A Wandering albatross (*Diomedea exulans*) nestling weighed by Tickell (1968) on Bird Island, South Georgia, shortly before its departure scaled 16·13 kg (35·48 lb).

The heaviest bird of prey is the Andean condor (*Vultur gryphus*), which ranges from Venezuela to Tierra del Fuego and Patagonia. Adult males scale 20–25 lb, which is the weight of a good-sized turkey, but one old male shot on San Gallan Island, off the coast of Peru, in 1919–20 weighed 26·5 lb (Murphy, 1925). In October 1965 a weight of 11 kg (24·2 lb) was reported for an Andean condor named "Friedrich" (hatched 1959) at Frankfurt Zoological Gardens, West Germany.

The now very rare Californian condor (*Gymnogyps californianus*) is only slightly smaller, and a weight of 22·75 lb has been reported for one individual.

The heaviest eagle is the South American Harpy eagle (*Harpia harpyja*). Adult females average 16–17 lb in weight, but they sometimes exceed 20 lb. Stanley E. Brock, manager of the vast Dadanawa Cattle Ranch in Guyana, owns a huge specimen which tips the scales at 27 lb. The male harpy eagle is much smaller than the female, weighing 9–10 lb.

Steller's sea eagle (*Haliaetus pelagicus*) of north-eastern Siberia is another huge bird, and Leslie Brown (1970) says weights up to 19·75 lb have been reported for females.

The wandering albatross has the largest wing-span of any living bird. (E. F. Pollock—F. Lane.)

The living bird with the largest wing-span measurement is the Wandering albatross (*Diomedia exulans*). Adult males average 10 ft 2 in with wings tightly stretched, while adult females rarely exceed 9 ft 6 in.

The largest recorded specimen was a male caught by banders in Western Australia in *c.* 1957 which measured 11 ft 10 in (Disney, *in litt.* 11.4.67). Another specimen found stranded on the beach at Bunbury, 110 miles south of Fremantle, Western Australia on 17th July 1930 had a wing-span of 11 ft 6 in (Whitlock, 1931).

Some unmeasured birds may reach or possibly just exceed 12 ft. Scoulet (1826) says he examined one bird with a wing-span of 12 ft, and the same measurement is quoted by Hutton (1865) for one of his specimens. According to Spry (1876) all the birds collected by him on Marion Island in the southern Indian Ocean measured from 11 to 12 ft, and Campbell (1877) claims he measured several birds of 12 to 13 ft in the Indian Ocean during the cruise of the *Challenger*.

Dr. Robert Cushman Murphy (1936), however, considers a measurement of 13 ft to be excessive. The largest specimen examined by him measured 11 ft 4 in, and he put the maximum wing-expanse of this species at "about 11½ feet" with the wings stretched out as tightly as possible.

According to Parkinson (1900) a wandering albatross with a wing-span of "17 feet 6 inches [*sic*]" is preserved in the Australian Museum in Sydney, but this figure is believed to have been a misprint for 12 ft 6 in. Dr. H. J. de S. Disney, Curator of Birds at the Museum, tells the author that the largest mounted specimen in his collection has a wing-span of 10 ft, although he says the bird is not fully adult.

The adult male Andean condor has an average wing-span of 9 ft 3 in, but a few reliable measurements in excess of 10 ft have been reported. The old male shot on San Gallan Island, for instance, measured a fraction of an inch over 10 ft, and Friedrich at Frankfurt Zoological Gardens has a wing expanse of 10 ft 1·25 in.

One bird killed in the Ilo Valley, southern Peru, in *c.* 1714 allegedly measured 12 ft 3 in, but this figure must be considered exaggerated.

Humboldt says he didn't see a single condor in Ecuador over 9 ft, and he was assured by the inhabitants of Quito that they had never shot any that exceeded 11 ft.

Paul Tschudi (1841), on the other hand, claims he saw several condors measuring 12 to 13 ft during his travels in Peru, and elsewhere he states: "I measured a very large male condor, and the width from the tip of one wing to the tip of the other was fourteen English feet and two inches, an enormous expanse of wing, not equalled by any other bird except the white albatross."

In discussing the size attained by the Andean condor, Philip Gosse (1861) writes: "Among birds the condor of the Andes has been the subject of greatly exaggerated reports of its dimensions. When it was first discovered by the Spanish conquerors of America, it was compared to the Rokh of Arabian fable, and by some even considered to be the identical bird, 'which is able to trusse an elephant'. Garcilasso states that some of those killed by the Spaniards measured fifteen *or* sixteen feet (the vagueness of the 'or' in what professes to be actual measurement is suspicious) from tip to tip of the extended wings. He adds that two will attack a bull and devour it, and that single individuals will slay boys of twelve years old.

"Desmarchais improves upon this; stretches the expansion of the wings to eighteen feet; a width so enormous that, as he says, the bird can never enter the forest; and he declares that a single one will attack a man, and carry off a stag.

"A modern traveller, however, soars far beyond these puny flights of imagination, and gravely gives forty feet as the measurement, carefully noted, as he informs us, 'with his own hand' from the actual specimen."

An Andean condor named "Joe" who lived in London Zoological

The marabou stork rivals the wandering albatross for expanse of wing.

Gardens from 1926 to 1939 was credited with a wing-span of 12 ft, but this figure was undoubtedly an over-estimate. He was, however, considerably larger than the other Andean condor living there at the same time which had a wing-span of 9 ft.

The adult male Californian condor has an average wing-span of 8 ft 6 in, but reliable measurements up to 9 ft 9 in have been reported.

In extreme cases the wing-span of the Marabou stork (*Leptoptilus crumeniferus*) may reach 11 ft (average span 9 ft), and an unconfirmed measurement of 13 ft 4 in has been reported for a specimen shot in Central Africa in the 1930s (Yelland *fide* Meinertzhagen, 1961).

In August 1939 a wing-span of 12 ft was recorded for a Mute swan (*Cygnus olor*) named "Guardsman" (died 1945) at the famous swannery at Abbotsbury, near Weymouth, Dorset. The average span is 8·5–9 ft.

The only other species of birds which have been reliably measured over 10 ft are the Trumpeter swan (*C.c. buccinator*) and the Griffin vulture (*Gyps fulvus*) with maximum expanses of 10 ft 2 in and 10 ft 0·5 in respectively (Breland, 1948; Dement'ev *et al.*, 1951). Both birds have an average span of 8·5–9 ft. The White pelican (*Pelecanus onocrotalus*) may also exceed 10 ft on occasion.

The greatest wing-span measurement recorded for an eagle (there are fifty-nine recognised species) is 8 ft 3 in for a female Australian wedge-tailed eagle (*Aquila audax*), but this measurement was exceptional. In one series of forty-three birds the span ranged from 6 ft 3 in to 7 ft 3 in (Brown, 1970). In December 1931 a span of 9 ft 2 in was reported for a wedge-tailed eagle killed at Molong, New South Wales (see page 114), but this measurement was probably exaggerated. The wing-span of the female Steller's sea eagle (*Haliaetus peagicus*) probably also exceeds 8 ft at times (average span 7·5 ft).

A female Golden eagle (*Aquila chrysaetos*) captured alive at Stockfield Park near Wetherby, Yorkshire on 29th November 1804 after being wounded by gunshot was credited with a wing-span of 9 ft 4·5 in (*Annual Register*, 1805), but this measurement must be considered excessive. The average expanse for females is 6–7 ft.

Although eagles are extremely powerful birds and can kill prey three or four times their own size, they cannot carry a load much in excess of their own body weight. Usually they kill animals half their own weight or less that can be carried away quickly.

According to Clarke (1969) a Natal mountaineer named Arthur Bowland once persuaded a Verreaux's eagle (*Aquila verreauxi*), a close relative of the golden eagle, to snatch a 20 lb pack while in flight, but the bird only managed to carry it a few yards before it was forced to let go.

Dan McCowan (quoted by Lane, 1955) says two hunters in the Canadian Rockies once saw an American bald eagle (*Haliaetus leucocephalus*) descend from a considerable height with a 15 lb mule deer fawn in its talons, which it dropped when the men shouted at it. There is also a reliable record of an American bald eagle carrying a lamb over a distance of 5 miles to its eyrie.

Stories of eagles carrying off human babies and even small children are legendary, but only one case has ever been fully authenticated.

On 5th June 1932, four-year-old Svanhild Hansen was playing in the yard of her parents' farmhouse in the small village of Leka, a few miles north of Trondheim, Norway, when a huge European sea eagle (*Haliaetus albicilla*) suddenly swooped down and carried her off. The bird headed for its eyrie, which was located 800 ft up on the side of a mountain more than a mile away, but in the end the load proved just a bit too much for it and the child was dropped on a narrow ledge about 50 ft below the eagle's nest.

The frantic parents immediately organised a search-party from the village and, guided by the eagle which was still soaring over the high ledge, they eventually found little Svanhild asleep and unharmed, except for some scratches and bruises (Storer, 1963).

Apparently the child was very small for her age, and Caras (1964) says the eagle hit a powerful upcurrent of air at precisely the right moment to give it the height needed for the incredible flight.

Svanhild, now married, still has the little dress she wore on that terrifying day, and the holes made by the eagle's talons are clearly visible.

Less reliable is a report from Syria that an eagle carried off a baby at Dowair, on the banks of the Assi River, near Damascus, in February 1953 while its mother was washing clothes. A search-party later found the baby unhurt in an eyrie on the side of a precipice, snuggled up warmly against three eaglets!

On 7th May 1959 a three-year-old boy was allegedly snatched from his father's side by an Imperial eagle (*Aquila heliaca*) on a mountain-side near Vienza, northern Italy. The child was later found unhurt on the 4,300 ft summit.

The bee hummingbird, the smallest bird in the world. (Cuban Academy of Science.)

The smallest bird in the world is the Bee hummingbird (*Mellisuga helenae*), also known as "Helena's hummingbird" or "the fairy hummer", which is found only in Cuba. An average adult male has a wing-span measurement of 28·4 mm (1·11 in), a body length of 58 mm (2·28 in) and weighs about 2 g (0·070 oz), which means it is lighter than a Sphinx moth (0·08 oz). Adult females are slightly larger than males.

The Bee hummingbird (*Acestruta bombus*) of Ecuador is about the same size as *M. helenae*, but is slightly heavier.

Hummingbirds (there are 319 recognised species) are extremely pugnacious creatures and will take on birds much larger than themselves. Greenwalte (1960) says they have even been known to engage hawks and eagles in aerial combat. Their weapon is their long needle-like bill which they use to attack the eyes of their enemies, and this, coupled with their ability to fly straight up, down, sideways and backwards makes them a very dangerous adversary.

Not surprisingly, hummingbirds have the highest energy output per unit of weight of any living warm-blooded animal (Greenwalte, 1960).

The smallest bird of prey is the African pygmy falcon *(Poliohierax semitorquatus)* of East and South Africa. Both sexes have a wing-span measurement of 110–119 mm (4·33–4·68 in) (Brown & Amadon, 1968).

The smallest resident British bird is the Goldcrest (*Regulus regulus*), also known as the "Golden-crested wren" or "Kinglet". Adult specimens measure 90 mm (3·5 in) in over-all length and weigh between 3·8 and 4·5 g. It is thus about half the size of the European wren (*Troglodytides troglodytes*), which is popularly thought to be the smallest bird in Britain. The Firecrest (*Regulus ignicapillus*) is of almost equal diminutiveness.

The most abundant species of bird is the Chicken, the domesticated form of the Red junglefowl (*Gallus gallus*) of South-East Asia. There are believed to be about 3,500,000,000 in the world, or nearly one chicken for every member of the human race. The fowl stock in Britain was estimated at 90,000,000 in 1965, producing nearly 200,000,000 chicks each year.

The most abundant species of wild bird is believed to be the Starling (*Sturnus vulgaris*) with an estimated world population of well over 1,000,000,000. In North America alone there are more than 500,000,000, and thereby hangs a sad tale. Starlings were imported into the United States in 1890 by an enthusiast of Shakespeare who wanted America to have all the birds mentioned in the Bard's works. He released sixty pairs in Central Park, New York, and followed it up with another forty pairs the following year. Since then the starlings have multiplied beyond all comprehension and do tremendous damage to fruit crops.

James Fisher (1940) estimated there are approximately 7,000,000 nesting starlings in England and Wales in early spring.

In November 1958 an estimated 3,000,000 starlings from Europe and the U.S.S.R. massed in three woods round the village of North Creake, Norfolk, and the following year another flock estimated to contain 2,000,000 birds invaded north Devon from behind the Iron Curtain.

On 16th February 1960 an enormous flock of starlings "so close you couldn't see between them" alighted on a field of winter wheat at Wolverley, near Kidderminster, Worcestershire. One observer calculated there were 29,000,000 birds in this flock, but this figure is much too extreme to be reliable. Another estimate put the number at a more reasonable 1,000,000.

The most numerous wild breeding birds in England and Wales, according to Fisher (1940), are the Blackbird (*Turdus merula*) and the Chaffinch (*Fringilla coelebs*), each with 10,000,000 individuals, followed by the Starling (*Sturnus vulgaris*) and the Robin (*Erithacus rubecula*) with 7,000,000 each. In 1959 the House sparrow (*Passer domesticus*) population of Britain was estimated at about 9,500,000

It was estimated in 1967 that 250,000 pigeon-fanciers owned an average of forty racing pigeons per loft, making a population of about 10,000,000 in Britain.

The most abundant sea bird, and also the smallest web-footed bird known (length 7–7·5 in) is Wilson's petrel (*Oceanites oceanicus*), which flies to the North Atlantic every summer from its breeding-grounds at the edge of the Antarctic.

No population estimates have been published for this species, but its numbers must run into hundreds—possibly thousands—of millions.

Another contender for the title is the Slender-billed shearwater (*Procellaria tenuirostris*). Flinders (1798) says he saw a single flock off Bass Strait, separating Australia and Tasmania, which took 1·5 hours to fly past him "at a speed almost equal to a flight of pigeons". He calculated that there were over 100,000,000 birds in this flock.

"Martha", the last recorded specimen of the passenger pigeon who died on 1st September 1914 in Cincinnati Zoo. (Smithsonian Institution.)

The most abundant species of bird ever recorded was the Passenger pigeon (*Ectopistes migratoria*) of North America. It has been estimated that there were between 5,000,000,000 and 9,000,000,000 of this species before 1840. Thereafter the birds were killed in vast numbers, and the last recorded specimen, a female named "Martha", died in Cincinnati Zoological Gardens, Ohio,

U.S.A. at 1 p.m. Eastern standard time on 1st September 1914 aged about twelve years. She had been collected with several others in Wisconsin in 1902 (Deane, 1908). The carcass of this bird was frozen in a 300 lb block of ice and shipped to Washington, D.C., where Shufeldt (1951) made a detailed examination. The mounted specimen is now on exhibition in the U.S. National Museum.

The sudden and complete disappearance of the passenger pigeon is probably the most remarkable in Zoological history.

At one time this pigeon formed an estimated 25–40 per cent of the total bird population of the United States and moved about in such incredible numbers as to stagger the imagination.

The first attempt to estimate the number of pigeons in a flock was made by Alexander Wilson (1832), who watched an immense column pass over his head near Frankfort, Kentucky, in 1808.

"They were flying with great steadiness and rapidity, at a height beyond gunshot, in several strata deep, and so close together, that could shot have reached them, one discharge could not have failed of bringing down several individuals. From right to left as far as the eye could reach, the breadth of this vast procession extended; seeing everywhere equally crowded. Curious to determine how long this appearance would continue, I took out my watch to note the time, and sat down to observe them. It was then half past one. I sat for more than an hour, but instead of a diminution of this prodigious progression, it seemed rather to increase both in numbers and rapidity; and, anxious to reach Frankfort before night, I rose and went on. About four o'clock in the afternoon I crossed the Kentucky river, at the town of Frankfort, at which time the living torrent above my head seemed as numerous and as extensive as ever."

According to Wilson the column measured at least 1 mile in breadth, and took four hours to pass overhead at the rate of 60 mile/h, which means that its entire length was 240 miles. He allowed three pigeons to each square yard of this moving body, and calculated that the flock contained 2,230,272,000 birds, although he thought that this figure was "probably far below the actual amount".

Another flock of pigeons seen by J. Audubon (1844) between Henderson and Louisville, Kentucky which took three hours to pass overhead and blotted out the sun was calculated by him to contain 1,115,136,000 birds.

An even larger flock was seen by Major W. R. King (1866) at Fort Mississisauga, Ontario, Canada. He says it took fourteen hours to pass overhead, and for several days afterwards smaller flocks of "weaker or younger birds" continued to fly past. Schorger (1955) has calculated that there were 3,717,120,000 pigeons in this huge column, which makes it the **largest flock of birds ever recorded.**

Their numbers on the ground were equally as impressive. Audubon saw a roost on Green River, Kentucky, which was 40 miles long and 3 miles wide, and Lincecum (1874) mentions another one which covered nearly 50 square miles. Trees were so overloaded by pigeons that some of the less firmly rooted examples just toppled over under the sheer weight. Even as late as 1871 says Schorger (1947) there were an estimated 136,000,000 pigeons in a concentrated nesting area in Wisconsin.

The passenger pigeon became extinct for two reasons. First of all, they were an extremely valuable source of food ("pigeon-pie" was a popular table dish); secondly, their habit of nesting in huge colonies made them an easy target for the guns and nets of the thousands of professional hunters who caught them for profit.

One hunter in Michigan said he frequently killed 70 pigeons with one shot when they were flying directly overhead in tight formation, and he usually killed 1,000 to 1,200 birds before breakfast. Another man in the same state killed 24,000 in ten days (Roney, 1879). In one three-year period 11,880,000 pigeons were shipped from western Michigan to New York. And when the food market eventually reached saturation-point the birds were fed to hogs or turned into fertiliser.

The most sought-after pigeons were the squabs (unfledged birds) because of their more delicate flavouring, and they were killed off at such an alarming rate that in the end the females were unable to raise sufficient enough young to replace those that had been massacred (only one egg is laid).

In 1881 one huge flock still nested in Michigan, but even that one was destroyed by a combination of hunters' guns and nets and a hailstorm that broke just at the critical hatching-stage. Several small flocks of pigeons were seen in Michigan, Wisconsin, Indiana and Nebraska from 1891 to 1894, but as this bird depended upon mass association its fate was sealed.

According to Schorger the last wild passenger pigeon was killed by a boy near Sargents, Pike County, Ohio, on 24th March 1900 (now preserved in the Ohio State Museum). Between 1901 and 1907 there were several sight records, but these were all wrongly identified Mourning doves (*Zenaidura*), which are similar in general appearance.

The Snowy owl, the most tenuously established British bird. (G. R. Austing— F. Lane.)

There are many claimants to the title of rarest bird in the world. Perhaps the strongest are the ten species last seen in the nineteenth century but still just possibly extant. They are: the New Caledonian lorikeet (*Vini diadema*) (New Caledonia before 1860); the Himalayan mountain quail (*Ophrysia superciliosa*) (eastern Punjab, 1868); the Forest spotted owlet (*Athene blewitti*) (central India, *c.* 1872); the Samoan wood rail (*Pareudiastes pacificus*) (Savaii, Samoa, 1873); the Fiji bar-winged rail (*Rallina poecilopterus*) (Ovalau and Viti Levu, 1890); the Kona "finches" (*Psittirostrata flaviceps* and *P. palmeri*) (Kona, Hawaii, 1891 and 1896); the Akepa (*Loxops coccinea*) (Oahu, Hawaii, 1893); the Kona "finch" (*P. kona*) (Hawaii, 1894); and the Mamo (*Drepanis pacifica*) (Hawaii, 1898) (Greenway, 1967).

The Puerto Rican nightjar (*Caprimulgus ruficollis*), believed extinct since 1888, was rediscovered in 1962.

There are thirty-six species of bird (eight of them unconfirmed) which have been recorded only once in the British Isles. That which has not recurred for the longest period is the Black-capped petrel (*Pterodroma hasitata*), also known as the "Diablotin". A specimen was caught alive on a heath at Southacre, near Swaffham, Norfolk, in March or April 1850. A Red-necked nightjar (*Caprimulgus ruficollis*) was shot at Killingworth, near Newcastle, Northumberland on 5th October 1856. The Egyptian vulture (*Neophron percnopterus*) has been recorded twice in the British Isles. The first, an immature bird, was shot near Kilve, Bridgwater Bay, Somerset, in October 1825. Another immature specimen was obtained at Peldon, Essex, on 28th September 1868 (Hallom, 1960). The most tenuously established British bird is now probably the Snowy owl (*Nyctea scandiaca*), now found only on Fetlar in the Shetland Islands. In 1971 only one pair was observed.

The rarest disclosed and regularly nesting British bird is the Osprey (*Pandion heliaetus*), also known as the "Sea hawk". Up to the latter part of the last century it bred commonly in the Scottish Highlands. But the assault of game-preservers and egg-collectors proved too much for it, and the last known Scottish nesting-site was at Loch Loyne, Inverness-shire, in 1910. In 1954 a pair of ospreys nested successfully in the same area. Four years later another pair attempted to breed in an old eyrie at Loch Garten, also in Inverness-shire, and almost succeeded. On the night of 2–3 June, however, at about 2.30 a.m., an egg-collector raided the eyrie right under the noses of the watchers and substituted two hens' eggs daubed with brown boot-polish. The intruder was spotted as he descended from the tree, but the eggs were dropped and smashed as he made good his escape into near-by cover.

The following winter an area by the loch was declared a bird sanctuary especially for the ospreys by the Royal Society for the Protection of Birds, and when the same pair returned in April and nested in a pine at the eastern end of the loch; the trunk of the eyrie tree was covered with barbed-wire and a round-the-clock watch maintained by members of the Society to prevent the nest being robbed again. Their vigilance paid off, and in the first week of August three fledglings left the eyrie. Two more young ospreys were raised in the same eyrie in 1960, three in 1961 and one in 1962. In 1964 vandals attempted to cut down the 40 ft Scots pine where the ospreys had been nesting and succeeded in sawing half-way through the trunk about 9 ft from the ground before they were disturbed. Three stout metal strips had to be riveted round the trunk to prevent it from cracking.

In 1969 four pairs of osprey were observed nesting in the Scottish Highlands, and it was thought that others were breeding in undiscovered eyries. In April 1970 a pair of ospreys returned to the traditional eyrie at the Royal Society's reserve at Loch Garten for the 12th successive year. Another pair nested at the Scottish Wildlife Trust preserve at Loch of

Britain's heaviest recorded horse, a champion Percheron stallion named "Saltmarsh Silver Crest", who weighs almost 1·25 tons. (G. Wood.)

The Fallabella of Argentina, the world's smallest breed of horse. Adult specimens usually stand about 8 hands. A 3 ft rule is shown for comparison. (J. Kennedy.)

Lowes, Perthshire for the first time, but the following month (May)
the eyrie was blown down by a gale and two eggs were found smashed.
That year four pairs of osprey nested in the Highlands and raised eight
young between them. In May 1971 raiders beat a round-the-clock guard,
electronic alarms and a 15ft high barbed wire fence and stole the three
eggs in the nest at Loch Garten. Despite this setback, however, seven pairs
of osprey nested in the Highlands last year and raised eleven young between them – a record.

In October 1971 the Royal Society for the Protection of Birds
reported that only one pair of Marsh harriers (*Circus aeruginosus*) nested
that summer at Minsmere, Suffolk, which now makes this species even
rarer than the osprey as a breeding bird.

Although birds are longer-lived than mammals on the average, very
few species exceed forty years, and reports that they sometimes live for a
hundred years or more should be treated with suspicion. An Egyptian
vulture (*Neophron percnopterus*) which died in the Menagerie at Schönbrunn,
Vienna, Austria, in 1824, for instance, was stated to have been 118 years
old. According to Flower (1925), however, the menagerie was not
founded until 1752, "so even if it were proved that it was one of the
original inmates of that famous collection, there is still a previous 36 years
to be accounted for". Other dubious records in the same age category
include an African grey parrot (*Pstittacus erythacus*) of 120 years, a Griffin
vulture (*Gyps fulvus*) of 117 years, a Golden eagle (*Aquila chrysaetos*) of 104
years and a Mute swan (*Cygnus olor*) of 102 years.

In July 1840 a mute swan named "Old Jack" died in St. James's Park,
London, reputedly aged seventy years. He was said to have been hatched
"on the piece of water attached to Buckingham Palace" in 1770 (*Morning
Post*, 16th July 1840).

On 6th August 1965 a white pelican named "Percy" died in Wellington Zoological Gardens, New Zealand, reputedly aged "at least 70", but
this record has not yet been fully substantiated. The bird was presented to
the zoo by the London Zoological Society in 1904.

A Greater sulphur-crested cockatoo (*Cacatua galerita*) which died at
London Zoo on 4th September 1936 after 29 years 3 months 4 days in
captivity (Flower, 1938) was stated to have been forty years old on arrival,
giving it a reputed age of sixty-nine; but this information was largely
based on hearsay.

Another greater sulphur-crested cockatoo named "Cocky Bennett",
owned by Mrs. Sarah Bennett, licensee of the Sea Breeze Hotel at Tom
Ugly's Point, near Sydney, New South Wales, Australia, was allegedly
over 120 years old when he died in 1916, but Kinghorn (1930) says there
is no authentic information available regarding the true age of this bird.
The cockatoo was in the possession of Mrs. Bennett for twenty-six years,
and had previously been owned by Captain George Ellis, skipper of a
South Seas sailing ship who said the bird was alive when he was only a
nine-year-old ship's apprentice. During the last twenty-five years of his
life Cocky Bennett was practically featherless, and he was often heard to
scream: "One more f . . . . . feather and I'll fly."

On 8th March 1968 the death was reported in the Nottingham Park
Aviary of another greater sulphur-crested cockatoo named "Cocky" aged
114 years, but this record is considered unreliable as several cockatoos of
this name had been kept in this aviary over the years.

Five and a half weeks later a Grey parrot (*Psittacus erythacus*) owned
by ex-seaman Ronald Dunstan of Bramcote, Nottinghamshire, died
allegedly aged ninety-nine years, but there are gaps in this bird's history.

In October 1969 the death was reported of another greater sulphur-crested cockatoo named "Cocky" at Bridge Sollers, Hertfordshire, reputedly aged 125 years, but as this bird was still in very good plumage at the time of its demise this record must be considered suspect (cockatoos start to look "tatty" around the 40th year.)

"Cocky", a sulphur-crested cockatoo which allegedly lived for 125 years. (Fox Photos.)

BIRD LONGEVITY RECORDS

Species	Age in years
European eagle-owl (*Bubo bubo*)	68*
Andean condor (*Vultur gryphus*)	65
Blue macaw (*Ara macao*)	64
Great white heron (*Ardea melanocephala*)	60
Ostrich (*Struthio camelus*)	59
Greater sulphur-crested cockatoo (*Cacatua galerita*)	56
Imperial eagle (*Aquila imperialis*)	56
Bateleur eagle (*Terathopsius ecaudatus*)	55*
Black vasaparrot (*Coracopsis vasa*)	54
White pelican (*Pelecanus onocrotalus*)	52
Golden eagle (*Aquila chrysaetos*)	50
Grey parrot (*Psittacus erythacus*)	49
Golden-naped parrot (*Amazona auropalliata*)	49
Australian crane (*Megalornis rubicunda*)	47
Adalbert's eagle (*Aquila adalberti*)	44
Grey crane (*Megalornis grus*)	43
Leadbeater's cockatoo (*Cacatua leadbeateri*)	42
Caracara (*Polyborus tharus*)	42
Chilean eagle (*Geranoaetus melanoleucas*)	42
White-tailed eagle (*Haliaetus albicillus*)	42
Sarus crane (*Megalornis antigone*)	42
Rough-billed pelican (*Pelecanus erythrorhynchos*)	41
Manchurian crane (*Megalornis japonensis*)	41
Asiatic white crane (*Megalornis leucogeranus*)	41
Banksian cockatoo (*Calyptorhynchus banksii*)	40
Bare-eyed cockatoo (*Cacatua gymnopis*)	40
Tawny eagle (*Aquila rapax*)	40
King vulture (*Sarcorhamphus papa*)	40
Western slender-billed cockatoo (*Licmetis pastinator*)	40

* Still alive.
Sources: Flower, 1938 and others.

It is interesting to note that Dr. Alex Comfort (1963) thinks the sixty-eight-plus years quoted by Flower for his longest-lived bird is "probably too low", and that the less fully authenticated records given by Gurney (1899) of birds living beyond seventy years are "probably substantially correct". These include an eighty-one-year-old greater sulphur-crested cockatoo and a seventy-two-year-old grey parrot.

The greatest authentic age recorded for a sea bird in captivity is forty-four years for a herring gull which lived in the Jardin des Plantes, Paris, from 1830 to 1874 (Gurney, 1899). Another specimen which died at Musselburgh, near Edinburgh, Scotland on 10th July 1937 was "41 years at least" (Professor James Ritchie, quoted by Flower, 1937).

*The Goldcrest (*Regulus regulus*), Britain's smallest resident bird. (J. Burton/B. Coleman Ltd.)*

*The Gentoo penguin (*Pygoscelis papua*) of the sub-Antarctic islands is the fastest swimmer among birds, having been timed at 22·5 mile/h under water.*

The European eagle-owl, the longest-lived bird of which there is authentic information.

Sea birds living under natural conditions do not generally attain such great ages as captive specimens, and information is only obtainable from ringed birds. Among the records given by Rydzewski (1962) are a herring gull of 31 years 11 months 10 days (25.7.29 to 5.7.61 Goteborg, Sweden) and a Black-headed gull (*Larus ridibundus*) of 30 years 3 months 12 days (23.6.32 to 5.10.62, Leiden, Holland).

The greatest authentic age recorded for a wild sea bird is exactly thirty-six years for a herring gull ringed on 29th June 1930 when about ten days old at Duck Rock, an islet just off Monhegan Island, Maine, U.S.A., and found dead on 20th June 1966 on the shore of Little Traverse Bay, Lake Michigan, Michigan, U.S.A.

The Wandering albatross (*Diomedea exulans*) and the Royal albatross (*D. epomophora*) are believed to live about twenty to thirty years in the wild, but Westerskov (1936) says the potential life-span may be as great as eighty years.

In January 1887 a wandering albatross was captured by the crew of the British frigate *Duchess of Argyll* near Cape Horn. Attached to its neck was a compass case containing the information that the bird had previously been caught in the North Atlantic by an American ship, the *Columbus*, on 8th May 1840. The bird was released again after a new case containing details of its second capture was attached to the albatross's neck (Rosenberg, 1887).

One of the shortest-lived birds is the Robin (*Etithacus rubecula*), which has an average life-span in the wild of only about one year.

A great deal of nonsense has been written about the *maximum* flying speeds attained by birds, the tendency being to exaggerate rather than underestimate the miles per hour. It is virtually impossible to time a bird accurately over a measured distance, even with theodolites at each end, because too many other factors are involved like wind velocity, gravity, angle of flight, etc., and other methods used to determine the speed like a car running on a parallel course or an aeroplane are not always reliable. The question is also complicated by the fact that *ground* speed is very different from *air* speed.

The *air* speed of a bird is defined as the velocity with which it flies in relation to the air, and *ground* speed as the velocity with which it flies in relation to the ground. Thus, a bird flying at 40 mile/h with a tail wind of 30 mile/h has an *air* speed of 40 mile/h, but the *ground* speed is 70 mile/h.

The spine-tailed swift, the fastest-moving living creature.

The fastest flying bird is the Spine-tailed swift (*Chaetura caudacuta*) of Asia. According to Gladkov (1942) air speeds up to 106·25 mile/h have been reliably measured in the U.S.S.R.

In 1934 ground speeds ranging from 171·8 to 219·5 mile/h were recorded by E. C. Stuart Baker (1942) with a stop-watch for spine-tailed swifts passing over his bungalow in the Cachar Hills, north-eastern India, to a ridge exactly 2 miles away behind which they *seemed* to dip into another valley, but scientific tests since have revealed that this species of bird cannot be seen at a distance of 1 mile, even with standard binoculars (Wing, 1956).

Gatke (1895), who spent fifty years in Heligoland studying bird migratory movements, was firmly of the opinion that much greater speeds were attained by birds flying at high altitudes than at low altitudes because of the more rarefied air, but his claim that birds like the plover, curlew and godwit reach speeds up to 240 mile/h at altitudes of 40,000 ft must be discounted because no bird can soar to this height (see highest-flying bird).

Ground speeds as high as 275 mile/h have been ascribed to the Peregrine falcon (*Falco peregrinus*) in a stoop, and 170–200 mile/h in level flight, but in recent experiments by British falconer Phillip Glasier, in which miniature air speedometers were fitted to the bird, the maximum recorded diving speed was 82 mile/h, and the top speed in level flight 60 mile/h (Lane, 1968).

Colonel Richard Meinertzhagen (1955) says the peregrine falcon cannot catch swift birds like the Racing pigeon (*Columba livia*) or the Sand-grouse (*Pterocles* sp.) in level flight.

Ground speeds in excess of 100 mile/h have also been reported for the golden eagle, but the pointed wings of this bird are best suited for slow, powerful, sustained flight.

According to the statement of one ornithologist there is a record of a Golden eagle dropping 5,000 ft in six seconds, which is "equivalent to a speed of 567·6 mile/h [*sic*]", but this must be dismissed as pure fantasy.

Leslie Brown (1953) once timed one of these birds in Scotland over a distance of 14 miles and found that its ground speed was 84 mile/h, but most of the time the eagle was gliding.

In September 1952 an African crowned eagle (*Stephanoaetus coronatus*) escaped from Dudley Zoo, Worcestershire. The following morning a patrolling policeman saw it in a tree in a near-by park and informed the zoo, but when keepers tried to net the bird it took off in a hurry. Ten minutes later the police received a report from Tamworth in Staffordshire, 20 miles away, that the eagle had just landed there.

BIRD AIR SPEED TABLE (level flight)

Species	Speed mile/h
Spine-tailed swift (*Chaetura caudacuta*)	106
Frigate-bird (*Fregata* sp.)	95
Spur-wing goose (*Plectropterus gambiensis*)	88
Red-breasted merganser (*Mergus serrator*)	80+
White-rumped swift (*Caffrapus caffer*)	77
Canvasback duck (*Nyroca valisineria*)	72
Eider duck (*Somateria mollissima*)	70
Teal (*Anas crecca*)	68
Pintail (*A. acuta*)	65
Mallard (*A. platyrhyncha*)	65
Golden plover (*Charadrius apricarius*)	60
Peregrine falcon (*Falco peregrinus*)	60
Canada goose (*Branta canadensis*)	60
Racing pigeon (*Columba livia*)	60
Quail (*Lophortyx* sp.)	57
Sandgrouse (*Pterocles* sp.)	55
Merlin (*Falco columbarius*)	55
Swan (*Cygnus* sp.)	55
Lapwing (*Vanellus vanellus*)	50
Snow goose (*Anser hyperboreus*)	50
Gannet (*Sula bassana*)	48

Sources: Meinertzhagen, 1955; Lane, 1955; Breland, 1963 and others.

The fastest flying sea birds are the Frigates or Man-o'-war birds (family Fregatidae). Stolpe and Zimmer (quoted by Lane, 1955) give a record of a frigate-bird flying at an air speed of 44 m/s (95·69 mile/h), but ground speeds in excess of 200 mile/h have been claimed.

In June 1928 a figure of 247 mile/h was attributed to a small group of

frigate-birds in level flight over a 25·25-mile course off the Cardagos
Garajos Islands, 250 miles north-east of Mauritius in the Indian Ocean
(Ricks, 1934), but this measurement must be considered excessive.

Air speeds up to 71 mile/h in level flight have been claimed for the
diminutive Hummingbird (family Trochilidae), but in wind-tunnel tests
the maximum speed was found to be 30 mile/h (Greenewalt, 1960).

The winner of the 186-mile Ulster race for pigeons in 1961 averaged
97·5 mile/h, but this was wind-assisted, and the average air speed was
about 45 mile/h. In level flight in windless conditions it is very doubtful if
any pigeon can exceed 60 mile/h, although Schorger (1955) says the
passenger pigeon had a potential speed of 70 mile/h when hard pressed.

The fastest standard game bird is the Spur-wing goose (*Plectropterus
gambiensis*), with a maximum recorded air speed of 88 mile/h.

Some species of bird can fly into a wind with a greater velocity than
their own maximum speed and *still move forward*, although the reasons
for this are not known. Meinertzhagen (1955) once saw a small group of
Eider duck (*Somateria mollissima*) perform this remarkable feat in South
Uist, Outer Hebrides, during a 90–95 mile/h gale. He says: "This particular wind was so strong that shooting was out of the question, wild
swans were grounded and unable to rise and we experienced the greatest
difficulty in walking against it. Eider Duck had come inland from the sea
and were sitting about on the short grass. When disturbed they would rise
into the wind and make headway against it at ground level, doing about
15–20 m.p.h. except for one bird who actually achieved a minus ground
speed and slowly backed towards us."

McNabb (1953) gives another record of a flock of Wood pigeons
(*Columba palumbus*) moving forward at 40 mile/h in the face of a 110 mile/h
gale when they should have been moving backwards!

The fastest ratite or running bird is generally conceded to be the Emu (*Plectropterus gambiensis*) of
Australia, which is second in size only to the ostrich among living birds
(i.e. 5–6 ft tall and up to 120 lb). This species has been credited with speeds
up to 40 mile/h over short distances, but the ostrich can probably exceed
this velocity when hard pressed (see largest living bird).

The fastest recorded wing-beat of any bird is that of the hummingbird *Heliactin cornuta* of tropical
South America with a rate of ninety beats a second. This rate is probably
exceeded by the Bee hummingbirds *Mellisuga helenae* and *Acestrura bombus*
(the number of strokes per second increases in proportion to the decrease
in size), but no figures have yet been published.

In 1951 wing-beats of up to 200 per second were reported for the
Ruby-throated hummingbird (*Archilochus colubris*) and the Rufous
hummingbird (*Selasphorus rufus*) of the eastern United States during
courtship flights, but these rates were for the narrow tips of the primaries
only and not the complete wing.

Large vultures (family Vulturidae) can soar for hours without beating
their wings, but sometimes exhibit a flapping rate as low as one beat per
second.

The fastest swimming bird is the Gentoo penguin (*Pygoscelis papua*) of Antarctica. In January 1913
Dr. Robert Cushman Murphy of the American Museum of Natural
History was able to time a few of these birds under water in a transparent
pool at the summit of a coastal hill south of the Bay of Isles, South Georgia.
"They dashed straight away under water the length of the pond and back
again, with a velocity which I then had an opportunity to compute as

about ten metres a second. They chased each other round and round, flashing into the air twice or thrice during their bursts of speed, every action plainly revealed through the clear quiet water."

Ten metres a second is equivalent to a speed of 22·3 mile/h, which is a respectable flying speed for some birds, but this penguin probably reaches 25 mile/h when fleeing from the deadly Leopard seal (*Hydrurga leptonyx*).

Speeds in excess of 16 knots (18·4 mile/h) have also been reported for the Adélie penguin (*Pygoscelis adeliae*).

The greatest depth reached by a diving bird has not yet been established, and a great deal of controversy surrounds this issue.

According to Faber (1826) Common and Black guillemots (*Uria salge* and *Cepphus grylle*) have been recovered from the stomachs of Spiny dogfish (*Squalus* sp.), which are rarely found in water less than 300 ft deep, and Forbush (1922) states that Crested auklets (*Aethia cristatella*) have been recovered from the stomachs of Cod (*Gadus callarias*) caught at a depth of 200 ft. These records, however, are discounted by Dewar (1924), who says there is no proof that these birds were actually swallowed by the fish on the sea bottom.

Clay (1911) claims he once saw several Baird's cormorants (*Phalacrocorax bairdii*) rise to the surface with kelp in their beaks from water with a reputed depth of over 80 fathoms (480 ft), but there is no evidence that this depth was reached in the course of the dive (kelp has been measured up to 195 ft in length).

There are also several records of diving birds drowning after getting entangled in fishermen's nets set at great depths. Faber, for instance, says Eider ducks (*Somateria mollissima*) have been captured this way at a depth of 30 fathoms (180 ft), and a depth of 240 ft has been reported for a Great northern diver (*Colymbus immer*). Yarrell (1845) records the capture of a Shag (*Phalacrocorax aristotelis*) at a depth of 20 fathoms (120 ft).

One of the finest divers is the King eider (*Somateria spectabilis*), which is able to reach mussels in 25 fathoms (150 ft) of water (Eaton, 1910), but a statement by Horring (1919) that this bird can descend to 72 fathoms (432 ft) in search of food must be discounted.

The Long-tailed duck (*Clangula hyemalis*) has also been credited with a dive of 150 ft in the Great Lakes, Canada (Schorger, 1947).

The great northern diver can remain under water for more than three minutes, and there is one authentic record of a wounded bird remaining submerged for fifteen minutes. The dives of the king eider generally last four to six minutes, but one bird remained below for nine minutes.

The greatest distance covered by a ringed bird during migration is 14,000 miles for an Arctic tern (*Sterna paradisaea*), which was banded as a nestling on 5th July 1955 in the Kandalaksha Sanctuary on the White Sea coast about 125 miles from Murmansk, European Russia, and was captured alive by a fisherman 8 miles south of Fremantle, Western Australia, on 16th May 1956 (Dorst, 1962).

Another Arctic tern banded as a nestling at Ikamint, western Greenland on 8th July 1951 was recovered in Durban Harbour, Natal, South Africa on 30th October 1951 after a flight of over 11,000 miles (Fisher & Lockley, 1954). This is an astonishing feat for a bird less than four months old.

Many other species also make long migratory flights. A Manx shearwater (*Procellaria puffinus*) ringed on Anglesey, north-western Wales in

The arctic tern, the most travelled of all birds. (N. Duerden—F. Lane.)

June 1966 was recovered in New South Wales, Australia in December 1966 after flying 12,000 miles.

A Mallard (*Anas platyrhynchos*) ringed at the Peakirk Wildfowl Trust near Peterborough, Northamptonshire in 1962 was shot in Alberta, Canada, in April 1966 after taking the 10,000-mile eastward route over Siberia.

The Slender-billed shearwater (*Puffinus tenuirostris*) flies 20,000 miles annually around the Pacific Ocean, and a nestling ringed at Babel Island, off Tasmania on 13th March 1955 was recovered off Tanoura, Shikoku Island, Japan, seventy-five days later (Serventy, 1957).

A Wandering albatross (*Diomedea exulans*) banded as a nestling on Kerguelen Island in the south Indian Ocean on 20th July 1952 was found at Patache, Chile, on 1st October 1953 and must have flown some 11,200 miles between the banding and recovery points (Angot, 1954).

Between breeding seasons the Sooty albatross (*Phoebetria fusca*) flies around the world at 40 degrees south latitude, covering a distance of 19,000 miles in some eighty days.

One of the longest journeys of a London ringed bird was that of a Tufted duck (*Aythya fuligula*) from St. James's Park, which died in the sea near Archangel, northern Russia, eight years later.

A Lesser yellow-legs or Yellowshank (*Tringa flavipes*) banded on Cape Cod, Massachusetts, U.S.A. on 28th August 1935 was killed six days later on the island of Martinique, in the West Indies, 1,900 miles away, which means it must have averaged 316 miles a day.

A banded Turnstone (*Arenaria interpres*) released at Heligoland was shot twenty-five hours later on the northern coast of France after covering a distance of 510 miles (Wing, 1956).

Griffin (1944) gives a record of a herring gull travelling 715 miles in less than twenty-four hours.

Most hummingbirds do not migrate very far, but the Ruby-throated hummingbird (*Archilochus colubris*), the Rufous hummingbird (*Selasphorus rufus*) and the Calliope hummingbird (*Stellula callipe*) of the south-western United States fly up to 2,000 miles from their breeding site to winter quarters. The ruby-throated hummingbird also makes non-stop migratory flights across the Gulf of Mexico to Yucatan, a distance of 500 miles (Greenewalt, 1960).

Migrating swallows (*Hirundo rustica*) often take a short-cut through the 4-mile-long Grand St. Bernard road tunnel from Italy to Switzerland rather than fly over the 8,000 ft high Alps!

The greatest recorded homing flight by a pigeon was made by one owned by the first Duke of Wellington (1769–1852). Released from a sailing-ship off the Ichabo Islands, West Africa, on 8th April, it dropped dead a mile from its loft at Nine Elms, London, on 1st June 1845, fifty-five days later, having flown an airline route of 5,400 miles, but an actual distance of possibly 7,000 miles to avoid the Sahara Desert.

The shortest bird migrations are made by species like the Black-capped chickadee (*Parus atricapillus*), Clark's nutcracker (*Nufifraga columbiana*) and the Rosy finch (*Leucosticte arctos*) of North America, which merely descend from exposed mountain ridges to the sheltered valleys below during the autumn months.

The longest migrations among flightless swimming birds are made by King penguins (*Aptenodytes patagonica*), which sometimes travel from the sub-Antarctic to the coast of Chile.

At one time it was believed that most birds flew at heights of 20,000 ft or more during migration because of the physical advantages of low pressure at high altitudes (see Gatke, 1895), but this theory no longer holds water. Most migrating birds, in fact, fly at relatively low altitudes (i.e. below 300 ft), and only a few dozen species fly higher than 3,000 ft.

The celebrated example of a skein of seventeen Egyptian geese (*Alopochen aegyptiacus*) photographed by an astronomer at Dehra Dun, northern India on 17th September 1919 as they crossed the sun at an estimated height of between 11 and 12 miles (58,080–63,360 ft) has been discredited by experts because the picture is not clearly defined (the calculation was based on the known diameter of the sun and the wing-span of a goose in flight) (Meinertzhagen, 1955).

The highest acceptable altitude recorded for a bird is 8,200 m (26,902 ft) for a small number of Alpine choughs (*Pyrrhocorax graculus*) which followed the successful British expedition led by Colonel John Hunt up Mount Everest in May 1953, but their take-off point may have been as high as 20,000 ft. In 1921 a Lammergeier (*Gypaetus barbatus*), a large member of the vulture family, was seen at 25,000 ft on the same mountain (Wollaston, 1922), and this magnificent bird probably sails over the summit on occasion (a dynamic soarer like the lammergeier does not need a great deal of oxygen for flight like other birds).

A Wall creeper (*Tichodroma muraria*) has been seen at 21,000 ft in the

Karakorum Range, northern India (Ingram, 1919), a Crane (*Grus* sp.) at
20,000 ft in the Himalayas, a Condor (*Vultur gryphus*) at 19,800 ft in the
Andes (Jack, 1953), and godwits, curlews and even jackdaws at 19,700 ft
on Mount Everest.

The highest flying song bird is probably the Rose-breasted rose finch (*Carpodacus puniceus*) of Asia
which may reach 18,000 ft.

On three separate occasions in 1959 a radar station in Norfolk picked
up flocks of small passerine night migrants flying in from Scandinavia at
altitudes up to 21,000 ft. Dr. David Lack (1960) of the Edward Grey
Institute, Oxford, says they were probably Warblers (Sylviidae), Chats
(Turnidae) and Flycatchers (Muscicapidae).

Birds have very large eyes for their size—the ostrich has the largest
eye of any terrestrial animal—because they are more dependent on sight
than other vertebrates, and the vision of some species like eagles, hawks
and falcons is extremely acute.

According to Leslie Brown (1970) a golden eagle can detect an 18 in
long hare at a range of 2,150 yd (possibly even 2 miles) in good light and
against a contrasting background, and a falcon can spot a pigeon at a
range of over 3,500 ft.

One day the American ornithologist E. H. Eaton was standing on a
lake shore when he saw an eagle which had been soaring high above his
head suddenly plunge in a dive-glide towards a distant part of the shore
where it seized a fish it had detected. Afterwards he measured the distance
between himself and the spot where the bird had seized its victim and found
that it was about 3 miles (Devoe, 1954).

The visual acuity of the large birds of prey is at least eight times as
great as that of human vision.

Some nocturnal birds of prey such as owls have a sensitivity to low
light intensities that is 50–100 times greater than that of human night
vision.

Tests have shown that under favourable conditions the Long-eared
owl (*Asio otus*) and the Barn owl (*Tyto alba*) can swoop on targets from a
distance of 6 ft or more in an illumination of only 0·00000073 ft-candle
(equivalent to the light from a standard candle at a distance of 1,170 ft)
(Dice, 1940), and the same birds can see prey (with difficulty) in an
illumination of 0·00000015 ft-candle, which is equivalent to the light from
a standard candle at a distance of 2,582 ft (Wing, 1956).

The largest egg produced by any living bird is that of the Ostrich (*Struthio camelus*). The average
example measures 6–8 inches in length, 4 to 6 inches in diameter and weighs
3·63 to 3·88 lb (equal to the volume of two dozen hen's eggs). It takes forty
minutes to boil. The shell is 0·0625 in thick and can support the weight of
an 18-stone (252 lb) man. Jackals are said to be able to break the eggs by
"kicking" one against another until they crack. On 8th August 1955 an
ostrich named "Emmie" at Ilfracombe Zoo, Devon, laid a 4 lb egg.

The largest egg laid by any bird on the British list is that of the Mute swan (*Cygnus olor*), which
measures from 4·3 to 4·9 inches in length and between 2·8 and 3·1 inches
in diameter. The weight is 12–13 oz.

The largest egg produced by a sea bird is that of the Wandering albatross (*Diomedea exulans*). The
average specimen measures 5·2 inches in length, 3·1 inches in diameter
and weighs about 1 lb, but weights up to 21 oz have been reported
(Murphy, 1936).

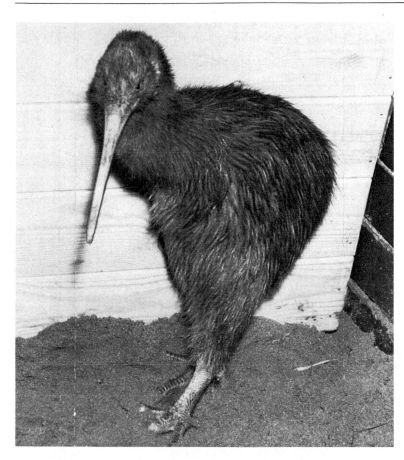

The kiwi of New Zealand lays a larger egg in proportion to body size than any other bird. (Reuter Ltd.)

The largest egg laid by any bird in proportion to its own size is that of the Kiwi (*Apteryx* sp.) of New Zealand. The egg sometimes weighs as much as 18 oz or one-fifth the body weight of the hen kiwi. Observers have reported that the hen staggers about as though drunk shortly before depositing the huge egg. The Bee hummingbird (*Mellisuga helenae*) (see below) is another strong contender. On this basis, the ostrich lays the smallest eggs of any living bird.

The smallest egg laid by any bird is that of the Bee hummingbird (*M. helenae*), the world's smallest bird. On 8th May 1906 two specimens were collected at Boyate, Santiago de Cuba by O. Tollin, who presented them to the U.S. National Museum, Washington, D.C., U.S.A. in 1909. One of these eggs has since been mis-laid, but the other one measures 11·4 mm (0·45 in) in length, 8 mm (0·32 in) in diameter and weighs 0·5 g (0·176 oz) (Watson, *in litt.* 5.7.67). This egg is closely matched in size by that of the Vervain hummingbird (*M. minima*) of Jamaica and Haiti. Two specimens collected by James Bond (*in litt.* 22.8.67) on Ile Tortue, Haiti, measure 11·6 × 8·4 mm (0·45 × 0·33 in) and 11·5 × 8·15 mm (0·45 × 0·32 in) respectively.

The smallest egg laid by any bird on the British list is that of the Goldcrest (*Regulus regulus*), which measures 12·2–14·5 mm (0·48–0·57 in) in length and between 9·4 mm and 9·9 mm (0·37 and 0·39 in) in diameter. The egg of the Firecrest (*Regulus ignicapillus*) measure between 12·7 mm and 14·2 mm (0·5 and 0·56 in) in length. The egg of the Wren (*Troglodytes troglodytes*) weighs between 1·37 and 1·59 g (between 0·048 and 0·055 oz).

The longest incubation period is that of the Wandering albatross (*Diomedea exulans*) with a normal range of seventy-five to eighty-two days, but Tickell (1968) says he observed two eggs on Bird Island, South Georgia, which took eighty-five days to hatch. The Royal albatross (*Diomedea epomophora*) has a normal range of seventy-five to eighty-one days, and the Common kiwi (*Apteryx australis*) seventy-five to eighty days.

The incubation period of the Mallee fowl (*Leipoa ocellata*) of Australia is normally sixty-two days, but Petersen (1963) gives a record of an egg taking ninety days to hatch.

The incubation period of the Ostrich (*Struthio camelus*) is about forty-two days.

The shortest incubation periods are to be found among the passerines or perching birds. In the case of the Hawfinch (*Coccothraustes coccothraustes*) this is only nine to ten days, and the Skylark (*Alauda arvensis*) and the Cuckoo (*Cuculus canorus*) usually hatch out in eleven days.

The number of eggs laid by a bird in a "single clutch" varies considerably among species and is largely related to food supplies and the physical condition and age of the hen.

The Bobwhite (*Colinus virginianus*) of North America is generally credited with laying the largest clutches with a normal range of twelve to twenty-four eggs, but this clutch size is closely matched by the Partridge (*Perdix perdix*) which usually lays twelve to twenty eggs. Removal of *most* eggs from a nest, however, has resulted in a Grouse (family Tretraonidae) laying 36 eggs and a bobwhite 128 before stopping (Wing, 1956).

On 12th July 1970 a Muscovy duck (*Cairina moschata*) named "Spike" owned by M. T. Spurr of Starbuck Farm, Beighton, Sheffield, Yorkshire hatched out twenty-one ducklings.

Some birds produce a single clutch that weigh considerably more · than themselves. A 1 lb Ruddy duck (*Oxyura jamaicensis*), for instance, will lay a clutch of fourteen to fifteen eggs weighing over 3 lb (Petersen, 1963).

The highest price ever paid for a bird's egg (excluding prehistoric examples) is £330·75 for a specimen of the now extinct Great auk (*Alca impennis*), a flightless North Atlantic sea bird, sold in London on 15th November 1934.

The largest nests (i.e. constructed of sticks or twigs) are built by the Bald eagle (*Halliaetus leucocephalus*) of the United States. One nest built by a pair of birds in Vermilion, Ohio and possibly their successors over a period of thirty-five years measured 8 ft 6 inches in width and 12 ft in depth. When it finally crashed to the ground during a storm (killing the eaglets inside) its weight was estimated at 2 tons. Another example built by a pair of bald eagles near St. Petersburg, Florida had a width of 9 ft 6 in and a depth of 20 ft (Petersen, 1963).

The incubation mounds of dry sandy earth with a core of vegetable matter built by the Megapodes or Scrubfowl (family Megapodidae) of the Indo-Pacific region are much larger. One mound reportedly measured 20 ft in height and 50 ft in diameter.

The smallest nests are built by Hummingbirds (family Trochilidae). That of the Bee hummingbird (*Mellisuga helenae*) is about the size of a thimble, and the nest of the Crested tree swift (*Hemiprocne mystacea*) of Malaysia and Australia is almost equally as diminutive.

The most valuable nests are those built by the little Cave swiftlets (*Collocalia esculenta*) of South-East Asia and Indonesia which produce the raw material for bird's-nest soup. The most sought-after nests are those made entirely of salivary secretion which do not require extensive cleaning (nests made of secretion mixed with feathers or vegetable matter fetch lower prices).

The stuffed great auk sold at Sotheby's, London in 1971 for a record £9,000. (United Press International.)

The highest price ever paid for a stuffed bird is £9,000 for a specimen of the Great auk (*Alca impennis*) in summer plumage collected in Iceland in *c.* 1821. The bird was purchased at Messrs. Sotheby & Co., London on 5th March 1971 by the Director of the Iceland Natural History Museum, who later said that his museum would have gone as high as £23,000 for this magnificent example. The last great auk was killed on Eldey, Iceland in 1844. The last British sightings were at County Waterford in 1834 and St. Kilda in *c.* 1840.

The Japanese long-tailed fowl, cock birds of which have tail coverts measuring up to 20 ft in length.

The longest feathers grown by any bird are those of the cock Long-tailed fowl or Onagadori (a strain of *Gallus gallus*) bred at Kochi in Shikoku, Japan, which have tail coverts measuring up to 20 ft in length.

The number of feathers on a bird varies with the species and the season (most abundant immediately after a moult). In general, however, large birds have more feathers than small ones. A Whistling swan (*Cygnus columbianus*) was found to have 25,216 feathers, 20,177 of which were on the head and neck and 5,039 on the body; a Pied-billed grebe (*Podilymbus podiceps*) 15,016; a Mallard (*Anas platyrhynchos*) 11,903; and a Domestic chicken (*Gallus gallus*) 9,325. The House sparrow (*Passer domesticus*) has about 3,500 in winter and 3,000 in summer. A Ruby-throated hummingbird (*Archilochus colubris*) had only 940, although hummingbirds have more feathers per area of body surface than any other living bird (Wetmore, 1936; Wing, 1956).

The normal blood temperature of awake but inactive birds is usually about 41·1 °C (106 °F), and 39·4 – 40 °C (103–104 °F) when asleep, but it rises during intense activity.

The highest blood temperature ever recorded for a bird is 44·8 °C (112·7 °F) for a Western pewee (*Myiochanes richardsoni*). This is closely matched by the Spine-tailed swift (*Chaetura caudacuta*), the fastest-moving living creature, which has a blood temperature of 44·7 °C (112·5 °F).

The lowest blood temperatures are found in torpid birds. In the case of hummingbirds (family Trochilidae) readings as low as 13·3 °C (56 °F) have been recorded (Chaplin, 1933), and a Nuttall's poorwill (*Phalaenoptilus nuttallii*) found hibernating in a rocky crevice in a deep canyon in the Chuckawalla Mountains, California, U.S.A. in December 1946 had a blood temperature of only 18·1 °C (64·6 °F) (normal active temperature 106 °F) (Jaeger, 1948).

The lowest normal blood temperature recorded for a bird, excluding torpid birds, is 37·7 °C (100 °F) for a Kiwi (*Apteryx* sp.) (Wetmore, 1921). A figure of 38·5 °C (101·3 °F) has been reported for the Western grebe (*Aechmophorus occidentalis*).

For parental energy in supplying food to its young, the Wren (*Troglodytes troglodytes*) probably takes some beating. One mother was observed to feed her young 1,217 times in a day of nearly sixteen hours (Wing, 1956), and there is another record of a pair of Great tits (*Parus major*) feeding their young 10,685 times during a fourteen-day period.

The most aerial of all birds is the Common swift (*Apus apus*), which remains airborne for at least nine months of the year and possibly much longer. There is no truth in the claim, however, that it sleeps on the wing, although Lockley (1970) says it "somehow manages to get enough rest during the night-flight to enable it to maintain a steady level without exhaustion".

It has also been calculated that the Chimney swift (*Chaetura pelagica*) of eastern North America flies 1,350,000 miles during its nine years of life (Wing, 1956).

It is unlikely that the Cuckoo (*Cuculus canorus*) has ever been *heard and seen* in Britain earlier than 10th March, on which date one was observed in Devon in 1884 and another in Wiltshire in 1938 (Harting, 1938). Richard Lydekker, in a letter published in *Field* on 8th February 1913, says he heard a cuckoo in Harpenden, Hertfordshire on 4th February 1913, and it was heard by several of his neighbours during the next four or five days. Later, however, he discovered that the call had been made by a bricklayer's labourer working on a new house near by who was an expert bird mimic! The two latest dates recorded are 16th December 1912 at Anstey's Cove, Torquay, Devon and 26th December 1897 or 1898 in Cheshire (Parker, 1943).

The largest domesticated bird (excluding the ostrich) is the Turkey (*Meleagris gallapavo*), which was introduced into Britain via Germany from Mexico in 1549.

The heaviest specimen on record was a White Holland stag named "Tom", owned by a breeder in California, U.S.A., who scaled 70 lb at the time of its death in December 1966. Unconfirmed weights up to 80 lb have been reported.

Several years ago a Mississippi showman toured the southern United States with what he claimed was a "220 lb turkey [*sic*]", but the bird was believed to have been an ostrich in disguise!

The heaviest weight recorded for a British turkey is 65 lb 4 oz for a stag shown at the International Poultry Show in London on 14th December 1971. It was bred by British United Turkeys at Hockenhull Hall Farm, Tarvin, Cheshire.

The longest lived domesticated bird is the Domestic goose (*Anser anser domesticus*) which normally lives about twenty-five years. Flower (1938) gives a record of one living thirty-five years, and unconfirmed ages up to eighty years have been reported (Gurney, 1899).

The Domestic pigeon (*Columba livia domestica*) and the Domestic dove (*Streptopelia risoria*) are also long lived, the average life-span being twenty years. Two specimens owned by John R. B. Masefield of Rosehill Cheadle, Staffordshire were thirty years old when they died, but Flower says the maximum age claimed for the Domestic dove is forty-two and a half years.

The Domestic fowl (*Gallus gallus*) rarely lives longer than thirteen or fourteen years, but Flower (1938) says there are reliable records of birds living twenty-two, twenty-three, twenty-four, twenty-five and even thirty years.

The turkey has a shorter life-span than the Domestic fowl, which is rather surprising considering its much greater size. Very few birds live longer than six years, although Oustalet (1899) says one specimen died in the Jardin des Plantes, Paris, on 7th December 1846 aged 12 years 4 months 19 days. Professor Lucien Cuenot (1911) gives the maximum age as sixteen years.

The Domestic duck (*Anas platyrhynchos domestica*) has a normal life-span of ten years, but ages in excess of eighteen years have been reliably recorded. A duck named "Bibbler", hatched by an adopted mother hen in 1942 at Barnham, Sussex, died in April 1965 aged twenty-three years. The mounted specimen is now preserved in Bognor Museum, Sussex (Cutten, *in litt.* 14.8.70).

The longest-lived small cagebird is the Budgerigar (*Melopsittacus undulatus*). The average life-span is six to eight years, but there are several records of birds living beyond sixteen years. In March 1971 a budgerigar owned by Mrs. Dolan of Loughton, Essex, was reportedly still alive at the age of 22 years 4 months. Another specimen named "Bluey", owned by Mrs. Dorothy Riddell of Findern, near Derby, celebrated his twenty-first birthday on 10th January 1955.

The highest authenticated rate of egg-laying by a domestic bird is 361 eggs in 364 days by a Black Orpington in an official test at Taranki, New Zealand in 1930 (Breland, *in litt.* 17.6.67).

(The artificially propagated quail has been induced to lay 365 eggs in one year in Japan.)

The U.K. record is 353 eggs in 365 days in a National Laying Test at Milford, Surrey, in 1957 by a Rhode Island red owned by W. Lawson of Welham Grange, Tetford, Nottinghamshire.

On 26th March 1967 a white leghorn laid seventeen eggs within six hours in Colombo, Ceylon.

A two-year-old hen named "Penny", owned by Clifford White, aged twelve, of Aston Clinton, Buckinghamshire, laid seven eggs in one day and twenty in a week in October 1971.

The largest egg reported is one of 16 oz with double yolk and double shell laid by a white leghorn at Vineland, New Jersey, U.S.A. on 25th February 1956. The largest in the United Kingdom was one of 8·25 oz laid by "Daisy", owned by Peter Quarton, aged eight, at Lodge Farm, Kexby Bridge, near York in March 1964. In April 1970 a bantam owned by Mrs. Beryl Bagshaw of Prees, near Whitchurch, Yorkshire, laid an egg weighing 6 oz, and in May 1971 another bantam owned by Tom Handley of Wickford, Essex laid one weighing 6·75 oz.

The smallest egg on record was one weighing only 1·29 g (0·044 oz), or 98 per cent less than the average weight (Szuman, 1926).

The Boas

SECTION III

Reptiles

(class *Reptilia*)

A reptile is a cold-blooded, air-breathing vertebrate covered with protective scales or bony plates. Unlike mammals and birds it has no effective mechanism for the regulation of body heat, and its temperature rises and falls according to the temperature of the surrounding air or water. The brain is small and poorly developed. Paired limbs, when present, are generally short and project so awkwardly from the sides of the body that the animal is compelled to crawl. Young are usually produced from eggs deposited on land, but in some species of lizard the eggs are retained within the oviduct of the mother and the young are born alive.

The earliest known reptiles were Hylonomus, Archerpeton, Protoclepsybrops and Romericus which lived about 290 million years ago. Their remains have been discovered in Nova Scotia.

There are about 5,175 living species of reptile and the class is divided into four orders. These are the Rhynchocephalia (the tuartara); the Squamata (lizards and snakes); the Crocodilia (crocodiles, alligators and gharials); and the Chelonia (turtles, tortoises and terrapins). The largest order is Squamata, which contains about 4,900 species or 94 per cent of the total number.

The estuarine crocodile is the largest living reptile.

The largest of all reptiles is the Estuarine or Salt-water crocodile (*Crocodylus porosus*), which ranges from India and Ceylon, southern China and the Malay Archipelago to northern Australia, New Guinea, the Philippines and the Solomon Islands.

Adult bulls average 12–14 ft in length and scale about 1,100 lb, but old specimens may be half as heavy again.

As with many other large animals the size attained by the estuarine crocodile has often been exaggerated. Sir Samuel Baker (1890), for instance, says those found in Ceylon were usually larger than those found on the Indian coast, and lengths of 22 ft were quite common, but this measurement has never been substantiated. According to Deraniyagala (1939) the official record (between pegs) for the whole of Ceylon is 6 m (19 ft 7 in) for a notorious man-eater shot in Eastern Provinces, and he also gives details of another one killed at Dikvalla, Southern Provinces, which measured 5·4 m (17 ft 8·5 in). In 1924 a length of 6·4 m (21 ft) was reported for a crocodile shot by game wardens at Kumana, Northern Province who said it was so huge that a man could only leap over the carcass with difficulty! This must have been a "curve" measurement, however, because the preserved skull of this specimen is only 28·54 inches in length (the head of a large crocodile accounts for one-eighth of the total length).

A 27·5 in long crocodilian skull preserved in the Raffles Museum, Singapore is said to have belonged to a 22 ft animal, but the overall length was more probably in the region of 18 ft 6 in.

In former times, before heavy persecution, this species reached a greater size than it does today because it was allowed full opportunity for uninterrupted growth, but reports of crocodiles measuring 30 ft or more in length can be discounted.

In this category can be included the much-quoted record of a 33 ft crocodile killed in the Bay of Bengal in 1840 which had a girth round the belly of 13 ft 8 in—the body was probably distended by internal gases—and weighed an estimated 3 tons. Fortunately the skull of this giant saurian was preserved and later presented to the British Museum of Natural History, London by Mr. Gilson Row (Boulenger, 1889), and its dimensions suggest that it must have come from a crocodile measuring about 24·5 ft in length which, nevertheless, is still an enormous size.

In 1895 an estuarine crocodile allegedly measuring 29 ft 6 in was shot by a Mr. Brunton on the Malabar coast, India ("Moidart", 1898), but this length was exaggerated. The preserved skull at Cochin measures 34·875 in, which means that its owner must have had a length of just over 23 ft in the flesh.

Two other records which can also be dismissed as fanciful are a 32-footer shot in the Pioneer River near Mackay, eastern Queensland, Australia before 1933, and one measuring 30 ft and weighing an "estimated 4 tons [sic]" killed in the Daintree River, northern Queensland in October 1964.

According to Ion Idriess (1946) a professional crocodile hunter named Frank Wyndham of East Kimberley, Western Australia once caught a huge crocodile in one of his traps with the intention of shipping it to Taronga Zoo, Sydney. The saurian, however, unleashed such fury that it smashed the stout planks of the trap and escaped into the Gulf of Cambridge still looped by the rope and dragging half a ton of timber with it.

"The crocodile was 26 ft 9 in long", says Idriess. "It was measured by the simple expedient of measuring the length of its tail which protruded from the trap before it got away. The trap was 20 ft long; the length of tail which protruded was 6 ft 9 in."

The greatest authentic measurement recorded for an estuarine crocodile is 27 ft for the notorious man-eater killed by Paul de la Gironière (1854) and George R. Russell with "antiquated arms" at Jala Jala near Lake Taal on the Philippine Island of Luzon in 1823 after a struggle lasting nearly an hour. This monstrous saurian measured 11 ft in girth just behind the forelimbs (the girth around the belly was considerably larger but there was some distention owing to the release of body gases) and stood over 5 ft at the shoulder. The weight of its severed head was given as 450 lb. Judging by its girth and length, this crocodile must have weighed a full 2 tons, which is very nearly the weight of an adult bull hippopotamus.

It is interesting to note that every single authority who has quoted this record since has wrongly given the length of the crocodile as 29 ft, which just goes to show that you can't do better than consult the original account!

The skull of the Jala Jala crocodile, now preserved in the Museum of Comparative Zoology at Harvard University, Cambridge, Massachusetts, U.S.A. measures 39 × 19 × 13 in, which makes it the largest

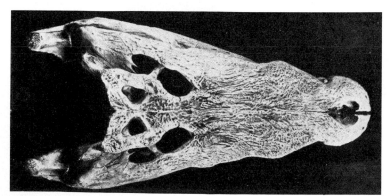

The largest crocodilian skull on record, excluding fossil remains. (Museum of Comparative Zoology, Harvard University, Cambridge, Massachusetts, U.S.A.)

crocodilian skull on record if we exclude fossil remains.

(In 1944 Dr. Karl P. Schmidt, Curator of Reptiles at Chicago Natural History Museum, Illinois, U.S.A. announced that the owner of the above-mentioned skull could not have measured more than 22·5 ft in the flesh, but he did not examine the trophy personally and based his calculation on a length of only 30 in!)

The Jala Jala skull is closely matched in size by a skull in the Indian Museum, Calcutta which measures 38 × 18 × 13·5 in and weighs 54 lb. Nothing is known of the history of this exhibit, but it must have come from an estuarine crocodile measuring at least 25 ft in length. Another huge crocodilian skull in the United Services Club, Calcutta measures 33·5 × 16 × 11·5 in (Prashad, 1931).

Dunbar Brander (1931) says he examined a crocodilian skull in the Elgin Museum, Morayshire, Scotland which measures 37 × 18·5 × 12·5 in, but the custodian (in litt. 21.5.71) informs me that they no longer have this exhibit. According to Brander the skull came from an estuarine crocodile measuring 27 ft in length and 12 ft in girth.

Major Moulton, Chief Secretary to the Government of Sarawak, told Barbour (1926) that he had a reliable Bornean record of a salt-water crocodile measuring 23 feet, and as recently as April 1966 a specimen measuring 20 ft 9 in was shot at Liaga on the south-east coast of Papua.

The largest estuarine crocodile ever held in captivity was probably a bull named "Goliath" in Frankfurt Zoological Gardens, Germany who measured 5 m (16 ft 5 in) in September 1936 (Flower, 1937).

The estuarine crocodile is normally a denizen of estuaries and coastal swamps, but it has been observed far out to sea. Gardiner (1919) says one 15-footer was captured alive at Rotuma, 260 miles north of Fiji, which means it must have crossed "at least 600 miles of open, landless sea" from the Solomon Islands.

Lengths up to 30 ft have also been claimed for the slender-snouted Gharial or Gavial (*Gavialis gangeticus*) of the Ganges, Indus, Brahmaputra and Irrawaddy Rivers of India. Lorenz Hagenbeck told Ditmars (1936) that one of his friends had shot a 30 ft gharial which looked like a stranded whale "as it bloated under the tropical sun", but this measurement must be considered excessive. The average length is 12–15 ft. A gharial measuring 21 ft 6 in was killed in the Gogra River at Fyzabad, United Provinces in August 1920 (Pitman, 1925), and this length probably represents the maximum size. Another large example measuring 16 ft 6 inches in length and 6 ft 6 inches in maximum bodily girth was shot at the mouth of the Maingtha stream about 40 miles south of the Sheweli River in July 1927 (Barton, 1929).

The average length of the Orinoco crocodile (*Crocodylus intermedius*) is 10–12 ft, but Bates states that "it grows to a length of eighteen or twenty feet and attains an enormous bulk". A huge specimen shot by Alexander von Humboldt in 1800 while he was exploring the course of the Orinoco measured 22 ft 4 in, but this was exceptional.

The American crocodile (*Crocodylus acutus*) of the southern United States, Central America, the West Indies and northern South America is about the same size as *C. intermedius* (i.e. 10–12 ft), but one outsized individual killed in Venezuela measured 23 ft.

F. A. Mitchell Hedges (1923), the English big-game fisherman and explorer, claims he shot five American crocodiles measuring from 18 ft 6 in to 23 ft in a single day's shoot on the Bayano River, Panama, in 1921, but photographic evidence suggests that their lengths were nearer 15 ft.

Although the American alligator (*Alligator mississipiensis*) of the south-eastern United States has an average length of only 8–10 ft, E. H. McIlnenny (1934) shot two 18-footers and one measuring 19 ft 2 inches in Louisiana.

The maximum length attained by the Nile crocodile (*Crocodylus niloticus*) of Africa and Madagascar is a matter of some dispute. Ditmars (1922), Schmidt (1944) and Pope (1957) all state that this species (average length 11–12 ft) never exceeds 16 ft, but Cott (1960) lists several reliable records from Central and southern Africa of crocodiles measuring between 16 and 19 ft. They include a 16 ft 7 in specimen shot by L. E. Vaughan, a senior game warden, in Northern Rhodesia; one measuring just over 17 ft 5 in shot by W. Hubbard in the Kafue River, also in Northern Rhodesia; an 18 ft 2 in example killed by a game ranger on the Semliki River, Uganda in 1950; a female measuring 18 ft 4 in shot on the same river in June 1954; and one measuring 18 ft 10 in shot by C. C. Yiannakis near Chipoko, Nyasaland (now Malawi).

Another crocodile shot by a professional hunter named Erich Nowotny near Nungwe, Lake Victoria, east Central Africa in 1948 measured exactly 21 ft, and Cott says Douglas Jones killed one in the Juba River, Somaliland which was just over 21 ft long and weighed about 1 ton.

In March 1903 a length of 25 ft was claimed by a German hunter named Hans Besser for a crocodile he had shot in Uganda which had lost a quarter of its tail. He said this monster had a girth of 14 ft and a skull measuring 4 ft 7 inches in length and 37 inches in width [*sic*] (Grzimek, 1970). These figures, however, must be dismissed as fanciful because the owner of a skull of these dimensions would have to measure nearly 40 ft in length in order to be proportional!

Another record that can also be discounted is that of a 27-footer reportedly killed in Lake Kyoga, Uganda in the 1920s.

According to Foran (1958) the largest of the 1,406 crocodiles killed by the commercial hunters Glover and Van Bart on the Kafue River, Northern Rhodesia in 1950–51 measured 17 ft 8 in but the average length was only 9 ft 6 in. Other reliable records over 17 ft given by the same writer include a 19 ft crocodile killed in the Kunene River, South-West Africa, and one measuring 17 ft 3 in shot by a policeman at Bentiu, in the Sudan, in September 1947. He also says a crocodile measuring 23 ft in length was shot on the Zambesi River near Test in Portuguese East Africa, but further details are lacking.

In 1953 a crocodile measuring 19 ft 9 in was shot on the Semliki River, Uganda (Clarke, 1969).

As recently as November 1968 a crocodile measuring 19 ft 3 in was shot in the Okavango Swamp, Botswana. The weight of this saurian was estimated at 1·5 tons (probably nearer 1 ton), and in its stomach were found the remains of a zebra, a donkey, two goats and an African woman who had been missing for seventeen days.

The largest accurately measured Nile crocodile on record was probably one shot by the Duke of Mecklenberg in 1905 near Mwanza, Tanganyike (now part of Tanzania) which, according to Hubbard (1927) measured 6·5 m (21 ft 4 in).

The Madagascar crocodile (*Crocodylus robustus*), now believed to be extinct, was credited with lengths up to 30 ft (in 1802 the French naturalist Pierre Denys de Montfort said he had trustworthy accounts of individuals measuring up to 60 ft!), but judging from the size of sub-fossil skulls (i.e. 27–30 in long) the maximum length of this species must have been about 20 ft.

At least six of the twenty-five recognised species of crocodilian will attack and eat man if given the opportunity, and several of the others are large enough to inflict serious injury or even death.

The most notorious man-eater of them all is undoubtedly the estuarine crocodile. Although no figures are available it probably kills well over 2,000 people annually.

The most horrifying example of this reptile's penchant for human flesh—in fact the greatest mass attack on man by any large animal on record—occurred on the night of 19th–20th February 1945 on Ramree Island in the Bay of Bengal. British troops had trapped more than 1,000 Japanese infantrymen in a coastal mangrove swamp, and the noise of the battle and the smell of blood had attracted hundreds of estuarine crocodiles from miles around to the area.

Shortly after nightfall the crocodiles moved in *en masse*, attacking the dead, wounded and healthy alike, and the terrible screams of the dying men were heard by the British troops waiting just outside the swamp throughout the night. When they moved in the following morning only twenty survivors were found (Wright, 1962; Caras, 1964).

The Nile crocodile also has a very bad reputation and probably kills nearly 1,000 people (mostly women and children) annually, although at one time the figure may have been as high as 20,000. One 15 ft 3 in crocodile shot in the Kihange River, Central Africa reportedly killed 400 people over the years (Clarke, 1969).

The strength of the crocodile is quite appalling. According to Deraniyagala (1939) a crocodile in northern Australia once seized and dragged into a river a magnificent 1-ton Suffolk dray horse which had recently been imported from England, despite the fact that this breed can exert a pull of more than 2 tons. Captain F. C. Selous (1908) once saw a full-grown black rhinoceros lose a tug-of-war with a crocodile in the Tana River, Kenya, and C. S. Stokes (1953) says there is an authentic record of a crocodile accounting for *three lions* drinking close together with a single sweep of its tail; the first lion crashing into the second from the force, and the second into the third until "the three, their balance lost, fell into the river, which seemed suddenly to become alive with great jaws".

Frank Lane (1955) says that tests carried out in France to determine the jaw strength of a 120 lb crocodile revealed that this animal could exert a force of 1,540 lb. On this basis, a crocodile weighing 1 ton could exert a force of nearly 13 tons!

Sometimes, however, even crocodiles over-estimate their own strength. One day in the 1860s a hunter named Lesley was a witness when a saurian seized the hind-leg of a large bull African elephant while it was bathing in a river in Natal. The crocodile was promptly dragged up the bank by the enraged tusker and then squashed flat by one of his companions who had hurried to the rescue. The victorious elephant then picked up the carcass with its trunk and lodged it in the fork of a near-by tree (Stokes, 1953). Oswell (1894) says he twice found the skeletons of crocodiles 15 ft up in trees by the river's bank where they had been thrown by angry elephants. Another elephant seized by the trunk near Murchison Falls, Uganda yanked the crocodile clean out of the river (albeit a painful operation) and then trampled it to death (Hallett, 1967).

Crocodilians have considerable diving endurance, and large specimens often remain submerged for over an hour when they are frightened. Reports of crocodiles remaining submerged for seven hours or more at a time, however, must be discounted.

Although the maximum life-span of the crocodilians has not yet been established, it is probable that some species live longer than fifty years in the wild. On the basis of its comparatively slow growth rate Cott believes that very large Nile crocodiles (i.e. 18 ft or over) must be at least 100 years, and that the largest recorded specimens may be as much as 200 years, but further research is needed in this field before any definite statements can be made. It can be stated, however, that very large crocodiles are very old because they continue to grow as long as they live.

The greatest authentic age recorded for a crocodilian is fifty-six years for an American alligator received at Dresden Zoological Gardens, Germany in 1880 and still alive in September 1936 (Flower, 1927).

Another specimen known as "Jean-qui-rit" (Laughing John), allegedly received at the Jardin des Plantes, Paris in 1852, was still alive on 2nd October 1936, but Flower doubts the validity of this record. The same authority also quotes a reliable record of fifty years for a Chinese alligator (*Alligator sinensis*) which was still living in Frankfurt Zoological Gardens on 8th September 1936, and Lederer (1941) says another one lived in Leipzig Zoological Gardens, Germany for fifty-two years.

The rarest crocodilian in the world is believed to be the Cuban crocodile (*Crocodylus rhombifer*) which, through over-hunting for its skin, is now confined to the tiny Zapata Swamp in Las Villas province, central Cuba. In 1965 there were only 500 of these animals left, and the area has since been declared a sanctuary (Fisher *et al.*, 1969).

The largest reptile (excluding snakes) found in Britain is the Slow worm (*Anguis fragilis*). A female collected in Midhurst, Sussex measured 460 mm (18·11 in) in length (Smith, 1951).

The smallest species of reptile is believed to be *Sphaerodactylus parthenopiom*, a tiny gecko found only on the island of Virgin Gorda, one of the British Virgin Islands, in the West Indies. It is known from only fifteen specimens, including some gravid females, found between 10th and 16th August 1964. The three largest females measured 18 mm (0·71 in) from snout to vent, with a tail of approximately the same length (Thomas, 1965).

Another Gecko (*S. elasmorhynchus*), may be even smaller. The type specimen, an apparently mature female with a snout–vent length of 17 mm (0·67 in) and a tail the same measurement was found among the roots of a tree in the western part of the Massif de la Hotte in Haiti on 15th March 1966 (Thomas, 1966).

A species of Dwarf chameleon (*Evoluticauda tuberculata*), found in Madagascar and known only from the type specimen, has a snout–vent length of 18 mm (0·71 in) and a tail length of 14 mm (0·55 in) (Angel, 1942), but this minute chameleon may have been only half grown.

The best criterion for determining the smallest reptile is *weight*, but none of the species already mentioned were weighed (the maximum volume for *S. parthenopion* has been estimated at no more than 0·3 cm³). Chameleons, however, are bulkier animals than geckos.

The smallest reptile found in Britain is the Viviparous or Common lizard (*Lacerta vivipara*). Adult specimens have an overall length of 108–178 mm (4·25–7 in).

The highest speed ever recorded for a reptile on land is 18 mile/h for a Six-lined racerunner (*Cnemidophorus sexlineatus*) pursued by J. Southgate Hoyt (1941) in a car

The six-lined racerunner lizard, which has been timed at 18 mile/h on land. (Mrs. D. Dwight Davis.)

near McCormick, South Carolina, U.S.A. This lizard maintained its speed on all four legs for more than a minute before darting off the clay road into the undergrowth. The Desert iguana (*Dipsosaurus dorsalis*) and the Gridiron-tailed lizard (*Callisaurus draconoides*), also of the United States, are probably equally as swift (Belkin, 1961), and the Komodo monitor (see below) may be even faster.

The largest of all lizards is the Komodo monitor or Ora (*Varanus komodoensis*), a dragonlike reptile found on the Indonesian islands of Komodo, Rintja, Padar and Flores.

Adult males average 8 ft in total length and weigh 175–200 lb, and adult females 7 ft 6 in and 150–160 lb.

Like crocodiles, the size attained by this lizard has often been exaggerated in the past.

Major P. A. Ouwens, the Curator of the Botanical Gardens at Buitenzorg, Java who first described this lizard in 1912, was informed by J. K. van Steyn van Hensbroek, Governor of Flores, that a "boeaya-darat" (land crocodile) measuring 4 m (13 ft 1·5 in) in length and weighing over 182 kg (400 lb) had been shot by a policeman on near-by Komodo, and the Governor also said that two Dutchmen working for a pearl-fishing company on the same island had told him that they had killed several specimens measuring between 6 and 7 m (between 19 ft 8 in and 23 ft). Another "dragon" seen by a Swedish zoologist on the shores of Komodo in 1937 was estimated by him to have "measured 23 feet [*sic*]", and the following year an American journalist reported that he had seen one measuring 14·5 ft.

All of these statements, however, were based on estimates or referred to estuarine crocodiles.

According to Ouwens the type specimen, now mounted in the museum at Buitenzorg, measured 2·9 m (9 ft 6·17 in) between pegs. Another specimen collected by De Rooij (1915) on the west coast of

Flores in 1915 measured 2·66 m (8 ft 8·75 in) in length, and the largest of the four monitors collected by the Duke of Mecklenburg on Komodo in 1923 was just under 3 m (9 ft 10 in). Of the fifty-four specimens collected by the Douglas Burden Expedition to Komodo in 1926, the largest measured 2·76 m (9 ft 0·5 in), and the largest collected by the Dutch zoologist De Jong (1937) on his second visit to the island measured exactly 9 ft. David Attenborough (1957) says he saw a "dragon" on Komodo which he estimated was "a full twelve feet", but in the light of the scientific measurements already quoted this length must be considered excessive.

The largest accurately measured Komodo monitor on record was probably the male which was put on exhibition in the St. Louis Zoological Gardens, Missouri, U.S.A. for a short period in c. 1937. This specimen measured 10 ft 2 inches in length and weighed 365 lb. (Breland, in litt. 26.4.66). Nothing is known of this lizard's earlier history, but it may have been the same animal as one that was presented to an American zoologist by the Sultan of Bima in 1928 which measured 3·05 m (10 ft 0·8 in).

According to Wendt (1956) two monitors over 11 ft long were collected by Dutch and German expeditions to Komodo before 1927 and presented to European zoos, but these lengths were exaggerated. Flower (1937) says a specimen received at the Berlin Zoological Gardens on 11th June 1927 measured 2·41 m (7 ft 11 in).

A male Komodo monitor named "Sumbawa" received at London Zoological Gardens on 6th June 1927, along with another male named "Sumba", measured 9 ft in length at the time of his death on 29th January 1934. During his life at the zoo this particular monitor struck up a friendship with an invalid woman named Miss Proctor who was a regular visitor to the gardens, and he often used to follow her round in her wheelchair.

A pair of young Komodo monitors presented to Kebun Binatang Jogjakarta in 1959–60 from Kebun Binatang Surabaja, Indonesia, each measured about 1 m (39·37 in) in length. In April 1966 the male measured 2·75 m (9 ft 0·3 in) and the female 2·50 m (8 ft 2·5 in) (Osman, 1967).

Another pair of Komodo monitors collected on Komodo Island and received at Taronga Zoological Gardens, Sydney, New South Wales in February 1963, measured 8 ft 4 in (male) and 7 ft 6 in (female) respectively in January 1966. Their weights were given as 200 lb and 160 lb.

In March 1964 the Indonesian Government presented a pair of adult Komodo monitors to the National Zoological Park, Washington, D.C., U.S.A. The male measured 9 ft in length and weighed 200 lb, and the female 6 ft and 125 lb. The male died twenty-nine days later from amoebiasis (Gray et al., 1966).

Young Komodo monitors (i.e. under 4 ft in length) are extremely fast-moving animals and can outrun a speedy dog over a level distance of 200–300 yd. But adult specimens are not nearly so active.

In the mid-1950s the total population of the Komodo monitor was estimated at 2,000 individuals, and the figure is about the same today. The species is strictly protected by the Indonesian Government and it cannot be killed for museums or exported alive for zoos. In 1965 there were only seven specimens in zoos outside Indonesia (Fisher et al., 1969).

The Komodo monitor's closest rival for size among the lizards is the slim-bodied Two-banded or water monitor (*Varanus salvator*) of Malaya which has been measured up to 9 ft. The Perenty (*V. giganteus*) of northern and central Australia and the Nile monitor (*V. niloticus*) of Africa both have a maximum length of 8 ft.

The greatest authentic age recorded for a lizard is "more than 54 years" for a male Slow worm (*Anguis fragilis*) kept in the Zoological Museum in Copenhagen, Denmark from 1892 until 1946 (Curry-Lindahl, *in litt.* 14.11.67). At the age of forty-five-plus this specimen mated with a female known to be at least twenty years old (Smith, 1951).

No other species of lizard lives anywhere near as long. The closest approach is probably made by the Komodo monitor which lives twenty to thirty years in the wild, but the greatest authentic age recorded for a specimen in captivity is 9 years 3 months (Flower, 1937). The Gila monster (*Heloderma suspectrum*) has lived for twenty years in captivity (Conant & Hudson, 1949).

The largest of all chelonians is the Pacific leatherback turtle (*Dermochelys coriacea schlegelii*), also known as the "Leathery turtle" or "Luth". The average adult measures 6–7 ft in overall length (length of carapace 4–5 ft), about 7 ft across the front flippers and weighs between 660 and 800 lb.

In 1923 an 8 ft 7 in long leatherback turtle weighing 1,286 lb was captured off the coast of California, U.S.A. (Pope, 1934), and a straggler weighing 1,450 lb was killed near Bojo Reef in Nootka Sound, Vancouver Island, British Columbia, Canada in August 1931 (MacAskie & Forrester, 1962).

There is also a record of a Pacific leatherback turtle measuring 7 ft 8 inches in overall length and weighing 1,575 lb (Carr, 1952).

The Pacific leatherback turtle, the largest of all chelonians. (J. C. Harris— F. Lane.)

The greatest authentic weight recorded for a Pacific leatherback turtle is 1,908 lb for a specimen captured off Monterey, California, U.S.A. in 1961, which is now on permanent display at the Wharf Aquarium, Fishermans Wharf, Monterey.

Another huge turtle measuring 9 ft in overall length and weighing 1,902·5 lb was caught in a fisherman's net near San Diego, California, U.S.A. on 20th June 1907.

In January 1951 a female leatherback turtle allegedly weighing a ton (2,240 lb) was caught in a fisherman's net at Bermagui, near Sydney, New South Wales, Australia and sent to the Australian Museum for preservation, but this weight was exaggerated.

In a letter to the author dated 5th March 1968 J. R. Kinghorn, former Assistant Director of the Museum, wrote: "The truck on which the turtle was transported weighed so much, as registered, and with the Luth weighed nearly a ton more. However, there was some other gear on board when it reached the museum, and that included some heavy timber struts, some steel bars, and other small items, all weighing about two or three hundred pounds I should guess. It measured a little over eight feet from head to tip of tail, and about seven feet across the flippers. . . . The luth was sawn open and all the innards, including many eggs, removed. . . . If I remember, the weight of the preserved specimen was about fifteen hundred pounds."

The Atlantic leatherback turtle (*Dermochelys coriacea coriacea*) rarely exceeds 800 lb, although much larger specimens have been reported. One turtle captured at Stonington, Connecticut, U.S.A. in July 1875 was 7 ft long and weighed about 1,000 lb, and Babcock (1919) says three other leatherbacks taken in Long Island Sound about the same time also scaled "about 1,000 pounds". In 1891 a turtle weighing 1,400 lb was caught in a fish trap in Buzzards Bay, near Woods Hole, Massachusetts, U.S.A. Another huge leatherback caught by the fishing schooner *Fannie Belle* off Sequin, near Portland, Maine, U.S.A. on 20th or 25th September 1919 and stated to have measured nearly 7 ft in length and 12 ft across the flippers, allegedly tipped the scales at 1,600 lb, but these figures are not compatible.

Louis Agassiz (1857) says he saw specimens weighing more than a ton (U.S. short ton of 2,000 lb), but he was probably being over-generous in his estimate.

In 1960 an unconfirmed weight of 2,000 lb was reported for a straggler captured near Westport, Connecticut, U.S.A.

On 8th May 1958 an Atlantic leatherback turtle measuring more than 7 ft long and weighing 997 lb was caught by a French fishing trawler in the English Channel. Another one described as weighing "nearly a ton" was netted off the Isles of Scilly on 18th June 1916, and a specimen reportedly weighing 1,345 lb was caught by a fishing vessel in the North Sea on 6th October 1951.

The adult Loggerhead turtle (*Caretta caretta*) of tropical and subtropical seas averages about 200–250 lb, but much heavier individuals have been captured. True (quoted by Pope 1934) describes one taken in 1871 that had a front flipper span of 9 ft and weighed 850 lb. Pritchard (1967) says there is a huge skull in the Bell Collection at Cambridge University which must have belonged to a loggerhead turtle weighing about 1,200 lb.

The largest freshwater turtle in the world is the Alligator snapping turtle (*Macrochelys temminckii*) of the south-eastern United States. The normal upper weight limit for this species is about 200 lb, but one monster caught in the Neosho River in Cherokee County, Kansas in 1937 scaled 403 lb (Hall & Smith, 1947).

The smallest freshwater turtles in the world are the Mud and Musk turtles (family Kinosternidae) of North and Central America. The Striped mud turtle (*Kinosternida baurii baurii*), which is confined to Key West and a few offshore islands in Florida has a maximum carapace length of only 3·82 in (Oliver, 1955).

Several species of turtle are renowned for their aggressive nature. Probably the most vicious of them all is the loggerhead turtle, which is known as the "Nai amai" or "dog turtle" in Ceylon because it bites savagely when caught (Deraniyagala, 1939).

On 3rd September 1905 the *New York Herald* published an exciting account of a battle between a small party of fishermen and an angry loggerhead in Long Island Sound. The 610 lb turtle had earlier been captured, but it had escaped from its pen at South Norwalk Market and headed for the harbour. A reward of $50 was offered for its recapture, and five local fishermen set out after the turtle in a rowing boat. The party eventually found it asleep on the surface, and one of the men tried to harpoon it. The turtle promptly attacked the boat and tried to overturn it with its flippers. The crew beat it desperately over the head with their oars, but the angry chelonian crunched through them as though they were toothpicks and then tore a long gash in the arm of one of its assailants with a blow from a flipper.

After an hour-long fight the turtle disappeared, apparently none the worse for its encounter, leaving behind a waterlogged boat and an injured man, who by now had lapsed into unconsciousness. It took the other four fishermen another two hours to paddle back to shore using the remnants of their oars, and they all swore they would never try to capture another loggerhead again, reward or no reward.

The alligator snapping turtle also has an evil temper and is well named. Raymond L. Ditmars (1936), Curator of Reptiles at the Bronx Zoo, New York complained that he could never take a photograph of this species without being confronted by a pair of wide-open jaws, and on one occasion an angry specimen bit a leg off his tripod.

The greatest authentic age recorded for a turtle is fifty-seven years for an alligator snapping turtle in Philadelphia Zoological Gardens, Pennsylvania, U.S.A. which was still alive in 1948. Another specimen at the same zoo was forty-seven (Conant & Hudson, 1949).

A small group of Atlantic loggerheads lived in the Vasco de Gama Aquarium at Lisbon, Portugal from 1898 to 1931. Flower (1937) says they all died suddenly during a heat-wave.

The leatherback turtles probably live up to fifty years in the wild state, but no large specimens have survived more than a few weeks in captivity.

A Hawksbill turtle (*Eretmochelys imbricata*) ringed by a Dutch officer in 1794 was found on the same Atlantic beach thirty years later.

The fastest swimming tetrapod (four-legged animal) is probably the Pacific leatherback turtle which has been timed at 22 mile/h. Frank Lane (1955) says a speed of 22 mile/h has also been reported for the Green turtle (*Chelonia mydas*).

The largest living tortoise is *Geochelone gigantea*, which is found only on Aldabra Island in the Indian Ocean. Adult males regularly exceed 500 lb in weight, and a specimen weighing 900 lb was collected in 1847.

A large male preserved in the Rothschild Museum at Tring, Hertfordshire has a carapace measuring 46·5 inches in length, and Lord Rothschild (1915) says this animal weighed 593 lb when alive.

The Elephant tortoise (*G. elephantopus*) of Indefatigable Island in the Galapagos group, 600 miles west of Ecuador, is another exceptionally large tortoise. One example with a 4 ft long carapace tipped the scales at 500 lb, and another one collected in 1830 required six men to lift it into a boat. There is also a record of a giant tortoise collected on nearby Porter's Island which had a carapace measuring 5 ft 6 inches in length and 4 ft 6 inches in width (Noel-Hume and Noel-Hume, 1954).

Although tortoises are the longest lived of all vertebrates, including man, claims that they sometimes survive for 200 or even 300 years can be discounted. Many exaggerated estimates have been based on the mistaken beliefs that (1) tortoises have a very slow rate of growth, and (2) scarred

A giant tortoise from Aldabra Island with a smaller relative. ("Planet News".)

The royal Tongan tortoise "Tu'imalilia", which reputedly lived for nearly 200 years. (Rob Wright.)

and rubbed shells are reliable evidence of great age.

On 19th May 1966 the death was reported of "Tu'imalilia" or "Tui Malela" (King of the Malilia), the famous but much battered Madagascar radiated tortoise (*Testudo radiata*) reputedly presented to the King of Tonga by Captain James Cook (1728–79) in 1773, but this record lacks proper documentation. In May 1923 the tortoise was examined by Captain E. T. Pollock, Governor of American Samoa, who later told the U.S. Navy Department that the creature was blind and showed signs of extreme age (Flower, 1937).

Another tortoise presented to Queen Victoria in 1850 by a family living at the Cape of Good Hope was stated to have been 179 years old (Dumeril, 1861), but this figure was largely based on hearsay.

In September 1969 "Samir", the oldest giant tortoise at the Giza Zoological Garden, Cairo, Egypt allegedly celebrated his 269th birthday [*sic*], but this information is largely based on hearsay. According to the story the tortoise, born in France, was presented to the Khedive, Isma'il Pasha, Turkish ruler of Egypt, by Eugenie Bonapart, wife of Napoleon III, on the occasion of the inauguration of the Suez Canal on the 16th November 1869. Shortly afterwards the Khedive presented the tortoise, which in Egypt is considered a symbol of good luck, to Giza Zoological Garden. Thus up to 1969, the animal had been continuously observed for *only* 100 years.

"Samir", the oldest tortoise at the Cairo Zoo, who allegedly celebrated his 269th birthday in 1969. (Associated Press.)

The greatest authentic age recorded for a tortoise is 152-plus years for a male Marion's tortoise (*T. sumeirii*) brought from the Seychelles to Mauritius in 1766 by the Chevalier de Fresne, who presented it to the Port Louis army garrison. This specimen (it went blind in 1808) was accidentally killed in 1918 (Boulenger, 1909; Flower, 1925, 1937).

Other reliable records over 100 years include a Common box tortoise (*T. carolina*) of 138 years (Oliver, 1955) and a European pond-tortoise (*Emys orbicularis*) of 120-plus years (Rollinant, 1934).

A Mediterranean spur-thighed tortoise (*T. graeca*) died at Lambeth Palace, London in 1730 or 1753 aged 102 or 125 years (Flower, 1937).

The greatest proven age of a continuously observed tortoise is 116-plus years for a Mediterranean spur-thighed tortoise which died in Paignton Zoo, Devonshire in 1957.

Extreme longevity data based on dates carved in the shells of tortoises are not generally considered reliable because they may have been put there by practical jokers, but one or two records may be genuine. According to Ditmars (1934) an ancient female common box tortoise found in Connecticut, U.S.A. in June 1927 was marked with the date 1809, but the carapace was so smooth that the figures could only be read with difficulty.

With the possible exception of chameleons (family Chamaeleonidae) tortoises move slower than any other reptile. Tests carried out on a giant tortoise (*Geochelone gigantea*) in Mauritius revealed that even when hungry and enticed by a cabbage it could not cover more than 5 yd in a minute (0·17 mile/h). Over longer distances its speed was greatly reduced.

The Desert tortoise (*Goperhus agassizi*) of the western United States is not much faster. One specimen tested in Utah walked at a rate of 0·13 to 0·30 mile/h.

Freshwater turtles usually move faster on land than tortoises, but there is a record of two Common snapping turtles (*Chelydra s. serpentina*) covering a distance of 1,830 ft in two and a half hours, which means they were walking at a rate of 0·138 mile/h (Klimstra, quoted by Oliver, 1955).

The rarest tortoise in the world is probably the Short-necked tortoise (*Pseudemydura umbrina*), which is found only in a small swamp area at Bullsbrook, some 20 miles north-east of Perth, Western Australia. In 1967 the total population was estimated at 200–300 animals. It is now strictly protected, and a small group are being studied at Perth Zoological Gardens (Fisher *et al.*, 1969).

The anaconda, the longest and heaviest of all snakes.

The longest (and the heaviest) of all snakes is the Anaconda (*Eunectes murinus*), also called the "Water boa", of tropical South America.

This snake has probably been the subject of more exaggerated claims concerning its size than any other living animal. The early Spanish settlers called it "matatora" (bull-killer) and spoke of individuals measuring 60–80 ft, but even larger specimens have been reported. In 1948, for instance, a "sucuriju gigante" (giant boa) measuring 115 ft in length was allegedly killed by army machine-gun fire at Fort Abunda, in the Guapore District, south-western Brazil (Heuvelmans, 1958), and six years later a measurement of 120 ft was reported for another snake killed by a Brazilian Army patrol at Amapa on the French Guiana border (Gregory, 1962). Needless to say, nothing was preserved of either of these two outsized carcasses!

Fortunately some of the early explorers and naturalists who visited South America were more critical in their accounts of this giant snake. Captain J. G. Stedman (1813), for example, who travelled extensively in the Guianas between 1772 and 1777, says the largest anaconda killed by him measured just over 22 ft in length; while Alfred Wallace (1876), who explored large parts of Amazonia, wrote that he never saw an anaconda measuring more than 20 ft, although he was told by his native bearers that they were sometimes 60 to 80 ft long.

Professor A. Hyatt Verrill (1937), another man very familiar with the fauna of South America, was firmly of the opinion that the anaconda never exceeded 20 ft and believed that the exaggerated lengths claimed for this snake by explorers and Indians alike was due entirely to the inability of the human eye to judge the length of a moving and writhing creature accurately.

To prove his point, Verrill once asked the other members of an animal-collecting expedition he was leading in Guiana to estimate the length of an anaconda they had spotted curled up on a rock:

"The camera man, who had never before been in the jungle, said sixty feet. The missionary who had spent seven years in the interior and had seen scores of big snakes was more conservative and said thirty feet. The Indians' estimates varied from twenty to forty feet; my camp boy, who had accompanied a party of snake collectors a few years earlier, said thirty feet, while the grizzled old 'captain' remarked, 'Takin' all de fac's of da case in consi'ation, I don't can state posritively, chief, but Ah knows for de truf tha' camudi (anaconda) is jus' too long.'

"A twenty-two rifle bullet through the head brought an end to the big anaconda's career and when he was straightened out and measured he proved to be exactly nineteen feet and six inches in length. But what a monster! About his middle he measured thirty-three inches and a fraction and he weighed over 360 pounds[?] and was a heavy load for five Indians. So huge were his proportions that even after we had measured the creature it was difficult to believe that he was so 'small'."

Other extreme measurements have been based on the length of skins, but these records are unreliable. According to Oliver (1958) it is impossible to remove the skin of a snake without stretching it, and in the case of the anaconda and other heavy snakes he says the *unintentional* stretching may add as much as 25 per cent to the original length. Mole (1924), for instance, killed a 17 ft 3 in anaconda in Trinidad which yielded a 19 ft 6 in skin, and Verrill says the skin of an 18-footer measured 23 ft. An unscrupulous trader could stretch a skin even more.

The American Consul at Iquitos, Peru told Leonard Clark, the American explorer that many of the anaconda skins brought to the city by skins traders each year measured 40 ft, and Thomas Barbour, the American naturalist, says he once saw a 45 ft skin (Perry, 1970). Victor Norwood (1954), the English adventurer, goes even further and states that the skin of a 60 ft monster killed by an American naturalist near the head-waters of the Essequibo River, British Guiana in 1936 is "now in the custody of a New York museum", but the American Museum of Natural History (presumably the museum referred to) does not possess an anaconda skin even half that length. The Butantan Institute at São Paulo, Brazil has a skin measuring 10 m (32 ft 9½ in) which has not been over-stretched (i.e. the markings are not distorted), and Dr. Bernard Heuvelmans says its owner must have been "at least 26 feet long". The skin of another anaconda measuring 36 ft collected on the Berbice River, British Guiana is reported to be preserved in "the museum" at The Hague in the Netherlands (Clark, 1926), but the author has not been able to confirm this claim.

Raymond L. Ditmars, Curator of Reptiles at Bronx Zoo, New York personally offered $1,000 to anyone who could supply him with an anaconda's skin measuring over 40 ft in length, but the money was never claimed (the largest skin submitted to him measured 21 ft 4 in). Ex-President Theodore Roosevelt (through the New York Zoological Society) made it even more sporting and offered $5,000 for the skin or vertebral column of an anaconda measuring more than 30 ft, but even this noble sum has never been collected.

It is now generally agreed by herpetologists that the average adult length of an anaconda lies somewhere between 17 and 20 ft, and that measurements over 25 ft are exceptional. Some say it never exceeds 30 ft, but there are exceptions and Pope (1961) has suggested that unusually large individuals might belong to a sub-species with a limited range.

The largest accurately measured anaconda on record was probably the 37·5 ft example shot by Roberto Lamon, a petroleum geologist working for the Richmond Oil Company, and other members of his team while they were exploring for oil on the Upper Orinoco River, eastern Colombia in 1944. When the huge snake stopped writhing the men dragged the 1,000 lb carcass out of the water on to the bank and measured it with a steel surveyor's tape. Later, however, when they went back to skin the animal they found to their astonishment that it had disappeared. Apparently the snake had only been stunned by the bullets from their ·45-calibre automatics (Dunn, 1944).

Fred Medem, herpetologist at the National University of Colombia, told Dr. James Oliver (1958) that another anaconda measuring 10·25 m (33 ft 7·5 in) was killed on the Lower Rio Guaviare in south-eastern Colombia in November 1956, but he did not see the snake personally and he said nothing of it was preserved.

Dr. Afranio do Amaral, Director of the Butantan Institute in São Paulo and a distinguished herpetologist, who reviewed many of the reports of giant anacondas in his paper "Serpentes Gigantes" (1948) accepted a Brazilian record of an 11·28 m (37 ft) specimen, and he said another snake killed in the Matto Grosso in c. 1913 measured just over 38 ft. After a thorough examination of the evidence he came to the conclusion that the maximum length attained by the anaconda was somewhere between 12 and 14 m (between 39 ft 4·5 in and 45 ft 11 in).

Algot Lange (1914) claims he shot a 56 ft anaconda on the Javari River, north-eastern Peru in 1910 which yielded a 54 ft 8 in skin when dried. The skin was reportedly crated and shipped to New York, but it apparently disappeared *en route*!

The colossal snake shot by Colonel P. H. Fawcett (1963) on the Rio Abunda not far from the confluence of the Rio Negro, western Brazil in 1907, was stated by him to have measured 62 ft (45 ft out of the water and 17 ft in it), but as this anaconda had a maximum diameter of only 12 in (=circumference of 37·7 in) this length must be considered excessive (a 24-footer shot by Paul Fountain in Brazil had a maximum bodily girth of 42 in).

Because anacondas are more difficult to keep in captivity than other constrictors, very few large specimens have been exhibited in zoos. On 8th July 1892 an anaconda measuring 18 ft 0·5 inch in length died in the Jardin des Plantes, Paris (Flower, 1925). Ditmars (1931) says the largest specimen ever held in the Bronx Zoo, New York was a 19 ft female which had a girth of 36 in and weighed 236 lb shortly before giving birth to seventy-two young. On 10th July 1960 a length of 20 ft 7 in was reported for an anaconda in Highland Park Zoological Gardens, Pittsburg, Pennsylvania, U.S.A. (Barton & Allen, 1961). Another specimen in Rio de Janeiro Zoological Gardens, Brazil measures 8 m (26 ft 3 in).

The anaconda's closest rival for size is the Reticulated python (*Python reticulatus*) of South-East Asia, Indonesia and the Philippines, which has also been credited with some astonishing measurements.

Lengths up to 50 ft have been reported, and Daniell (quoted by Gosse, 1861) speaks of one enormous snake killed by a small group of fishermen on the bank of the Ganges River which measured "sixty-two feet and some inches in length".

One of the largest pythons on record was killed in Penang, Malaya in October 1859:

"A monster boa-constrictor was killed one morning this week by the overseer of convicts at Bayam Lepas, on the road to Telo' Kumbar. His attention was attracted by the squealing of a pig, and on going to the place he found it in the coils of the snake. A few blows from the changkolf of the convicts served to despatch the reptile, and, on uncoiling him, he was found to be twenty-eight feet in length, and thirty-two inches in girth" (*The Times*, 1st November 1859).

Another python shot near Taiping, Perak, Malaya measured 27 ft in length and yielded a 33 ft skin which is now preserved in the British Museum of Natural History, London, and Oliver (1957) says a snake reputedly measuring 30 ft was killed near Penang in 1844. There is also an unconfirmed record of a 33 ft python from Java.

The greatest authentic length recorded for a reticulated python is exactly 10 m (32 ft 9·5 in) for a monster shot near a mining camp on the north coast of Celebes Island, in the Malay Archipelago, in 1912. An account of this killing was given by Henry C. Raven (1946), the American explorer and animal collector:

"I crossed the Strait of Macassar in my little schooner and sailed along the north coast of Celebes. Stopping near a mining camp at a place where there was a good harbour, I left the schooner and went inland a short distance to camp on the mountains, which were covered with virgin jungle.

"The white men at the mine told me of a huge python one of their natives had killed a few days before my arrival, and showed me a very poor photograph of it after it had been killed and dragged to camp. Though the print was dull, you could see a man standing on the huge body, which was about a foot thick. The civil engineer told me it was just ten metres . . . I asked him if he had paced off its length, but he said, no, he had measured it with a surveying tape. No part of the animal was preserved. It had been rainy weather when it was killed, and on account of the dampness not even the skin was kept. I visited the place where the carcase had been cast aside. There was only the odour, and a few little pieces of bone left."

On 31st August 1799 the *Bombay Courier* carried a story of a Malay sailor who had been "crushed to death" ·by a python on the same island. His companions, hearing his screams, went to his assistance, but they arrived too late to save the poor man. They did, however, succeed in killing the snake. The length of this monster was given as 30 ft, and its girth "that of a moderate-sized man".

Unlike anacondas, several large reticulated pythons have been kept in captivity. In 1904 a 28 ft specimen weighing 250 lb was received at Carl Hagenbeck's Tierpark, Hamburg, Germany. Another one which died in London Zoological Gardens on 14th December 1911 measured 24 ft in length and weighed 168 lb (Flower, 1925). The reticulated python "Rex"

Despite its diminutive size, the ruby-throated hummingbird has tremendous powers of endurance and during migration it makes a non-stop 500-mile flight across the Gulf of Yucatan. (R. Austing/ F. Lane.)

*The very rare Philippine monkey-eating eagle (*Pithecophaga jefferyi*), which rivals the Harpy eagle (*Harpia harpyja*) of Central and South America for the title of largest living eagle. (F. Lane.)*

*The Andean condor (*Vultur gryphus*), which has the greatest wing area of any living bird. (R. van Nostrand/F. Lane.)*

exhibited in New York by the First International Snake Exposition of
1936 measured 27 ft 3 in and weighed 191 lb 1 oz (Pope, 1962), and the
same authority says the largest specimen exhibited in the National Zoological Park, Washington, D.C., U.S.A. was 25 ft long and weighed
305 lb. In 1961 a length of 24 ft 5 in (weight 247 lb) was reported for a
male reticulated python in the Houston Museum of Natural History,
Houston, Texas, U.S.A.

Another reticulated python caught by Charles Mayer, the French
animal collector, in the State of Negri Sembilan, Malaya and brought
back by him to Europe was stated to have measured 32 ft in length. This
snake later came into the hands of Henry Trefflich, the American animal
dealer who confirmed this length after running a string along the curve
of the body (it took eight men to hold and straighten out this snake on the
floor), but Oliver says he sold it as a 34-footer.

The largest snake ever held in a zoo was probably a female reticulated python named "Colossus",
who died in Highland Park Zoological Gardens, Pittsburgh, Pennsylvania,
U.S.A. on 15th April 1963. She arrived at the zoo on 10th August 1949,
after being shipped to the United States from Singapore. Her length then
was 22 ft. In June 1951 she measured 23 ft 3 in, and by February 1954 her
length had increased to 27 ft 2 in (weight 295 lb). On 15th November 1956
she measured 28 ft 6 in, when she was said to be still growing at the rate
of just over 10 in per year (?). Her maximum bodily girth before a feed was
measured at 36 in on 2nd March 1955 and she weighed 320 lb on 12th
June 1957 (Barton & Allen, 1961). Shortly before her death the length of
this snake was believed to have been in excess of 30 ft, but this measurement
was not borne out by posthumous examination.

In a letter to the author dated 23rd April 1966, William B. Allen, Jr.,
Curator of Reptiles at Highland Park Zoo, wrote: "The snake was
measured after its death but it was fairly hard to get a good measurement.
It was stiffened up and vertebrae had pulled together shrinking the
snake. We had a measurement of over 24 feet, but this being put on the
same ratio as a smaller snake dying and shrinking, we could add the
difference that would have given us our 28 feet alive. . . . It was not
weighed because of its stiffened condition, but it weighed over 200 lbs., as
it took several men all they could do to move it, by dragging and pulling."

An autopsy revealed that several segments of the vertebrae were
eaten almost completely through, along with several rib sections, by
reptilian tuberculosis, and it was this factor, along with a lung infection
and possibly old age, that contributed to this snake's death.

*The female reticulated
python "Colossus", the
largest snake ever kept in a
zoo. (Highland Park
Zoological Gardens,
Pittsburgh, Pennsylvania,
U.S.A.)*

A reticulated python with an alleged length of 30 ft being stretched out at Singapore Zoo.

Twenty-two-foot-long python skins hanging up to dry in a London warehouse.

*The White pelican (*Pelecanus onocrotalus*) of eastern Europe, equatorial Africa and parts of Asia has one of the largest wing-spans of any living bird, adult specimens commonly measuring 8–8·5 ft. (G. Wood.)*

*The largest flying bird found in Britain is the Mute swan (*Cygnus olor*). One outsized specimen had a wing-span of 12 ft. (F. Quayle.)*

The African rock python (*Python sebae*) is another large constrictor whose size has been grossly exaggerated.

According to the historians of Ancient Rome the army of Attilus Regulus, while laying siege to Carthage (near modern Tunis), was attacked by an enormous serpent which was destroyed only after a tremendous battle. The skin of this monster, measuring 120 ft in length, was sent to Rome where it was preserved in one of the temples.

Suetonius says another specimen exhibited in front of the Comitium in Rome measured 50 cubits or 75 ft.

As recently as 1932 a python allegedly measuring 130 ft in length was killed in the Semliki Valley, Central Africa but the snake was converted into stew by the local Bwambwa tribe before any reliable measurements could be taken!

In reality, the adult African rock python averages about 16 ft, but specimens measuring over 20 ft have been reliably reported.

Arthur Loveridge (1929) measured the freshly removed skin of a python speared by natives on the banks of the Nigeri Nigeri River near Morogoro, Tanganyika (now part of Tanzania) and found that it was exactly 30 ft in length. He estimated that the snake must have measured about 25 ft in the flesh and said he was quite prepared to believe that this species sometimes reached 30 ft.

Three years later he was proved right when Mrs. Charles Beart shot an African rock python measuring 9·81 m (32 ft 2·25 in) in the grounds of a school at Bingerville in the Ivory Coast (Pope, 1961). This must have been an outsized freak, however, because no specimens even remotely approaching this length have been reported since (in the early 1950s a Johannesburg newspaper published a picture of what was claimed to be a 26 ft python, but the appearance was achieved by pushing the tail of a 13 ft specimen into the mouth of another of approximately the same length and then covering the joint with sand!).

The Amethystine python (*Python amethystinus*) of northern Australia, New Guinea and the Philippines has also been reliably measured over 20 ft (average adult length 15 ft), and Eric Worrell (1954) says one gigantic individual shot by Louis Robichaux at Greenhills near Cairns, Queensland measured 28 ft. This length, however, has never been fully substantiated.

The largest snake found in Britain is the Grass snake (*Natrix natrix*), also known as the "Ringed snake", which is found throughout southern England, parts of Wales and in Dumfries-shire, Scotland. Adult males average 2 ft 6 inches in length, and adult females 3 ft 3 in.

A fine specimen of the grass snake, the longest British snake. (Francis Pitt.)

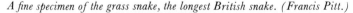

The largest accurately measured specimen on record was a female killed in the New Forest, Hants, which measured 1,700 mm (5 ft 6·9 in) (Smith, 1951). Eric Parker (1943) says he saw an enormous grass snake in his garden at Hambledon, Surrey which he calculated was "just about 6 ft. in length", but the animal was never captured.

The king cobra, the longest venomous snake in the world. This specimen measures 16 ft 6 in. (Fox Photos.)

The longest venomous snake in the world is the King cobra (*Naja hannah*), also called the "Hamadryad", of eastern India, China, the Malay Archipelago and the Philippines. Adult specimens average 12–13 ft in length and weigh about 15 lb.

In April 1937 an enormous individual measuring 18 ft 2 inches in length was captured alive near Fort Dickson, in the State of Negri Sembilan, Malaya and kept in captivity for a time by a Mr. J. Leonard of Ruthkin Estate (Gibson-Hill, 1948). Later it was sent to London Zoological Gardens where a measurement of 18 ft 4 in was recorded for it shortly after arrival. At the time of its death a few days before the outbreak of the Second World War (all the poisonous snakes at the zoo were killed as a safety precaution) it measured 18 ft 9 in (Ball, *in litt.* 16.3.71).

Another huge king cobra shot by a Dyak hunter in the Nakhon Sritamart Mountains, southern Siam (Thailand) in 1924 measured 18 ft 4 in, but a gun-barrel was used to obtain the length (Smith, 1943). The head of this snake is preserved in the Museum of Comparative Zoology, Harvard University, Cambridge, Massachusetts, U.S.A.

The heaviest snake is the anaconda (see page 181).

The heaviest venomous snake is the Eastern diamondback rattlesnake (*Crotalus adamanteus*), which is found in the south-eastern United States. A 7 ft 9 in specimen killed by Rutledge (1946) weighed 34 lb. Another one killed by two boys in the Big Santee Swamp, South Carolina reportedly measured 8 ft 4 inches in length and tipped the scales at 40 lb (Wallace, 1950), but Klauber (1956) has questioned the accuracy of this claim. The largest specimen measured by Ditmars (1907) was 8 ft 3 in long but no weight was quoted.

The Western diamondback rattlesnake (*Crotalus atrox*) is also of comparable size. A 7 ft 5 in specimen (excluding rattle) killed near Brownsville, Texas on 6th July 1926 weighed 24 lb (Klauber, 1956). Less reliable lengths up to 8 ft have been claimed.

This poundage *may* be matched by the bulky Bushmaster (*Lachesis mutus*) of Nicaragua, Costa Rica and Brazil, which has been measured up to 12 ft in length.

In 1950 a weight of 26·5 lb was recorded for a 15 ft 7 in king cobra captured alive on Singapore Island and taken to Raffles Museum (because of its exceptionally large size this snake was mistaken for a python by the three men who captured it by *hand!*).

A 5 ft 8·5 in female Gaboon viper (*Bitis gabonica*) killed in the Mabira Forest, Uganda in September 1933 scaled 18 lb with an empty stomach (Pitman, 1938), which means this species is proportionately heavier than the eastern diamondback rattlesnake.

The shortest snake in the world is probably the Thread snake (*Leptotyphlops bilineata*), which is found on the islands of Martinique, Barbados and St. Lucia in the West Indies. It has a maximum recorded length of 11·9 cm (4·7 in) Emin's thread snake (*L. emini*) and Jan's thread snake (*L. conjuncta*) of south-eastern and eastern Africa are not much longer, measuring 4–6 in (Pitman, 1938).

Thread snakes this size can glide through a cavity only 0·125 inch in diameter, such as the hole left in a standard sized pencil after the lead has been removed.

The shortest venomous snake in the world is probably Peringucy's adder (*Bitis peringueyi*) of South-West Africa which has a maximum recorded length of 12 in. This size is closely matched by the Striped garter snake (*Elaps dorsalis*) of South Africa.

When food is plentiful snakes often eat prodigious meals. They are able to do this because their jaws are highly elastic and can be stretched to a remarkable degree. Oliver (1958) says he once owned a 14 in long Cottonmouth moccasin (*Ancistrodon piscivorous*) which swallowed a very slender 29 in Ribbon snake (*Thamnophis sauritus*) sharing the same cage, and he quotes another case of a 38 in King snake (*Lampropeltis getulus*) disposing of an 8 in DeKay's snake (*Storeria dekayi*), a 15 in Grass lizard and a 40 in Corn snake (*Elephe guttata*) in the space of one day.

According to Raymond Ditmars (1951) the head keeper in the reptile house at the Bronx Zoo, New York once kept a record of the footage in snakes devoured by a 14 ft king cobra from July to the following March and found that it added up to 145 ft!

There is also a record of a 13 ft king cobra being shot as it was in the process of swallowing an 8 ft python.

When it comes to eating *heavy* meals, however, the giant constrictors are the undisputed champions, although the actual size of the prey they swallow is sometimes exaggerated.

The largest recorded animal to be swallowed by a snake was a 130 lb Impala (*Aepyceros melampus*) which was removed from a 16 ft African rock python (Rose, 1955). The weight of the snake was not given, but it was probably not much heavier than its victim.

Gustav Lederer (1944) once got a 24 ft reticulated python to swallow a 120 lb pig, and a Collared peccary (*Tayassu angulatus*) weighing an estimated 100 lb was removed from an anaconda measuring 25 ft 8 in killed in French Guiana (Pope, 1961). Rose believes that the ceiling for any constrictor is 150 lb, but Pope believes a very large African rock python (i.e. 25 to 30 ft) could probably surpass this poundage.

Instances of constrictors attacking and then swallowing human beings are extremely rare.

Felix Kopstein (1927), a student of East Indian reptile fauna, cites the case of a 14-year-old boy who was attacked and swallowed by a 17 ft reticulated python on Salebaboe Island in the Taland group, and he also says there is an authentic record of an adult woman being devoured by a python over 30 ft long.

In 1927 a Calcutta newspaper carried the following news item:

"Maung Chit Chine, a Burmese salesman for a firm of European jewellers, was shooting in the Thaton district, when he was attacked and swallowed by a large python. Another member of the party found Maung's hat near the python which was still asleep. He killed the python, opened it and found Maung's body inside. He had been swallowed feet first."

Rose has queried the authenticity of this story, but Oliver points out that many of the races found in South-East Asia are noted for their small stature and physique.

Sometimes large constrictors misjudge the size of a prospective meal and pay for their mistake with their lives.

Dr. James Oliver (1958) gives an account (taken from a newspaper) of a dramatic tug-of-war between a huge reticulated python and an elephant calf in a jungle clearing. The snake had seized its "victim" by a hind-leg and then anchored itself to a near-by tree. For several hours the fight see-sawed round the clearing while the local villagers looked on. Eventually, however, the giant snake managed to swallow the terrified pachyderm's leg and couldn't get any further. The villagers then moved in and hacked the python to pieces.

Reticulated python after swallowing a large bush pig.

The land snake which possesses the most toxic venom is probably the Tiger snake (*Notechis scutatus*) of southern Australia, which grows to a length of 4–5 ft. F. G. Morgan (1956) of the Commonwealth Serum Laboratories in Melbourne found that the *dried* venom of twelve black specimens (possibly a sub-species) collected on Reevesby Island had a lethal dose of 0·00087 mg per 100 g of body weight when injected subcutaneously in guineapigs, which means that the fatal dose for an average 70 kg (154 lb) man would be 0·609 mg. This extremely high potency is exceptional, however, and is more than twice as toxic as the venom found in mainland tiger snakes (i.e. 0·0002 mg per 100 g of body weight). In earlier tests Fairley (1929)

The tiger snake, the most deadly of all venomous snakes. (Australian News and Information Bureau.)

had established that the average venom yield of the tiger snake at one milking (26·2 mg) was sufficient to kill 118 sheep, and that the maximum yield recorded for this species was enough to kill 387 sheep.

The venom of the much larger Taipan (*Oxyuranus scutellatus*) of northern Australia and south-eastern New Guinea is also extremely potent, the toxicity being 0·0025 mg per 100 g of body weight, and Morgan says this snake is even more dangerous than the tiger snake because its extremely long fangs are "capable of injecting at a bite an enormous dose of highly potent neurotoxic venom".

Both these Australian snakes produce a poison which is four times as toxic as that of the Death adder (*Acanthopis antarcticus*), 20 times that of the Asiatic cobra (*Naja naja*), and 100 times that of Russell's viper (*Vipera russeli*).

The Kraits (genus *Bungarus*) of South-East Asia and the Malay Archipelago are also very high up on the list of contenders. The Indian krait (*B. caeruleus*) is particularly dangerous because it has a venom of very high toxicity for man (the lethal dose is 4 mg), but the venom of the Javan krait (*B. javanicus*), which is known only from the type specimen, is probably even more potent (Kopstein says three natives died soon after being bitten in quick succession by this snake).

The only snake in the Western Hemisphere which has a venom comparable in toxicity to that of any of the snakes already mentioned is the Island viper (*Bothrops insularis*), which is confined to the small rocky island of Queimada Grande off the south-eastern coast of Brazil. According to Ditmars this snake feeds entirely on small birds, for which it has developed an extremely powerful venom that kills its victim before it can fly away and be lost in the sea.

Mention should also be made of the Tropical rattlesnake (*Crotalus terrificus*), the venom of which is second in potency only to *B. insularis* among New World vipers.

The most venomous snake in Africa is the much feared Black mamba (*Dendroaspis polylepis*), but although it secretes a highly toxic venom the potency is not unusually high when compared to that of the tiger snake and the taipan.

The venoms of some of the sea snakes (family Hydrophidae) are also extremely toxic. The most venomous of the fifty known species are the

Beaked sea snake (*Enhydrina schistosa*) and the Banded small-headed sea snake (*Hydrophis fasciatus*), both of which are found in the Indo-Pacific region. Tests on laboratory specimens have shown that the fatal dose for an average-sized man (154 lb) is about 1·5 mg, which puts these two snakes on a par with the tiger snake for toxicity of venom.

The most dangerous snake in the world is probably the King cobra (*Naja hannah*). Its venom is not as potent as that of the tiger snake or the taipan, but the combination of great size, intelligence and aggressive spirit found in this animal makes it a much more deadly adversary.

Rodolphe Meyer de Schauense of the Academy of Natural Sciences of Philadelphia, Pennsylvania, U.S.A. said that shortly before he arrived at Chieng Mai in northern Siam (Thailand) a large elephant tusker working in the near-by teak forest had died after being bitten by a king cobra. He was told that at least two or three valuable elephants belonging to the teak companies were killed in this region annually by the hamadryad, and that the snake achieved this seemingly impossible task by puncturing the tender skin at the tip of the trunk or on the foot at the juncture of the nail. The elephant usually died about three hours after being bitten (Ditmars, 1951).

The snake with the largest yield of venom is the Eastern diamondback rattlesnake (*Crotalus adamanteus*) of the south-eastern United States, with a normal range of 370–720 mg (dried). The venom yield of the Western diamondback rattlesnake (*C. atrox*) of the south-western United States is usually half that amount (i.e. 175–325 mg) but Dr. Laurence Klauber (1956), the leading authority on rattlesnakes, says he "milked" one specimen which yielded an astonishing 1,145 mg or sufficient to kill forty-five people.

The Bushmaster (*Lachesis mutus*) of Central and South America and the Asiatic cobra (*Naja naja*) are also big yielders, with 280–450 mg and 170–325 mg respectively.

At the other end of the scale, the Eastern coral snake (*Micurus fulvius*) of the southern United States has a venom yield of only 2–6 mg, and the Banded small-headed sea snake (*Hydrophis fasciatus*), one of the most venomous snakes in the world, less than 1 mg.

The greatest number of people reportedly killed by a single venomous snake is eleven. This was the figure attributed to an 11 ft 9 in black mamba shot in the Barotse Valley, Northern Rhodesia after a reign of terror lasting three years (Pitman, 1938). Another rogue black mamba killed in Southern Rhodesia was credited with the deaths of five natives and 200 geese, chickens, goats, calves and dogs! (Fitzsimons, 1932).

It is estimated that between 30,000 and 40,000 people die from snakebite each year, 75 per cent of them in densely populated India where some 400,000 people are bitten annually by venomous and non-venomous snakes. Burma has the highest mortality rate, with 15·4 deaths per 100,000 population per annum, but Swaroop and Grab (1956) say the rate in some districts is as high as 30 or more per 1,000 (in Sagaing District the figure is 37 deaths per 1,000 people!). The mortality rate for Australia, on the other hand, which harbours some of the most deadly snakes on earth, is extremely low, the annual rate being 1 in 2,000,000 or six deaths a year, but this is explained by the sparse population (13,000,000).

The only venomous snake in Britain is the Adder (*Vipera berus*), which is found throughout southern England, parts of Wales and Scotland.

The longest recorded specimen was one of 38 in killed on Walberswick Common, east Suffolk on 8th July 1971. Another adder killed in Kingstone, Herefordshire on 18th June 1968 was credited with a length of 36·5 in, but this snake was not preserved for scientific examination.

Since 1890 nine people have died from snakebite in Britain, including five children. The most recently recorded death was on 13th May 1957 when a fourteen-year-old boy was bitten on the right hand at Carey Camp, near Wareham, Dorset. He died in Poole Hospital three hours later from cardio-respiratory failure due to anaphylactic shock.

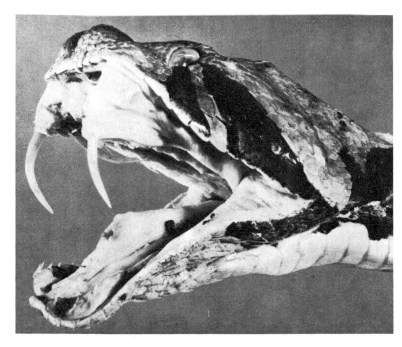

The Gaboon viper has the longest fangs of any snake, measurements up to 2 in having been recorded. (Philadelphia Zoological Gardens, Pennsylvania, U.S.A.)

The snake with the longest fangs is the highly venomous Gaboon viper (*Bitus gabonica*) of tropical Africa. In a 4 ft 3 in specimen they measured 29 mm (1·14 in), and in a 6 ft snake they were 50 mm (1·96 in) (Minton, 1969). Despite this formidable armament, however, the Gaboon viper is not an aggressive snake and will allow itself to be handled without attempting to bite.

As in everything, though, there are exceptions. At 9.50 a.m. on 31st December 1928 R. Marlin Perkins, Curator of Reptiles at St. Louis Zoological Gardens, Missouri, U.S.A. was bitten by a Gaboon viper while treating it for parasites and nearly died as a result. Only prompt medical attention saved his life (Ditmars, 1931).

Venomous snakes are not immune to their own venom. On 12th February 1963 a Gaboon viper bit itself to death in the Philadelphia Zoological Gardens, Philadelphia, Pennsylvania, U.S.A. Keepers of the Reptile House found the snake with its fangs deeply embedded in its own back. They think it tried to scratch itself with the handiest thing around— its fangs.

Sir Harry Johnston (1902) describes how a Gaboon viper he kept in a cage with three huge African rock pythons killed the constrictors after they had annoyed it by constantly rolling their huge bulk over its body:

"When they were particularly exasperating, it would turn and bite

them, and a bite with its formidable fangs would be followed by the
spurting forth of two little streams of blood. Nevertheless, the death of the
pythons did not follow as instantaneously as we knew would have been
the case with warm-blooded creatures; they only became ill, and lingered
for two days before they finally died."

The only other venomous snake which has fangs of comparable size
is the Bushmaster (*Lachesis muta*) of Central and South America. Those of
an 11 ft 4 in specimen measured 1·375 in (Cochran, 1943).

THE 20 MOST VENOMOUS LAND SNAKES IN THE WORLD*

Species	Location
Tiger snake (*Notechis scutatus*)	**Australia**
Taipan (*Oxyuranus scutellatus*)	**Australia**
Island viper (*Bothrops insularis*)	**Brazil**
Javan krait (*Bungarus javanicus*)	**Java**
Tropical rattlesnake (*Crotalus terrificus*)	**Central and S. America**
Indian krait (*Bungarus caeruleus*)	**India and W. Pakistan**
Barba Amarilla (*Bothrops atrox*)	**Central and S. America**
Saw-tailed viper (*Echis carinatus*)	**Africa and Asia**
Black mamba (*Dendroaspis polylepis*)	**Africa**
Death adder (*Acanthophis antarcticus*)	**Australia**
Asiatic cobra (*Naja naja*)	**India and Ceylon**
Gaboon viper (*Bitis gabonica*)	**Africa**
Jararacussu (*Bothrops jararacussu*)	**S. America**
King cobra (*Naja hannah*)	**South-East Asia**
Boomslang (*Dispholidus typhus*)	**Africa**
Australian brown snake (*Demansia textilis*)	**Australia**
Yellow cobra (*Naja nivea*)	**Africa**
Mojave rattlesnake (*Crotalus scutulatus*)	**U.S.A. and Mexico**
Many-banded krait (*Bungarus multicinctus*)	**Burma, China and Formosa**
Puff adder (*Bitis arietans*)	**Africa**

---

* Not listed in order of venom toxicities.
Sources: Ditmars (1931); Cochran (1943); *Venoms* (1956); Oliver (1958);
Poisonous Snakes of the World (1965); and Caras (1964).

Like growth, the longevity of snakes has been much exaggerated, and
this largely stems from the ancient belief that periodic sloughing of the
skin was a form of rejuvenation. That is why, in mythology, snakes are
often 1,000 years old.

The greatest irrefutable age recorded for a snake is 34 years 1 month in the case of an Indian
python (*Python molurus*) at Philadelphia Zoological Gardens, Philadelphia,
Pennsylvania, U.S.A. which was still alive on 1st January 1971. It was
formerly in the private collection of Mrs. Eugenia S. Shorrock of
Massachusetts (Shaw, *in litt.* 13.1.71).

There is also an authentic record of a female Anaconda (*Eunectes
murinus*) living for more than thirty-one years. This specimen was received
at Basle Zoological Gardens, Basle, Switzerland on 18th August 1930,
and died on 8th May 1962 (Wackernagel, *in litt.* 25.5.66). A boa constrictor (*Boa constrictor*) owned by Mrs. Shorrock also lived thirty-one
years.

The oldest venomous snake on record was an African black-lipped cobra (*Naja melanoleuca*). It was hatched in San Diego Zoological Garden, San Diego, California, U.S.A. on 1st October 1928, and died there on 12th November 1957 aged 29 years 42 days.

Other longevity records over twenty-five years include an Indian python (*Python molurus*) of 28 years 3 months (San Diego Zoo); a Timber rattlesnake (*Crotalus horridus*) of 28 years 1 month (Charlotte College); an Anaconda (*E. murinus*) of 28 years 9 days (National Zoological Park, Washington, D.C.); a Short-tailed python (*P. curtus*) of 27 years 10 months (San Diego Zoo); an African rock python (*P. sebae*) of 26 years 6 months (San Diego Zoo); and a Gopher snake (*Drymarchon corais couperi*) of 25 years 11 months (John G. Moore Collection) (Shaw, *in litt.* 13.1.71).

Although snakes give the impression of fast movement as they glide smoothly through grass or bushes, the velocity at which they travel over the ground has been greatly exaggerated. Except for short bursts, the vast majority of them cannot even keep pace with a man walking at a fairly rapid rate, and their endurance is such that they tire very rapidly.

In the 1930s Walter Mosauer (1935) carried out some locomotion tests on several species of desert snake in California. The results were extremely disappointing. The maximum speed recorded was 3·6 mile/h for a Colorado desert whip snake (*Masticophis flagellus piceus*), while the allegedly swift Sidewinder rattlesnake (*Crotalus cerastes*) could only notch up 2·04 mile/h. The slowest of the six snakes tested was the Rosy boa (*Lichanura roseofusca*) with a miserable 0·224 mile/h (its "prowling" speed was 0·10 mile/h!).

In a similar series of speed trials carried out in Australia with snakes known as "racers" (family Elapidae) the maximum speed was 3·5 mile/h (Kinghorn, 1956).

Even if we make due allowance for the fact that snakes rarely travel in a straight line between two points (Parker says a snake's meandering course can add 25–35 per cent to the measured distance it has to travel), it is still doubtful whether the faster serpents like the whip snakes and the racers ever exceed 5–6 mile/h.

The fastest-moving land snake in the world is probably the slender Black mamba (*Dendroaspis polylepis*). It has been claimed that this species can keep up with a galloping horse (about 30 mile/h), but this belief is based solely on the evidence of a few cases of men who have been bitten as high up as the thigh when mounted on horseback (in most instances the horse was stationary or moving at a slow trot).

On 23rd April 1906 Colonel Richard Meinerzhagen timed an angry black mamba at a speed of 7 mile/h over a measured distance of 47 yd near Mbuyuni on the Serengeti Plains, Kenya. This specimen (later shot), however, was only 5 ft 7 inches in length, so it is probable that a large individual (i.e. 12 ft) could reach 10 mile/h on level ground.

When it is in a "real hurry" (e.g. escaping from a bush fire) the black mamba is said to touch 20 mile/h over a short distance, but this is when it is rushing downhill. The maximum speed over a level surface is about 15 mile/h.

Some observers maintain that the African fork-marked grass snake (*Psammophis furcatus*), also called the "lebitsi", can travel even faster than the black mamba, but no statistics are available.

The British grass snake (*Natrix natrix*) has a maximum speed of 4·2 mile/h, which classifies it as one of the "sprinters" of the serpentine world.

The black mamba is the fastest-moving snake.

Snakes are highly tenacious of life and are difficult to kill. Dr. Klauber once decapitated thirteen rattlesnakes of six different races to determine the reactions of the severed heads and bodies, and the results were positively frightening. He found that the heads were dangerous for twenty to fifty minutes after severing. Up to forty minutes after decapitation the fangs would erect at the approach of a hand and the pupils of the eyes would contract, and at forty-three minutes one head bit a stick which had been thrust into its mouth and discharged its venom.

The headless bodies were even more persistent of life, although their movements were less functional. One specimen turned on its back succeeded in righting itself seven hours forty-three minutes after losing its head, and even when all bodily movement had ceased the heart continued to beat strongly for several hours. In one case it was still active after fifty-nine hours.

The lizard-like Tuatara (*Sphenodon punctatus*), found on twenty rocky islands in Cook Strait and off the north-east coast of North Island, New Zealand is the sole survivor of an ancient group of reptiles which flourished some 150,000,000 years ago.

Adults measure 19–28 inches in length and weigh several pounds.

The most distinctive feature of this living fossil is its rudimentary third or pineal eye, which is situated on the top of its head, but nothing is known of its function.

The tuatara is one of the longest lived of all reptiles. In the wild it reportedly lives well over fifty years, and there is an unconfirmed report of a captive specimen living for seventy-seven years (the oldest captive tuatara listed by Flower, 1937, was twenty eight).

In addition, its incubation period of thirteen to fifteen months is the longest of all reptiles.

Flower (1925) says this animal is susceptible to music, and Drummond (1923) gives an interesting account of tuataras coming out of their burrows to listen to a child's voice.

The tuatara is strictly protected by the New Zealand Government, and the total population has been estimated at between 20,000 and 30,000 animals.

SECTION IV

Amphibians

(class *Amphibia*)

An amphibian is a cold-blooded, air-breathing vertebrate which lives both in the water and on land. It normally has four legs and is distinguished from reptiles by its naked and moist skin which is used in respiration. Throughout the class the brain is of a very low type. The majority of young are hatched from eggs deposited in water and breathe by means of external gills during the larval stage. At the completion of the metamorphosis the gills close up and breathing is transferred to the skin and lungs so that the animal can live on land. In cold weather it burrows into the earth or mud at the bottom of a lake or pool where it passes into a state of hibernation.

The earliest known amphibian and the first quadruped was Ishthyostega which lived about 350,000,000 years ago. Its remains have been discovered in Greenland.

There are about 2,000 living species of amphibian and the class is divided into three orders. These are the Salientia (frogs and toads); the Urodela (newts and salamanders); and the Gymnophiona (the wormlike caecilians). The largest order is Salientia, which contains about 1,800 species or 90 per cent of the total number.

The largest amphibian in the world is the Chinese giant salamander (*Megalobatrachus davidianus*), which is found in the cold mountain streams and marshy areas of north-eastern, central and southern China. Adult specimens of both sexes average 1 m (39·37 in) in total length and scale 11–13 kg (24·2 to 28·6 lb) the weight depending on the amount of water contained in the body. Abbé Armand David (1875), who gave his name to the species, says he collected examples weighing 25 to 30 kg (55 to 66 lb) and saw others even larger.

The largest Chinese giant salamander on record.

The largest accurately measured giant salamander on record was a huge individual collected in Kweichow (Guizhou) Province in southern China in the early 1920s and described by Arthur Sowerby (1925) who says it measured 5 ft from the tip of the snout to the tip of the tail between pegs, and 5 ft 9 in along the curve of the body. Unfortunately this animal was not weighed, but it must have scaled nearly 100 lb.

The Japanese giant salamander (*Megalobatrachus japonicus*), found in the cold mountain streams of southern Japan proper, is slightly smaller than its Chinese counterpart, but its tail is proportionately longer. Adult specimens of both sexes average 3 ft in total length. Apart from size Ch'eng-Chao Liu (1950) also says the two species can be distinguished by the character of the tubercles on the head, those of *M. davidianus* being smaller and fewer than those of *M. japonicus*.

According to Flower (1936) a very large Japanese salamander which died in Leipzig Zoological Gardens, Germany on 31st May 1930 measured 1·44 m (4 ft 8·69 in) in a straight line and 1·64 m (5 ft 4·56 in) along the curve of the body. This specimen weighed 40 kg (88 lb) when alive and 45 kg (99 lb) after death, the body having absorbed water from the aquarium. Another one called "Geerts" who died in the Jardin des Plantes, Paris on 14th June 1925 measured 1·4 m (4 ft 7·11 in) in a straight line and weighed 34 kg (74·8 lb).

The only other salamander which approaches *Megalobatrachus* in length is the eel-like Three-toed amphiuma (*Amphiuma* means *tridactylum*) of the south-eastern United States, which has been measured up to 1,015 mm (39·96 in) (Bishop, 1943). The Hellbender (*Cryptobranchus alleganiensis*), also of the southern United States, is not so long (maximum length 27 in), but it is a much bulkier creature than *A.m. tridactylum* and runs second to *Megalobatrachus* for weight.

The Waltl newt, the largest species of newt, grows to a length of 15·74 in. (Zoological Society of London.)

The largest newt in the world is the Pleurodele or Ribbed newt (*Pleurodeles waltl*), which is found in Morocco and on the Iberian Peninsula. The average total length is 15–20 cm (5·9 to 7·87 in), and the weight about 3 oz, but specimens measuring up to 40 cm (15·74 in) in total length (Hellmich, 1956) and weighing nearly 1·5 lb have been reliably reported.

The largest British amphibian is the Warty or Great crested newt (*Triturus cristatus*). The two largest specimens (one male and one female) collected by Boulenger (1894) at Hampton, Middlesex measured 14·4 cm (5·66 in) and 16·2 cm (6·37 in) respectively, and Evans says the largest pair collected by him at Dunbar, East Lothian, Scotland weighed 10·6 and 9·4 g (0·373 and 0·33 oz).

Another female captured at Tring, Hertfordshire and kept by Flower for nearly six years (1911–17) was measured by Dr. Boulenger at the British Museum of Natural History, London shortly after its death and was found to have a total length of 170 mm (6·69 in).

The largest frog in the world is the rare Goliath frog (*Rana goliath*) of Cameroun and Spanish Guinea, West Africa. On 23rd August 1960 a female weighing 3,305 g (7 lb 4·5 oz) was caught by Jorge Sabater Pi, Curator of the Centro de Ikunde in Bata, Rio Muni, in the rapids of the River Mbia, Spanish Guinea. It had an overall length of 81·5 cm (32·08 in) and measured 34 cm (13·38 in) snout to vent. According to Pi (1969) weights up to 13 lb and snout–vent lengths up to 2 ft have been claimed for this species, but he considers these figures to be exaggerated.

The rare Goliath frog, the largest known species of frog.

Another female with a snout–vent length of 35·6 cm (14·01 in) and weighing 3·1 kg (6·82 lb) was collected by Dr. Paul Zahl (1967) in Spanish Guinea in December 1966.

In December 1960 another giant frog known locally as "agak" or "carn-pnag" and said to measure 12–15 in snout to vent and weigh over 6 lb, was reportedly discovered in central New Guinea, but no specimen of this frog has ever reached a scientific collection.

In 1969 a new species of giant frog was discovered in Sumatra, but no measurements have yet been published.

The American bullfrog (*R. catesbeiana*) has been measured up to 200 mm (7·87 in) snout to vent, and weights up to 1 lb 4 oz have been recorded (Oliver, 1955).

The largest species of tree frog is *Hyla vasta*, found only on the island of Hispaniola (Haiti and the Dominican Republic) in the West Indies. The average snout–vent length is about 9 cm (3·54 in), but a female collected from the San Juan River, Dominican Republic by Gerritt S. Miller, Jr. for the U.S. National Museum, Washington, D.C. in March 1928 measured 14·3 cm (5·63 in) (Cochran, *in litt.* 1.6.67).

The largest frog found in Britain is the introduced Marsh frog (*R.r. ridibunda*). Adult males have been measured up to 9·6 cm (3·77 in) snout to vent, and adult females up to 12·6 cm (4·96 in), the weight ranging from 60 to 95 g (2·11 to 3·3 oz). In eastern Europe lengths up to 17 cm (6·69 in) and weights up to 300 g have been quoted for this species (Smith, 1951).

The largest "native" British frog is the Common frog (*R. temporaria*), which has been measured up to 9·5 cm (3·74 in) snout to vent in Scotland (Boulenger, 1893). The average snout–vent length is 4–4·5 cm (1·57 to 1·77 in).

The largest toad in the world is probably the Marine toad (*Bufo marinus*) of tropical South America. An enormous female collected on 24th November 1965 at Miraflores, Vaupes, Colombia and later exhibited in the reptile house at Bronx Zoo, New York had a snout–vent length of 23·8 cm (9·37 in) and weighed 1,302 g (2·70 lb) at the time of its death (Hutchison, *in litt.* 5.10.67). This specimen is now preserved in the American Museum of Natural History in New York.

This size is closely matched by the Blomberg toad (*B. blombergi*) of Colombia. The type specimen was collected by Rolf Blomberg in the vicinity of Nachao, province of Narino, south-western Colombia on 11th September 1950. It measured 20·7 cm (8·14 in) snout to vent and weighed 1,000 g (2·2 lb). Another one collected by Blomberg in the same area in May 1951 was slightly larger, measuring 21·5 cm (8·8 in) snout to vent (Myers & Funkhouser, 1951).

Peter Knobel (1962) gives the snout vent length of a female *B. blombergi* named "Berta" living in the aquarium at Ruhr-Zoo, Gelsenkirchen, West Germany as 25 cm (9·84 in) and says it weighed 1,125 g (2·47 lb).

The Rococco toad (*Bufo paracnemis*), found in Brazil and northern Argentine, has been credited with snout–vent measurements up to 25 cm (9·84 in), but this figure needs confirming. One specimen collected in Brazil had a snout–vent length of 20·5 cm (8·07 in).

There is also a record of a Malayan giant toad (*B. asper*) measuring 21·5 cm (8·8 in) snout to vent (Boulenger, 1912), and Six (quoted by Boring and Liu, 1934) says a giant toad of the sub-species *B. b. gargarizans* collected at Mokanshan, near Hangchow, eastern China had a snout–vent length of 22·8 cm (9 in).

Giant toads appear to be widely distributed, and in most parts of the world there is at least one species which reaches an exceptional size.

The common toad and the natterjack toad, the largest and the smallest species of toad found in Britain. (D. English— F. Lane.)

The largest toad found in Britain is the Common toad (*B. vulgaris*). Adult males have an average snout–vent length of 6·3 cm (2·5 in) and adult females 8·8 cm (3·5 in), but measurements up to 7 cm (2·75 in) and 10·2 cm (3·94 in) respectively have been recorded (Smith, 1951).

In southern Europe the Common toad reaches a much greater size. Fatio (1872) says one female collected in Sicily had a snout–vent length of 15·3 cm (6·02 in), and another female from Serra Gerez, Portugal measured 13·5 cm (5·31 in) (Gadow, 1896). According to Mina-Palumbo this species has been measured up to 18 cm (7·08 in) snout to vent, but this figure has been queried by both Boulenger and Gadow.

The smallest known amphibian is the Arrow-poison frog *Sminthillus limbatus*, found only in Cuba. Full-grown specimens have a snout–vent length of 8·5–12·4 mm. (0·33–0·48 in) (Barbour & Shreve, 1937).

This size is rivalled by the Little chorus frog (*Pseudacris ocularis*) of the south-eastern United States, adult specimens ranging from 11·5 to 17·5 mm (0·45–0·68 in) (Wright & Wright, 1949).

The Nyasaland (Malawi) frog (*Phrynobatrachus ukingensis*) has been credited with a snout–vent length of 13 mm (0·51 in) when fully grown (Hoffman, 1944), but females measuring up to 22·2 mm (0·87 in) have been collected since (Loveridge, 1953).

Camp's frog (*Syrrhophus campi*) of the southern United States is also diminutive, the average adult snout–vent length being 19 mm (0·74 in) (Wright & Wright, 1949).

The smallest tree frog in the world is the Least tree frog (*Hyla ocularis*) of the south-eastern United States, with a maximum snout–vent length of 15·8 mm (0·62 in).

The smallest toad in the world is the sub-species *Bufo taitanus beiranus*, first discovered in c. 1906 near Beira, Mozambique, East Africa. Adult specimens have a maximum recorded snout–vent length of 24 mm (0·94 in) (Poynton, 1964).

Two other toads found in the Upemba National Park in the Congo (*Kinshasa*) are almost equally as tiny. One of them, *B. ushoranus*, has been measured up to 25·3 mm (0·99 in), and the other, *B. melanopleura*, up to 25·1 mm (0·98 in) (Schmidt & Inger, 1959).

Rose's toad (*B. rosei*), which lives on the slopes above Cape Town, South Africa, has also been credited with the title of "smallest living toad", but female specimens up to 38·5 mm (1·51 in) have been recorded (Parker, *in litt.* 6.7.67).

The smallest salamander in the world is the Pygmy salamander (*Desmognathus wrighti*), found only in Tennessee, North Carolina and Virginia, U.S.A. Adult specimens measure from 37 to 50·8 mm (1·45–2·0 in) in total length (King, 1936). This size is closely matched by *Thorius minutissimus*, which is known only from the State of Oaxaca, Mexico. Specimens measuring only 39 mm (1·53 in) in total length have been recorded (Turner, *in litt.* 4.5.66), but it is not yet known whether these samples were fully adult.

The smallest newt in the world is believed to be the Striped newt (*Notophthalmus perstriatus*) found in the south-eastern United States. Adult specimens average 51 mm (2·01 in) in total length.

The smallest amphibian found in Britain is the Palmate newt (*Triturus helveticus*). Adult specimens measure 7·5–9·2 cm (2·95–3·62 in) in length and weigh up to 2·39 g (0·083 oz). The Natterjack or Running toad (*B. calamita*) has a maximum snout–vent length of 8 cm (3·14 in), but it is a bulkier animal.

The greatest authentic age recorded for an amphibian is about fifty-five years for a male Japanese giant salamander (*Megalobatrachus japonicus*) which died in the

*The largest living bird is the North African ostrich (*Struthio camelus camelus*). Adult males reach 345 lb in weight and stand up to 9 ft tall.*

*The Kori bustard (*Otis kori*) of South Africa, the world's heaviest flying bird. Cock birds sometimes exceed 40 lb. (P. Carol/F. Lane.)*

aquarium at Amsterdam Zoological Gardens on 3rd June 1881. It was brought to Holland in 1829, at which time it was estimated to be three years old (Flower, 1936). According to Schneider (1932) a female Japanese giant salamander which died in Leipzig Zoological Gardens, Germany on 31st May 1930 had spent sixty-five years in captivity (originally received at Berlin Zoological Gardens in 1865), but Flower refused to accept this record. He said this specimen was one of two received at Berlin Zoo in 1884, which means it was about forty-six years old at the time of its death.

Another giant salamander owned by Lord Rothschild, which died at Tring Park, Hertfordshire on 2nd August 1934 after having lived there for over forty-four years, was estimated to have been fifteen to twenty years old on arrival, but this seems unlikely (giant salamanders reach adult size at five years).

On 28th March 1936 a Japanese giant salamander died in Blackpool Aquarium after having lived there for over forty-five years. Its date of arrival was not recorded, but Flower says it was fully grown in 1890, which means it must have been at least fifty-one years old.

In a letter to Flower dated 8th May 1935, Dr. C. H. Townsend of the New York Aquarium said that he knew of at least six giant salamanders which had "attained ages of between fifty and sixty years", but he did not go into details.

Toads, too, are also long lived, having survived for more than thirty years in captivity (the record is held by a Common toad which lived under a front-door step for thirty-six years until it was killed by a tame raven), but claims that specimens found in cavities of wood or solid rock are sometimes hundreds of years old must be discounted.

In 1821 a live toad was removed from a stone step at the home of Mr. F. Ross of Broadway House, near Topsham, Devon after an alleged incarceration of forty-five years (Gosse, 1895).

On 26th November 1825 Dr. Buckland, the famous English naturalist, decided to put the longevity of the toad to the test and enclosed two dozen specimens of different sizes in separate airtight compartments made of compact sandstone or porous limestone which he buried in his garden. When he examined them again on 10th December 1826 he found that all the toads in the sandstone compartments were dead and very much decayed, while most of the others in the larger cells of porous limestone were still alive although emaciated. The survivors were buried again for a further twelve months, but at the end of this period they were all found to be dead.

In May 1844 workmen cutting down a fir-tree in Kingston, Kent found a toad completely buried in the centre which crawled away after being exposed to the air for a few hours. The tree was twenty-five years old.

About 1900 a hollow flint containing a dead toad was discovered at Lewes, Sussex. The creature was exhibited at a meeting of the Linnean Society in London and later handed over to the Brighton Museum.

It was suggested that this unfortunate amphibian had made its way into the cavity a few million years ago [sic] when it was only partly developed by way of a small hole at one end of the flint, which it could not have passed through when it was fully grown!

In May 1919 a miner working in Netherseal Colliery was holing in the dirt beneath the coal when his pick broke into a "pocket" and a live toad came rolling out.

"The creature", said a newspaper of the day, "is about three inches in length and has a skin of dirty brown colour. Its eyes were open, but it was obvious that it could not see at first. Two days afterwards it gave indications of returning to normal. The toad has no mouth, but there are evidences that it once possessed this useful member. On the same day as the sight began to return the toad also started to leap about in a clumsy manner. The webbed feet differ from present well-known varieties. The spot where it was found is 200 yards below the surface. The toad has been sent to Birmingham University."

In July 1933 a live toad with eyes but no mouth was found in the solid chalk face of a greystone lime pit at Dorking, Kent. It was discovered after blasting operations 50 ft from the surface and 4 ft into the face of the cliff. The animal was about 1·25 in long. When found it was pink in colour, but gradually got darker. It was later taken to the British Museum of Natural History, London for examination.

Toad eggs often filter down through the soil and rock with surface water and get lodged in limestone, sandstone and coal cavities where the temperature is sufficient for them to hatch. The young animals feed on the insects which accumulate in these cavities until eventually they become too big to get out through the narrow aperture they had entered.

On 27th February 1963 Moscow Radio announced that geologists working in northern Siberia had revived two four-toed tritons (a kind of newt) which they had found frozen in the ice at depths of 25 and 13 ft respectively. They estimated that the animals had been "asleep" for about 5,000 years. The radio added that one of the tritons had died after three weeks, but the geologists had managed to keep the other one alive for a whole summer, during which time it showed no fear of humans and "ate wild berries and flies out of their hands".

Two days later Professor Lev Losino-Losinsky, head of a cosmic laboratory in Leningrad, whose name had been linked to the claim, declared that the story was "pure fantasy". He said that he had carried out a number of experiments to discover if creatures could be kept alive by freezing for long periods, and they had all been unsuccessful.

The greatest authentic age recorded for a newt is twenty-eight-plus years for a female Warty newt (*Triturus cristatus*) which died in the Horniman Museum, London in 1928. A Japanese newt (*T. pyrrhogaster*) received at the Museum of Natural History, Magdeburg, Germany in May 1903 was still alive in April 1929 (Flower, 1936).

The finest jumpers among amphibians are frogs, the abilities of which are largely dependent on body weight, hind-leg length and the surface from which they take off.

The jumper par excellence, not only for distance covered but also in terms of snout–vent length, is the 2 in long South African sharp-nosed frog (*Rana oxyrhyncha*). On 16th January 1954 a specimen named "Leaping Lena" (later discovered to be a male) covered a distance of 32 ft 3 inches in three consecutive leaps on Green Point Common, Cape Town. The feat was witnessed by Dr. Walter Rose, Curator of Reptiles at the South African Museum. The frog was released after its record-breaking performance.

At the annual Calaveras County Jumping Frog Jubilee at Angels Camp, California, U.S.A. in May 1955 another male of this species made an unofficial *single* leap of over 15 ft when being retrieved for placement in its container.

The greatest distance achieved in the annual Frog Olympics at Elsburg, Transvaal, South Africa is 20 ft 8 in (the total of three jumps) by a male named "Fanjan" on 6th November 1965. The greatest distance reached in the annual

*The Viviparous or Common lizard (*Lacerta vivipara*), Britain's smallest reptile. Adult specimens average about 4·5 inches in total length. (W. Rohdich/F. Lane.)*

*The Common toad (*Bufo bufo*) probably has the widest range of habitat of any living animal. Specimens have been found at altitudes of 26,200 ft in the Himalayas and at a depth of 1,115 ft in a mine. (R. Riches/F. Lane.)*

contest at Angel's Camp is 19 ft 3·125 in by an American bullfrog named "Ripple" on 23rd May 1966 before an audience of 65,000. Another frog named "Hottie" achieved 22 ft 10 inches in the qualifying rounds on 21st May 1966.

The greatest number of consecutive jumps attributed to a frog is 120 for a freshly caught adult Spring peeper (*Hyla crucifer*) placed by A. S. Rand (1952) on a grassy lawn. He also observed that the distance between each hop gradually decreased.

The leaping ability of toads is not nearly so impressive, although they probably have more stamina than frogs. Rand tested a small number of Fowler's toads (*Bufo woodhousi fowleri*) on the same lawn and found that they jumped from 12 to 22·5 in per hop; on sand the distance covered was only 6–14·5 in.

One of the strongest contenders for the title of "poorest jumper" is Ricord's frog (*Eleutherodactylus ricordi planirostris*) of the southern United States. One specimen tested by Oliver (1955) with a snout–vent length of 1·25 inches could only manage a personal best of 4·75 in, or just under four times its own length.

The maximum distance covered by a Gliding frog (family Rhacophoridae) between trees is about 100 ft. These animals, found in Malaya, Sarawak and Borneo, are able to volplane because they have a larger area of webbing on their feet than other species of frog.

The greatest altitude at which an amphibian has been found is 8,000 m (26,246 ft) for a Common toad (*B. bufo*) collected in the Himalayas. This species has also been found at a depth of 340 m (1,115 ft) in a coal-mine.

The most poisonous animal ever recorded, the kokoi arrow poison frog of Colombia. (Photo-Reportage Ltd.)

The most active known poison is the batrachotoxin derived from the skin secretions of the Kokoi (*Phyllobates latinasus*), an arrow-poison frog found in north-western Colombia, South America. Only about 0·0001 g (0·0000004 oz) is sufficient to kill a man.

The Choco Indians catch these 1 in long frogs by imitating their call.

When one replies it gives away its location. Back in the village the frogs are pierced through the mouth and body with a specially cut stick and then held over an open fire. The heat contracts the skin and forces the poison out in droplets which is collected in a jar. The natives dip the tips of their arrows in the secretion and then leave them to dry. One frog produces enough poison to tip fifty arrows.

The Chocos use the arrows to hunt animals like the jaguar, deer and monkey. The poison causes immediate paralysis, and the victim dies soon afterwards (Marki & Witkop, 1963).

The poison of the kokoi is ten times more powerful than the deadly tetrodotoxin produced in the body of the Japanese puffer fish (*Tetraodon hispidus*) (see page 240), which causes rapid respiratory paralysis in humans and has no known antidote (Halsted, 1956).

The tetrodotoxin produced by the abundant and well-developed glands of the California newt (*Taricha torosa*) is also particularly virulent, and experiments have shown that 9 mg (0·0003 oz) is sufficient to kill 7,000 mice.

Some frogs and toads lay more eggs than any other land vertebrate. According to Oliver the record is held by a Woodhouse's toad (*Bufo w. woodhousei*) which laid 25,650 eggs, and he also cites a figure of 20,000 for the American bullfrog (*Rana catesbeiana*). Other species of frogs have been credited with even higher egg counts, but these have not been substantiated.

At the other end of the scale, Camp's frog (*Syrrhophus campi*) only lays six to twelve eggs at a time, and Ricord's frog (*Eleutherodactylus ricordi planirostris*) nineteen to twenty-five eggs.

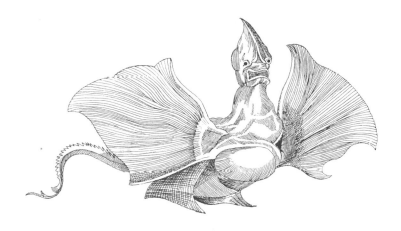

SECTION V

Fishes

(classes *Marsipobranchii, Selachii, Bradyodonti, Pisces*)

A fish is a cold-blooded vertebrate which lives in water and breathes air by means of gills. Usually it has a muscular, streamlined body covered with scales and limbs modified into paired fins for swimming, but in some species the skin is unprotected or concealed by bony plates, and others have no recognisable fins at all. A few primitive fish also move on land and breathe with lungs. The brain is basically a primitive structure, but bony fish are capable of association and show a capacity for learning. The majority of young are hatched from eggs deposited in the water.

The earliest known fish, and the first vertebrate, was Agnathans, a jawless fish, which lived about 480,000,000 years ago. Its remains have been found near Leningrad, U.S.S.R.

There are about 30,000 living species of fish, 2,300 of them fresh water, and they are divided into four very distinct classes. These are the Marsipobranchii (lampreys and hag-fishes); the Selachii (skates, rays and sharks); the Bradyodonti (chimaeras); and the Pisces (bony fishes). The largest class is Pisces, which contains over 95 per cent of living species.

The world's largest fish, the whale shark. This specimen measures 30 ft in length. (Associated Press.)

The largest fish in the world is the rare plankton-feeding Whale shark (*Rhineodon typus*), which is found in the warmer areas of the Atlantic, Pacific and Indian Oceans. It was first discovered in April 1828 when a 16 ft 6 in specimen (one of the smallest on record) was harpooned by fishermen in Table Bay, Cape of Good Hope, South Africa after they had noticed its unusual coloration (i.e. greenish grey with white spots). The shark was examined by Dr. Andrew Smith, a military surgeon attached to the British troops stationed at Cape Town, who published a brief description the following year and a more detailed one in 1849. The dried skin, which Dr. Smith purchased for £6 sterling, is now preserved in the Natural History Museum, Paris.

More than forty years elapsed before *Rhineodon* was heard of again. In 1868 a young Irish naturalist named E. Perceval Wright spent six months in the Seychelles, a group of islands in the western Indian Ocean. During his stay there he heard of a monstrous fish called the "Chagrin" and offered a reward of $12 for the first specimen to be harpooned and delivered to him on shore. Eventually two examples measuring 18 and 20 ft respectively were secured, both of which he photographed and dissected. Two years later, in Dublin, he wrote: "I have seen specimens that I believed to have exceeded fifty feet in length, and many trustworthy men, accustomed to calculate the length of the Sperm whale (one of the most important stations for this cetacean is off Ile Denis, one of the Seychelles Group) have told me of specimens measuring upwards of seventy feet in length."

He also said that Mr. Swinburne Ward, Civil Administrator of the islands, had informed him that he had measured one whale shark personally at slightly over 45 ft in length.

Since then about 100 whale sharks of varying sizes have been stranded or harpooned in different parts of the world, but only a few of them have been scientifically examined.

The largest accurately measured whale shark on record was a 59 ft specimen which got jammed in a bamboo stake-trap set in 50 ft of water at Koh Chik, on the eastern shore of the Gulf of Siam (Thailand) in 1919 (Dr. Hugh M. Smith, Fisheries Adviser to the Siamese Government, quoted by Gudger, 1953). The weight of this immense fish was not recorded, but it must have scaled about 90,000 lb (42·4 tons).

Another whale shark measuring 60 ft in length and 35 ft in maximum bodily circumference was reportedly washed ashore near Chittagong, East Pakistan (formerly part of Bengal, British India) on 8th April 1934, but in a letter to the author dated 26th December 1967, Dr. G. Ramakrishna of the Zoological Survey of India in Calcutta said the dead animal had been identified as a Fin whale (*Balaenoptera physalus*).

According to Dr. Bernard Heuvelmans (1965) a 53 ft whale shark was washed ashore in Kommetjie Bay, Cape Province, South Africa in 1934, but the South African Museum in Cape Town have no record of this fish, and it is not mentioned by the late Dr. E. W. Gudger, the world authority on the whale shark, in any of his papers.

In 1905 a whale shark measuring "not less than 57 feet in length" was impaled on the bow of the liner *Armadale Castle* during an Atlantic crossing. It was held there by pressure for about fifteen minutes before slipping back into the depths (*Illustrated London News*, 11th February 1905).

A similar incident occurred in September 1934 when the liner *Maurganui* collided with a *Rhineodon* 60 miles north-north-east of Tikehau Atoll in the South Pacific and "cut so deeply into the body of the fish that it was literally impaled on the bow". According to Gudger (1940) about 15 ft of the shark hung on one side of the bow, and another 40 ft on the other, making a total length of 55 ft.

Nearly two dozen such collisions have been recorded around the world, and they are attributed to the sluggish nature of this surface-feeder and its apparent indifference to danger.

Zane Grey (1925), the famous writer of Westerns and big-game fisherman, once had an exciting encounter with a 50 ft whale shark off Cape San Lucas, Lower California, Mexico. He and his crew first tried to capture the animal by fixing a gaff hook in its tail ("the fish did not appear to be aware of our ambitions and evil attempts"), but it simply swam on, dragging the boat in its wake. Finally they resorted to the harpoon, but it took three attempts before an iron finally lodged home. The shark then went into a steep dive, and after taking out 1,600 ft of rope the hook and the harpoon pulled out.

During the summer of 1926 Mack Sennett, one of the pioneers of screen comedy, organised a fishing expedition in the Gulf of California and took along with him a newly invented underwater camera to film the marine life in the area. While the party was in Los Frales Bay, about 40 miles inside the gulf, an enormous whale shark suddenly came into camera range and swam around the fishing boat for several minutes. Sennett later told Gudger (1927), who saw the film he had shot in New York, that the shark had measured an estimated 65 ft in length and 10 ft across.

Gudger also heard from a man living in Puerto Rico that in 1889 or 1890 a whale shark had followed a schooner from Cuba to Puerto Rico and taken up residence outside San Juan Harbour, where it remained, on and off, for several years. When it eventually died and was washed ashore its length was found to be 20 m (67 ft 7 in).

Another huge individual known as "Sapodilla Tom", who frequented the waters off Honduras for fifty years, was estimated to measure 60 to 70 ft in length, and fisheries inspector Frederick Wallace (1923) was told by the red-snapper fishermen working in the Gulf of Campeche on the western Yucatan Peninsula that a local whale shark known as "Big Ben" was more than 75 ft in length!

The most publicised whale shark on record was a 38-footer killed by Captain Charles Thompson and some local fishermen just below Knight's Key, southern Florida, U.S.A. in May 1912. They took nine hours to beach this monster, and it only succumbed after a piece had been cut out of its head and the small brain pierced by a knife attached to a long pole. The huge carcass was then towed to Miami, where it has hauled out of the water and placed on a railway flat-car, which promptly collapsed under the weight. The fish was later purchased by an enterprising promoter who had it skinned and stuffed—a job taking several months—and then toured the eastern United States with it.

Gudger worked out the weight of this shark as 26,594 lb (11·8 tons), basing his calculation on a length of 38 ft and a circumference of 18 ft, but this latter figure is low for a whale shark of this length and leads one to suspect that the circumference was taken at the first gill-slit instead of directly behind the pectoral fins. Another 38 ft whale shark captured by fishermen off the coast of Karachi, Pakistan in 1949 had a more reasonable circumference of 23 ft just behind the pectorals and must have weighed—using Gudger's formula—about 43,420 lb (19·3 tons).

Other reliable records over 30 ft (most of them taken from Gudger) include: a 10 m (32 ft 9·75 in) example caught in a drift-net off Cape Inubo, on the south-east coast of Japan in June 1901 (the stuffed fish measured 26 ft 3 inches in length and 11 ft 11·75 inches in circumference); one measuring 31 ft taken near Cape Sable, Florida, U.S.A. on 11th June 1919, and another of 31·5 ft killed near Marathon in the Florida Keys on 9th June 1923 after a fight lasting fifty-four hours; a 10 m (32 ft 9·75 in) specimen caught at Salinas, in Cavite Province, Luzon in the Philippines, on 19th January 1925; one measuring 36 ft stranded at Silay, Negros Occidental Province, Negros, in the Philippines about the same time; a 32-footer stranded at Jaimanitas, a village situated about 5 miles west of Havana, Cuba on 20th November 1927 (this fish was weighed piecemeal and totalled about 18,000 lb or 8·03 tons); one measuring 34 ft captured off Cojimar, a village situated about 5 miles east of Havana, on 10th March 1930; a *Rhineodon* measuring about 40 ft stranded in Southport Harbour, North Carolina, U.S.A. on 6th June 1934 (the most northerly recorded); a 35 ft specimen which blundered into a fish trap off Fire Island Light, on the south shore of Long Island, N.Y., U.S.A. on 9th August 1935 (examined by Dr. Gudger who estimated its weight at 16,000 lb or 7·13 tons); a 41·5 ft specimen captured off the Baba Baba Islands off the coast of Karachi, Pakistan in November 1949; one measuring 37 ft and weighing an estimated 20,000 lb (8·9 tons) caught off Bimini in the Bahamas in 1958 and towed to Miami; and a 32-footer caught in the Arabian Sea in 1959 and towed to Mangalore, India after an epic struggle (the weight of this fish was estimated at 5 tons, but judging from photographic evidence it was probably nearer 8–9 tons).

A 34 ft whale shark taken off the coast of Ceylon in *c.* 1889 is now on display in the Fish Gallery at the British Museum of Natural History, London.

An interesting account of the capture of a large whale shark appeared in the March 1951 issue of *Nature*. Although the capture occurred on 23rd November 1940, near Pangkor Island, off the west coast of the Malayan Peninsula, it became known only in 1950 when the director of the Fisheries Department at Penang examined some records of the Japanese occupation.

The fish measured 35 ft in length and 23 ft (?) between the outstretched pectorals. It was caught in a beach seine, about a mile in length, operated by the Madras fishermen who migrated to Malaya. They tried to weigh it piecemeal, but after recording just over 13,000 lb (5·7 tons) of flesh they grew tired and dumped the rest of the carcass in the sea.

According to Clark (1963) a young whale shark weighing "several thousand pounds" was exhibited for several months at the Mito Aquarium in south-eastern Japan many years ago. It was kept in a small bay which was separated from the open sea by a wide-mesh net. This specimen was probably the largest fish ever held in captivity (in October 1969 a weight of 3 tons was reported for an ocean sunfish named "Jennie" who spent ten days in captivity at the Manly Aquarium, New South Wales, Australia before being released, but judging from a published photograph this tonnage was exaggerated).

Apart from being the largest fish in the world, **the whale shark also has the thickest skin of any living animal**. In a 30 ft specimen it is 4 in thick, and in a 60-footer about 9 in, and the skin has been likened to the solid rubber tyre of a heavy truck. But that's not all. When it is harpooned this fish can strengthen its "armour plating" by tightening its dermal muscles, with the result that other irons simply bounce off its body.

On one occasion Dr. William Beebe (1938) was aboard his yacht *Zaca* in the Gulf of California when a whale shark (estimated length 42 ft) was sighted. He ordered the vessel to draw alongside, and it kept pace with the great fish for several hours. Eventually two of his brawny Samoan crew leapt on to the animal's back from the deck and rammed home a large harpoon which was attached by a long line to an empty petrol drum. The shark immediately went into a crash dive, and when it reappeared fifteen minutes later the large drum was crushed in the middle, the result of the tremendous pressure encountered at great depths. Two more attempts were made to harpoon this fish, but each time the irons came back buckled "as if they had struck steel".

"A strong man may drive a sharp fine-pointed harpoon into a whale shark's skin if the point strikes at a right angle to it," says Dr. Gudger (1941), "but I doubt if he could drive it *through* it. Time after time I have seen a harpoon, thrown by a strong man, rebound from the fish's back. When the whale shark is fired at with buckshot, these simply rebound. So also will shots from a high-powered rifle, unless the shots strike the skin properly—i.e. perpendicularly. Clad in this well-nigh impervious armour, *Rhineodon* fears no man."

The only other fish which compares in size with the whale shark is the Basking shark (*Cetorhinus maximus*), another plankton-feeder, which is found in all temperate waters of the world, although it is most common in the North Atlantic.

Adult specimens average 26–29 ft in length and weigh 5·25 to 6·5 tons —two basking sharks measuring 28 ft and 30 ft landed at Monterey, California, U.S.A. in 1931 reportedly weighed 6,580 lb and 8,600 lb respectively, but these poundages are unusually low—but much larger sizes have been reported.

In 1806 a basking shark measuring 36 ft 6 inches in length and weighing an estimated 8 tons was washed ashore at Brighton, Sussex. Another

*The basking shark, the
largest fish found in British
waters. This young
specimen measures 18 ft
in length. (Central Press.)*

specimen measuring 32 ft 10 inches in length and 18 ft in maximum bodily
circumference was captured near Brown's Point, Raritan Bay, New Jersey,
U.S.A. in 1821 (Lesueur, 1822), and one measuring 40 ft 3 in was trapped
in a herring gill net in Musquash Harbour, New Brunswick, Newfoundland, Canada in 1851 (Perley, 1852). In 1865 a 40-footer was captured at
Povoa de Varzim, Portugal, and three years later a specimen measuring
35 ft was stranded at Eastport, Maine, U.S.A. The ten largest basking
sharks taken on the Norwegian coast during the period 1884 to 1905
measured 45 ft (the largest recorded specimen), 40 ft, 40 ft, 40 ft, 36 ft,
32 ft 2 in, 32 ft, 31 ft, 30 ft 6 in and 30 ft 3 in respectively (Collett, 1905).

Other reliable records over 30 ft include: a 30 ft 6 in shark (maximum
bodily circumference 20 ft) stranded at Portland, Victoria, Australia in
November 1883; one measuring 34 ft stranded near San Francisco, California, U.S.A. in *c.* 1896 (this shark was embalmed and put on exhibition);
a 36-footer taken in Monterey Bay, California, in *c.* 1915; one measuring
38 ft captured near Concarneau, north-western France, in 1917; a 32 ft
specimen caught in a cod-trap at Petty Harbour, near St. John's, Newfoundland, Canada in 1934; a 40 ft individual taken off Portland, Maine,
U.S.A. on 2nd August the same year; a 31-footer taken at Long Point,
near Provincetown, Massachusetts, U.S.A.; one measuring 35 ft washed
up on Chesil Beach, Portland, Dorset on 1st October 1935; a 40-footer
trapped in a herring weir on Grand Manan Island, New Brunswick,
Newfoundland in July 1958; one measuring 35–40 ft caught in a salmon
gill-net in Portugal Cove, Conception Bay, Newfoundland on 15th July
1961; a 32-footer entangled in a net at Grand Bruit, Newfoundland in
July 1962; and one measuring 40 ft caught at Burgeo, Newfoundland in
August the same year (McCoy, 1885; Bigelow & Schroeder, 1948;
Templeman, 1963; Heuvelmans, 1965).

The largest basking shark seen by the late Gavin Maxwell (1952) at
his shark fishery on Soay in the Inner Hebrides between 1945 and 1949
measured 31 ft 5 in, but he says he narrowly missed capturing another one
between Uisenish and Lochboisdale, South Uist (Outer Hebrides) which
was "a full forty feet".

On the 6th May 1935 a basking shark allegedly measuring 48 ft in
length and 26 ft in maximum bodily circumference was killed by rifle-fire

off Mutton Island, Galway Bay, western Ireland after becoming entangled in a fisherman's net, but subsequent inquiries revealed that the actual length of this fish was 39 ft.

In October 1808 the rotting carcass of an unknown marine animal was washed up on the island of Stronsa (now called Stronsay) in the Orkneys. It was serpentine in appearance, measuring 55 ft in total length, 12 ft in circumference and having a 15 ft long (maned) neck.

Details of this monster and part of the skull were forwarded to the Royal Museum of Edinburgh University, and at a meeting of the Wernerian Society in Edinburgh on 19th November 1808 Mr. Patrick Neill, a well-known naturalist and secretary of the society, read "an account of a great sea-snake, lately cast ashore in Rothiesholm Bay, in the Island of Stronsa".

At a later meeting he described the unique specimen as a new genus, *Halysdryus pontoppidiani*, in honour of Bishop Erik Pontoppidan, who fifty years earlier had described a similar beast in his *Natural History of Norway*.

Eventually news of the strange creature reached the ears of Sir Everard Home, the celebrated surgeon and anatomist of the Royal College of Surgeons in London, who was also a competent ichthyologist, and he asked Malcolm Laing, M.P., a Justice of the Peace in Orkney, if he could borrow some of the remains. A few weeks later he received several vertebrae and part of the pectoral fin, and after a close study he announced that they came from a large basking shark. He also queried the length of 55 ft quoted for this animal, saying that the vertebrae corresponded in size with those of a 30 ft 6 in specimen he had recently examined at Hastings (Home, 1809).

The vertebrae of this fish are now preserved in the Royal Scottish Museum in Edinburgh. In November 1933 they were examined by the late Commander Rupert T. Gould of Loch Ness monster fame (quoted by Dinsdale, 1966), who said that their huge size—they measure 6 inches in diameter—led him to believe that the length of 55 ft originally reported for this shark was reliable. He was mistaken, however, in thinking that these particular vertebrae were exceptionally large. In fact, they were slightly smaller in diameter than the largest vertebrae of a 25 ft basking shark washed up on a beach near Provincetown, Massachusetts, U.S.A. in 1939 (Schroeder, 1940).

The rotting carcass of a basking shark provides the basis for more than 90 per cent of the "monster on the beach" stories that appear in the world's Press. This is not altogether surprising, because when the body of one of these great selachians is found in an advanced state of decomposition it does *look* more like a sea serpent than a basking shark. This is because the gill apparatus and the massive lower jaw have long dropped off and been washed away by the sea, leaving behind a tiny box-like cranium and a fleshy backbone which could pass as a small head on a long, slender neck (shades of Plesiosaurus!). And the mane? That is made up of thousands of threads from the disintegrating muscle fibres.

As recently as November 1970 a 30 ft long "unknown" marine animal described by local police as a sea serpent was washed up on a beach near Scituate, Massachusetts, U.S.A. It reportedly weighed "between 15 and 20 tons [*sic*]" and looked like "a giant camel without legs". Later it was positively identified as—a basking shark!

The largest carnivorous fish (excluding plankton-eaters) is the comparatively rare Great white shark (*Carcharodon carcharias*), also called the "Man-eater", which is found mainly in tropical and sub-tropical waters. Adult specimens (females are slightly larger than males) average 14–15 ft in length and generally scale

The great white shark is the largest carnivorous fish in the world. (Miami Seaquarium, Florida, U.S.A.)

between 1,150 and 1,700 lb, but much heavier weights have been reported. For instance, one tremendously bulky 15-footer captured at San Miguel Island off the coast of California, U.S.A. weighed more than 3,000 lb (1·33 tons) (Kenyon, 1959).

Another great white shark caught on rod and line in South African waters, where it is known as the "Blue pointer", measured 13 ft 3 inches in length and weighed 2,175 lb (*Illustrated London News*, 14th July 1928), and weights up to 2,400 lb (1·07 tons) have been reported for 13-footers taken off the Washington coast, U.S.A. (Bonham, 1942).

In 1964 Captain Frank Mundus killed a huge carcharodon off Montauk Point, at the tip of Long Island, New York, N.Y., U.S.A. after a five-hour struggle which measured 17 ft 6 inches in length and weighed 4,500 lb (2·009 tons). Norman and Fraser (1948) give another record of a female great white shark caught at Agamy near Alexandria, Egypt which measured 14 ft in length and "weighed 2·5 tons [*sic*]", but this weight is impossible for a shark of this length (the nine fully developed young in this female were all credited with a length of 2 ft and a weight of 108 lb, but the latter figure must mean the *total* weight).

These marked variations in poundage reflect the physical condition of the shark.

Although the general literature on sharks abounds with stories of enormous carcharodons, there are very few *authentic* records of specimens reaching or exceeding 20 ft in length. In October 1907 a "White pointer" (as it is known in Australia) with a maximum bodily circumference of 18 ft 6 in (?) was harpooned by a whaleman named Archer Davidson from a 10 ft dinghy at Eden, New South Wales and dispatched with a boat spade handle (Caldwell, 1937). Another 20-footer measuring 10 ft 9 inches in maximum bodily circumference and weighing an estimated 3,000 lb was killed by rifle-fire near Fremantle, Western Australia after it had eaten two 5 ft sharks and was in the process of swallowing a third (Andrews, *in litt.* 17.7.65).

A blue pointer harpooned from a whale catcher about 100 miles off the coast of Durban was also credited with a weight of 3,000 lb (1·33 tons) (Davis, 1965), but the length of this fish was not given.

In 1758 a carcharodon measuring 20 ft in length, 9 ft across the pectoral fins and weighing 3,924 lb (1·75 tons) was harpooned from a French frigate in the Mediterranean after swallowing a sailor who had fallen overboard.

Another man-eater caught by fishermen near Aix, southern France in 1829 measured 22 ft in length and weighed over 4,000 lb (Smith, 1833).

This length was exceeded by another carcharodon trapped in a herring weir at Harbour de Loutre, Campobello Island, New Brunswick, Canada in November 1932 which measured 26 ft (Piers, 1934).

William Travis (1963) says a carcharodon caught by him in the Seychelles and raised to within 20 ft of the surface was only 3 ft shorter than his shark cutter, which measured 32 ft, but the line holding this monster eventually snapped under the tremendous strain and the fish escaped.

According to the Russians a 9 m (29 ft 5·25 in) long great white shark weighing 4 tons was caught by the trawler *Gizhiga* in the north Pacific in November 1970, but this record needs confirming.

Dr. David Starr Jordan (1896), the foremost American ichthyologist of his day, says a 30 ft carcharodon captured off Soquel, California in 1880 had a 100 lb sea lion in his stomach, but this record is not considered reliable.

In a letter to the author dated 7th July 1964, Dr. Stewart Springer of the U.S. Fish and Wildlife Service, said:

"I can find no confirmation of the measurement of this shark and rather doubt that Jordan saw it. Perhaps he accepted the report on hearsay, feeling that if it could swallow a hundred pound sea-lion entire, it was really very large. But of course a 14- to 16-foot White shark can swallow a hundred-pound sea-lion, or two for that. Consequently I doubt that the record of this 30-foot carcharodon is valid."

Another man-eater stated to have measured 32 ft in length was reportedly caught at Santa Monica, California, after 1950, but further details are lacking.

The popularly held view is that the largest carcharodon on record (of which there is evidence) was a 36·5 ft monster captured off Port Fairy, Victoria, Australia in 1842, the jaws of which are preserved in the British Museum of Natural History, London. This measurement, however, has also been queried by Dr. Springer, who had an opportunity to examine the teeth of this shark several years ago. He told me he was "greatly surprised" to find that they were about the same size as those of a 16-footer he had measured (the longest tooth in the upper jaw measures 2·2 in).

"I think it likely that the specimen really was somewhere around 16 feet long, perhaps 18 feet or even 20 feet, but certainly not 36½ feet", he concluded.

Such monsters do exist, however, for in June 1930 a carcharodon measuring a staggering 37 ft in length was found trapped in a herring weir at White Head Island, New Brunswick, Canada.

This shark, identified by Dr. Vadim Vladykov (1935), is the largest accurately measured great white shark on record.

According to Zane Grey (1957) a 39 ft carcharodon was stranded at Montague Island, in the Tasman Sea in *c.* 1923 after swallowing a small shark that had been hooked on a set line, but he didn't see this shark personally, and the record appears to be largely based on hearsay.

Captain J. S. Elkington of Queensland told the late David Stead (1963) that one day in 1894 an enormous carcharodon drew alongside his launch just outside Townsville Breakwater and lay there virtually motionless for half an hour. He said the shark was at least 4 ft longer than his 35 ft launch.

Lawrence Green (1958), the well-known South African writer, says another man-eater measuring 43 ft in length was caught in False Bay, Cape Province, many years ago after it had followed a ship in with plague on board.

In a letter to the author dated 6th July 1966 he said: "I gathered a great deal of information on whaling and shark fishing in those waters from a Tristan islander named George Cotton who settled at Simonstown towards the end of the last century. He died only a few years ago, almost a centenarian.

"Cotton was very vivid and accurate in his descriptions, but vague about dates. Thus it would be almost impossible to give the date of the 43-footer. In any case the newspapers of those days gave little or no space to such events."

The most amazing story of all, however, comes from Australia. One morning in 1918, writes Stead (1963), the crayfish men at Port Stephens, New South Wales, were fishing near Broughton Island when they suddenly saw something in the water that was so colossal that it sent cold shivers down their spines. They immediately weighed anchors and fled back to port, and for several days afterwards they refused to put to sea.

"The men had been at work on the fishing grounds—which lie in deep water—when an immense shark of almost unbelievable proportions put in an appearance, lifting pot after pot containing many crayfishes, and taking, as the men said, 'pots, mooring lines and all'. These crayfish pots, it should be mentioned, were about 3 feet 6 inches in diameter and frequently contained from two to three dozen good-sized crayfish each weighing several pounds. The men were all unanimous that this shark was something the like of which they had never dreamed of. In company with the local Fisheries Inspector I questioned many of the men very closely, and they all agreed as to the gigantic stature of the beast. But the lengths they gave were, on the whole, absurd. I mention them, however, as an indication of the state of mind which this unusual giant had thrown them into. And bear in mind that these were men who were used to the sea and all sorts of weather, and all sorts of sharks as well. One of the crew said the shark was 'three hundred feet long at least'! Others said it was as long as the wharf on which we stood—about 115 feet! They affirmed that the water 'boiled' over a large space when the fish swam past. They were all familiar with whales, which they had often seen passing at sea, but this was a vast shark. They had seen its terrible head which was 'at least as large as the roof of the wharf shed at Nelson's Bay'. Impossible, of course! But these were prosaic and rather stolid men, not given to 'fish stories' nor even to talking at all about their catches. Further, they knew that the person they were talking to (myself) had heard all the fish stories years before! One of the things that impressed me was that they all agreed as to the ghostly whitish colour of the vast fish. The local Fisheries Inspector of the time, Mr. Paton, agreed with me that it must have been something really gigantic to put these experienced men into such a state of fear and panic."

In Stead's view the fishermen had seen a very rare example of the *Carcharodon megalodon*, an enormous ancestor of the white pointer, which swam in Miocene seas between 1,000,000 and 25,000,000 years ago (see

Prehistoric Animals) and *might* still exist today. Teeth dredged from the bottom of the Pacific Ocean indicate it reached a length of at least 80 ft.

He may be right of course, but the fact that the fishermen told him that the creature had an enormous head (in comparison to its barrel-like body the head of the white pointer is quite small) leads the author to suspect that the animal was more probably a very large albino sperm whale in the mould of Herman Melville's famous "Moby Dick".

On 21st August 1951 a 55 ft long completely white sperm whale was killed off the coast of Peru (Budker, 1958).

The largest fish ever caught on a rod was a great white shark weighing 2,664 lb (1·18 tons) and measuring 16 ft 10 inches in length taken on a 130 lb test line by Alf Dean at Denial Bay, near Ceduna, South Australia on 21st April 1959. Mr. Dean has also caught five other carcharodons over a ton. They weighed 2,536 lb (16 ft 9 in), 2,372 lb (15 ft 11 in), 2,344 lb (15 ft), 2,333 lb (16 ft 3 in) and 2,312 lb (16 ft 1 in) respectively. In 1952 he nearly caught another huge individual nicknamed "Barnacle Lil" whom he estimated measured 20 ft in length and weighed 3,000 lb, and in 1954 he played a carcharodon weighing an estimated 4,000 lb for five and a half hours before losing it.

SHARKS (maximum size and weight)

Species	Length ft	Length in	Weight lb
Whale shark (*Rhineodon typus*)	59	0	90,000*
Basking shark (*Cetorhinus maximus*)	45	0	32,000*
Great white shark (*Carcharodon carcharias*)	37	0	24,000*
Greenland shark (*Somniosus microcephalus*)	21	0	2,250
Tiger shark (*Galeocerdo cuvieri*)	20	10	2,070
Great hammerhead shark (*Sphyrna mokarran*)	18	4	1,860
Thresher shark (*Alopias vulpinus*)	18	0	1,100
Six-gill shark (*Hexanchus griseus*)	15	5	1,300
Grey nurse shark (*Ginglymostoma cirratum*)	14	0	1,225
Great blue shark (*Prionace glauca*)	12	7	550
Mako (*Isurus oxyrinchus*)	12	0	1,200
Dusky shark (*Carcharhinus obscurus*)	11	11	850
Whaler shark (*Eulamia brachyura*)	11	8	768
Whitetip shark (*Carcharhinus longimanus*)	11	6	750
Porbeagle (*Lamna nasus*)	10	0	500
Bull shark (*Carcharhinus leucas*)	10	0	400

Sources: Hedges, 1923; Bigelow & Schroeder, 1948; McCormick *et al.*, 1963 and others.
* Weight estimated.

Apart from its impressive size, the great white shark is also the man-eater par excellence.

According to Rondelet (1554) whole men in armour have been found in large individuals caught off Nice and Marseilles in the Mediterranean, and he says "two tunny and a fully-clothed sailor" were removed from the stomach of another shark.

Thomas Pennant (1776), in his account of this species, writes: "This grows to a very great bulk, Gillius says to the weight of four thousand pounds; and that in the belly of one was found a human corpse entire, which is far from incredible considering their vast greediness after human flesh.''

Muller and Henle (1838–41) go even further and claim that a 750 kg (1,650 lb) man-eater caught off the island of Sainte-Marguerite near Cannes, south-eastern France contained the body of "a complete horse" which had probably been dumped overboard by a passing ship, but this feat of swallowing would be impossible for a carcharodon of this size.

Sometimes the man-eater is killed by its own greed. In 1957 a 10 ft specimen was found stranded on a beach in the Gulf of Mexico, the body of a man lodged in its throat. It had choked to death after trying to swallow its victim (Helm, 1961).

Every year about 100 people are attacked by sharks round the world, half of whom die as a result.

In the three-month period July to September 1959 a 6 ft shark which could have been a small carcharodon killed five people and injured thirty others at Machgaon, near the mouth of the Devi River, southern India (Coppleson, 1962).

The voracious nature and indiscriminate feeding habits of the carcharodon have resulted in many unusual objects being found in its stomach.

One individual caught in the Adriatic had three overcoats, a nylon raincoat and a motor car licence inside it, and a fur coat was removed from another shark (Coppleson, 1962). A man-eater taken near Port Jackson, New South Wales, Australia yielded half a ham, several legs of mutton, the hindquarters of a pig, the head and forelegs of a bulldog with a rope tied round its neck, a quantity of horseflesh, a piece of sacking and a ship's iron scraper. A 16-footer captured in Hobson's Bay near Brighton, Victoria, Australia in 1877 after looking through the fence surrounding the ladies' bathing section in "a disagreeable manner", contained a large Newfoundland dog which had disappeared the previous day (McCoy, 1882). Bricks, bottles, tin cans and even a porcupine have been found in the stomachs of other carcharodons.

On 18th April 1968 Henri Bource, a twenty-eight-year-old Australian skin-diver, was shooting an underwater film about sharks in the sea off Melbourne, Victoria when he was attacked by a white pointer which bit off his artificial left leg and swallowed it! His original left leg had also been lost to a shark of the same species.

Perhaps the strangest meal ever recovered from a man-eater's stomach was a set of ship's papers which eventually led to the condemnation of a brig and her cargo as a prize of war.

The incident occurred in the Caribbean towards the end of August 1799 when Great Britain and America were at war.

The cutter H.M.S. *Sparrow*, commanded by Lieutenant Hugh Whylie, was patrolling off the island of Haiti when she sighted the 125-ton American brig *Nancy* out of Baltimore on a blockade-run. The *Nancy* immediately crowded on sail and a chase ensued. Eventually the brig was overhauled and a shot put across her bows, but not before her Yankee skipper, Captain Briggs, had dumped the ship's papers overboard and replaced them with forgeries obtained at Curaçao which indicated that the vessel was owned by a Dutchman. When Lieutenant Whylie boarded the brig with some of his men the confident Captain Briggs threatened legal proceedings, but Lieutenant Whylie paid no attention. He sealed the ship's papers, told Captain Briggs that he and his brig were now a prize of war, and ordered some of his men to sail the *Nancy* to Port Royal, Jamaica where the case could be settled by the Vice-Admiralty.

The jaws of the shark which swallowed the papers of the U.S. brig "Nancy". ("Evening News", London.)

In Port Royal the Advocate-General filed a suit for salvage against "a certain brig or vessel called Nancy, her guns, tackle, furniture, ammunition, and apparel and the goods on board her, taken and seized as property of some person or persons being enemies of our Sovereign Lord the King and good and lawful prize on the high seas".

A few days later Captain Briggs filed a counter-suit in which he stated that "no papers whatever were burnt, torn, thrown overboard, cancelled, concealed or attempted so to be . . . that all the papers on board said brig were entirely true and fair".

In court the false papers were carefully studied, but officials could find nothing wrong with them that could justify seizure of the *Nancy* as a prize of war, and it looked as though Captain Briggs would be discharged and get high costs from his pending counter-action.

But he hadn't accounted for a strange quirk of fate. . . .

On 30th August, the day after Lieutenant Whylie had captured the *Nancy* and sent her to Port Royal, the crew of another British ship, H.M.S. *Ferret*, discovered a dead bullock floating in the sea near the island of San Domingo. It was surrounded by sharks who were jerking and tearing at the carcass. One of the brutes was a particularly large individual, and the ship's commander, Lieutenant Michael ("Fighting") Fitton, who was a keen fisherman, decided to have a go at catching this fish. He ordered the bullock to be taken into tow, and a few minutes later the shark rose to the bait and was hoisted on to the deck by the crew. Inside its stomach the men found the *Nancy*'s papers tied up with string, which they handed over to their skipper. By a strange coincidence Lieutenant Whylie was due to come aboard the *Ferret* that very morning to have breakfast with Lieutenant Fitton, and when he heard about the find and examined the surprisingly well-preserved papers it didn't take him long to realise what had happened. The two commanders at once set course for Port Royal, and they arrived there with their strange evidence just in time to prove the true ownership of the *Nancy* and condemn Captain Briggs and his crew.

After the case the "Shark Papers" as they became known were placed on exhibition in the Institute of Jamaica in Kingston, where they are still preserved today. The shark's jaws are preserved in the Royal United Service Institution in London.

In November 1959 a thirst-crazed African bull elephant waded into the sea off the east coast of Kenya and headed for near-by Lamu Island in a desperate search for water. About 7 miles from the mainland it was attacked by a number of sharks, some of them carcharodons. Fishermen at the scene said the elephant didn't stand a chance. As the great pachyderm lunged desperately at its attackers with its long tusks the sharks swept in and tore great chunks out of the stricken animal. Within a few minutes the elephant was dead. This appears to be the only fight (if you can call it that) on record between the largest terrestrial animal and sharks.

In October 1949 a cow hippopotamus was observed to plunge into the sea at St. Lucia on the north Natal coast, South Africa and seize a 300 lb blue pointer which was lazing in the surf. The shark was hurled up on to the beach where the hippo trampled it to death.

The heaviest bony or "true" fish in the world is the Ocean sunfish (*Mola mola*), which is found in all tropical, sub-tropical and temperate waters. Adult specimens average 6 ft from tip of snout to tip of tail fin, 8 ft between the dorsal and anal fins (vertical length) and weigh up to 1 ton.

On 3rd September 1919 a very large example was captured off the Santa Catalina Islands, California, U.S.A. by Van Campen Heilner (1920). It measured 10 ft 11 inches in length, 10 ft 9 in between the dorsal and anal fins, and nearly 4 ft in maximum thickness. Its weight was not recorded, but on the basis of its other measurements it must have scaled over 1·5 tons.

Another sunfish of approximately the same dimensions taken off the coast of southern California in 1910 is now mounted in the American Museum of Natural History in New York. It measures 10 ft in length and 11 ft between the dorsal and anal fins (Dean, 1913).

During a gale in the North Atlantic on 17th October 1926 a semi-adult sunfish landed on the deck of the American liner *Republic* after crashing through the guard rail. According to Gudger (1928) it measured 6 ft in length, 6 ft 10 in between the dorsal and anal fins, and weighed an estimated 800 lb.

*The largest ocean sunfish
on record.*

The largest ocean sunfish ever recorded was a monstrous specimen accidentally struck by the S.S. *Fiona* shortly after 1 p.m. on 18th September 1908 off Bird Island some 40 miles from Sydney, New South Wales, Australia.

A full account of this incident appeared in the *Wide World Magazine* for 10th December 1910:

". . . all hands were alarmed by a sudden shock, as though the steamer had struck a solid substance or wreckage. The result was strange and remarkable, for the port engine was brought up 'all standing'. The starboard engine was quickly stopped and a boat lowered and sent to investigate. On getting under the steamer's counter the boat's crew were astonished to find that a huge sun-fish had become securely fixed in the bracket of the port propeller. One blade was completely embedded in the creature's flesh, jamming the monster firmly against the stern-post of the vessel. It was impossible to extricate the fish at sea, so the boat was hoisted on board again and the steamer proceeded on her passage to Sydney with the starboard engine only working. On reaching Port Jackson, the Fiona was anchored in Mosman Bay, where all hands were set to work to remove the fish. After much difficulty and with the aid of the steamer's winch, the sun-fish was hoisted clear and swung on board."

The fish was later taken to a near-by wharf and put on a weigh-bridge, where it recorded a weight of 4,928 lb (2·24 tons). It measured 10 ft in length and 14 ft between the dorsal and anal fins.

The largest ocean sunfish ever recorded in British waters was a specimen washed ashore at Kessingland near Lowestoft, Suffolk on 19th December 1948. It measured 6 ft 6 in between the anal and dorsal fins and weighed 672 lb. Another specimen weighing 500 lb was taken in Plymouth Sound in 1734, and one measuring 7 ft between the anal and dorsal fins (weight not recorded) was caught off the Dorset coast in 1846.

Like the whale shark, the ocean sunfish is very tough skinned. Gilbert Whitley (1940) reports that one large individual caught in Botany Bay, New South Wales, Australia was impervious to bullets fired from Winchester rifles. Another one encountered off Montevideo, Uruguay resisted all attempts to harpoon it and was only secured after a harpoon had been inserted into its gill-cleft.

The longest bony fish in the world is the Russian sturgeon (*Acipenser huso*), also called the "Beluga", which is found in the temperate areas of the Adriatic, Black and Caspian Seas, but enters large rivers like the Volga and the Danube for spawning.

The average adult female measures about 7 ft in length and weighs 310–360 lb (the average weight of 1,977 adult males caught in the Don River in 1934 was 165–198 lb), but exceptional fish may measure up to 14 ft in length and weigh 2,000 lb.

In former times, when it was more abundant, this species attained a much greater size. Seeley (1886) says sturgeons measuring 24 ft and upwards in length were quite common in the Danube and fishermen sometimes caught fish "so large that they were unable to drag them from the river". One female caught at Saratov on the west bank of the Volga in 1869 scaled 2,760 lb.

According to Dr. Leo S. Berg (1948), the Russian ichthyologist, the largest beluga on record was a gravid female taken in the estuary of the Volga in 1827 which measured 24 ft in length and weighed 1,474·2 kg (3,250·5 lb). Another gravid female caught in the Caspian Sea in 1836 scaled 1,460 kg (3,212 lb), and one weighing 3,200 lb was taken at Sarepta (now called Krasnoarmeisk) on the Volga in 1813.

The Russian sturgeon or beluga, the longest of the bony fishes. This one measures 14 ft 2 in, but lengths up to 26 ft have been reliably reported. (F. Hansen.)

Vogt-Hofer (quoted by Mohr, 1952) refers to a 9 m (29 ft 6·5 in) female which weighed 1,300 kg (2,860 lb), but a more acceptable length of 8 m (26 ft 3 in) has also been quoted for this specimen.

The Russian *Encyclopaedia* says belugas have been measured up to 8 m (26 ft 3 in) in length and weighed up to 1,600 kg (3,520 lb).

On 11th May 1922 a female weighing 1,200 kg (2,648 lb) was caught in the estuary of the Volga. The head weighed 288 kg (633·6 lb), the body 667 kg (1,467 lb) and the eggs or caviare 146·5 kg (322·3 lb). Another female weighing 1,228 kg (2,701 lb) caught in the Tikhaya Sosna River, in the Biruch'ya Kosa region, in 1924 had 7,700,000 eggs weighing 541 lb in her ovaries (Babushkin, 1926).

The Kaluga or Daurian sturgeon (*Huso dauricus*) of the Amur River and adjacent lakes of eastern Siberia also reaches a great size. The largest one listed by Soldatov (1915) measured 4·18 m (13 ft 11 in) in length and weighed 541 kg (1,190 lb), but Berg (1932) quotes weights of 820 kg (1,804 lb) and 1,140 kg (2,508 lb) for two others.

A White sturgeon (*Acipenser transmontanus*) caught in the Columbia River at Astoria, Oregon, U.S.A. in 1892 and exhibited at the World's Fair in Chicago the following year was stated to have weighed "more than 2,000 pounds", but Gudger (1934) says he was unable to confirm this weight. There are also two claims for a 1,500 lb white sturgeon on record: one reportedly taken from the Weiser River, Washington, in 1898, and the other from Snake River, Oregon in 1911 (Brown, 1962).

The official record is held by a 12·5 ft fish taken in the Columbia River near Vancouver, Washington in May or June 1912 which weighed 1,285 lb.

The largest sturgeon found in British waters is the slender Common sturgeon (*A. sturio*). The heaviest recorded specimen was a female measuring 10 ft 5 inches in length and weighing 700 lb netted by the trawler *Ben Urie* off the Orkneys and landed at Aberdeen on 18th October 1956. Another female measuring 12 ft in length and weighing 672 lb was caught by the trawler *King Athelstan* in the North Sea and landed at Lowestoft, Suffolk on 4th April 1937. The largest river specimen was a female weighing 460 lb taken in the Esk, Yorkshire in 1810. Another fish reportedly weighing "over 500 lb" was caught by a Mr. J. Legge in the Severn at Lydney, Glos. on 1st June 1937 and sent to Billingsgate, London, but further details are lacking.

The largest fish which spends its whole life in fresh or brackish water is the European catfish or Wels (*Silurus glanis*), which is widely distributed in central and eastern Europe. Large individuals measure 5–6 ft in length and weigh 200 lb or more.

In earlier times, before it was over-fished, this species attained a much greater size, but claims that it sometimes grew to 20 or even 22 ft in length can be discounted. According to Kessler (1856) the catfish found in the Dnieper River reached a length of 8 to 14 ft and weighed up to 600 lb, and he says the largest one on record measured 15 ft in length and tipped the scales at 720 lb.

Seeley (1886) writes: "It is often from six to nine or ten feet long, and occasionally reaches a length of thirteen feet. In the Danube it often attains a weight of four hundred or five hundred pounds, and in South Russia may exceed six hundred pounds. With age it increases chiefly in circumference, and sometimes is as much as two men can span."

The largest accurately measured catfish of which there is reliable evidence is a 3 m (9 ft 10 in) female caught in the Danube in Rumania which is now preserved in the Museum of Natural History, Paris (Pellegrin, 1931). Another specimen from Rumania measured 2·85 m (9 ft 4·25 in) in length and weighed 170 kg (374 lb).

The heaviest Russian example listed by Berg (1949) was taken in the Desna River 6 miles from Chernigou in the Ukraine in September 1918. It weighed 256·7 kg (564·7 lb). Another one caught in the Dnieper River near Kremenchug allegedly weighed 300 kg (660 lb), but further details are lacking. Berg says catfish weighing 200 kg (440 lb) are not a rarity in the Syr-Darya and Chu Rivers.

Lord Rothschild told Flower (1929) he saw a catfish on exhibition at Hercules Bath in July 1907 which weighed 250 kg (551 lb). The fish had been caught in Hungary.

In 1937 a wels weighing 162 kg (356·4 lb) was taken in the Volga near the Seroglazinskaya stanitsa (Dobrokhotov, 1940).

This size is closely matched by another giant catfish known as the Pla buk (*Pangasianodon gigas*), which is found in the Mekong River of Thailand and Indochina. According to Seidenfaden (1923) this fish attains a length of 3 m (9 ft 10 in) and a weight of 240 kg (528 lb), and he says he saw one personally which measured 2·5 m (8 ft 2·5 in) in length, 1·7 m (66·9 in) in maximum bodily circumference and weighed 180 kg (396 lb).

Another specimen caught at Chiengsen, on the Mekong, in northern Thailand in 1931 measured 8 ft 4 inches in length, 4 ft 6 inches in maximum bodily circumference and weighed an estimated 400 lb (Smith, 1931), but this poundage is probably too high.

The Pla tepa (*Pangasius sanitwongseii*) of the Menam River, Thailand also grows to a great size. Smith (1931), in describing this species, writes: "In point of size this fish rivals the celebrated Pangasius of the Mekong basin called Pla Buk by the Siamese. In former times fish 3 m (9 ft 10 in) in length were sometimes taken, and at least one fish of that size has been recorded within eight years. In recent years, examples over 1·5 metres in length have been rare."

There are also several huge catfishes in South America. The longest, although not the heaviest, is the Lau-lau (*Brachyplatystoma filamentosum*), found in the rivers of Guiana as well as the Amazon, which has been credited with a maximum length of 12 ft (Hillhouse, 1825), but 8 ft is a more realistic figure. Dr. William Beebe and John Tee-Van told Dr. Gudger (1943) that the two largest specimens taken by them at Kartabo at the junction of the Cuyuni and Mazaruni Rivers in British Guiana in 1927 measured 74 and 75·5 inches in length (these measurements did not include the tail fins which would add about another 12 in) and weighed 200 and 210 lb respectively. Eleven years earlier Beebe had measured another lau-lau caught at Kartabo at 83 in (about 95 in with the tail fin).

The Pirahyba (*Piratinga piraiba*) of the Amazon River, which is closely related to the lau-lau, has been called the goliath of catfishes, but very little information has been published on its size and weight. Ex-President Theodore Roosevelt (1914) was told by the doctor attached to his Brazilian expedition that while he was working at Itacoatira, a small town at the mouth of the Madeira River, he had seen a pirahyba measuring 3 m (9 ft 10 in) in length. It had been killed by two men with machetes after it had attacked their canoe.

Another specimen collected by Dr. J. D. Haseman (quoted by Gudger, 1943) in the Guapore tributary of the Mamore River in 1909–10 for the Carnegie Museum, Pittsburgh, Pennsylvania, U.S.A. was so heavy that it required the efforts of four sturdy men to pull it up on to a sandbar. This fish measured 6 ft 1 inch in length and weighed an estimated 350 lb. Dr. Haseman put the maximum length and weight of this species at 7 ft and 400 lb.

The largest catfish of the La Plata and its tributaries is the Manguruyu (*Paulicea lutkeni*). In his account of this mysterious fish Dr. Gudger (1943) says: "How large this great catfish grows is not known. The Dorado Club in Buenos Aires in its *Guide* for 1937 has unverified reports of very large ones. One measured sixty-six and one half inches in length, forty and one half inches girth, and the head length thirty-one inches—nearly half the length of the fish. Its weight was not taken but it was estimated at about 200 pounds. Another, when caught and pulled to the surface, was so huge that a horse was required to drag it ashore. It was reported to be seven feet long and to weigh 220 pounds.

"A third when hooked pulled the fisherman out of his canoe, but he hung on and was rescued by his friends. Then the fish took charge of the canoe and towed it down stream about seven miles and was subdued only after a three-hour fight. No length is given, but the fish is said to have weighed 308 pounds."

The same writer also mentions a huge manguruyu skull discovered by Sir Christopher Gibson after a receding flood which measured over 6 ft in length and was adjudged to have come from a fish measuring 13 or 14 ft in length and weighing about 660 lb. Unfortunately the skull was not preserved, but Dr. Gudger says Sir Christopher's measurements must have also included a fused mass known as the "complex vertebra" which is so firmly attached to the base of the true skull that it looks like part of it. He concluded that "the true skull must have measured less than four feet and the length of the fish that bore it must have . . . been about eight feet in length."

The largest freshwater fish in the world is probably the pike-like Arapaima (*Arapaima gigas*), also called the "Pirarucu", which is found in the Orinoco as well as the Amazon and its tributaries. When Schomburgk (1841) visited Brazil in

1836 the natives of the Rio Negro told him they had caught pirarucu measuring 15 ft in length and weighing 400 lb (?), but the German naturalist did not see any fish even approaching that length. The two longest specimens collected by him measured 8 ft 1·5 in and 7 ft respectively, the former weighing an estimated 325 lb.

Paul Fountain (1914) says he killed an arapaima on the Rio Negro which weighed 628 lb piecemeal, but this poundage must be considered excessive.

Dr. Haseman told Gudger (1943) that he measured an 8 ft arapaima at Meura on the Rio Negro which weighed 120 kg (265 lb), and he heard from the local fishermen that they had caught a 10-footer weighing 200 kg (440 lb) in the same spot a few days earlier.

"Haseman did not see the fish," says Gudger, "but he did see the head. This was so much larger than the head of the one he measured that he thought the report of length and weight 'reasonably accurate'."

Allen (1942) caught an arapaima in the Upper Amazon which measured 7 ft 2 inches in length and weighed 165 lb (now preserved in the Museum of Comparative Zoology at Harvard University), and another specimen collected by the same expedition measuring exactly 7 ft in length weighed 246 lb.

Dr. Godfrey Davidson informed Leander J. McCormick (1949) that he had caught arapaima in the pools on the east bank of the Uaca River in the Guianas which were "too long and wide to fit into a fifteen-foot canoe", but this statement must be considered exaggerated.

Three specimens caught by Edward McTurk, a rancher at Karanambu, on 13th May 1947 were 6 ft 11·75 in and 203 lb, 6 ft 8 in and 148 lb and 5 ft 11 in and 110 lb. He told McCormick (1949) that he once killed a fish measuring 9 ft, but it was not weighed.

The arapaima, the largest freshwater fish in the world.

The largest freshwater fish found in North America is the Alligator gar (*Lepisosteus spatula*) of the Mississippi River and its tributaries. The largest specimen listed by Gudger (1942) was a female taken in Belle Island Lake, Vermilion Parish, Louisiana in *c.* 1925 which measured 9 ft 8·5 inches in length and weighed 302 lb. Another one caught by Dr. Henry Thibault in the Arkansas River near Little Rock measured 9 ft 2 in and weighed 232 lb. At one time this fish probably attained lengths of 10 or 11 ft, but today anything over 7 ft can be considered exceptional.

The shortest known fish, and the shortest of all vertebrates, is the Dwarf pygmy goby (*Pandaka pygmaea*), a colourless and nearly transparent creature found in the streams and lakes of Luzon in the Philippines. Adult males measure 7·5–9·9 mm (0·29–0·38 in) in length and weigh 4–5 mg (0·0014–0·0017 oz), and adult females 9–11 mm and 5–6 mg (Herre, 1927). This fish is so tiny that it has to be studied with a microscope rather than a strong magnifying glass.

The Sinarapan (*Mistichthys luzonensis*), another goby found in Lake Buhi, in southern Luzon is almost equally as diminutive. Adult males measure 10 to 13 mm in length, and adult females 12 to 14 mm (Smith, 1902).

Surprising as it may seem, the latter fish is much in demand as a *food* and has considerable commercial importance. The natives of the region catch them with large close-web nets, pack them tightly into woven baskets until the water drains out leaving a compact mass, and then sell them in dried cake form (a 1 lb cake contains about 70,000 fish!).

"Conditions in the Philippines and especially in Luzon have produced an extraordinary variety of gobies," writes Dr. Herre (quoted by Gudger, 1941), "but it is remarkable that the island of Luzon should have produced the two smallest specimens of fish in the world, both gobies."

The smallest freshwater fish found in South America according to Garman (1895) is the carp-toothed *Heterandria minor*. Of several hundred specimens collected at the confluence of the Beni and Mamore Rivers in northern Bolivia, adult males averaged 17·5 mm in length, and adult females 19–20 mm.

North America's shortest freshwater fish is the Top minnow (*H. formosa*), found in the rivers and lakes of the south-eastern United States. Adult males average 19 mm in length, and adult females 25–29 mm (Garman, 1895).

The shortest recorded marine fishes are the Marshall Islands goby (*Eviota zonura*) measuring 12–16 mm and *Schindleria praematurus* from Samoa, measuring 12–19 mm, both in the Pacific Ocean. Mature specimens of the latter fish, which was not described until 1940, have been known to weigh only 2 mg, equivalent to 14,175 to the ounce—the lightest of all vertebrates and the smallest catch possible for any fisherman.

The smallest fish found in British waters is the Diminutive or Scorpion goby (*Gobios scorpoides*), which measures 20 to 25 mm in length (Jenkins, 1925).

The longest lived species of fish is difficult to determine as aquaria are of too recent origin. Early indications are that it is the Lake sturgeon (*Acipenser fulvescens*). Between 1951 and 1954 the ages were assessed of 966 specimens caught in the Lake Winnebago region, Wisconsin, U.S.A. by examination of the growth rings (annuli) in the marginal ray of the pectoral fin. The oldest sturgeon was found to be one measuring 6 ft 7 inches in length which was eighty-two. The next oldest was a 6-footer aged forty-nine (Probst & Cooper, 1954). Another lake sturgeon measuring 6 ft 9 inches in length and weighing 215 lb caught in the Lake of the Woods, Kenora, Ontario, Canada on 15th July 1953 was believed to be 152 years old based on a growth ring count (Anonymous, 1954), but this extreme figure has been questioned by some authorities.

A 7 ft 7 in White sturgeon (*A. transmontanus*) caught in the lower part of the Fraser River, British Columbia, Canada in the summer of 1962 was believed to be seventy-one years old based on an annuli count (Semakula & Larkin, 1968).

According to Petrov (1927) a 4·2 m (13 ft 11 in) Russian sturgeon caught on 3rd May 1926 in the estuary of the Ural River and weighing over 1,000 kg (2,200 lb) was about seventy-five years old, and Soldatov (1935) quotes a figure of fifty-five years for a 656 kg (1,443 lb) kaluga.

A Sterlet (*A. ruthensus*) lived in the Royal Zoological Society Aquarium in Amsterdam for 69 years 8 months (Nigrelli, 1959).

Stories about Methuselah fish are legendary. The most classic of them all is probably the one about an enormous pike which was caught in the Kaiserwag Lake in Württemburg, Germany in 1497. This fish, states Gesner (1558), had a copper ring round its "neck" with an inscription saying it had been put in the lake in 1230, which made the creature 267 years old. Its length was given as "17 ft and its weight as 350 lb [*sic*]". The *alleged* skeleton of this monstrous fish was later preserved in Mannheim Cathedral. In the nineteenth century a celebrated German anatomist examined the bones and discovered that they came from several different fish!

Another pike taken in the River Meuse in 1610 bore a copper ring on which was engraved the name of the city of Stavern and the date 1448.

Apparently it was the custom in some countries to put rings into the gills and round the necks of fishes.

In 1865 a pike measuring between 4 and 5 ft in length and *believed* to be 100 years old was caught in the Loire at Saint-Paul-en-Cornillon. In its stomach were found a double-bladed knife, a small key and the steel snap of a purse. The fish was later presented to the museum at Saint-Etienne.

Exaggerated claims apart though, the pike is still one of the longer-lived fishes. Francis Bacon (1645) says it sometimes lives "to the fortieth year", and this view is shared by Dr. C. Tate Regan (1911), who remarks that "it is probable that fish of sixty or seventy pounds weight are at least as many years old".

Dr. Alex Comfort (1964), on the other hand, is more cautious and refers to a record of a 34 lb pike caught in 1961 which had a scale reading of only thirteen to fourteen years, while Frost and Kipling (1959) give the maximum scale reading for 5,000 pike taken in gill-nets from Lake Windermere from 1944 to 1957 as "slightly in excess of 15 years". This is a big reduction; nevertheless even fifteen years is a good age for a fish.

Some staggering life-spans have also been attributed to carp under favourable circumstances. Gesner says one in the Swiss Palatine lived for 100 years; others introduced into the ponds at Versailles during the reign of Louis XIV (*c.* 1690) were reportedly still alive early in 1830, and some of those living in the ponds at Fontainbleau before the French Revolution were allegedly 400 years old.

According to Regan (1911), however, the carp lives up to fifty years under artificial conditions, but only twelve to fifteen years under natural conditions.

"Clarissa", London Zoo's famous 44 lb Mirror carp (*Cyprinus carpion*), who died in May 1971 after spending nineteen years in the Aquarium, was estimated to have been about thirty years old at the time of her arrival, which means she was aged about forty-nine years at death. Another specimen received at the same aquarium on 18th June 1925 after being "previously in captivity in a washing bath for thirty-seven years", was still alive in 1935 aged about forty-seven years (Flower, 1935).

After the sturgeons, the European catfish (*Silurus glanis*), the European freshwater eel (*Anguilla anguilla*) and the Halibut (*Hippoglossus hippoglossus*) are probably the longest-lived fishes.

Flower says two European catfish placed in a pond at Woburn in 1874 were still alive on 16th January 1935 aged sixty-plus years, and he also cites records of forty, forty-two and fifty-five years for the European freshwater eel. In 1957 a female halibut measuring 10 ft in length and weighing 504 lb was caught in the North Sea and landed at Grimsby. Its age was given as sixty-plus years on a scale reading.

The life-span of most sharks is less than twenty-five years. One exception is the Australian school shark (*Galeorhinus australis*), females of which take twelve years to mature and probably live thirty years. The virtually indestructible whale shark (*Rhineodon typus*) may live sixty years or more.

In September 1966 the death was reported of a Brook trout (*Salmo trutta fario*) which had lived in a farmer's well at Fisnes, northern Norway for thirty years. It was four years old when originally caught. Shortly afterwards another farmer living at Egge reported that he had kept a trout in a well for thirty-nine years (1909–44), and a figure of forty-two years was claimed for a specimen kept in a well at Nordekvaal.

The exhibition life of a Goldfish (*Carassius aurktus*) is normally about seventeen years (Comfort, 1964), but much greater ages have been reliably reported. Bateman (1890) quotes a record of 29 years 10 months 21 days for a specimen kept in an aquarium at Woolwich, London from 20th May 1853 until 11th April 1883, and Mennel (1926) gives details of several others which lived twenty-five years. On 22nd August 1970 Mrs. I. M. Payne, of Dawlish, Devon announced that her pet goldfish had just celebrated its thirty-fourth birthday. There is also a record of a goldfish living in a water-butt for forty years (Comfort, 1956), but further information is lacking.

There are several contenders for the title of **shortest-lived fish**. One of them is the Transparent or White goby (*Latrunculs pellucidus*), which hatches, grows, reproduces and dies in less than a year. Other "annuals" include the Top minnow (*Gambusia holbrookii*), the Sea horse (*Hippocampus hudsonius*), the Dwarf pygmy goby (*Pandaka pygmaea*) and the Ice fishes (family Chaenichthyidae) of the Antarctic.

Because of the practical difficulties of measurement very little accurate data has been published on the speeds attained by fishes. A good insight to rate of performance is provided by the shape of the tail and body. Fishes with deeply forked or crescent-shaped tails and cigar-shaped bodies thickest in the middle are capable of high speeds; slow swimmers, on the other hand, usually have square or round tails and short, laterally compressed bodies.

Most ichthyologists share the view that the fastest fish in the world over a short distance is the highly streamlined Sailfish (*Istiophorus platypterus*), which is found in all tropical waters. The maximum velocity reached by this species is not known for certain, but Hamilton M. Wright (quoted by Hunt, 1935) says that in a series of trials carried out with a stopwatch at the Long Key Fishing Camp, Florida, U.S.A. between 1920 and 1925 one sailfish took out 100 yd of line in three seconds, which is equivalent to a speed of 68·18 mile/h (cf. 60 mile/h for the cheetah!).

"The speed of the sailfish", writes Wright, "is sometimes such that I have known a man on his first fishing trip to think that there were two fish when only one was on the line, because the fish reappeared on the surface so quickly in another quarter."

When it is travelling at high speed the long dorsal fin of the sailfish folds back into a slot in the back, and the pectoral and ventral fins are pressed flush against the body to cut down drag to a bare minimum. The same technique is also used by other fish of the family Istiophoridae.

The Swordfish (*Xiphias gladius*) has also been credited with amazing bursts of speed, but the evidence is based mainly on bills that have been found deeply embedded in ships' timbers. A speed of 50 knots (57·6 mile/h) has been calculated from a penetration of 22 in by a bill into a piece of timber, but this figure has been questioned by some authorities. According to Sir James Gray (1968) a 600 lb swordfish travelling at 10 mile/h would hit a wooden vessel travelling at the same speed in the opposite direction with a force of about half a ton, all of it concentrated into the 1 in² tip of the bill. This, he says, would be equivalent to a 1 lb projectile hitting the vessel at a speed of 30 mile/h.

The Pacific black marlin is one of the fastest of all fishes. (D. J. Sprungman— F. Lane.)

When the American whaling ship *Fortune* returned to Plymouth, Massachusetts in 1826 from an expedition in the Pacific the stump of a swordfish's bill was found protruding from her hull. The bill had "penetrated through the copper sheathing, an inch board sheathing, a three inch hard wood plank, the solid white oak timber of the ship 12 in. thick, through another two and a half inch hard oak ceiling-plank, and lastly had perforated the head of an oil cask, where it remained immovably fixed so that not a single drop of oil had escaped" (Smith, 1843).

There is also a record of a bill penetrating a ship's hull to a depth of 30 in (*New York Herald*, 11th May 1871), but Gudger (1940) thinks that the major portion of this blade projected into the hold.

Most experts put the maximum speed of the swordfish at between 30 and 35 knots (35–40 mile/h). Anything higher, they say, would be impossible because the drag from this fish's non-depressible dorsal fin and long bill would be too great.

Gudger also suspects that most of the accounts of "swordfish" attacks on ships refer to marlins or spearfishes (genus *Tetrapturus*) which grow to a much greater size and have a heavier and stronger bill.

Since 1800 there have been *at least* six authentic cases of men being killed by swordfish. The earliest account is given by William Daniel (1813), who says: "In the Severn near Worcester, a Man bathing was struck and actually received his Death-wound from a Sword-fish. The fish was caught immediately afterwards and the fact was ascertained beyond a doubt."

Two other cases are given by Gudger (1940). One of the victims was Captain F. D. Langsford, who sailed out of Lanesville, Massachusetts, U.S.A. on 9th August 1886 in the 12-ton schooner *Venus* in search of swordfish.

"About 11 a.m. . . . in Ipswich Bay, a fish was seen. The captain, with one man, taking a dory, gave chase, and soon harpooned the fish, throwing over a buoy with a line attached to the harpoon, after which the fish was left and they returned to the vessel for dinner. About an hour later the captain, with one man, again took his dory and went out to secure the fish. Picking up the buoy, Captain Langsford took hold of the line, pulling his boat toward the swordfish, which was quite large and not badly wounded.

"The line was taut as the boat slowly neared the fish, which the captain intended to lance and thus kill it. When near the fish, but too far away to reach it with the lance, it quickly turned and rushed at and under the boat, thrusting its sword up through the bottom of the boat 23 inches. As the fish turned and rushed towards the boat the line was suddenly slacked, causing the captain to fall over on his back; and while he was in the act of rising the sword came piercing through the boat and into his body. At this time another swordfish was in sight near by, and the captain, excited and anxious to secure both, raised himself up, not knowing that he was wounded. Seeing the sword, he seized it, exclaiming, 'We've got *him*, any way!' He lay in the bottom of the dory, holding fast to the sword, until his vessel came alongside, while the fish, being under the boat, could not be reached. Soon the captain said, 'I think I am hurt, and quite badly.' When the vessel arrived he went on board, took a few steps, and fell, never rising again.

"The boat and fish were soon hoisted on board, when the sword was chopped off to free the boat, and the fish was killed on the deck of the vessel. The fish weighed 245 pounds after its head and tail were cut off and the viscera removed; when alive it weighed something over 300 pounds. Captain Langsford survived the injury about three days, dying on Thursday, August 12, of peritonitis" (Wilcox, 1887).

The other fatality occurred off the coast of Freetown, Sierra Leone, West Africa: "On December 19th, 1902, Jno. Pearce was returning with three others from a fishing trip, and was sitting on the gunwale of the sailboat when he was spitted by a swordfish, apparently a Xiphias. He was stabbed in the back, the point of the sword projecting from the abdomen. His fellows testified 'that they heard a sudden rush from the water, and Pearce fell inside the boat and cried that he was killed'" (Renner, 1903).

The wounded man was taken to hospital in Freetown and operated on to remove the sword, but he died thirty hours later.

In April 1936 a fisherman trawling about 12 miles off the Gold Coast, West Africa was stabbed through the head by an angry swordfish as he tried to draw the hooked fish in and died a few minutes later.

On 30th November 1957 a fisherman died after being speared through the back by a swordfish off the coast of Baja California, Mexico, and in July 1959 another man died in a Tokyo hospital after being stabbed in the back by a swordfish he had caught in his deep-sea net.

In July 1967 a swordfish rammed the three-man American research submarine *Alvin* and damaged some of its electrical equipment. The

16-ton vessel was forced to surface to make repairs, and the trapped 200 lb fish was hauled aboard a research ship lying at anchor near by where it was later served for dinner. The crew of the submarine were presented with the sword as a "battle trophy".

There is also the strange case of the three dead swordfish without their swords which were washed ashore at East London, Cape Province, South Africa in May 1947. Ichthyologists were puzzled—until a bale of raw rubber drifted ashore further down the coast with three swords buried in it. Apparently the fish had attacked the rubber in mistake for an enemy (e.g. a shark) and then been held fast until they died of exhaustion and the swords had snapped.

Some American fishermen believe that the Bluefin tuna (*Thunnus thynnus*) is the fastest fish in the sea, and speeds up to 65 mile/h have been claimed.

The bluefin tuna of the North Atlantic has been scientifically clocked at 43·4 mile/h., making it one of the fastest fishes in the sea. This specimen, weighing 798 lb, was caught off Scarborough, Yorkshire in 1932. (Associated Press.)

Certainly its body is beautifully streamlined for speed, and when it is travelling flat out its first dorsal, pectoral and pelvic fins are withdrawn into grooves in its body to facilitate swimming (the second dorsal and anal fins remain fixed because they have to act as stabilisers).

The question of how fast a bluefin tuna can swim was answered by H. Earl Thompson off Liverpool, Nova Scotia, Canada in 1938. Using a device he and a friend had invented called a "Fish-O-Meter", which consisted of a motor-cycle speedometer, a flexible cable and V-pulley mounted on a rod and reel, Thompson hooked a young bluefin weighing 59·5 lb which registered a speed of 43·4 mile/h in a twenty-second dash. He said that specimens weighing 500 to 600 lb were the fastest swimmers (Patterson, 1939).

Some sharks are also very swift over short distances, but a claim by Hans Hass that they reach speeds of "between 40 and 70 knots" must be considered excessive. Pelagic sharks normally cruise at 3–5 knots, but this speed can be increased fourfold in an emergency. One of the fastest-swimming species is the Mako shark (*Isurus oxyrinchus*). One 12-footer chased by Thomas Helm (1961) and a colleague in the Florida Keys kept ahead of their speedboat travelling at 27 knots (31 mile/h) for half a mile before sounding. Frank Lane (1955) cites another record of a 600 lb mako leaping nearly 30 ft out of the water, and as it has been calculated that a shark this size would require a starting speed of at least 22 mile/h just to clear the surface (Lineaweaver and Backus, 1970), this particular specimen must have been moving at nearly 40 mile/h (the leading edges of the mako's fins are severely swept back in an effort to cut down drag).

It has also been claimed that the mako is faster than the swordfish because the flesh of this fish has been found in the stomachs of captured specimens (a swordfish weighing 120 lb was found in the stomach of a 730 lb mako caught near Bimini in the Bahamas, but *Xiphias gladius* is a fighter and would not normally flee from such an adversary.

The Great blue shark (*Prionace glauca*) can also reach a very high velocity. In one experiment carried out by Magnan and Sainte-Legue (1928), in which the fish was tethered by an extremely fine thread to a tachometer, a great blue shark measuring 6 ft 6 inches in length and weighing 70·65 lb registered a speed of 21·3 knots. In another experiment using water current a very young great blue shark measuring 2 ft in length and weighing only 1·3 lb held its own against a current of 26 ft/s (24·5 mile/h), and in short bursts of speed reached an astonishing 43 mile/h (Budker, 1971).

According to McCormick *et al.* (1963) an underwater spearfisherman hunting off Cape Cod, Massachusetts, U.S.A. once speared a shark which took off like an arrow, towing the luckless man behind it. Eventually a pursuing speedboat overtook the half-drowned diver and his seemingly tireless quarry, but it had to clock 14 knots to do so! The shark was not identified, but it was probably a great blue shark.

The great white shark is another swift species, but the statement by Riedman and Gustafson (1969) that it swims "constantly" at 10 knots is probably an over-estimation.

One day Captain Jacques Cousteau and a member of his team were diving off the Cape Verde Islands off the bulge of West Africa when a 25 ft carcharodon appeared out of the gloom some 40 ft in front of them. Suddenly it saw the two divers. "His reaction", writes Cousteau (1953), "was the least conceivable one. In pure fright, the monster voided a cloud of excrement and departed at an incredible speed."

The Wahoo (*Acanthocybium solandri*) and the Bonefish (*Albula vulpes*) are also magnificent sprinters. Walters and Fiersteine (1964) timed a wahoo running out a light line in open water at 48·5 mile/h, and Lane (1955) says Zane Grey once hooked a bonefish which dashed off at a calculated speed of 40 mile/h.

The Four-winged flying fish (*Cypselurus heterurus*) of the tropical Atlantic may also reach 40 mile/h during its rapid rush to the surface before take-off (the average speed in the air is about 35 mile/h.

The Atlantic bonefish, one of the fastest fish in the sea. (Fox Photos.)

To perform a leap like this the salmon has to leave the water at a speed of 20 mile/h. (R. Thompson– F. Lane.)

The swiftest domestic fish is probably the Atlantic salmon (*Salmo salar*). One specimen which made a leap of 11 ft 4 in over a waterfall on the Orrin River in Ross-shire, Scotland was calculated to have had an initial velocity of 20 mile/h as it left the water at the foot of the fall (Calderwood, 1931). The Pike (*Esox lucius*) is also capable of rapid acceleration, but only for very short distances. According to Hertel (1966) this fish can cover 7·5 to 12·5 times its own length in one second when lunging at prey, and Bainbridge (1958) says fish up to 1 m (39·37 in) should be able to swim ten times their own body length per second. On this basis, a 3 ft pike could cover 22·5 to 37·5 ft/s, which is equivalent to 15·3 to 25·5 mile/h.

The fastest fishes in the world over a sustained distance are the Marlins (genus *Tetrapturus*). According to Norman and Fraser (1948) they can swim at a very rapid rate for several hours, and Bandini (1933) writes: "One minute there is nothing, the next they are all around you, and a minute afterward the sea is empty once more."

FISH SPEED TABLE

Species	Maximum speed recorded (mile/h)
Sailfish (*Istiophorus platypterus*)	68·18
Marlin (*Tetrapturus* sp.)	50·00
Wahoo (*Acanthocybium solandri*)	48·50
Bluefin tuna (*Thunnus thynnus*)	43·40
Great blue shark (*Prionace glauca*)	43·00
Bonefish (*Albula vulpes*)	40·00
Swordfish (*Xiphius gladius*)	40·00
Four-winged flying fish (*Cypselurus heterurus*)	35·00
Tarpon (*Megalops attanticus*)	35·00
Mako (*Isurus oxyrinchus*)	31·00
Needlefish (*Strongylura* sp.)	30·00

Sources: Patterson, 1939; Lane, 1954; Helm, 1961; Budker, 1971.

The slowest-moving marine fishes are the Sea horses (family Syngnathidae). Some of the very small species measuring less than 1 inch in length probably never get above 0·01 mile/h, even in an emergency!

The greatest depth from which a fish has been recovered is 7,130 m (23,392 ft) for a 6·75 in long brotulid of the genus *Bassogigas* sledge-trawled by the Royal Danish Research Vessel *Galathea* in the Sunda Trench, south of Java, in about September 1951 (Brunn, 1956). The previous record had been held by another brotulid, *Grimaldichthys profundissimus*, caught by Prince Albert of Monaco south of the Cape Verde Islands at a depth of 6,035 m (19,799·5 ft) (Idyll, 1964). In 1970 another brotulid of the genus *Bassogigas* was reportedly dredged from "nearly five miles down" in the Puerto Rico Trench by the research vessel *John Elliott* of Pittsburg, operating under the joint National Geographic Society-University of Miami Deep-Sea Biological Programme, but further information is lacking. In 1910 the Norwegian Michael Stars Expedition trawled several Rat-tailed fishes (family Macrouridae) from a depth of 4,700 m (15,420 ft) in the North Atlantic (Marshall, 1954). There is also a record of a Deep-sea eel (family Synaphobranchus) in a stage of metamorphosis being taken at a depth of 4,040 m (13,254 ft) in the Indian Ocean.

At 1306 hours on 24th January 1960 Dr. Jacques Piccard and Lieutenant Don Walsh, U.S. Navy, sighted a sole-like fish about 1 ft long (tentatively identified as *Chascanopsetta lugubris*) from the bathyscaphe *Trieste* at a record depth of 35,802 ft in the Challenger Deep (Mariana Trench) in the western Pacific. "Slowly, very slowly," says Piccard (1960) "this fish . . . moved away from us, swimming half in the bottom ooze, and disappeared into the black night, the eternal night which is its domain."

At this depth the fish would have been subjected to a weight of 16,000 lb to the square inch. This sighting has been questioned by some authorities, who still regard the brotulids of the genus *Bassogigas* as the deepest-living vertebrates. The two men had earlier sighted and photographed a bathypterois, which is related to lantern-fishes, and a haloporphyrus at 23,000 ft.

Some fishes lay an enormous number of eggs, fecundity increasing with weight. A carp (*Cyprinus* sp.) had 2,000,000 in its ovaries; a halibut (*Hippoglossus hippoglossus*) 2,750,000; a cod (*Gadus morhua*) 6,652,000; a Turbot (*Scophthalmus maximus*) 9,000,000; a Conger eel (*Conger conger*) 15,000,000; and a Common ling (*Molva molva*) 28,361,000. The most prolific fish of them all, however, is the ocean sunfish (*Mola mola*). According to Johannes Schmidt, the famous Danish marine zoologist, the ovaries of one female contained 300,000,000 eggs, each of them measuring about 0·05 inch in diameter. It has also been established that there is a greater size difference between a newly born ocean sunfish (i.e. 0·1 in long) and an adult than between any other living animal. Gudger (1936) says "the larval sunfish is to its mother as a 150-lb. rowboat is to 60 Queen Marys".

The bony fish which produces the least number of eggs is probably the guppy *Lebistes reticulatus*. The average yield is forty to fifty, but one female measuring 1·2 inches in length had only four in her ovaries, while another measuring 2 in had 100.

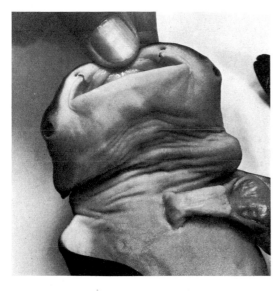

The whale shark lays the largest egg of any living animal. This infant was removed from an egg 11 in long and 5 in wide.

The largest egg produced by any living animal is that of the Whale shark (*Rhineodon typus*).

On 29th June 1953 Captain Odell Freeze of the shrimp trawler *Doris* was fishing 130 miles south of Port Isabel, Texas, U.S.A. at a depth of 31 fathoms (186 ft) when he noticed a very large egg case in one haul of the net.

"I saw this thing in the net and, on picking it up, felt something kicking around in it. When I opened it with a knife, out flopped this little shark, very much alive!"

The egg case measured 12 in by 5·5 in by 3·5 in, and the embryo was 13·78 inches in total length (Baughman, 1955).

In 1910 sixteen egg cases were found in one of the oviducts of a whale shark stranded on the coast of Ceylon, but no measurements were taken.

The most venomous fishes in the world are the hideous-looking Stonefishes (family Synanceidae) of the tropical waters of the Indo-Pacific region. These creatures administer their neurotoxic poison through the thirteen spines of their fins, and direct contact causes excruciating pain, followed by delirium and often death.

Dr. J. L. B. Smith (1951) writes: "Pain starts almost at once and rapidly becomes intolerable. Within ten to fifteen minutes the victim either collapses or becomes delirious and maniacal, raving and thrashing about in a boat or on the ground. If stabbed whilst wading, it generally takes three or four men to hold him and get him to shore without drowning. The intense agony lasts from 8 to 12 hours, after which it gradually diminishes, but the victim is weak and exhausted.

"Those who die generally do so within a time assessed at about six hours. Swelling starts soon after the stab and continues to increase for 'some days'. Legs may attain elephantine proportions.

"Some victims are able to walk after 3 weeks, but mostly it is said to be 'a long time' before the limb is usable. Often large blisters form and sloughing of large areas of skin occurs. Sometimes the dark pigment is destroyed and the skin of the blistered area remains light pink. Stabs in fingers and toes have led to the loss of those digits which turn black and 'fall off'. Some persons are still sick as long as a year afterwards."

According to Roughley (1952) a stonefish victim at Bundaberg, Queensland, Australia in January 1950 was saved by inhaling trilene (trichlorethylene) which served to numb the body and therefore counteract the shock.

Rather surprisingly, stonefishes have enemies. They are sometimes eaten by bottom-feeding sharks and rays without apparent ill-effects, and young ones often fall victim to large conches like *Strombus goliath* and *S. gigas*.

The most venomous fish found in British waters is the Lesser weever (*Trachinus vipera*), which is usually found in shallow bays. It buries itself in the sand on the bottom with its poisonous dorsal fin projecting and is easily trodden on by unwary bathers. The resultant wound is so excruciatingly painful that fishermen at sea have been known to try to throw themselves overboard, and there is at least one record of a man cutting off his own finger to obtain relief. People with heart complaints have reportedly been known to die within minutes of being stung.

In October 1961 Dr. David Carlisle, head of the Plymouth Marine Biological Association, blamed the lesser weever for many of the 200 mysterious drownings that had occurred in the shallow waters off the south and west coasts of England in the previous three years.

"It has a powerful poison that causes acute pain and immediate panic. I believe that many of the drowned people have been poisoned and have then fallen headlong in the sea." He added: "Woe betide the swimmer who accidentally touches one. It will chase and poison, usually under the armpit."

This venom potency may be matched by that of the Sting ray (*Dasyatis pastinaca*), which is quite common in the English Channel. In addition, the sting or dagger of this fish can also cause severe lacerations which may result in permanent damage to the affected limbs. Fatalities, however, are extremely rare.

The most poisonous fish in the world is the Japanese puffer fish (*Arothron tetraodon*), also known as the "Deadly death puffer fish". The internal organs, skin and muscles of this species contain a very powerful nerve poison called tetrodotoxin which produces respiratory paralysis, and most human victims die within twenty-four hours. The minimum lethal dose for rabbits is 3–4 mg per kg of body weight, and Dr. Bruce Halstead (1956) says there is no known antidote.

*The largest lizard in the world, the Komodo monitor or Ora (*Varanus komodoensis*) of Indonesia, which has been measured up to 10 ft 2 inches in length. (F. Lane.)*

*The Tuatara (*Sphenodon punctatus*) of New Zealand, the only surviving member of the order Rhynchocephalia which flourished 150,000,000 years ago. (F. Lane.)*

The deadly Japanese puffer fish is the most poisonous fish in the world. (Fox Photos.)

Extraordinary as it may seem the flesh of this fish and other puffers is considered a great delicacy in Japan, and in restaurants where it is served special cooks are employed who are skilled at removing the poisonous parts without contaminating the rest of the fish.

Despite these precautions, however, "fugu" as it is called is still the main cause of food poisoning in Japan each year (over 60 per cent of the victims die), and there is a saying in that country: "Great is the temptation to eat fugu, but greater is the dread of losing life" (Caras, 1964).

The most powerful electric fish in the world is the Electric eel (*Electrophorus electricus*), which is found in the rivers of Brazil, Colombia, Venezuela and Peru. An average-sized specimen can discharge 400 V at 1 A, but a measurement of 650 V has been recorded by Dr. C. W. Coates (1937) for a 90-pounder in the New York Aquarium (Bronx Zoo). This latter discharge would be sufficient to kill a man on contact or stun a horse at a distance of 20 ft.

Charles Holder (1886) describes how the natives of Calabozo, Venezuela, catch thousands of electric eels in the surrounding streams and lakes by a remarkable method known as "embarbascar con caballas" (intoxicating by means of horses).

"Mules, horses, and other animals are used, and the scene, though frightfully cruel, is made the occasion of great festivities. The poor animals are driven by shouts and blows into the water, where they dash about as if aware of their danger. Great eel-like, yellow bodies appear, their backs flashing in the sun, darting about, hurling themselves against the terrified beasts, which with staring eyes and trembling frames are completely paralysed by the electric discharges. Some are killed as if by lightning, and fall among the writhing mass; others endeavour to break through the howling throng of natives upon the banks, but are beaten back to terrible death or torture. The eels seem to be aware of the most vulnerable points of attack, as they strike the poor brutes near the heart, discharging the whole length of their battery. The terrible struggles last from twenty to thirty minutes, and then those horses that have survived the ordeal seem to grow careless of the attacks. The fishes have exhausted their electric supply for the time; and now the natives step to the fore. The eels, finding their power on the wane, seek the bottom of the lake; the natives, mounting the horses, rush wildly about among the fleeing animals, striking them with their long spears, and dragging them ashore, or anon rolling from their horses, paralysed by unexpected shocks that dart up the wet lines. Great numbers of eels are captured, and it is always found that, though they soon exhaust their force, if an attack is intended the next day the same precautions are necessary, their recovery of vital force being extremely rapid."

Baron Alexander von Humboldt (1852) says the South American Indians use the shock-giving power of the electric eel to treat paralysis and other ailments of the body, and one specimen sent from Surinam to Stockholm, Sweden at the end of the nineteenth century was used to treat rheumatism. People would queue up to touch it in the hope of being cured. This fish reportedly lost all its electrical power shortly before its death four months later, which is hardly surprising considering the amount of work it had to put in!

In 1941 two Indians died in the State of Amazonas, Brazil when the plank they were walking across slipped and they fell into a pool containing a number of electric eels. They were killed instantly (Caras, 1964).

The Electric catfish (*Malapterurus electricus*) of the rivers and lakes of tropical Africa can also produce a powerful discharge, and measurements up to 350 V at 1 A have been recorded.

The electric catfish of Africa. (W. J. Howes.)

The most powerful electric marine fishes are the Torpedo rays (genus *Torpedo*), which are found in all warm and temperate waters. The Black torpedo ray (*T. nobiliana*) of the Mediterranean and adjacent parts of the eastern Atlantic, including the English Channel, normally produces 50–60 V at 1 A, but discharges up to 220 V have been measured. Marine electric fishes do not need very

*The Adder (*Vipera berus*) is the only venomous snake found in Britain. It is confined mainly to southern England. (J. Burton/B. Coleman Ltd.)*

*The American common snapping turtle (*Chelydra serpentina*) is an extremely aggressive animal and has powerful hooked jaws capable of inflicting serious injury. (F. Lane.)*

high voltages to stun or kill their prey because salt water is a better conductor of electricity than fresh water.

The most ferocious fish in the world are the Piranhas of the genera *Serrasalmus*, *Pygocentrus* and *Pygopristis*, which live in the *sluggish* waters of the large rivers of South America. These utterly fearless cannibals have razor-sharp teeth, and their jaw muscles are so powerful that they can bite off a man's finger or toe like a carrot. They move about in large shoals numbering anything up to a thousand strong and will attack with lightning speed any creature in the water, whatever its size, if it is injured in any way and they can smell blood. There is a record of a 100 lb capybara being reduced to a skeleton in less than a minute, and cows have been reduced to the same state in under five minutes.

Colonel Candido Rondo, who himself lost a toe to one of these demons,

A piranha fish caught by David Attenborough during his zoo quest to Guiana. (David Attenborough.)

told ex-President Theodore Roosevelt (1914) that on one of his previous expeditions into the Brazilian interior a member of his party had been attacked by piranhas while wading across a narrow stream and bitten on the thighs and buttocks. Bleeding profusely the man managed to stagger to the near-by bank and heave himself out of the seething water by means of an overhanging branch, but his injuries—he lost over 3 lb of flesh—were so severe that it took him six months to recover.

On another army expedition a stream was dynamited to secure food, and the men waded in to pick up the stunned fish floating on the surface. One of them, a young lieutenant, picked up a fish in each hand and stuffed a third head-first in his mouth. Unfortunately it was a *piranha*, and just as he reached the shore the fish recovered its senses and promptly bit a large piece out of his tongue. The man very nearly died from the resulting haemorrhage.

There are also a number of reports of people being killed and eaten by piranhas, although many of these stories are based on hearsay.

One of the most gruesome stories comes from Colonel Percy Fawcett

(1953). According to this famous explorer a red-trousered soldier was fishing from a canoe in the Corumba River, central Brazil one day when he was suddenly pulled into the water by his catch. He clung to the side of the canoe shouting for a while and then fell silent. Eventually another canoe put out from the shore to rescue the man, only to discover that the hands still gripping the gunwale belonged to a dead person. From the waist down the soldier was just a skeleton.

On 4th February 1966 seven children were reportedly eaten alive by piranhas when their canoe capsized on the Madre de Dios River in Peru. A fisherman who went to their rescue also suffered the same fate.

In July 1971 a gangster told a U.S. inquiry how he once kept a piranha in a bowl at his Boston gambling den. Debtors were given the chance of paying up—or having a hand nicked by a razor and then shoved into the bowl!

The most ferocious marine fish is the Bluefin (*Pomatomus saltatrix*), which is found in most of the warm seas of the world. This fast-moving species, which travels in large schools, has been described by Professor Spencer F. Baird (1871) of the United States Commission for Fish and Fisheries as "an animated chopping machine whose sole business in life is to cut to pieces and destroy as many other fish as possible in a given space of time".

It will attack mackerel, weakfish and herring with unbelievable ferocity, leaving behind a trail of oil, blood and pieces of its victims, and often destroys ten times as many fish as it can eat. In fact, its gluttony is so great that when its stomach is full to bursting point (up to forty fish have been removed from captured specimens) it often disgorges the contents and starts the slaughter all over again just for the sheer joy of it. It has been calculated that an average-sized bluefin weighing 5 lb will eat nearly a ton of fish a year.

The coelacanth, the "living fossil fish with arms". This specimen was caught near Madagascar in December 1952. (Sport and General.)

The most interesting and important zoological find of this century was the discovery of a live Coelacanth, an archaic marine fish believed to have been extinct for 70,000,000 years and thought to be the missing link between man and primitive life.

The type specimen was caught in a mixed trawl catch of food-fishes and sharks in about 40 fathoms (240 ft) of water near the mouth of the

Chalumna River, Cape Province, South Africa on 22nd December 1938 and lived for some time after capture. The captain of the trawler described the fish as being a brilliant, steel-blue colour when alive, with large dark-blue eyes. It was 5 ft long, weighed 127 lb and was unusually oily.

On reaching port the fish was acquired by Miss Courtenay-Latimer, the inquisitive Curator of the East London Museum, who drew a sketch of the strange creature and sent it to Professor J. L. B. Smith, the famous ichthyologist at Rhodes University College, Grahamstown to see if he could identify the specimen. He was on holiday at the time so that the letter did not reach him for ten days, and by then the fish had been skinned and mounted by a local taxidermist. Unfortunately the body, which had began to decay, was thrown away though the skull was kept.

Later Professor Smith identified the fish from its external characteristics and scale structure as a coelacanth and gave it the generic name of Latimira in honour of the curator.

"It was", he says, "a sensational scientific discovery", and soon afterwards he began circulating the East African region with descriptive leaflets offering £100 reward to anyone who could supply him with another specimen.

Fourteen years went by, however, before another coelacanth was captured.

In December 1952 a second specimen, also measuring 5 ft in length and weighing 120 lb, was caught by a native fisherman off Anjouan Island in the French Comoro group some 200 miles west of Madagascar and preserved in formalin by Captain Eric Hunt, English skipper of a 150-ton trading schooner, who died tragically in a shipwreck four years later.

Professor Smith appealed to the South African Prime Minister Daniel Malan for assistance in acquiring this very valuable fish, and the Premier laid on a special military transport plane to fly the ichthyologist the 2,000 miles to the island. As a result, the grateful scientist named the coelacanth *Malania anjouanae* in the mistaken belief that he had discovered a new species.

While he was on the island the native fishermen told Professor Smith that the coelacanth was well known to them and that they often used its tough scales to roughen the punctured inner tube of a bicycle before carrying out repairs.

On 24th September 1953 another coelacanth was caught off Anjouan Island after a thirty-minute battle. This time, however, the 4 ft 4 in long fish went to the Madagascar Institute of Scientific Research at Tananaviro, because by now the French Government was also offering a reward of £100 to anyone who could supply them with a coelacanth. Two more specimens caught off Great Comoro Island in January 1954 were also sold to the institute, and by 1956 they had ten of these fish (eight males and two females). Today there are more than twenty examples preserved in various museums and institutes, including one measuring 4 ft in length and weighing 70 lb caught in the Comoro Islands on 24th March 1969 which was purchased by the Royal Scottish Museum, Edinburgh for an undisclosed sum.

Among the peculiar characteristics exhibited by the coelacanth are three sets of fins remarkably like stunted arms and legs and a backbone like a long tube. Above the mouth is a large section of bone and the tooth-plates are covered with tiny sharp teeth. The bones differ from the general arrangement in modern species and the large scales are covered with an enamel-like substance known as ganoin, found only in primitive forms.

SECTION VI

Echinoderms

(phylum *Echinodermata*)

An echinoderm is a spiny-skinned marine invertebrate or animal without a hard internal skeleton. It occurs in all depths of the sea, and the shape and size of the body is exceedingly varied. The main characteristic is the water-vascular system, which is connected with the hollow tube feet and serves as a means of locomotion and respiration. Another feature is the strongly developed external skeleton of chalky plates embedded just under the surface of the skin. Nearly all echinoderms are symmetrically radial in form, which means the various parts of the body are arranged round a central axis or disc. Most species lay eggs in the sea and these hatch into free-swimming larvae.

Echinoderms are a very ancient order of animal, and their fossil remains have been found in rocks dating back 600,000,000 years.

There are about 6,200 living species of echinoderm and the phylum is divided into five classes. These are the Asteroidea (starfishes); Ophiuroidea (brittlestars and basketstars); Echinoidea (sea-urchins); Holothuroidea (sea-cucumbers); and the Crinoidea (sea-lilies). The largest class is Ophiuroidea, which contains about 2,100 species or 33 per cent of the total number.

The largest of the 1,600 known species of starfish is probably the five-armed *Evasterias echinosomo* of the North Pacific. In June 1970 a Russian expedition from the Institute of Marine Biology in Vladivostock collected a huge specimen in the flooded crater of a volcano in Broughton Bay, Semushir, one of the Kurile Islands. It measured 96 cm (37·79 in) in total diameter—more than twice the width of an average dustbin lid—and weighed just over 5 kg (11 lb) when alive (Dr. Vladimir Lukin, *in litt.* 25.11.70). In February 1958 two New Zealand scientists announced that they had found starfish (? *Labidiaster*) measuring up to 48 inches in total diameter in McMurdo Sound, in the Ross Sea, Antarctica, but further information is lacking.

The heaviest known starfish is *Oreaster reticulatus* of Florida, the Bahamas and the West Indies. Although it has a maximum total diameter of only 20 in, it is a massive animal and has a very large disc (Buchsbaum & Milne, 1960).

The largest starfish found in British waters is the Northern sun star (*Solaster endeca*), which has been measured up to 40 cm (15·74 in) in total diameter. This size is closely matched by the very rare *Odontaster mediterraneus*, which has been measured up to 39 cm (15·35 in). The Spiny starfish (*Marthasterias glacialis*) usually measures 9 inches in total diameter, but measurements up to 13·75 in have been recorded (Mortensen, 1927).

The smallest known starfish is the North Pacific deep-sea species *Leptychaster propinquus*, which has a maximum total diameter of only 1·83 cm (0·72 in) (D'yakonov, 1968). *Marginaster capreensis*, found in the Mediterranean, measures up to 2 cm (0·78 in).

The smallest starfish found in British waters is the Cushion starfish (*Asterrina gibbosa*), which has a maximum total diameter of 6 cm (2·36 in). The very rare *Ceramaster balteatus* is smaller, i.e. 4·4 cm (1·73 in), but this species is normally confined to the Mediterranean and the adjacent waters of the eastern Atlantic.

Starfishes are generally short-lived animals, most species surviving for only three to four years, but Comfort (1964) gives details of a Spiny starfish (*Marthasterias glacialis*) and a Common starfish (*Asterias rubens*) which reached seven and six years respectively. There is also a record of an *Astropecten irregularis* living for six and a half years (Feder & Christensen, 1960). According to McGinitie and McGinitie (1949) *Pisaster ochraceus* may live for twenty years in areas where it develops slowly, but this needs confirming.

The greatest depth from which a starfish has been recovered is 7,630 m (25,032 ft) for a specimen of *Eremicaster tenebrarius* collected by the Galathea Deep Sea Expedition in the Kermadec Trench, in the Central Pacific, in 1951 (Bruun, 1956).

The most destructive starfish in the world is the "Crown of Thorns" (*Acanthaster planci*) of the Indo-Pacific region. This giant starfish (12–24 inches in total diameter) feeds on the polyps which make up coral reefs, and a single individual can destroy up to one square yard of coral a day.

Until 1960 this starfish was rarely seen, but then there was a massive population explosion in the South Pacific. In two and a half years an estimated 200,000 starfish destroyed 25 miles or 90 per cent of the coral reef along the north coast of Guam (*Science*, 18th July 1969), and already large parts of the 1,250-mile-long Great Barrier Reef off the coast of Queensland, Australia have gone the same way.

Starfish ravages have also been reported from Borneo, New Guinea, Fiji, the Solomon Islands and—moving west—Malaysia, Ceylon and the Red Sea.

Once the polyps are destroyed and the empty coral cups become overgrown with algae the edible fish in the area move to new habitats, and with them goes the shallow-water fisheries on which many small islands in the South Pacific depend for a living. Then the wind and sea begin to break up the reef itself, and this is followed by severe erosion of the coastline.

Efforts have been made by skin-divers in Guam, Queensland and the Malay Peninsula to kill the "Crown of Thorns" with injections of formaldehyde, paraffin and methylated spirit, but although the starfish usually die within a few hours as a result their numbers are too prodigious at the present time for this method to have any real impact.

In 1970 scientists at the Max Planck Institute in Frankfurt, West Germany, discovered that the 2 in long shrimp Hymenocera would attack and kill this starfish by boring holes into it, but it is not yet known whether this shrimp will repeat the performance outside of the laboratory.

The fastest-moving starfish, and the fastest of all echinoderms, is probably the giant nineteen-armed sun star *Pycnopodia helianthoides*. One specimen observed by Kjerskog-Agersborg (1918) covered 115 cm (45·2 in) in one minute, which is equivalent to a speed of 0·0356 mile/h, but Feder and Christensen (1966) say this rate of movement was measured down an incline. On a level surface this starfish is probably about one-third slower, which means it can cover about 75 cm (29·5 in) in a minute (0·027 mile/h). A speed of 75 cm a minute has also been reported for *Luidia sarsi* (Fenchel, 1965), and Feder and Christensen are of the opinion that large *Luidia* species are the speediest of all starfishes.

Most of the 1,900 known species of ophiuroid average less than 0·5 inch in disc diameter and only 4–5 inches in total diameter, but some like the tropical species *Ophiarachna increassata* have been measured up to 20 inches in total diameter. The Antarctic species *Astrotoma agazzizii* is even larger. One specimen with its arms missing had a disc diameter of 57 mm (2·24 in), and Fell (1966) says it must have measured about 1,000 mm (39·37 in) in total diameter. Another one with its arms missing collected from South Georgia had a disc diameter of 60 mm (2·36 in) (Mortensen, 1936).

The largest ophiuroid found in British waters is the Gorgon's head basketstar (*Gorgonocephalus caput-medusae*). The diameter of the disc sometimes reaches 90 mm (3·54 in), and the total diameter 350 mm (13·78 in). This size is closely matched by *Ophiophrixus spinosus*, which has been measured up to 300 mm (11·81 in) in total diameter (Mortensen, 1927).

The smallest known ophiuroids are some species of *Ophiomisidium* which measure only 3–5 mm (0·11–0·19 in) in total diameter.

Very little information has been published on the life-spans of ophiuroids. Comfort (1964) gives a record of a *Ophiothrix fragilis* living for five years, and five to six years has been reported for *Ophiura texturata* (Mortensen, 1927). According to Buchanan (1964) *Amphiur chiajei* lives for ten to fifteen years, and Fell (1966) thinks that it is not improbable that large ophiuroids like *Astrotoma* and *Gorgonocephalus* may survive twenty or even thirty years.

The greatest depth from which an ophiuroid has been recovered is 6,660 m (21,653 ft) for a specimen of *Ophiura loveni* collected by the Galathea Deep Sea Expedition in the Kermadec Trench in 1951 (Bruun, 1956).

The largest of the 800 known species of sea-urchin is the extremely rare *Sperosoma giganteum* of Japan, which has a horizontal test (shell) diameter of just under 13 in. The Black sea-urchin (*Diadema setosum*) has been credited with measurements up to 18 in, but the 5 in long spines were included.

The largest sea-urchin found in British waters is *Aroeosoma fenestratum*. One specimen had a test diameter of 280 mm (11·02 in) (Mortensen, 1927), but the average diameter is 140–180 mm (5·5–7·08 in).

The smallest known sea-urchin is probably *Echinocyamus scaber* of New South Wales, Australia which has a test diameter of only 5·5 mm (0·21 in) (Clark, 1925).

Longevity records for the echinoids are few. Boolootian (quoted by Moore, 1966) says an *adult specimen* of *Eucidaris tribuloides* lived for seven years in captivity, which means it must have been at least ten years old at the time of its death, and Comfort (1964) mentions a *Echinus esculentus* which lived for eight years under natural conditions. According to

Buchanan (1967) a study of the growth curves of two settlements of *Echinocardium cordatum* indicate a longevity of about fifteen years, and ten to twelve years has been reported for *Cucumaria elongata*.

The greatest depth at which a sea-urchin has been recovered is 7,250 m (23,786 ft) for an unidentified specimen collected by the Galathea Deep Sea Expedition in the Banda Trench near Indonesia in 1951 (Bruun, 1956).

The most venomous echinoderm in the world is probably the sea-urchin *Toxopneustes pileolus* of the Indo-Pacific region. Its sting can produce a curare-like paralysis, and deaths from drowning have been reported (Halstead, 1956).

The largest of the 1,000 known species of sea-cucumber are two members of the genera *Actinopyga* and *Stichopus* which have been measured up to 40 inches in length and 8 inches in diameter (Buchsbaum & Milne, 1960). Some of the worm-like sea-cucumbers of the genus *Synaptula* may reach 36 in, but they only measure 0·5 inch in diameter.

The largest sea-cucumbers found in British waters are *Cucumaria frondosa* and *Stichopus tremulus*, both of which have been measured up to 500 mm (19·68 in) (Mortensen, 1927).

The smallest known sea-cucumber is *Rhabdomolgus ruber*, found in the North Sea (Heligoland) and the eastern Atlantic (Brittany), which does not exceed 10 mm (0·39 in) in length. This species will probably be found sooner or later in British waters, but until that time the smallest native sea-cucumber is *Echinocucumis hispida*, which does not exceed 30 mm (1·18 in) in length.

As with echinoids, longevity records for holuthurians are few.

According to Mitsukuri (quoted by Pawson, 1966) the Japanese species *Stichopus japonicus* has been known to live for five years, and Tao (1930) says the Pacific species *Paracaudina chilensis* takes three to four years to attain maximum size.

The greatest depth from which an echinoderm has been recovered is 10,190 m (33,431 ft) for an unidentified sea-cucumber collected by the Galathea Deep Sea Expedition in the Philippine Trench in 1951 (Bruun, 1956).

The largest of the 550 known species of crinoid is the Feather star (*Helimoetra glacialis*), which is confined to the western part of the Sea of Okhotsk, an inlet of the north-west Pacific Ocean. This species has been measured up to 36 inches in total diameter.

The largest stalked crinoids or sea-lilies have a maximum length of 500 mm (19·68 in).

The smallest crinoids are certain species of feather star which have a total diameter of only 30 mm (1·18 in).

Some crinoids like *Promachocrinus kerguelensis* do not reach maturity until the tenth year, and Fell (1966) puts the maximum life-span at somewhere in the region of twenty-plus years.

The greatest depth from which a crinoid has been recovered is 8,210 m (26,935 ft) for a single specimen (species not identified) collected by the Galathea Deep Sea expedition in the Kermadec Trench in 1951.

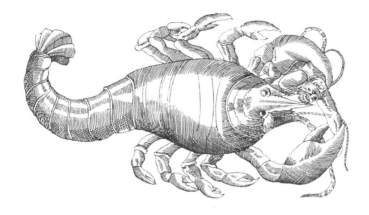

SECTION VII

Crustaceans

(class *Crustacea*)

A crustacean is an aquatic invertebrate which breathes through gills. It has a segmented body, paired jointed limbs and a tough outer integument or shell which is pliable at the joints. This external skeleton, which is incapable of growth, is periodically cast off and replaced by a lime-impregnated coat. Another characteristic is the two pairs of antennae in front of the mouth which are used as feelers. The young are produced from eggs shed freely into the water or carried by the female.

The earliest-known crustacean was the twelve-legged Karagassiema which lived about 650,000,000 years ago. Its remains have been found in the Sayan Mountains in the U.S.S.R.

There are about 26,000 living species of crustacean, and the class is divided into eight subclasses. These are the Cephalocardia (cephalocarids); the Branchiopoda (branchiopods); the Ostracoda (mussel or seed shrimps); the Copepoda (copepods); the Mystacocarida (mystacocarids); the Branchiura (fish lice); the Cirripedia (barnacles); and the Malacostraca (shrimps, prawns, lobsters, crabs and woodlice). The largest subclass is the Malacostraca, which contains about 18,000 species or 69 per cent of the total number.

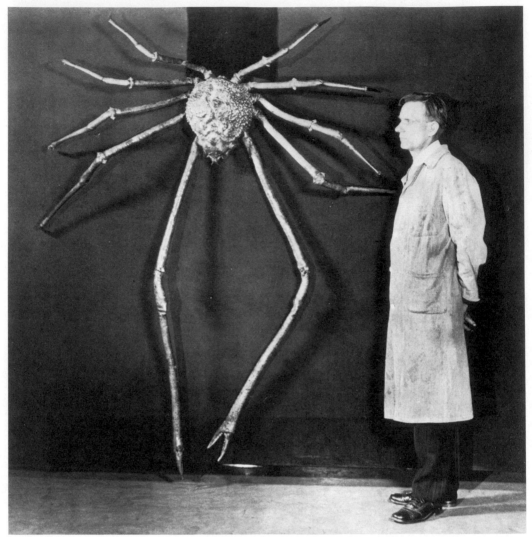

The giant spider crab of Japan, the largest of all crustaceans. (American Museum of Natural History, New York.)

The largest of all crustaceans is the Giant spider crab (*Macrocheira kaempferi*), also called the "Stilt crab", which is found in the deep waters off the south-eastern coast of Japan. Mature specimens usually have a 12–14 in wide body and a claw-span of about 8–9 ft. A specimen with a claw-span of 12 ft 1·5 in weighed 14 lb.

The maximum size attained by this bizarre creature has not yet been established with any degree of certainty. One huge individual caught in a fisherman's net in November 1921 reportedly had a claw-span of 19 ft and weighed 40 lb, and Holder (1886) says the first European to set eyes on one of these crabs saw two biting claws leaning against a fisherman's hut which both measured 10 ft in length and must have belonged to a specimen with a claw-span of 22 ft! (at first the traveller thought they were "some curious toy or grotesque plaything made in exaggerated imitation of the common rock crab").

Because of its strange shape, the giant spider crab can only move about in the very still waters found at great depths (i.e. up to 1,000 ft). On dry land it is completely helpless and cannot raise itself erect.

The Australian giant spider crab (*Leptomithrax spinulosus*) has also been credited with great size, but this species rarely exceeds 3 ft claw to claw, although unconfirmed measurements up to 7 ft have been reported.

In April 1932 two monster crabs (species not identified) weighing "nearly 80 lb each [*sic*]" were reportedly caught by the trawler *Coolgwai* off the Tasmanian coast. The larger of the two was stated to have measured 27 in across the shell and been armed with 14 in long claws, but these dimensions are not compatible with a crab of this alleged poundage.

The largest crab found in British waters is the Edible or Great crab (*Cancer pagurus*), adult specimens averaging 5–6 in across the shell and 1–2 lb in weight. In 1895 a crab measuring 11 in across the shell and weighing 14 lb was caught off the coast of Cornwall. Another giant caught off the Norfolk coast by Cromer fishermen on 7th September 1958 weighed 9 lb and had *16·5 in long claws*.

The largest spider crab found in British waters is the Spiny spider crab (*Maia squinado*). Specimens measuring up to 7 in across the shell and weighing 4 lb have been recorded.

The largest land crab in the world is the Coconut crab (*Birgus latro*) of the Pacific Ocean. It sometimes measures more than 12 in across the shell, and weights up to 9 lb have been recorded.

The smallest crabs in the world are the Pea crabs (family Pinnotheridae), which are so called because their bodies are usually about the size of a pea. Some species have a shell diameter of only 0·25 in, including *Pinnotheres pisum*, which is found in British waters.

Female crabs are great travellers. One caught off Whitby, Yorkshire in 1962 turned up in a seine-net in Aberdeen Bay, about 175 miles away, eighteen months later. Another specimen tagged about the same time covered 124 miles from Norfolk to Yorkshire in twenty-one months. The distance record, however, is held by a female crab which travelled 230 miles from Whitby to Fraserburgh, Aberdeenshire in under two years.

The speed record is held by a female which covered 13 miles in twenty-three days (average 995 yards a day) in 1962. Another individual tagged the same year covered 45 miles in 114 days (average 694 yards a day). In September 1925 an edible crab with distinctive markings escaped from a covered basket at Sennen Cove, Cornwall and was recaptured two days later just over two miles away! Male crabs are much less venturesome, preferring to stay where they are.

The slowest-moving crab is probably *Neptunus pelagines*. According to Professor Grunel (1931) of the Museum of Natural History, Paris, one specimen tagged in the Red Sea took twenty-nine years to travel the 101·5 miles to the Mediterranean via the Suez Canal at an average speed of 3·5 miles a year. Compared to this, the snail's speed (roughly 1 mile a fortnight or 26 miles a year) is that of an express train to a pedestrian!

Crabs are long-lived animals, as evidenced by the one just mentioned. Another crab caught by French fishermen off Saint-Nazaire on 4th

October 1959 had apparently travelled 62 miles in thirty years. The words "Job Le Roux" scratched on its shell were identified by Monsieur Joseph Le Roux, who said he had caught the crab in 1929 further south and inscribed his name on its shell before throwing it back into the sea.

In February 1951 building-workers at Hermosa Beach, California, U.S.A. reportedly found a crab—still alive—embedded in the mortar of a brick wall which had been built in 1915, but this story must be put in the same category as that of the Methusaleh toads already mentioned in Section IV.

Crabs can be extremely pugnacious animals when they want to. G. W. Walker (*Aquarist*, July–August 1930) describes how 1,400 Masked crabs (*Corystes cassivelaunus*) in the Brighton Aquarium, Sussex divided themselves into two armies and fought a pitched battle, in which 400 were killed.

"These 1,400 living caricatures were placed in one of the aquarium tanks, and for some reason best known to themselves they refused to 'mix', quickly grouping themselves into two camps several feet apart.

"It wasn't long before the opposing armies adopted extended order, and then, as though at a given signal, the two straggling lines simultaneously hurled themselves together in deadly combat. The engagement was short—a matter of minutes—but while it lasted the struggle was fiercely contested. No quarter was asked or given.

"It was a unique experience to watch this remarkable conflict, a wild fantasia of whirling claws and waving feelers, beneath which, capering and tottering on puny legs, the unchanging, expressionless human faces [masked crabs have shells resembling grotesque human faces] bobbed about like evil things in a submarine orgy of hate.

"In ten minutes the doughty warriors were fraternising with their late enemies. The battlefield was strewn with discarded claws and legs, among which 'Red Cross' parties were busily engaged in moving disabled combatants.

"No more fighting has since occurred."

The largest species of lobster, and the heaviest of all crustaceans, is the American or North Atlantic lobster (*Homarus americanus*). Although a good-sized specimen weighs only 3–4 lb, there are several authentic records of lobsters weighing over 20 lb.

Dr. Francis Herrick (1895) describes a very large male captured in Penobscot Bay, near Belfast, Maine on 6th May 1891 which was weighed in the presence of several witnesses and scaled just over 23 lb. This lobster—now preserved in the Museum of Adelbert College, Cleveland, Ohio—measures 20 in from the rostrum to the end of the tail-fan and has a maximum girth of 16·5 in. Its crushing-claw is nearly 14 in long, and Herrick says "it was probably powerful enough to crush a man's arm at the wrist".

Another male caught at Salem, Massachusetts in 1850 and now preserved in the Peabody Academy of Science, weighed 25 lb when alive, and one weighing 24·5 lb was captured at Lubec, Maine in September 1892. Fragments of another lobster captured with hook and line on the coast of Delaware and stated to have weighed over 25 lb are preserved in the Smithsonian Institute in Washington, D.C.

In the summer of 1890 a male lobster weighing nearly 25 lb was taken in a trawl off Monroe Island, some 5 miles east of Rockland, Maine (the crushing-claw of this specimen measured 16 inches in girth). Another male weighing 27 lb was caught off Breton Reef, Newport, Rhode Island in June 1894, and one weighing 30 lb was taken in a hoop-net in Golden Cove, in Vinal Haven Harbour, Maine in 1858.

According to Rathbun (1887) a lobster found on the beach in Boothbay Harbour, Maine at low tide in *c.* 1856 weighed between 30 and 40 lb but Herrick, who examined the mutilated shell of this specimen in the Land Office at Boothbay Harbour where it is preserved, put its weight at a more conservative 20–22 lb.

Other *unreliable* records include a 39-pounder caught off Gloucester, Massachusetts before 1845 (the crushing-claw of this lobster preserved in the Peabody Academy of Science is only slightly larger than that of the 23-pounder taken at Belfast, Maine); a male weighing 35–40 lb captured off Provincetown, Massachusetts in August 1894 (after examining the preserved specimen at the St. Nicholas Hotel in Boston, Dr. Herrick came to the conclusion that this animal "could not have much exceeded 20 pounds"); a 33 lb 11 oz male taken at Cape Breton before 1881 (the crushing-claw of this lobster is slightly smaller than that of the 23 lb Belfast specimen); and a 39-pounder caught off Boston, Massachusetts, in March 1823 (the length and maximum girth of the crushing-claw of this lobster preserved in the Zoological Museum at Yale University indicate a more reasonable weight of 22–23 lb).

In 1897 an enormous lobster was caught off Atlantic Highlands, New Jersey. It measured 23.75 in from the rostrum to the end of the tail-fan (3 ft 4 in over all) and weighed 34 lb when alive (Firth, 1939).

This record stood until the autumn of 1934 when Captain Charles

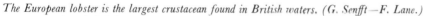
The European lobster is the largest crustacean found in British waters. (G. Senfft—F. Lane.)

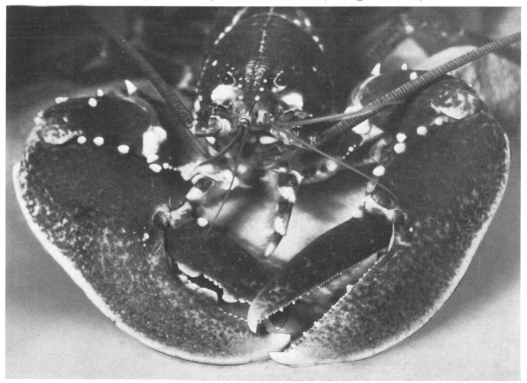

Wheeler of the smack *Hustler* caught a lobster weighing 42 lb 7 oz in 100 fathoms (600 ft) of water off the Virginia Capes, Virginia. A few months later Captain Wheeler caught another monster weighing 38 lb 12 oz in the same area. Both these specimens, known as "Mike" and "Ike", are now on display in the Museum of Science, Boston, Massachusetts (Gurney, 1950).

In the summer of 1939 an unconfirmed weight of 47 lb was reported for a lobster taken off the coast of New Jersey (Firth, 1939), and another specimen allegedly weighing 48 lb was caught off Chatham, New England in 1949. There is also a record of a lobster weighing 64 lb, but this poundage must be considered excessive.

The largest crustacean found in British waters is the Common or European lobster (*Homarus vulgaris*), which averages 2–3 lb in weight.

The maximum size attained by this species has been much exaggerated in the older literature. Olaus Magnus (1555), for instance, says some of the lobsters found between the Orkneys and the Hebrides were so enormous that they could catch a strong swimmer and crush him to death in their claws, and Erik Pontoppidan (1753), Bishop of Bergen, claims that one lobster seen by fishermen near Utvaer in the Bay of Erien, Norway was so huge (it reportedly had a claw-span of over 6 ft!) that no one dared to attack it.

It is now known, however, that the common lobster is considerably smaller than its American cousin (largely due to overfishing) and rarely exceeds 9 lb in weight. Buckland (1877) quotes a record of a lobster weighing 13 lb taken at Durgan, and he says another specimen weighing 12 lb was caught in Saints Bay, Guernsey, in the Channel Islands in May 1875.

On 30th July 1842 a gigantic lobster measuring 2 ft 5·5 inches in total length and having a crushing-claw 14 in long and 16 inches in maximum girth was exhibited at Billingsgate, London (these dimensions are proportional to a weight of 20 lb), but this was probably a specimen of *Homarus americanus*.

The largest common lobster on record is probably the specimen preserved in the Museum of the Academy of Natural Sciences of Philadelphia, Pennsylvania, U.S.A. which has a total length of 32·5 in (crushing-claw 13·1 in). "Unfortunately," writes Dr. Herrick, "it is not known where or when it was captured, nor what its living weight was; but from the measurements given . . . I would conclude that it weighed from 21 to 22 pounds. . . . This specimen has been carefully examined by Professor Ryder, who writes that there is no doubt of its belonging to the European species . . . that it was normal in every respect, and that the skeleton is in an admirable state of preservation."

(In actual fact, this specimen was taken off the coast of Norway in 1850. It measured 19·4 in from the rostrum to the tip of the tail-fan and weighed 18 lb.)

Other reliable records over 9 lb include: an 11·25 lb lobster caught off Guernsey and exhibited in Bond Street, London in August 1873; one weighing 10·5 lb caught off Tenby, Pembrokeshire, South Wales (presented to the Francis Buckland Museum in 1876); and a 14-pounder taken in a trammel-net off the coast of Cornwall in 1875 (total length 1 ft 11·25 in).

On 13th August 1935 a lobster weighing 12 lb 4 oz was caught by a Largs (Scotland) fisherman near Skelmorlie Bay. Another specimen measuring 2 ft 3·5 inches in total length and weighing 13·25 lb was caught off Gothenberg, Sweden in October 1949, and one measuring 4 ft 5 in from the tip of its feelers to the end of its tail-fan and weighing 13 lb was caught by fishermen at Lorient, Brittany, northern France in February 1952. In August 1956 a 9·5 lb lobster was caught by hand at Salcombe, Devon (later presented to Plymouth Aquarium), and another one weighing 11 lb 10 oz was caught on rod and line at the entrance to Wooton Creek, Isle of Wight, the following month (Brighton Aquarium tried to secure this giant for exhibition, but it was cooked and eaten before they could make contact!). On 25th August 1957 a lobster weighing 10·5 lb and "nearly 3 ft. long" was taken on a conger-line off Truro, Cornwall. Another one weighing 11 lb 5 oz was caught on a hand-line off Southampton in October 1959 and one weighing 11 lb was taken in Cardigan Bay in November 1960. In July 1962 two skin-divers caught a lobster measuring nearly 3 ft in total length (crushing-claw 10 in long and 12 inches in maximum girth) and weighing nearly 11 lb in a wreck off Berry Head, Brixham, Devon.

On 20th June 1964 an enormous crushing-claw was collected in a trawl near Skagen (the northernmost tip of Jutland) at a depth of 40 m (131 ft). It measured 35·1 cm (13·81 in) in length and 40 cm (15·74 in) in maximum girth.

In a letter to the author dated 9th June 1967, Dr. Torben Wolff, Chief Curator of the Universitetets zoologiske Museum in Copenhagen, Denmark, said: "When comparing with the list of giant American lobsters . . . the living weight of the whole animal must have been about 13 kg. or 30 pounds or perhaps somewhat more as the claws of the American lobster are somewhat larger compared to the body than those of the European lobster."

Thirty pounds is probably an over-estimate, however, because the crushing-claw is no larger than that of the lobster exhibited at Billingsgate, London in 1842 which weighed an estimated 20 lb.

On 19th April 1966 a lobster allegedly measuring more than 5 ft in total length (including feelers?) and weighing 35 lb was caught by fishermen at Bastia, Corsica, but this record has never been substantiated.

On 17th August 1967 a skin-diver caught a lobster weighing 14·5 lb off St. Ann's Head, Pembrokeshire, Wales (now mounted in the bar of the Amroth Arms, Amroth, Pembrokeshire). **This specimen, and the one taken off Cornwall in 1875, are the two largest lobsters ever recorded in British waters.**

In August 1969 a lobster measuring nearly 3 ft in total length and weighing 11 lb 11 oz was caught off Oban, on the west coast of Scotland, by a skin-diver. The live specimen was later presented to Flamingo Park Zoo, at Kirby Misperton, Yorkshire.

The Spiny lobster (*Jasus verreauxi*), also known as the "Green crayfish", which is found in the waters off the coast of eastern Australia, averages between 10 and 15 lb at maturity, but specimens weighing up to 25 lb have been recorded.

The Spiny lobster or Crawfish (*Palinurus vulgaris*) of British waters measures 10–24 in from the rostrum to the end of the tail-fan and may weigh more than 8 lb.

The smallest known lobster is the Cape lobster (*Homarus capensis*) of South Africa which usually measures 10–12 cm (3·93–4·72 in) in total length. Buckland (1875) says the "chicken lobsters" caught off Bognor, Sussex averaged fourteen to twenty to the pound, but this diminutiveness (the lobsters were in fact *Homarus vulgaris*) was due to overfishing.

The largest freshwater crustacean in the world is the Crayfish *Astacopsis franklini*, which is found in small streams in Tasmania. Weights up to 9 lb have been recorded.

Britain's largest native freshwater invertebrate is the Whiteclaw (*Astacus fluviatilis*), which measures up to 6 inches in total length and may weigh 1 lb.

The smallest known crayfish is the freshwater species *Tenuibranchiurus* of Queensland, Australia which does not exceed 25 mm (1 in) in total length. (François, 1960).

The longest-lived of all crustaceans is the American lobster (*Homarus americanus*). Very large specimens may be as much as fifty years old (Herrick, 1911). The European lobster may live for thirty years, and the European crayfish (*Astacus fluviatilis*) for twenty-five years.

The fastest-moving crustacean is probably the American lobster. Herrick (1911) says it can "shoot backward through the water with astonishing rapidity", and he quotes one observer as saying it can cover 25 ft in less than a second (more than 17 mile/h). The Common lobster (*Homarus vulgaris*) is also a rapid mover. Travis (1768) writes: "In the water they can run nimbly upon their legs or small claws and, if alarmed, can spring tail forward to a surprising distance as swift as a bird can fly. The fishermen see them pass about 30 feet, and by the swiftness of their motion suppose that they go much farther."

The greatest depth at which a crustacean has been seen is 35,802 ft for an unidentified red shrimp sighted from the bathyscaphe *Trieste* in the Challenger Deep on 24th January 1960.

The greatest depth from which a crustacean has been recovered is 9,790 m (32,119 ft) for an amphipod (order Amphipoda) collected by the Galathea Deep Sea Expedition in the Philippine Trench in 1951 (Brunn, 1956).
    The Marine crab *Ethusina abyssicola* has been recovered from a depth of about 14,000 ft.

The smallest known crustaceans are water fleas of the genus *Alonella*, which may measure less than 0·25 mm (0·0098 in) in length. They are found in British waters.

The most ferocious freshwater fish in the world is the Piranha (Serrasalmus sp.), which is found in the large rivers of South America. It will attack anything that looks remotely edible. (F. Lane.)

The most venomous known fish are the Stonefish (Synanceja sp.) of the tropical Indo-Pacific oceans. They administer their neurotoxic poison through the spines of their fins and there have been a number of human fatalities. (F. Lane.)

SECTION VIII

Arachnids

(class *Arachnida*)

An arachnid is a terrestrial invertebrate which breathes through gill-like structures called "book-lungs" or by means of a network of air-filled tubes. The body is divided into two main parts: the cephalothorax (head and thorax fused together) bearing four pairs of legs and two pairs of pincer-like appendages, and the abdomen which is limbless. It has a rigid external skeleton which it casts off periodically but no antennae. The function of these organs is served instead by the sensory bristles which cover the body and appendages. The young are usually hatched from eggs after leaving the female, but some are born alive.

The earliest known arachnids were probably scorpions, some species of which lived 400,000 years ago. The earliest known spider was *Palaeostenzia crassipes*, which lived about 370,000,000 years ago.

There are about 110,000 living species of arachnid, and the class is divided into ten orders. These are: the Scorpionida (scorpions); the Pseudoscorpionida (pseudoscorpions); the Solifugae (camel spiders); the Palpigradi (micro-whip scorpions); the Uropygi (whip scorpions); the Amblypygi (amblypygids); the Araneae (spiders); the Ricinulei (ricinuleids); the Opilones (harvestmen); and the Acarina (mites and ticks). The largest order is Araneae, which contains about 40,000 species or 36 per cent of the total number.

Theraphosa leblondi, *the largest spider in the world. (American Museum of Natural History, New York.)*

*The notorious "Black Widow" spider (*Latrodectus mactans*) of the United States, females of which have a venomous bite capable of killing a human being. (R. Cassell/F. Lane.)*

*The South American bird-eating spiders (*Mygalomorpha*) are the largest living spiders. Some specimens may have a leg-span of 10 in when fully extended and a body length of 3·5 in. (R. Kinne/B. Coleman Ltd.)*

The largest known arachnid is the "Bird-eating" spider *Theraphosa leblondi* of northern South America. A male specimen with a leg-span of 10 in when fully extended and a body length of 3·5 in was collected by Mrs. Joseph H. Sinclair at Montagne la Gabrielle, French Guiana in April 1925 (now preserved in the American Museum of Natural History in New York). There is also an unconfirmed record of a female with a leg-span of 28 cm (11·02 in).

In discussing the large South American bird-eating spiders (Mygalomorphae), and in particular *Mygale avicularia* of Brazil, H. W. Bates (1863), the English naturalist, writes: "Some Mygales are of immense size. One day I saw the children belonging to an Indian family who collected for me with one of these monsters secured by a cord round its waist, by which they were leading it about the house as they would a dog."

On 7th March 1938 a bird-eating spider measuring 8 in across the extended legs was found in a consignment of bananas in Exmouth Street Market, London and bit a fruiterer on the thumb before it was killed. The man was taken to hospital in great pain, but recovered after treatment.

Another Mygalomorph spider (*Selenotypus plumipes*) with a leg-span of 9·5 in and a body as big as a bantam's egg was collected in the Australian interior in November 1938.

Some of the wolf spiders (Pisauridae) are also very large, and *Cupiennius sallei* of Central America, which has exceptionally long legs, has been measured up to 10 in across.

Ivan Sanderson (1937) says he collected a "giant hairy spider" in the Assumbo Mountains in the British Cameroons, West Africa in 1932 for the British Museum of Natural History, London which covered an enamel dish measuring 12 in by 8 in when its legs were fully extended in all directions, but these dimensions are incorrect. In a letter to the author dated 12th August 1971 the late D. J. Clark, of the Department of Entomology at the British Museum of Natural History, London said: "The largest spider sent by Mr. Sanderson measures 2½ inches body length, 3 inches if you count the chelicerae [pincers], and has a leg spread of, at most, 7 inches. This spider belongs to the genus *Hysterocrates*. The largest African spider is probably *Hysterocrates hercules*, with a body length of 3 inches, 3½ inches if the chelicerae are included, and a leg spread of 8 inches."

A male specimen of *Grammostola mollicoma* collected in Brazil and preserved in the British Museum of Natural History, London measures 9·5 in across the legs (Clark, *in litt.* 12.8.71).

The heaviest spider ever recorded was a female of the genus *Lasiodora* (twenty-three species) collected by Tom Gilliard at Manaos, Brazil in 1945. It measured 9·5 in across the legs and weighed almost 3 oz (Gertsch, 1949).

A "tarantula" of the species *Dugesiella crinita* collected by Dr. William J. Baerg (1958) in Tlahualilo, northern Mexico in 1935 had a body length of 85 mm (3·32 in) and weighed 54·7 g (1·92 oz).

The most extreme weight claimed for an arachnid is "4 lb. [*sic*]" for a Wolf spider (*Lycosa tarentula*) killed in the Cathedral at Milan in 1751 as it was lapping up lamp-oil (for the record, says Bristowe (1947) spiders cannot tolerate oil or any other greasy liquid).

In 1868 a Mr. Rautenbach of Elands River, Natal reportedly killed a tarantula spider as big as a *turkey cock* which killed three dogs and had three charges of shot fired into it before it died!

Of the 610 known British species of spider covering an estimated population of more than 500,000,000,000, the Cardinal spider (*Tegenaria parietina*), a species of house spider, has the greatest leg-span, males sometimes exceeding 5 in (length of body up to 0·75 in). This spider is found only in southern England. The well-known "Daddy Longlegs" spider (*Pholcus phalangiodes*) rarely exceeds 3 inches in leg-span, but Savory (1928) says one outsized specimen collected in England measured 6 in across (length of body 0·031 in).

The heaviest spider found in Britain is the very bulky Orb weaver *Araneus quadratus* (formerly called *Araneus reaumuri*). An *average-sized* specimen collected in October 1943 weighed 1·174 g (0·041 oz) and measured 15 mm (0·58 in) in body length (Bristowe, 1947). This weight may be matched by the Six-eyed spider (*Segestria florentina*) of southern England, which has been measured up to 23 mm (0·905 in) in body length and has been referred to as "the largest British spider" (Locket & Millidge, 1951) and more especially by the bulky Wolf spiders, *Dolomedes fimbriatus* of southern England and *D. planitarius* of East Anglia, both of which have been measured up to 22 mm (0·86 in) (Duffey, 1956; Bristowe, 1958).

The smallest known spider is *Microlinypheus bryophilus* (family Argiopedae), the scientific name of which is about fifty times longer than its actual length! Adult males of this species, which was first discovered in Lorne, Victoria, Australia in January 1928, have a body length of 0·6 mm (0·023 in), and females 0·8 mm (0·031 in) (Butler, 1932).

The smallest recorded spider in Britain is the Money spider *Glyphesis cottonae*, which is known only from a swamp near Beaulieu Road Station (New Forest), Hants. (Locket & Millidge, 1951) and Thurley Heath, Surrey. Adult specimens of both sexes have a body length of 1 mm (0·039 in). Another Money spider (*Saloca diceros*), found among mosses in Dorset and Staffordshire, and the widely distributed Comb-footed spider (*Theonoe minutissima*), are almost equally as diminutive, their body lengths being 1–1·2 mm (0·039–0·047 in) and 1–1·25 mm (0·039–0·049 in) respectively (Bristowe, 1958).

The largest spider webs are the aerial ones spun by the tropical orb weavers of the genus *Nephila*. Several examples found by Captain W. S. Sherwill (1850) in the Karrakpur Hills near Monghyr, central Bihar, India measured 5 ft in diameter (= 15 ft 8·5 inches in circumference) and had supporting guy-lines up to 20 ft in length, and A. E. Pratt (1906) reports seeing webs in New Guinea measuring up to 6 ft in diameter (= 18 ft 9·5 inches in circumference).

According to Bock (1932) a nephila spider can easily produce up to 300 m (984 ft) of silk, and he says lengths up to 700 m (2,296 ft) have been reported, but these impressive measurements represent very little weight.

A web measuring 60 cm (23·62 in) in diameter weighed only 0·002 g, and it has been calculated that a single spider's thread long enough to circle the world would weigh less than 6 oz.

The silk produced by nephila spiders is incredibly strong and possesses great elasticity. Keith McKeown (1952) says it is not unusual for a man to have his hat knocked off his head by one of these snares, and Francis Ratcliffe (quoted by Lane, 1955) describes how he once blundered into a huge web "and almost literally bounced off". But statements that the thread is *as thick as darning wool* are exaggerated.

Not surprisingly, small birds and lizards are often entrapped, and E. J. Banfield (quoted by McKeown, 1936) reports finding a bat hopelessly entangled in a web on Dunk Island off the Queensland coast.

In New Guinea, the Papuans use the webs of the nephila spiders for fishing-nets. A native goes to the forest where the spiders are most abundant and sticks upright in the ground the stem of a long and pliant bamboo, the top end of which has been bent over and tied so as to form a large loop. This loop makes a convenient frame in which to build a web, and a spider soon takes advantage. Later the native takes the net which has been presented to him to a near-by stream and catches fish weighing up to 1 lb in it. The beauty of the "net" is that the water does not seem to damage it, because the threads are coated with a gummy substance that is waterproof, and the more twisted and matted the net becomes the tougher it makes the fabric (Pratt, 1906).

The nephila, however, are not the only spiders that spin webs of great tensile strength.

"On the evening of the 13th inst." writes S. Cummings (1835), "a gentleman in this village [Batavia, New York] found in his wine cellar, *a live striped snake*, nine inches long, suspended between two shelves, by the tail, by spiders' web. The snake hung so that his head could not reach the shelf below him by about an inch; and several large spiders were then upon him, sucking his juices. The shelves were about two feet apart; and the lower one was just below the bottom of a cellar window, through which the snake probably passed into it. From the shelf above it, there was a web in the shape of an inverted cone, eight or ten inches in diameter at the top, and concentrated to a focus, about six or eight inches from the under side of this shelf.

"From this focus there was a strong cord made of the multiplied threads of the spider's web, apparently as large as common sewing silk; and by this cord the snake was suspended.

"Upon a critical examination through a magnifying glass, the following curious facts appeared. The mouth of the snake was fast tied up, by a great number of threads, wound tight around it, so tight that he could not run out his tongue. His tail was tied in a knot, so as to leave a small loop or ring, through which the cord was fastened; and the end of the tail, above the loop, to the length of something over half an inch, was lashed fast to the cord, to keep it from slipping. As the snake hung, the length of the cord from his tail, to the focus, to which it was fastened, was about six inches; and a little above the tail, there was observed a round ball, about the size of a pea. Upon inspection this appeared to be a green fly around which the cord had been wound as the windlass, with which the snake had been hauled up; and a great number of threads were fastened to the cord above, and to the rolling side of the ball to keep it from unwinding, and letting the snake down. The cord therefore must have been extended from the focus of the web, to the shelf below, where the snake was lying when first captured; and being made fast to the loop in his tail, the fly was carried and fastened about midway, to the side of the cord. And then, by rolling this fly over and over, it wound the cord around it, both from above and below, until the snake was raised to the proper height, and then was fastened, as before mentioned.

"In this situation the suffering snake hung, alive, and furnished a constant feast for several large spiders, until Saturday forenoon, the 16th, when some persons, by playing with him broke the web above the focus, so as to let part of his body rest upon the shelf below. In this situation he lingered; the spiders taking no notice of him, until Thursday last, eight days after he was discovered; when some large ants were found devouring his dead body."

A similar drama occurred in a shed in St. Charles, Illinois, U.S.A. in October 1932 when a spider succeeded in enmeshing a 10 in long garden snake in its web. The luckless snake died twenty-four days later.

There are also several records of mice being snared by spiders.

In 1932 Professor C. E. Inglis of Cambridge University carried out some strength tests on a spider's web and discovered that a filament had a strength of 70 tons per square inch. He added: "If a cable of this strength and weight could be manufactured, a clear span bridge across the Straits of Dover would almost become a possibility."

Over the centuries several attempts have been made to use spider silk for commercial purposes (a few pairs of stockings and gloves were produced by a Frenchman in 1709), but none have been successful. In 1710 René Reaumur, one of France's greatest entomologists, was commissioned by the Academy of Sciences in Paris to investigate the possibility of establishing a spider silk industry. But he found the spiders temperamental and unco-operative. They became excited and resented their food so much that they ate each other instead. And the silk they did produce was much more delicate than that of the silkworm and difficult to spin.

De Reaumur also calculated that it would take 663,522 spiders to produce just 1 lb of silk, which ruled out any possibility of competition with the silkworm.

The smallest webs in the world are spun by spiders like *Glyphesis cottonae*, etc., which are about the size of a postage-stamp.

Some of the large spiders like the bird-eating varieties lay an enormous number of eggs. According to Gertsch (1949) *Theraphosa leblondi* is reputed to lay up to 3,000, each of which measures about 4 mm (0·157 in) in diameter, and he says large orb weavers and wolf spiders have been found with 2,200 in a single sac (these spiders often have two or more egg-sacs).

In addition, Bristowe (1947) cites a record of a 0·33 g *Araneus quadratus* which laid 935 eggs totalling more than double her own body weight!

Small spiders, on the other hand, produce very few eggs. The Cave spider (*Telema tenella*), for instance, lays only one egg measuring about 0·4 mm (0·015 in) in diameter, and the Six-eyed spider (*Oonops pulcher*) just two (Bristowe, 1958).

The longest-lived of all spiders are the primitive Mygalomorphae (tarantulas and allied species). One mature female tarantula collected by Baerg (1958) at Mazatlan, Mexico, in 1935 and estimated to be ten to twelve years old at the time, was kept by him for sixteen years, making a total of twenty-six to twenty-eight years in all, and he believed that this was the normal life-span for females. Another female tarantula lived in the British Museum of Natural History, London, for fourteen years and was thought to have been about twenty at the time of her death (Vesey-Fitzgerald, 1967), and Petrunkevitch (1955) says a female tarantula lived in the Museum of Natural History in Paris for twenty-five years. Most male tarantulas reach maturity in eight to nine years and die a few months later, but Baerg says he has reared specimens of the Arkansas species *Dugesiella hentzi* under laboratory conditions which lived for ten, eleven and even thirteen years.

Some of the Funnel web spiders (*Atrax* sp.) are also long-lived and Barrett (quoted by McKeown, 1952) mentions one which occupied a cavity in a staghorn fern in his garden at Elsternwick, Victoria, Australia, for seventeen years.

The longest-lived British spider is probably the Purse web spider (*Atypus affinis*). Bristowe (1958) says he kept a specimen in a greenhouse for nine years. The House spider (*Tegenaria derhamii*) is another long-lived spider, and two specimens kept by Dr. Oliver of Bradford survived for five and seven years respectively (Savory, 1928). Some large wolf spiders (Lycosidae and Pisauridae) may also live as long as seven years.

The majority of spiders complete their life-cycle in ten to twelve months. **One of the shortest-lived species** is the deadly Black widow spider (*Latrodectus mactans*), which must come as a relief to many people! A number of males reared under laboratory conditions lived on an average about 100 days, while females averaged 271 days (Deevey & Deevey, quoted by Gertsch, 1949). Very tiny spiders like *Microlinypheus bryophilus* may have an even shorter existence, but further information is needed.

The highest speed recorded for a spider on a level surface is 1·73 ft/s (1·17 mile/h) in the case of a specimen of *Tegenaria atrica* (Bristowe, 1958). Like all large spiders, however, it is very short on stamina and cannot maintain this "furious pace" for much longer than fifteen seconds. The crab spiders of the family Selenopidae are probably even faster, but no speed records have yet been published.

The most elusive of all spiders (and the most primitive) are the atypical tarantulas of the genus *Liphistius*, which are found only in South-East Asia. These trapdoor spiders live in narrow silken tubes buried in sandy ground and are extremely difficult to detect.

The most elusive spider in Britain is the handsome crimson and black Lace web eresus spider (*Eresus niger*), found in Hampshire, Dorset and Cornwall, which is known only from eight specimens (seven males and one female). In 1934 an eresus spider was seen at Kynance Cove in Cornwall (Bristowe, 1958), and in the 1950s another one was seen at Sandown on the Isle of Wight (Savory, 1966).

The highest altitude at which a spider has been found is 22,000 ft for a jumping spider (family Salticidae) collected by R. Hingston, the British naturalist-mountaineer on Mount Everest in 1924, but immature specimens probably "balloon" even higher in their own gossamer.

The most venomous spider in the world is *Latrodectus mactans* of the Americas, which is better known as the "black widow" in the United States. Females of this species (the much smaller males are harmless) have a bite capable of killing a human being, but fatalities are rare. According to Thorp and Woodson (1945) there were 1,291 *reported* cases of black widow bites in the United States during the period 1726 to 1943 (578 in California), but only 55 proved fatal and most of these were children or elderly people living in rural areas (black widow spiders like to make their homes under outdoor toilet seats).

In August 1952 a four-month-old baby was bitten by a black widow at Logansport, Indiana, U.S.A. and died four days later.

The venom of this spider attacks the nervous system. The bite, says Gertsch (1949) has been described as "intense, violent, agonizing, exquisite, excruciating, griping, cramping, shooting, lancinating, aching and numbing, and was either continuous and incessant, or paroxysmal and intermittent".

In 1936 D'Amour, Becker and Van Riper carried out a series of experiments to determine the toxicity of this spider's venom and found that on a dry-weight basis it was fifteen times more potent than that of the Prairie rattlesnake (*Crotalus terrificus*). It has even been claimed that it is the most highly toxic of all venoms, but although this may be true snakes like *C. terrificus* are much more dangerous because they can inject much more massive doses of venom into a victim.

The eggs of the black widow spider are also extremely toxic, and Blair (1934) says that two of them crushed and emulsified in a drop of saline and injected intraveneously into an adult mouse killed the animal very quickly. A rabbit injected intraveneously with a few drops of the same emulsion died within two minutes.

At one time, write Chamberlin and Ivie (1935), the Gosiutes of Utah smeared their arrow-heads with a lethal mixture of macerated black widow and rattlesnake poison.

According to some newspaper stories black widow spiders have even been used in suicide and murder attempts.

On 3rd June 1935 a young man died in a hospital in Worcester, Massachusetts, from what was claimed to be the self-induced bite of a black widow spider.

Apparently the man, despondent over his failure to obtain employment and rejected by the woman he loved, had ordered the spider by post from California. Later he was found unconscious in his room, the perforated cardboard box containing the deadly creature beside him. A note read: "I feel the effects now. The room is going around and around. I can barely see what I am writing. Maybe it is the end. Who knows? I do not care. It is very pleasant. Yes. No."

At the post-mortem inquiry, however, doctors revealed that the man had died from an overdose of sleeping tablets and not the venom of the black widow spider as supposed.

In July 1962 police at La Puente, California, charged a thirty-three-year-old man with attempting to kill his wife by holding a jar containing black widow spiders to her neck. The man said he did it to scare her!

Just before the Second World War there were five examples of this spider living in London Zoological Gardens, but they were responsible for so many questions in the House of Commons that when war was declared they were all destroyed as a precautionary measure just in case they escaped during a bombing raid.

At least two people have been bitten by the black widow in Britain. In November 1970 an American sergeant stationed at the U.S. Air Force Base at Lakenheath in Suffolk and a middle-aged woman living near by were attacked in embarrassing circumstances (see page 269). Both bites left an ulcerating wound which was treated at hospital, but other than that there were no complications. The spider was never caught, but it is understood to have been brought into the country accidentally aboard an American Air Force plane.

The Brown recluse spider (*Loxosceles reclusa*) of the Central and Southern States of the U.S.A. has also been credited with the title of the world's most venomous spider, but only one death has been attributed to this species and that was a four-year-old boy (Breland, 1963). The bite produces an ulcerating wound which often turns gangrenous, and infections are common.

The venom toxicity of the black widow spider may be matched by that of the Funnel web spider (*Atrax robustus*), which is found only in New South Wales, Australia. This spider first made the news in 1927 when a two-year-old boy was bitten by one and died within ninety minutes. Since then five other deaths have been reported, the latest being a seventeen-year-old pregnant woman who died in Sydney in 1970 after being bitten on the breast.

The Jockey or Red-back spider (*Latrodectus hasseltii*), which ranges from Arabia right across southern Asia and the Pacific islands to Australia and New Zealand where it is known as the "katipo" or "night stinger", is also extremely venomous. According to McKeown (1952) this variety of *L. mactans* has killed *at least* ten people in Australia this century, including a three-month-old baby and a man who died after thirty days, and there have been five fatalities in New Zealand in the past fifty years (two of these were children who died after hundreds of katipo invaded the country town of Raetahi in June 1969 after a minor earthquake).

In February 1967 a man was bitten on the left hand by one of these spiders while he was cutting grass at Port Moresby, New Guinea and died two days later.

The Button spider (*Latrodectus indistinctus*) of South Africa, another variety of *L. mactans*, also has a very potent venom, but only one fatality has been reported since the Second World War, and that was an eight-year-old girl (Clark, 1969).

Spiders of the genus *Phoneutria* have also been credited with deaths in Brazil (*P. fera* has a nerve venom equal in toxicity to that of the rattlesnake *C. terrificus*), but Bucherl (1956) says most of the victims have been children under six years of age. The Podadora (*Glyptocranium gasteracanthoides*) of Argentina and the Black tarantula (*Sericopelma communis*) of Panama are also dangerous spiders and fatal cases have been known.

On 19th April 1934 Reuters reported that huge, poisonous spiders of an unknown species were invading the town of Antofagasta in Chile and biting the inhabitants. According to the news agency twenty people, including nine children, were already in hospital with severe wounds and an SOS had been sent to the public health authorities in Santiago.

Although the bird-eating spiders of South America and elsewhere can inflict a deep wound with their formidable jaws, the venom they secrete is generally of a low potency and has only a local effect in man. There are exceptions, however. One of the most dangerous species is the Funnel web tarantula (*Trechona venosa*), which has a neurotoxic venom very similar to that of the black widow spider (Gertsch, 1949). The Australian tarantula (*Euctimsna tibialis*) also has a very powerful venom, and Butler (1934) says at least one person has died from its bite since 1926.

In December 1925 a man (age not given) died in Aberavon, South Wales after being bitten by a large bird-eating spider he had found in a barrel of apples. Another death from a spider bite was reported from Duisburg-Hamborn, West Germany in October 1930 when a sixty-year-old woman was taken ill in the street after finding a bird-eating spider in a bunch of bananas. An autopsy revealed that she had been bitten on the arm.

The venom of *Lasiodora* sp., the world's heaviest and most formidable-looking spider, is only deadly to cold-blooded animals and appears to have little or no effect on man; nevertheless, the spiders of this genus can still inflict a very nasty wound.

Finally, mention should also be made of the notorious Tarantula or Wolf spider (*Lycosa tarantula*) of southern Europe, whose bite was believed to have been responsible for the peculiar disturbance known as "tarantism" which swept through Europe during the Middle Ages (the first case was recorded in the seaport town of Taranto in 1370).

The symptoms of this strange phenomenon were acute pain and swelling of the limbs, followed by nausea and vomiting, and then delirium and intense melancholy which sometimes ended in death. The only cure, said physicians of the day, was music and wild dancing which served to "sweat" the venom out of the system.

It has since been established, however, that tarantism was nothing more than a form of mass hysteria, and that this spider is no more virulent than other spiders of the same genus.

According to Kobert (1901), the Italian physician Sanguinetti once allowed himself to be bitten on the arm by two tarantulas in the presence of witnesses, but apart from some inflammation about the wound and slight ulceration, there were no ill effects.

The largest of the 700 known species of scorpion is *Pandinus imperator* of West Africa. In October 1931 an exceptionally large specimen was received at the London Zoological Gardens from the Gold Coast (now Ghana). It measured 9 in from the tip of the head to the end of the sting and was described as the biggest and most perfect specimen in living memory. A specimen of *P. dictator* preserved in the British Museum of Natural History, London measures 8·5 inches in length, but this measurement also includes the 2·5 in long claws. Another large scorpion of the family Heterometrus from South-East Asia measuring 8 inches in length was received at London Zoological Gardens in December 1953 from Malaya. A length of 8 in has also been reported for an African rock scorpion (*Scorpion viatoris*), but the average length is 4 in. The slender lobster scorpion of Sumatra has been credited with measurements up to 10 in, but these lack confirmation.

In September 1959 two dozen scorpions, each allegedly "nearly a foot long", were found in the Slany area north-west of Prague, Czechoslovakia, but as scorpions only attain their maximum size in tropical countries, this report must be considered exaggerated.

During an unseasonal heat-wave in February 1937 a workman discovered an African rock scorpion measuring nearly 5 inches in length clinging to a wall at Plymouth Gas Works. He knocked the creature down with his cap and sent it to the Plymouth Museum.

The smallest scorpion in the world is *Microbuthus pusillus* from the Red Sea coast, which measures about 13 mm (0·51 in) in length (Savory, 1964). *M. fagei* from the coast of Mauritania reaches about 17–18 mm (0·66–0·70 in).

Very little information has been published on the ages reached by scorpions. Most species take about a year to reach maturity and probably live two to three years.

Although the scorpion has a very evil reputation it is largely undeserved because the venom of most species produces only a mild to severe local reaction in man.

The world's most dangerous scorpion is probably the large North African species *Androctonus australis*. This scorpion can deliver a massive dose of neurotoxic venom which has been known to kill a man in four hours and a dog in about seven minutes.

Between 1936 and 1950 *A. australis* was responsible for nearly 80 per cent of the 1,300 *reported* cases of scorpion stings in Algeria, 377 of which proved fatal, but the death-roll would have been much higher if the patients hadn't been treated with an antitoxin produced by the Pasteur Institute in Algiers. In September 1938 seventy-two cases of dangerous scorpion stings were reported *in one day* from districts near Cairo!

The scorpions of the genus *Centruroides*, found in the south-western

United States and Mexico, also have a very bad reputation. According to Caras (1964) *C. sculpturatus* and *C. gertschi* were responsible for sixty-four deaths in Arizona between 1929 and 1948 (about 2,500 people are stung by scorpions in this State each year), and Breland (1963) says approximately 1,600 people died in Mexico from scorpion stings over a period of thirty-five years (in most cases the sting entered the sole of the naked foot).

Deaths have also been attributed to the Brazilian scorpion *Tityus serrulatus*, the venom of which is reported to be even more toxic than that of the phoneutria spiders. Bucherl (1956) and Clarke (1969) say a number of soldiers fighting on both sides in the Western Desert, North Africa, during the Second World War died after being stung by scorpions of the genus *Buthacus*.

In February 1936 a plague of scorpions (*Buthacus* spp.) descended on Malmesbury, Cape Province, and stung three African children to death, and in November 1959 a two-year-old African girl died in the village of Kenhardt, Cape Province, ten minutes after being stung by one of these creatures.

Rather surprisingly, the huge *Pandinus imperator* of West Africa has been responsible for very few deaths, although it probably has the largest sting of any scorpion and can inject a massive dose of venom.

The most venomous scorpion in the world is *Leiurus quinquestriatus* of the Sudan, but the amount of venom it delivers is so small that the only lives endangered are those of young children.

Despite its formidable armament there is at least one animal that knows how to kill scorpions with impunity, and that is the adult Chacma baboon (*Papio porcarius*) of South Africa. As soon as it discovers one of these creatures under a stone it pounces on it like a flash and neatly rips off the sting. The scorpion is then torn to pieces and devoured at leisure.

At one time it was strongly believed that the scorpion would sting itself to death if surrounded by a ring of fire, but as scorpions are resistant to their own venom and also lack the power to reason this must be put down to faulty observation. When it is threatened a scorpion—not unnaturally—will lash out with its tail, and these actions can easily be interpreted as self-induced stinging.

Experiments by French scientists have revealed that scorpions can survive massive doses of atomic radiation for weeks on end.

Their immunity, reports Professor Maxime Vachon of the Museum of Natural History in Paris, was first noticed following France's atomic bomb tests in the Sahara. It was discovered that scorpions in the area were unaffected by sustained doses of gamma rays up to 100,000 roentgen, and subsequent experiments showed that the scorpions only succumbed when the radiation level reached 150,000 roentgen. This is an astonishingly high level, says Professor Vachon, when compared to the 700 roentgen dose usually fatal to man and the higher animals.

SECTION IX

Insects

(class *Insecta*)

An insect is primarily a terrestrial invertebrate which breathes through a system of air tubes. The body is divided into three main parts, the head, thorax and abdomen, and is covered by a horny covering or external skeleton which is shed periodically. The head bears a pair of antennae and three pairs of feeding appendages, and there are usually one or two pairs of wings rising from the thorax and three pairs of legs. The capacity for flight is one of the most striking features of adult insects, but not all species have wings. The young usually hatch from eggs after leaving the female, but some are born alive as fully developed larvae.

The earliest known insect was Rhyniella proecursor, which lived about 370,000,000 years ago. Its remains have been found in Aberdeenshire, Scotland.

There are about 1,000,000 living species of insect, and the class is divided into twenty-nine orders. The largest order is Coleoptera (beetles), which contains about 300,000 species or 30 per cent of the total number.

The Goliath beetle, the bulkiest of all the insects. (L. C. Chace—F. Lane.)

The heaviest insect in the world is the Goliath beetle *Goliathus giganteus* of Equatorial Africa. One specimen measuring 14·85 cm (5·85 in) in length (jaw to tip of abdomen) and 10 cm (3·93 in) across the back weighed 3·52 oz. This size is closely matched by another Goliath beetle (*G. regius*), found in West Africa, which also exceeds 5 inches in length.

The Longhorn beetles (*Titanus giganteus*) of South America and *Xinuthrus heros* of the Fiji Islands are also massive insects. Both have been measured up to 15 cm (5·9 in) in length, and 95 per cent of this is solid beetle.

The heaviest aquatic insect is the Giant water-bug (*Lethocerus indicus*), also known as the Electric-light bug because it is attracted to bright light, of northern South America and Trinidad. It has a body length of up to 5 in and weighs nearly 2 oz.

The great silver water-beetle is the heaviest ground insect found in Britain.

The heaviest insect found in Britain is the rare Great silver water-beetle (*Hydrophilus piceus*) of southern England, which measures up to 48 mm (1·88 in) in length, 22 mm (0·86 in) across the back and weighs 8–9 g.

This length is exceeded by the equally bulky male Stag-beetle (*Lucanus cervus*), now confined to Hampshire, which usually measures 38–50 mm (1·5–1·96 in), but the mandibles account for about 30 per cent of the length (in June 1969 a stag-beetle measuring 3 inches in length was captured at Priest Hill, Caversham).

The longest insect in the world is the stick-insect *Pharnacia serratipes*, females of which have been measured up to 33 cm (12·99 in) in length. A female *P. maxima* with a body length of 27 cm (10·63 in) preserved in the British Museum of Natural History, London has a total length of 51 cm (20·07 in) with legs fully extended (Meadows, *in litt.* 10.9.71). A female specimen of *Phobaeticus fruhstorferi* from Burma preserved in the U.S. National Museum, Washington, D.C. measures 30 cm (11·81 in) in length.

The largest African stick-insects are among the genus *Palophus*. A female specimen of *P. titan* preserved in the British Museum of Natural History, London has a body length of 25 cm (9·84 in) and a total length of 39 cm (15·35 in) with legs extended. The males of this species have a body length of 17 cm (6·69 in) and a total length of 27 cm (10·63 in).

The wingless *Eurycantha horrida* of New Guinea is another large species, females measuring up to 10 inches in body length.

A giant stick insect.
(H. Spencer—F. Lane.)

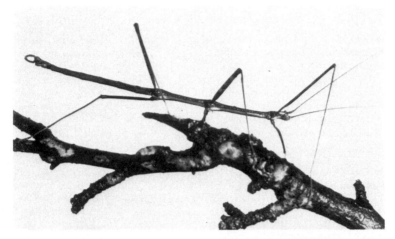

The longest stick-insect found in Britain is the Smooth stick-insect (*Clitarchus hookeri*), which was introduced from New Zealand some years ago. Females of this species measure up to 87 mm (3·42 in) in body length (Ragge, 1965).

The longest known beetle (excluding antennae) is the Hercules beetle (*Dynastes hercules*) of Central and South America, which has been measured up to 18 cm (7·08 in), but over half of this length is accounted for by the "prong" from the thorax. The two largest specimens collected by Dr. William Beebe (1947) in Avagua National Park, Venezuela, in 1954 measured 74 mm (2·91 in) and 76 mm (2·99 in) in *body length* and weighed 15 and 16·3 g respectively.

The Longhorn beetle *Batocera wallacei* of New Guinea has an overall length of 10·5 in, but 7·5 in of this is antenna.

The smallest insects recorded so far are the "hairy-winged" beetles of the family Trichopterygidae and the "battledore-wing fairy flies" (parasitic wasps) of the family Mymaridae. They measure only 0·2 mm (0·008 in) in length, and the fairy flies have a wing-span of only 1 mm (0·04 in). This makes them smaller than some of the protozoa (single-celled animals).

The male bloodsucking Banded louse (*Enderleinellus zonatus*), ungorged, and the Parasitic wasp *Caraphractus cinctus*, may each weigh as little as 0·005 mg, or 5,670,000 to an ounce. The eggs of the latter each weigh 0·0002 mg, or 141,750,000 to the ounce.

The greatest majority of insects live less than a year, but there are some Methuselahs. One of them is the North American cicada (*Megicica septemdecim*), which is also known as the seventeen-year locust. Northern broods of this species live underground in a larval state for about seventeen years before digging to the surface and living as adults for a few weeks; while southern broods have a life-cycle of about thirteen years.

Some beetles are also long-lived. In 1846 Sir John Richardson showed members of the British Association a specimen of the Burying or Sexton beetle (family Silphidae), which had been found embedded in concrete and must have been at least sixteen years old. The creature was still alive when it was brought to Sir John, and lived for another six weeks (Timbs, 1868). A Cellar beetle (*Blaps gigas*) kept by Labitte (1916) lived for 14 years 233 days.

In 1889 the 3 cm (1·18 in) long larva of a Metallic wood-boring beetle (*Bupretis splendens*) emerged from the step of a staircase in the library at the University of Copenhagen. The stairs, made from foreign pine-wood, were laid in 1860, which meant the beetle was at least twenty-nine years old (Meinert, 1889).

A similar case was reported in March 1966 when a 1 in long larva suddenly appeared from the step of a staircase in a house at Thorpe Bay, Essex, after living in the pine-wood for more than thirty years (the tree in which this beetle was born had been sawn up and shipped to Britain from Canada in 1936). The specimen, identified as *B. aurulenta*, was killed and sent to the Forest Products Research Laboratory in Princes Risborough, Bucks for analysis.

There is also a record of a specimen of *B. splendens* living in the wood of a pencil-box for thirty years (Burr, 1954).

Williams (1937) says there is "an authentic record" of a metallic wood-boring beetle living for thirty-seven years, and another mentioned by Packard reportedly lived for forty-five years, but further details are lacking.

Certain species of ant (*Formicoidea*) also have long life-spans. Sir John Lubbock (1894) says he kept a female Small black ant (*Formica fusca*) from December 1874 until August 1888, when it was at least fifteen years old, and Donisthorpe (1936) kept a queen Westwood's ant (*Stenamma westwoodi*), which must have been at least sixteen years when she died on 2nd October 1935 and was probably more. He had her in captivity for fifteen years and considers from the size and condition of her nest when he captured her that she was probably eighteen when she died.

The longest-lived insects are Queen termites (Isoptera), which are closely related to ants. Some have been known to lay eggs for up to fifty years. In 1872 the top of a 14 ft high termite nest of the Australian species *Nasutitermes triodiae* was broken off to make way for overhead telegraph wires in Queensland, and when it was examined again in 1935 it was still in a good state of repair and had a flourishing population. This means that the king and queen who founded this colony were probably still alive, because secondary reproductions are unknown in this species (Hill, 1942). Klots and Klots (1961) believe that some queen termites may live 100 years or more, but this has not yet been proven.

The shortest-lived of all insects is probably the Common house-fly (*Musca domestica*). In one study of over 8,500 specimens males had an average life-span of seventeen days, and females twenty-nine days (Rockstein, 1959). Adult honey-bees (*Apis mellifera*) live about six weeks (Pixell-Goodrich, 1920). Some mayflies (*Ephemeroidea*) survive only a few hours in the adult stage, but they spent two to three years as larvae. Nothing is known about the longevity of the insects of the families Trichopterygidae and Mymaridae (see smallest insects).

The male cicada, the loudest of all insects. (L. C. Chace—F. Lane.)

The loudest of all insects is the male cicada (family Cicadidae). The tymbal organs or membranes at the base of the abdomen, which vibrate from 120 to 480 times a second, produce a noise that is detectable more than a quarter of a mile away. The sound, says Pesson (1959) has been likened to a knife-grinder, a railway whistle and even fat spitting in a hot frying-pan, depending on the species.

According to scientists at Princeton University, New Jersey, U.S.A. the sound produced by thousands of cicadas under a single tree registered between 80 and 100 db at a distance of 60 ft.

The only British species is the very rare Mountain cicada (*Cicadetta montana*), which is confined to the New Forest area in Hampshire.

Some authorities claimed that the European cricket (*Brachytrypes megacephalus*) is even louder, and that it can be heard up to a mile away, but this needs confirming.

The most dangerous insect in the world is the Common house-fly (*Musca domestica*). It can transmit thirty diseases and parasitic worms to man, including cholera, typhoid, dysentery, bubonic plague, leprosy, cerebro-spinal meningitis, diphtheria, scarlet fever, smallpox and infantile paralysis.

The twenty or so species of malarial mosquito which form the genus *Anopheles* are also strong contenders. These tiny creatures kill at least 1,000,000 people a year in Africa and South-East Asia, and an estimated 600,000,000 people are constantly exposed to the disease although it has now been brought under control.

Four species of malarial mosquito are found in Britain, but they can only carry malaria if they come into contact with someone suffering from the disease. There are, however, several records of people dying in this country after being bitten by a mosquito on the face or neck.

If we exclude disease carriers, then the most dangerous insects are bees (family Apidae) and wasps (family Vespidae). Between them they kill more people each year than the estimated 40,000 who die from snake-bite. Take the United States, for example. According to the Office of Vital Statistics there were seventy-one deaths from snakebite and eighty-five deaths from bee and wasp stings in that country during the period

1950–54 (Caras, 1964). Clarke (1969) says the annual toll in Africa is well over 200, and in Britain these insects cause seven to eight deaths annually. In September 1970 seven people died from wasp stings in France, most of them women.

In September 1964 a young Rhodesian set up an unenviable world record when he was stung 2,243 times by bees.

He was attacked on a river bank by a swarm which settled in a 3 in layer on his head, shoulders and chest.

He jumped into the river and stayed there with only his head above water, but many bees got into his mouth and were swallowed. The youth was rescued barely conscious four hours later, his scalp, face, neck, trunk and arms black with stings. More than 2,000 were removed from his eyelids, lips, tongue and mouth alone. To the astonishment of everyone he made a complete recovery after five days in hospital.

The previous record had been set two years earlier by a Dutch tin-mine employee working 200 miles from Bulawayo, Rhodesia, who had 2,053 bee stings removed from his body in February 1962 after being attacked by maddened wild bees on the banks of the Gwaai River, a tributary of the Zambesi. His boxer dog was stung to death.

In July 1970 an eighty-year-old woman died after being attacked by a colony of bees she kept in her garden at Selsdon, Surrey. More than 300 stings were removed from her body.

In 1962 Mr. Nikolai Glushkov, Director of the Soviet Agricultural Institute in Moscow reported that there were 30,000,000 swarms of bees in the world. Of this total 10,000,000 were in the Soviet Union, 6,000,000 in the United States and 3,000,000 in China.

The common housefly, the most dangerous animal in the world. (L. C. Chace— F. Lane.)

The most destructive insect in the world is the Desert locust (*Schistocerca gregaria*), the locust of the Bible, whose habitat is the dry and semi-arid regions of Africa, the Middle East, Pakistan and India.

In the Book of Exodus (Chapter 10) we are told a plague of these locusts invaded Egypt and "covered the face of the whole earth so that the land was darkened, and they did eat every herb of the land and all the fruit of the trees which the hail had left: and there remained not any green thing in the trees, or in the herbs of the field, through all the land of Egypt."

The desert locust is also mentioned by Paulus Orosius (*fl.* 415 B.C.), the Spanish historian and theologian, who writes: "In the year of the world 3800 such infinite myriads of locusts were blown from the coast of Africa into the sea and drowned that, being cast upon the shore, they emitted a stench greater than could have been produced by the carcases of one hundred thousand men, and caused a general pestilence."

In 125 B.C. 800,000 people reportedly died of starvation after a swarm of desert locusts invaded the Roman colonies of Cyrenaica and Numidea in North Africa (Williams, 1958).

This species of locust, which in fact is a short-horn grasshopper, can eat its own weight in food a day, and during long migratory flights of anything up to 2,000 miles a large swarm will consume 3,000 tons of greenstuff a day and bring famine to whole communities.

In 1956 the desert locust was estimated to do over £30,000,000 of damage to crops a year, but the figure today is probably well over £100,000,000.

The greatest swarm of desert locusts ever recorded was one covering an estimated area of 2,000 square miles seen by Fletcher in South Africa in 1784. He says this swarm was blown out to sea by a strong wind, and when the tide washed back their bodies they formed a bank 4 ft high along the beach for 50 miles.

In 1889 another swarm covering an area of 2,000 square miles and containing an estimated 250,000,000,000 insects weighing about 500,000 tons was observed crossing the Red Sea.

Another very large swarm covering an area of 1,000 square miles invaded the Somali Peninsula, East Africa in December 1957.

There is also a record of a large infestation on the island of Cyprus

Part of a large swarm of desert locusts. (F.A.O.)

Nine-inch-long desert locust found alive in Shoreditch, London in July 1957. (Press Association.)

in 1881 which resulted in 1,300 tons of locust eggs being dug up and destroyed (Klots & Klots, 1959).

According to Williams (1958) a number of desert locusts turned up in south-western England in October 1869, the first ever recorded in Europe. Eighty-five years later, on 17th October 1954, two more were captured in the Scilly Isles and one just off Tranmore in Co. Waterford, Eire, followed by six more in the Scillies, southern Ireland and Cornwall.

Because of the practical difficulties of measurement very little reliable information has been published on the flight speeds of insects, but their general size gives them the false impression of being very much faster than they really are.

One of the first men to carry out experiments in this interesting field of research was Demoll (1918), the German entomologist. He released a number of different species in a room lit by a single window and timed them by stop-watch as they flew directly from the dark side of the room to the light. It was found that the swiftest flier was a hawk-moth (family Sphingidae) which travelled at a rate of 15 m/s (33·5 mile/h). A Horse-fly (*Tabanus bovinus*) and a dragon-fly (family Agrion) were not far behind with a speed of 14 m/s (31·25 mile/h). The other insects tested were much slower. A Common house-fly (*Musca domestica*) flew at a rate of 2·3 m/s (5·12 mile/h), a Honey-bee (*Apis mellifera*) at 3·7 m/s (7·26 mile/h) and a Bumble-bee (*Bombus lapidarius*) at 5 m/s (11·16 mile/h).

The most accurate lists of insect flying speeds published so far, how-ever, are those of Professor A. Magnan (1934), the French authority on animal velocities, who obtained his result by two methods. In one series of experiments he tethered the insect to a thread wound round a small drum mounted on ball-bearings, the revolutions of which were recorded on a kymograph as the creature was in flight. In another series he timed the insect with a chronometer (aided with cinephotography) as it flew between two markers set against a grid at a measured distance.

Of the thirty-two species of insect tested by Magnan, the fastest was a dragon-fly (*Anax parthenope*) which travelled at a rate of 8 m/s (17·86 mile/h). Next came another dragon-fly (*Aeschna mixta*) with 7 m/s (15·63 mile/h), followed by a Hornet (*Vaspa crabro*) with 6 m/s (13·39 mile/h). The latter speed is particularly interesting, because it means that the average cyclist attacked by one of these pugnacious wasps can easily outsprint his assailant.

The fastest of the five species of flies tested was a Horse-fly (*Tabanus bovinus*) which travelled at 4 m/s (8·93 mile/h).

As can be seen, Professor Magnan's speeds are considerable lower than those given by Demoll, but the French investigator does explain that the measurements he obtained do not represent the full maximum velocity of the insects as they fly in nature. In the final analysis he felt that certain insects could reach speeds of 10 m/s (22·33 mile/h).

From these observations, it would appear that sphinx moths, horse-flies and certain species of dragon-fly are the fastest-moving insects, all of which can exceed an *air speed* of 20 mile/h in level flight over short distances.

Dr. R. J. Tillyard (1917), the Australian entomologist, says he once timed a large dragon-fly of the species *Austrophlebia costalis* at 61·3 mile/h along a stretch of stream 80–90 yd long, but this must have been its ground speed.

According to the calculations of Hocking (1953) a dragon-fly this size could not possibly fly faster than 36 mile/h, even in short bursts, over a level course, and the absolute maximum air speed over a sustained distance would be about 24 mile/h. He does add, however: "This does not necessarily mean that Tillyard's observation is not reliable; a following wind, downhill flight and the short distance (850 × body length) taken together could account for the difference in the figures. It is well known that muscle may develop power much greater than normal for very brief periods. It is worth noting that even the great fossil species *Meganeura monyi*, with its 29-inch wing-span would on a similar basis only have been capable of 43 m.p.h.; indeed it probably had to fly at close to this speed in order to remain airborne."

Frank Lane (1955) says there are records of hawk-moths overtaking torpedo-boats travelling at more than 30 knots (34·7 mile/h), but the insects may have utilised air currents drawn along with the vessel.

The same writer also quotes Dr. C. H. Curran as saying that some of the horse-flies found in the tropics which are parasitic on birds may reach 70 mile/h when pursuing their intended hosts, but this figure is unacceptable because there are no species of bird living on or near the Equator capable of such high speeds.

In April 1926 Dr. Charles H. T. Townsend, an American zoologist, startled the scientific world by announcing that the Deer bot-fly (*Cephenemyia pratti*) was the fastest-moving living creature.

Writing in the *Journal* of the New York Entomological Society, he said: "On 12,000 foot summits in New Mexico I have seen pass me at an incredible velocity what were certainly the males of *Cephenemyia*. I could barely distinguish that some had passed—only a brownish blur in the air of about the right size for these flies and without a sense of form. As close as I can estimate, their speed must have approximated 400 yards per second."

This speed is "equal to 818 m.p.h. [*sic*]", which means that the fly could crash through the sound barrier (what no bang!) and outstrip the sound of its own buzz!

Astonishing as it may seem, a great number of people took this claim seriously, despite the fact that no instruments were used to measure the speed, and the figure was widely quoted for a number of years. It was eventually shot down in flames by Dr. Irving Langmuir (1938), the Nobel Prize-winner for chemistry in 1932, who carried out some calculations and experiments on a model of a deer-fly in his laboratory.

He said the fly would have to develop the equivalent of 1·5 hp and consume one and a half times its own weight in food per second to acquire the energy that would be needed to reach a velocity of 800 mile/h, and even if this was possible the fly would still be crushed by the air pressure and incinerated by the friction. He also revealed that a whirling piece of solder the same size as the fly was "barely visible" at 26 mile/h, "a very faint line" at 43 mile/h, and "wholly invisible" at 64 mile/h.

He deduced from these experiments that "a speed of 25 miles per hour is a reasonable one for the deer fly, while 800 miles is utterly impossible".

Despite these very careful calculations, however, Dr. Langmuir's figure of 25 mile/h is probably too low. This is because he carried out his tests in *normal* air conditions and used a model of a 10 mm (0·39 in) deer-fly (*Chrysops*) instead of a 15 mm (0·59 in) *Cephenemyia* (there was some confusion over identity). But even if we make due allowances for these differences, it is still doubtful whether this high-altitude fly ever exceeds 35–40 mile/h in level flight, even in the rarefied air of its normal habitat.

The frequency of wing-beat among insects varies enormously and is closely linked to bodily size. Generally speaking, the smaller the insect the faster it beats its wings . . . and the higher pitched sound it produces.

The higher frequency so far recorded for any insect under natural conditions is 1,046 c/s (= 62,760 a minute) by a tiny midge of the genus *Forcipomyia*. This measurement was based on an aural estimation by Dr. Olavi Sotavalta (1947), the remarkable Finnish entomologist, who has a sense of absolute pitch accurate to within 2·5 per cent of a cycle. Later he told Frank Lane (1955) that another specimen which had been truncated and exposed to a temperature of 37 °C (98·6 °F) produced a flight tone equivalent to a frequency of 2,218 c/s (= 133,080 a minute).

Measurements calculated from pitch-of-sound experiments, however, have been questioned by some authorities who contend that such values are 50 per cent too high.

The highest figure obtained by Magnan (1934), who used high-speed cinematography and a tuning fork in his tests, was 250 c/s (= 15,000 a minute) for a Honey-bee (*Apis mellifica*).

The lowest frequency of wing-beat reported for any insect is 5 c/s (= 300 a minute) for a specimen of the Swallowtail butterfly (*Papio machaon*) (Sotavalta, 1947). Most butterflies beat their wings at a rate of 460 to 636 a minute.

In proportion to their size, insects (especially beetles) are the strongest members of the animal kingdom. Lane (1955) gives a record of a Longhorn beetle (Cerambycidae) raising and lowering with its mandibles a foot-long rod 196 times heavier than itself, and the same writer also mentions a Scarabid beetle (Scarabeidae) which lifted a load on its back equivalent to 850 times its own weight.

The largest worker ant in the world is the Driver ant (*Dinoponera grandis*) of Africa with measurements up to 33 mm (1·31 in), but the males and queens of some of the genus

Dorylus are larger. Step (1924) says the huge wingless queens of the species *D. helvolus* of South Africa are sometimes "nearly two inches in length" after hypertrophy.

The largest of the twenty-seven species of ant found in Britain is the Wood ant (*Formica rufa*), males reaching 9 mm (0·35 in) and queens 11 mm (0·43 in) in length. The Blood-red robber ant (*F. sanguinea*) and the Meadow ant (*F. pratensis*) are also of comparable size, and a measurement of 11·5 mm (0·45 in) has been reported for a queen of the latter species (Donisthorpe, 1927).

The smallest ant in the world is the worker minor of *Oligomyrmex bruni* of Ceylon, whose total length is 0·8–0·9 mm (0·031–0·035 in) (Yarrow, *in litt.* 21.11.71).

The smallest ant found in Britain is *Solenopsis fugax*, whose worker measures 1·5–3 mm (0·059–0·18 in).

Ants are extremely tenacious of life. In one experiment carried out by Janet (1898) a wood ant worker survived for twenty-nine days without its head!

Although ants are not normally listed under the heading "dangerous insects", most of them have well-developed stings and/or large venom glands.

The most dangerous ant in the world is the Black bulldog ant (*Myrmecia forficata*) of the coastal regions of Australia and Tasmania, which uses its sting and jaws simultaneously when attacking. In November 1936 a fifty-year-old man died at Mount Macedon, Victoria after being "bitten" by one of these ants. Another fatality occurred in September 1963 when a woman was bitten on the foot by a black bulldog ant in her suburban garden at Launceston, Tasmania and died fifteen minutes later.

The Fire ants (Myrmicinae) of Argentina and *now* the southern United States also have a very unpleasant reputation, and Clarke (1969) says at least one death has been attributed to them.

The Texan and Western harvesters (*Pogonomyrmex barbatus* and *P. occidentalis*) are another species high up on the list of dangerous ants. Wheeler (quoted by Step, 1924) writes:

"The sting of these ants is remarkably severe, and the fiery, numbing pain which it produces may last for hours. On several occasions when my hands and legs had been stung by several of these insects while I was excavating their nests, I grew faint and almost unable to stand. The pain appears to extend along the limbs for some distance and to settle in the lymphatics of the groin and axillae. If it be true, as has been reported, that the ancient Mexicans tortured or even killed their enemies by binding them to ant-nests, *Pogonomyrmex barbatus* was certainly the species employed in this atrocious practice."

Despite the fact that many improbable stories have been told by white hunter-authors about the ferocity of army and driver ants, a colony of these creatures on the march *will* attack and devour any animal that is too slow to get out of the way, including an injured man or a baby in a cot (on 2nd March 1922 Professor Lefroy startled his audience at the Royal Institute in London by citing an authentic record of a baby which had been eaten alive by driver ants). For the most part, however, they feed on insects and often perform a valuable service to man by ridding his dwellings of vermin.

One of the most fascinating uses of ants is made by the Indians of South America, who employ the vice-like jaws of Leaf-cutting worker ants

(*Atta cephalotes*) in surgery. Instead of stitching up extensive wounds, a number of these ants are collected, and their jaws applied to the edges of the skin. As soon as the ants have taken hold and drawn the cut ends together, their bodies are snipped off and the row of jaws left hanging until the wound has healed. Gudger (1925) says the same practice is also well known in India.

Although ants have been credited with a high degree of intelligence— "Go to the ant, thou sluggard; consider her ways and be wise" (Proverbs, Chapter 6)—the modern view is that most of their actions are actuated by instinct. Sometimes, however, these actions are so ingenious that they go beyond the realms of instinct.

An interesting demonstration of ant "intelligence" was reported by Mme. Marguerite Combes, a scientist working at the Laboratory of Vegetable Biology at Fontainebleau, in 1930. In the garden adjoining the laboratory there were three separate colonies of Red ants (*Myrmica rubra*). One day Mme. Combes threw down a lighted match near each of the first two colonies. Their inhabitants immediately poured out as though panic-stricken. Many, pushing towards the front to see what the strange flame was, got themselves burnt to death.

When a lighted match was thrown down near the third colony, however, the result was quite different. The ants, having formed themselves into a solid brigade, advanced cautiously towards the flame and then, with one accord, began to squirt out formic acid on to the burning match. Many of them were seen pressing their stomachs in order to intensify the force of the jets.

Their efficiency as fire-fighters was proved by the fact that the match was not allowed to burn out. The flames were quenched when it was a little more than half consumed.

The experiment was repeated several times with a smouldering cigarette with the same result, and Mme. Combes then planted a lighted taper in the ant-hill, which the insect fire brigade also extinguished. A lighted candle was finally substituted for the taper, and the ants put this out in about a minute.

Twice, says Mme. Combes, over-keen ants which were in danger of being burned to death by approaching the flame too close were seized by other ants and dragged to safety.

The inhabitants of this third colony apparently had good reason to be efficient firemen. It transpired that one of the officials of the laboratory, in taking a favourite walk round the garden, had a habit of dropping lighted cigarette ends near the colony dwelling.

A long experience of these smouldering fragments had caused the ants of this particular settlement to constitute a kind of fire brigade of their own. They were thus able to meet quite calmly an emergency with which their fellows in the other colonies were incapable of dealing through lack of experience.

The master builders of the world are termites, commonly but erroneously called "white ants" because they are superficially ant-like and live like ants. Some of the mounds of these animals found in northern Australia measure up to 20 ft in height and nearly 100 ft in diameter at the base, and Howse (1970) has calculated that if termites were man-sized their largest citadels would be four times as high as the Empire State Building and measure 5 miles in diameter! The African termite *Macrotermes bellicosus* builds even taller mounds (heights up to 30 ft have been recorded in northern Kenya), but the bases are usually less than 10 ft in diameter (Harris, 1961).

Apart from their architectural ability, termites are best known as destroyers of wood which they digest with the aid of intestinal protozoa, and every year they cause hundreds of millions of pounds' worth of damage to materials like wooden frameworks of buildings, telegraph poles, railway sleepers, etc. They have even dictated the course of battles. . . .

In 1809 a force of British soldiers attacked a garrison on a French island in the Antilles in the West Indies and won a surprisingly easy victory because the enemy were unable to defend themselves. Apparently termites had eaten their way through the wooden parts of the garrison walls and just left an external shell as is their fashion, and when the French soldiers opened fire the whole lot collapsed round their ears. As a result the island became British (Burr, 1954).

The termite's insatiable hunger for wood has also affected sporting fixtures as well.

During a cricket match in India in 1949 the stumps were left out overnight. They were immediately attacked by termites which ate away the inside and left thin shells of wood covering the hollows they had made.

When cricket was resumed the next day the stumps looked perfectly normal. But the first fast ball shattered the stumps at one end into tiny fragments. As there were no more stumps available the match had to be abandoned.

The largest termite in the world is *Macrotermes bellicosus* of Africa which reaches 5 inches in length (Harris, 1961).

The smallest known termite is *Afrosubulitermes* sp., which measures about 3·5 mm (0·13 in) in length. Physogastric queen termites are the champion egg-layers in the insect world. Roonwal (1960) says one queen of the species *Odontotermes obesus* laid 86,400 eggs in one twenty-four hour period at the rate of one a second. There is also a record of an African queen termite laying 4,000 eggs a day and keeping it up for several years.

The largest of the 16,000 known species of bush-cricket is *Pseudophyllanax imperialis*, found on the island of New Caledonia, in the south-western Pacific Ocean. A female preserved in the British Museum of Natural History, London has a body length of 10·5 cm (4·13 in) including the ovipositor, or 12·5 cm (4·92 in) with wings folded. The wing-span is 24 cm (9·44 in). The antennal length is 15 cm (5·90 in), but these have been broken and could have been much longer (Meadows, *in litt.* 10.9.71). This size is closely matched by the rare *Phyllopora grandis* of New Guinea which has a wing-span measurement of up to 23 cm (9·05 in).

The largest bush-cricket found in Britain is *Tettigonia viridissima*. Adult males measure 28–33 mm (1·1–1·3 in) in body length, and adult females 32–35 mm (1·26–1·37 in). In August 1953 an enormous female measuring 77 mm (3·03 in) in body length was caught in a sand-pit at Grays, Essex and later presented to London Zoo.

The largest of the fourteen true grasshoppers found in Britain is *Mecostethus grossus*, females of which measure up to 39 mm (1·53 in) in body length.

The smallest grasshoppers are among the family Eumastacidae, where the males are often under 1 cm (0·39 in) in body length, and one specimen preserved in the British Museum of Natural History, London has a body length of only 6 mm (0·23 in).

The smallest grasshopper found in Britain is *Myrmeleotettix maculatus*, which has a maximum body length of 16 mm (0·63 in).

According to Graham Hoyle (1958) of Glasgow University a grasshopper, weight for weight, *has the most powerful muscle of any known animal.* He says slow-motion camera studies have shown that the muscle which operates the grasshopper's amazingly strong legs exerts a power 20,000 times its own weight (i.e. 0·04 g) when the insect is doing a high jump ten times its own body length and a long jump double that distance. This is equivalent to a man high-jumping 60 ft or long-jumping 120 ft.

In July 1949 an enormous swarm of grasshoppers covering an area of 3,000 square miles (75 miles × 40 miles) invaded Oregon and California, U.S.A. **This is the largest swarm of insects in recorded history.**

Another swarm containing an estimated 100,000,000 grasshoppers invaded the Talaud Islands, northern Indonesia in June 1971 and destroyed 3,000,000 coconut trees.

The largest of the 3,600 known species of dragon-fly and damsel-fly is probably *Tetracanthagyna plagiata* of north-eastern Borneo, which is known only from the type specimen preserved in the British Museum of Natural History, London. This dragon-fly has a wing-span of 19·4 cm (7·63 in) and an overall length of 10·8 cm (4·25 in) (Ward, *in litt.* 7.9.71).

This size is closely matched by the Damsel-fly *Megaloprepus caerulatus* of Central and South America which has been measured up to 19 cm (7·48 in) in wing-span and 12·7 cm (5 in) in overall length. The largest specimen preserved in the British Museum of Natural History, London has a wing-span of 18·8 cm (7·40 in) and an overall length of 11·8 cm (4·64 in).

The Australian dragon-fly *Petalura ingentissima* has been measured up to 16·5 cm (6·5 in) in wing-span (Stanek, 1969).

The largest of the forty-three species (twenty-seven dragon-flies and sixteen damsel-flies) found in Britain is the Golden-ringed dragon-fly (*Cordulegaster boltoni*), which has been measured up to 84 mm (3·3 in) in overall length and may have a wing-span of more than 100 mm (3·93 in).

The smallest damsel-fly in the world is probably *Agriocnemis naia* of Burma. A specimen preserved in the British Museum of Natural History, London has a wing-span of 17·6 mm (0·69 in) and an overall length of 18 mm (0·7 in).

The smallest dragon-fly found in Britain is the scarce Ischnura (*Ischnura pumilio*), which has an overall length of 25 mm (0·98 in).

Adult dragon-flies and damsel-flies have the biggest eyes in the insect world and can detect movement up to 50 ft away. In large species like *M. caerulatus* the optics are larger than those of a mouse.

In 1862 a swarm of dragon-flies (species not identified) estimated to contain nearly 2,500,000,000 insects was observed flying over Germany.

The largest known fly is the robber-fly *Mydas heros*, which is found in tropical South America. It has a body length of up to 60 mm (2·36 in) and a wing-span measurement about the same (Oldroyd, 1964).

Some of the daddy-longleg species of crane-fly like *Holorusia* of the tropics have a wing-span of nearly 100 mm (3·93 in) and a length with legs extended of about 20 mm (0·8 in), but these insects have very little bulk. A specimen of *H. brobdignagius* preserved in the British Museum of Natural History, London measures 9 in from the tips of the front legs to the tips of the hind-legs (Cogan, *in litt.* 13.10.71).

Most species of fly have a highly developed power of flight and can cover surprising distances considering their small size. One marked Common house-fly (*Musca domestica*) released near Dallas, Texas, U.S.A. travelled 13·14 miles, and a Screw-worm fly (*Chrysomyia macellaria*) 15·1 miles (Bishop & Laake, 1921). But the long-distance champions of this order are the Black-flies (*Simulium*), some species of which may fly more than 100 miles when wind-assisted.

Flies can also survive at very high altitudes. One specimen observed inside an unpressurised plane was "comfortable" at 18,000 ft but became erratic at 20,000 ft. Another fly became torpid at 30,000 ft, but recovered when the plane descended to 25,000 ft.

These records, however, are dwarfed by a fly which emerged apparently unscathed from a container after it had been subjected to an atmospheric pressure of 10 mb. This is equivalent to a height of 20 miles or 105,600 ft.

In September 1933 the inhabitants of Tokio caught a record "bag" of 117,530,000 flies in the annual Haotori or Fly-Catching Day, which is no longer celebrated for obvious reasons. It took officials of the Sanitary Department two weeks to total the results.

Various writers have tried to estimate the possible number of descendants a pair of common house-flies might have in a summer if all the individual flies survived. According to the calculations of Wardle (1929) there would be 5,598,720,000,000 progeny at the end of the season if each female laid 120 eggs, but this figure is far short of the maximum potential (one female laid 2,387 eggs!).

Fortunately the mortality rate of insects is enormously high.

The largest of the 1,830 described species of flea is one reported from Seattle, Washington, U.S.A. which measures 8 mm (0·31 in) in body length. Females of the species *Hystrichopsylla talpae* have been measured up to 6 mm (0·23 in) in body length. The mole-flea is reportedly even larger when gorged with blood.

The most dangerous flea in the world is the rat-flea (*Xenopsylla cheopis*), carrier of the dreaded bubonic plague bacterium (*Pastuerella pestis*). In the Middle Ages this blood-sucking parasite caused the death of 25,000,000 people in Europe, approximately one-quarter of the total population (the "Great Plague" of London in 1665 killed 68,596 people out of a population of 460,000), and in the great Indian plague of 1896–1917 over 10,000,000 people died.

Apart from their danger as carriers of disease, fleas are best known for their jumping abilities. In 1910 M. B. Mitzmain of the U.S. Public Health Service carried out some very careful experiments in this area of research and found that the jumper *par excellence* among fleas was the Common flea (*Pulex irritans*). One energetic performer allowed to leap at will executed a high jump of "at least" 7·75 in and a long jump of 13 in, but these measurements were exceptional (the mean average long jump of the five specimens tested was 7·75 in). In jumping 130 times its own height a flea subjects itself to a force of 200 g.

Although the entire life-cycles of some fleas can be as short as two weeks in hot, dry weather, life can be prolonged considerably in cool, moist conditions. Bacot (1914) found that *unfed* adults of the Common rat flea (*Ceratophyllus fasciatus*) lived for twenty-two months, those of the Common flea (*P. irritans*) for nineteen months, and the Dog flea (*Ctenocephalides canis*) for eighteen months in cool temperatures, but these fleas would have lived much longer if they had been supplied regularly with blood.

The longevity record for fleas appears to be held by a well-nourished Russian bird-flea (*Ceratophyllus* sp.) which lived for 1,487 days or 4 years 27 days.

The most popular "host" for fleas appears to be the Red squirrel (*Sciurus vulgaris*). More than 13,000 squirrel-fleas (*C. acutus*) were removed from one individual.

In 1969 Australia's Commonwealth Scientific and Industrial Research Organisation reported that the world's oldest flea and the missing link in flea evolution had been dug up near Melbourne, Victoria. This "super flea" had lived about 120,000,000 years ago clinging to the fur of a prehistoric bandicoot. The flea's fossilised remains show it was nearly 0·3 in long.

The largest bee in the world is the Leaf-cutter bee (*Megachile pluto*) which is found only on Batjan in the Moluccas or Spice Islands, Malay Archipelago. It measures up to 38 mm (1·49 in) in body length (Curran, 1945).

The largest bee found in Britain is the Large garden humble-bee (*Bombus ruderatus*), workers of which measure about 23·5 mm (0·93 in) in body length.

The smallest bee is *Trigona duckei*, a dwarf stingless variety found in Brazil which measures 2–5 mm (0·078–0·19 in) in body length. This size is closely matched by some of the *Turnerella* species of Australia (Yarrow, *in litt.* 21.10.71).

The smallest bee found in Britain is the Least mining-bee (*Halictus minutissimus*) which has a body length of 5 mm (0·19 in). The Neat mining-bee (*H. nitidiusculus*) measures 5·75 mm (0·22 in) (Step, 1932).

The largest animal ever killed by bees was a bull African elephant (*Loxodonta africana*) found dead by natives in Tanganyika (now part of Tanzania). Apparently the huge pachyderm had accidentally picked up a bees' nest with its trunk while foraging for food and tried to swallow the mass. The nest lodged in the animal's gullet, and it died from strangulation (Burr, 1954).

The largest wasps in the world are the spider hunting wasps of the genus *Pepsis* found in South America. *P. atrata* of Amazonia has a body length of 2·5 in (excluding the 0·5 in stinger) and a wing-span of 4 in (Zahl, 1959). *P. frivaldskii* is even larger. A specimen preserved in the British Museum of Natural History, London has a wing-span of 4·5 in (Yarrow, *in litt.* 21.10.71).

The largest wasp found in Britain is the Greater horntail (*Sirex gigas*), females of which have a body length of 40 mm (1·57 in) excluding stinger.

The smallest known wasps are the parasitic wasps of the family Mymaridae (see smallest insects).

The smallest wasp found in Britain is the Minute black wasp (*Diodontus minutus*) which has a maximum body length of 6·35 mm (0·25 in).

The largest wasps' nest on record was one found on a farm at Waimaukau, New Zealand in April 1963 which had grown so heavy that it had broken off and split into two pieces. It originally measured 12 ft in length and 5 ft 9 inches in diameter.

The largest known butterfly is the Giant birdwing *Troides victoriae* of the Solomon Islands (south-western Pacific), females of which may have a wing-span exceeding 12 in and weigh over 5 g. (0·176 oz).

The natives of these islands use them as adornments in their hair (Whitehouse, 1932).

The New Guinea birdwing (*T. alexandrae*) and the African giant swallowtail (*Papilio antimachus*) of West Africa and the Congo are also of comparable size, females of both species measuring up to 10–11 inches in wing expanse.

Butterflies of these dimensions are virtually impossible to catch with a net because they frequent the tops of high trees and fly very rapidly. Instead, collectors have to resort to "shooting" them with sporting guns loaded with dirt or water.

The largest butterfly found in the British Isles is the Monarch butterfly (*Danaus plexippus*), also called the Milkweed or Black-veined brown butterfly, a rare vagrant which breeds in the southern United States and Central America. Adult females average 1·5 inches in body length and have a wing-span of 3·5 in. In October 1937 a huge specimen with a wing-span of 5 in was caught in a garden at Lydney, Glos., and exhibited in Gloucester Museum. It weighed about 1 g.

The first monarch butterfly ever recorded in the British Isles was caught at Neath, South Wales, on 6th September 1876 by Sir John Llewelyn. Since then more than 200 specimens have been observed or captured.

The swallowtail, Britain's largest native butterfly.

The largest native butterfly (sixty-two recognised species) is the Swallowtail (*Papilo machaon*), females of which have a wing-span of 7–10 cm (2·75–3·93 in) and weigh 500–600 mg. This species is now confined to a small area of the Norfolk Broads.

The world's smallest known butterfly is the Dwarf blue (*Brephidium barberae*) of South Africa. It has a wing-span of 14 mm (0·55 in) and weighs less than 10 mg. The Pygmy blue (*Lycaena exilus*) of North America is another diminutive butterfly, having a wing-span of 18 mm (0·7 in).

The smallest butterfly found in the British Isles, and one of the smallest in the world, is the Small blue (*Cupido minimus*) which has a wing-span of 19–25 mm (0·75–1·0 in).

Some butterflies have extraordinary powers of flight and migrate great distances. The champion is the Painted lady (*Vanessa cardui*). In the early spring hundreds of thousands of these fragile insects leave their homes in North Africa and Asia Minor and fly across the Mediterranean and Europe to southern England, where they arrive in late May or early June after a journey of 2,000–3,000 miles. Some take a further trip to Scotland, and individual stragglers have even been seen in the extreme north of Iceland within a few degrees of the Arctic Circle, which means they must have flown nearly 4,000 miles! `

Monarch butterflies also cover enormous distances during migration. This species leaves the Canadian border in September and arrives in Florida, Mexico or California two months later after a journey of 2,000 miles. Then, after spending the winter in a state of semi-hibernation, they fly back to the Canadian border the following March.

They have also been found in the Hawaiian Islands, 2,000 miles from the American continent, where they were unknown until the milkweed, their favourite food, was first grown.

The occasional flights made by vagrant specimens across the Atlantic (about 3,200 miles) are not nearly so arduous because they are *carried* most of the way by strong westerly winds (this distance would probably be impossible for a monarch butterfly under normal conditions).

In January 1966 the B.B.C. Natural History Unit at Bristol released fifty marked monarch butterflies received from Toronto University near the city in an experiment to determine how far they would travel. One specimen, flying at 17 mile/h, reached Alvechurch, 80 miles away, in less than five hours.

Most butterflies live between two and eight months, depending on the time of year they were hatched, but some large migratory species like the monarch butterfly may live for twelve months or slightly longer.

In 1926 Father Cambouet, a missionary in Madagascar and a noted entomologist, reported to the Academy of Sciences in Paris that *decapitated butterflies live longer than those which are left intact*. He said he had found that when certain caterpillars were decapitated in such a way as to cause the minimum loss of blood, they could continue the natural course of their development and, after passing through the chrysalis stage, emerge as perfectly healthy but headless butterflies.

Scientists who have studied this phenomenon since have come to the conclusion that headless butterflies are longer lived because they lead a much less active life. A perfect butterfly quickly spends its strength in activity, whereas its headless companions, leading much more placid lives, wear out their vital forces at a slower rate and thus attain a comparatively ripe old age.

Like migrating locusts, butterflies often travel in huge swarms. One mass migratory flight of painted ladies observed moving on a 40-mile-wide front in the southern United States reportedly took three days to pass a given point, and Williams (1958) says he witnessed a single flight of the Pale form butterfly (*Catopsilia florella*) in East Africa in 1928–29 which continued steadily for more than three months!

The majority of butterflies fly 5–8 ft above the ground during migration, but some species travel at great heights. According to Williams (1958) dead Cabbage whites (*Pieris brassicae*) have been found in the Alps above the 12,000 ft mark, and butterflies of the genera *Cosmosalyrus*, *Lymanopoda* and *Pedaliodes* have been seen crossing the Andes at heights up to 4,700 m (15,419 ft) (Klots & Klots, 1958).

The greatest height reliably reported for migrating butterflies is 19,000 ft for a few "Small tortoiseshells" (probably *Aglais urticae*) seen flying over the Zemu Glacier (Sikkim) in the eastern Himalayas. This height is probably also reached by the Queen of Spain fritillary (*Argynnis lathonia*), which has been sighted at nearly 6,000 m (19,650 ft) in the Himalayas. The painted lady reaches 17,000 ft.

The rarest of all butterflies (and the most valuable) is the birdwing *Troides allottei*, which is found only on Bougainville in the Solomon Islands. A specimen was sold for £750 at an auction in Paris on 24th October 1966. The Butterfly of Paradise (*T. paradisea*) of New Guinea is another very rare birdwing and has fetched prices up to £120. In November 1955 a collector paid DM1,500 (then about £125) at the annual Insect Trading Day in Frankfurt for the only known example in Europe of a *Teinopalpus imperialis*, a butterfly found in the mountains of south-east China.

Abnormally coloured butterflies also fetch high prices. In 1921 Lord Rothschild paid £75 for a black swallowtail caught by a fisherman on the Norfolk Broads. At a London auction in April 1941 a collector paid £49 for an entirely white Marbled white (*Melanargia galathea*), and an all-black example was sold for £41. In 1958 a black Cabbage white (*Pieris brassicae*) was sold in London for £44, and in 1962 the British Museum of Natural History, London paid £50 for a Chalk Hill blue (*Lysandra coridon*) which was pure white.

The rarest native British butterfly is probably the Black hairstreak (*Strymonidia pruni*), which is restricted to a few small areas of Huntingdonshire, Oxfordshire, Northamptonshire and Buckinghamshire. In November 1965 a specimen was found in Keysoe Park Wood, Bedfordshire.

The Large blue (*Maculinea arion*), now found only in north Cornwall, and the Swallowtail (*Papilo machaon*) are also threatened species, and their numbers may be even smaller.

One of the greatest butterfly collectors of all time was James Joicey of Witley, Surrey who died in March 1932 aged sixty-one.

For over thirty years this man, the son of a millionaire, spent up to £10,000 annually in sending agents all over the world in search of rare specimens, and by 1913 his collection had become so important (later to become the third largest private collection in existence) that a special building was erected in the grounds of his magnificent home at Witley, where a curator and seven assistants were in constant attendance.

He was also an extremely generous benefactor of the British Museum of Natural History, London, and during his lifetime he presented to the trustees between 200,000 and 300,000 specimens.

In 1927 Joicey went bankrupt, and it was related in court that because of his "special hobby" he found it impossible to live on £20,000 a year.

It had always been the intention of this fanatical lepidoperist to bequeath his collection of 1,500,000 butterflies and moths estimated to be worth nearly £1,000,000 to the nation, but the involved conditions of his financial affairs at the time of his death made this impossible.

Joicey's proudest boast was that he had added 500 new species to the order.

M. Charles Oberthus, a French millionaire who died in 1924 aged seventy-five, was another famous butterfly collector. In 1927 the British Museum of Natural History, London acquired about 70 per cent of his total collection or some 1,140,000 specimens.

The largest privately owned collection of butterflies and moths on record was that of the late Lord Rothschild, which totalled over 2,000,000 specimens. This collection is now preserved in the Rothschild Museum at Tring in Hertfordshire, where it is maintained by the Trustees of the British Museum of Natural History, London.

Although butterflies are not normally recognised as being dangerous to man the larvae of several families are equipped with poisonous hairs and contact can cause severe irritation, swelling and burning of the affected skin. Adult members of the family Danaidae are also poisonous to birds (two monarch butterflies contain enough poison to kill a starling) and other insectivorous animals because the toxins of the milkweed plants they feed upon are retained in the bloodstream.

The Indian atlas moth has a wing-span of up to 12-in.

The largest known moth, and the heaviest of all flying insects if we exclude stick-insects, is the Hercules emperor moth (*Coscinoscera hercules*) of tropical Australia and New Guinea. Females measure up to 10·5 in across the outspread wings and have a wing area of more than 40 in². This insect is so large that it has been likened to a pigeon in flight!

The little-known Owlet moth (*Thysania agrippina*) of Brazil has been measured up to 30 cm (11·81 in) in wing-span, and the Atlas moth (*Attacus atlas*) of South-East Asia up to 28 cm (11·02 in), but both these species are less bulky than *C. hercules*.

The death's head hawk moth, the largest insect found in Britain. (Fox Photos.)

The death's head hawk moth. ("Daily Mail.")

The largest of the 21,000 species of insect found in Britain is the very rare Death's head hawk moth (*Acherontia atropos*), females of which have a body length of 60 mm (2·36 in), a wing-span of up to 133 mm (5·25 in) and weigh about 1,600 mg.

According to Newman (1965) this moth is extremely fond of honey and is a habitual raider of hives, but it often loses its life because of its greed. After gorging itself on the honey *A. atropos* frequently gets lost in the hive and is later found dead among the combs, having died from a surfeit of honey rather than from bee stings.

The largest native British moth is the Privet hawk moth (*Sphinx ligustri*), which has a body length of 50 mm (1·96 in) and a wing-span of over 110 mm (4·33 in). It is also interesting to note that weights up to 2,400 mg have been recorded for females of this species (Sotavalta, 1947), which makes it a *bulkier* insect than *A. atropos*.

The smallest of the 140,000 known species of Lepidoptera is the moth *Nepticula microtheriella*, which has a wing-span of 3–4 mm (0·11–0·15 in) and a body length of 2 mm (0·078 in) (Meyrick, 1928). It is found in Britain.

Some other species of the family Nepticulidae are almost equally as diminutive. *N. nylandrella*, *N. poterii*, *N. distinguenda* and *N. scomicrotheriella* all have a wing-span of 3–5 mm (0·11–0·19 in), and *N. plagicolella* measures 4–5 mm (0·15–0·19 in) (Jacobs, *in litt.* 4.12.68).

Although moths—like butterflies—are not normally considered dangerous to man, a large number of caterpillars have poisonous hairs or spines which produce varying degrees of irritation and swelling on contact with skin. One of the most feared species in the southern United States is the abundant "puss caterpillar" (*Megalopyge opercularis*). Children "stung" by larvae of this moth often develop a high fever and nervous symptoms (Riley & Johannsen, 1932), and the poison secreted by a closely related species, *M. lanata*, is stated to be *potentially* lethal, although no deaths have been reported.

Another dangerous moth, though for quite different reasons, is the recently discovered "vampire" moth (*Calyptra eustrigata*). Dr. Hans Banziger (1968), a Swiss entomologist working in Malaya, reports that this large moth uses its strong, barbed proboscis to extract blood from heavy mammals like water-buffalo, deer and tapir, and he says its nasty habit of regurgitating some of the blood it has drunk makes it a potential carrier of disease.

In the laboratory this moth can be induced to feed on man—human guinea-pigs have commented that "it felt like being stabbed with a hot needle"—but so far this performance has not been witnessed under natural conditions.

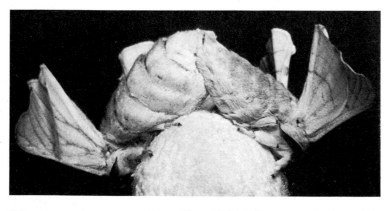

Close-up of two silkworm moths, males of which have the most acute sense of smell in nature. (R. Cassell —F. Lane.)

The most acute sense of smell exhibited in nature is that of the male True silkworm moth (*Bombyx mori*), which can detect the sex signals of the female at incredible distances. In 1961 some German scientists released a number of marked males from a moving train at regular intervals in an experiment to determine the maximum distance the love scent could be picked up, and they found that some of the specimens could trace the perfume to its source from the almost unbelievable range of 11 km (6·8 miles) (Droscher, 1964).

One female put in a cage near a window attracted 127 males from 2 miles away in the space of only a few hours.

This scent has been identified as one of the higher alcohols ($C_{16}H_{30}O$), of which the female carries less than 0·0001 mg, and even then only a very few molecules of this perfume are released into the air at any given time. Yet the male silkworm moth still manages to pick up these inconceivably minute traces in its antenna.

The largest known insect eggs are those of the polyphemus moths which have a diameter of 0·125 in. The smallest are those laid by the gall midge (*Dasyneura leguminicola*), which have a diameter of only 0·004 in.

The bulky Hercules emperor moth (Coscinoscera hercules) of Australia and New Guinea, the largest living moth. (G. Pizzey/B. Coleman Ltd.)

The Hercules beetle (Dynastes hercules) of Central America is one of the longest beetles in the world. Adult males have been measured up to 7·5 inches in length including the mandibles. (L. Chace/F. Lane.)

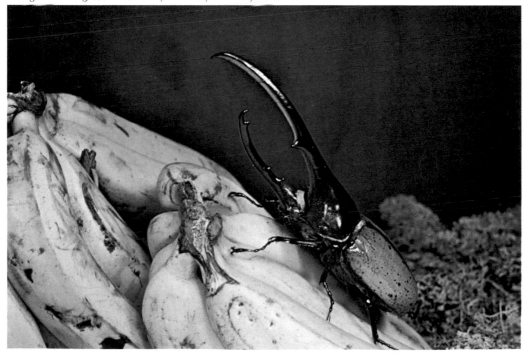

SECTION X

Centipedes

(class *Chilopoda*)

A centipede is a carnivorous land-dwelling invertebrate which breathes by means of trachae or air tubes distributed throughout the body. It has a distinct head bearing one pair of antennae and three pairs of jaws and an elongated body composed of many segments, each of which bears one pair of jointed walking legs. The appendages of the first body segment are modified into poison fangs. During growth the animal sheds its external skeleton or horny skin frequently. Young are hatched from eggs after leaving the female.

The earliest known centipedes lived about 350,000,000 years ago.

There are about 3,000 living species of centipede and the class is divided into four orders. These are: Geophilomorpha; Scolopendromorpha; Heterostigmata; and Scutigeromorpha.

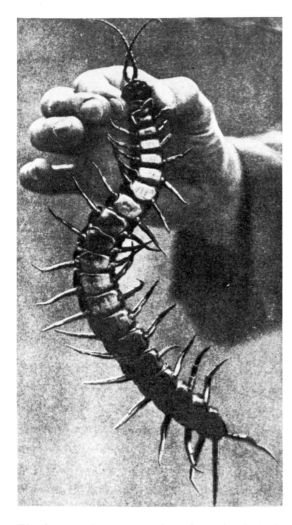

A giant centipede.
(Photo-Reportage Ltd.)

The longest known species of centipede is the forty-six-legged Giant scolopender (*Scolopendra gigantea*) of the rain forests of Central and South America. Specimens have been reliably measured up to 26·5 cm (10·43 in) in length and 2·54 cm (1 in) in diameter. Measurements of 12 and even 15 in have been claimed for individuals collected in British Guiana, but these figures need confirming. Baron Alexander von Humboldt (1769–1859), the famous German naturalist and explorer, says he saw centipedes in Venezuela measuring 18 in, but this length must be considered excessive.

Some of the giant centipedes found in India and Malaysia are also of comparable size. Wood (1935) writes: "In the Kubbo-Kale valley I saw a centipede 10 inches long. Its general colour was electric blue with bright coral red fangs. It was the most terrible thing I have seen in my tramps through the forest."

This centipede was probably a large variant of the widely distributed *S. morsitans* which normally measures 6–8 inches in length.

Another example collected in West Africa reportedly measured 12·5 inches in length, but this figure needs confirming.

*The male Cairns birdwing (*Troides*) of north-eastern Australia is one of the most beautiful butterflies in the world and is much sought after by collectors. (G. Pizzey/ B. Coleman Ltd.)*

*The recently discovered Vampire moth (*Calyptra eustrigata*) of Malaysia which uses its strong barbed proboscis to extract blood from large mammals like water-buffalo. In the laboratory it can be induced to feed on man.*

S. subspinipes, another widely distributed species, also grows to a great size, and Cloudsley-Thompson (1958) says one specimen collected in Brazil measured 10 in.

The longest centipede found in Britain is *Haplophilus subterraneus*, which has between seventy-seven and eighty-three pairs of legs and measures up to 70 mm (2·75 in) in length and 1·4 mm (0·005 in) across the body (Eason, 1964).

The shortest known centipede is an unidentified species which measures only 5 mm (0·19 in) in length.

The shortest centipede found in Britain is *Lithobius duboscqui*, which measures up to 9·5 mm (0·374 in) in length and 1·1 mm (0·043 in) across the body (Eason, 1964).

The centipede with the greatest number of legs is *Himantarum gabrielis* of southern Europe which has 171–177 pairs when adult.

Half of the known species of centipedes have only fifteen pairs of legs when adult, but they all start off life with about six pairs, including *H. gabrielis*.

The fastest-moving centipede is *Scutiger coleoptrata* of southern Europe which can travel at a rate of 50 cm (19·68 in) a second or 4·47 mile/h (Manton, 1952). It can thus outpace a fast-walking pedestrian.

Most centipedes live less than two years. The longest-lived species are the giant scolopenders which do not reach maturity until they are three years old and probably have a maximum life-span of five years.

The venomous bite of large tropical centipedes like *Scolopendra morsitans* can be extremely dangerous, and Caras (1964) says victims in India and Burma are sometimes laid up for as long as three months.

One of the most feared centipedes is a variety of *S. subspinipes* found in the Solomon Islands which reportedly has a bite that defies description. The pain is so acute that victims have been known to plunge their bitten hand into boiling water as a counter-irritant—the attempted cure being more disastrous in its effects than the original injury.

According to Remington (1950) the only authentic case of a fatal centipede bite on record is that of a seven-year-old child who died on Leyte Island, in the Philippines, twenty-nine hours after being bitten on the head. The centipede was probably *S. subspinipes*.

SECTION XI

Millipedes

(class *Diplopoda*)

A millipede is a herbivorous land-dwelling invertebrate which breathes by means of tracheae or air tubes. It has a distinct head bearing one pair of antennae like the centipede, but each segment of the elongated body has two pairs of legs instead of one. It also differs from the centipede in having two rows of stink glands down each side of the body which secrete an evil-smelling substance capable of repelling insect enemies. Young are hatched from eggs after leaving the female.

The earliest known millipedes lived about 400,000,000 years ago.

There are about 8,000 living species of millipede and the class is divided into ten orders. These are: Polyxenida; Glomerida; Glomeridesmida; Nematophora; Stemmiulida; Polydesmida; Julida; Spirobolida; Spirostreptida; and Cambalida.

The longest known species of millipede are *Graphidostreptus gigas* of Africa and *Scaphistostreptus seychellarum* of the Seychelles in the Indian Ocean, both of which have been measured up to 28 cm (11·02 in) in length and 2 cm (0·78 in) in diameter (Kaestner, 1968).

The longest millipede found in Britain is *Cylindroiulus londinensis* which measures up to 50 mm (1·96 in).

The shortest millipede in the world is the British species *Polyxenus lagurus*, which measures 2·1–4·0 mm (0·082–0·15 in). Another British species, *Macrosternodesnus palicola*, measures 3·5 mm (0·137 in).

Although the word millipede means "thousand-legged" very few species have more than 200. The record appears to be held by a South African millipede mentioned by Schubart (1966) which has 355 pairs (710 legs), but he does not name the species. Another millipede (*Siphonophora panamensis*) discovered by H. F. Loomis (1964) in Panama had 175 segments, but not every segment had two pairs of legs.

Millipedes start off life with even fewer legs than centipedes, the usual number being three pairs.

The rarest species of millipede found in Britain is *Isobates littoralis*, which lives on the sea-shore between high and low tides. It is known from only three specimens collected from the Isle of Man, Lancashire and Llandudno, Caernarvonshire. *Cylindroiulus parisiorum* is known only from four specimens, all of them collected in churchyards (Glower, *in litt.* 6.11.71).

No speeds have been published for millipedes, but they move at a much slower rate than centipedes.

Most species of millipede live one to two years, but some like *C. londinensis* may live up to seven years.

SECTION XII

Segmented Worms

(phylum *Annelida*)

A segmented worm is a soft-bodied invertebrate which lives on land or in water and breathes through the skin or by means of gills. Its body is divided into equal parts, and the muscular part of each segment is covered by a thin transparent skin from which bundles of horny bristles protrude. The main function of these bristles is to aid locomotion, but they are also used to anchor the worm firmly in its burrow. Young are hatched from eggs deposited on land or shed in water.

The earliest known segmented worms lived about 500,000,000 years ago.

There are about 6,800 living species of segmented worm and the phylum is divided into three classes. These are: the Polychaeta (bristleworms); the Oligochaeta (earthworms); and the Hirudinea (leeches). The largest class is Polychaeta, which contains about 4,000 species or nearly 32 per cent of the total number.

The longest known species of earthworm, and the longest recorded segmented worm, is *Megascolides australis*, first discovered in Brandy Creek, southern Gippsland, Australia in 1868. An average-sized specimen measures 4 ft in length (2 ft when contracted) and nearly 7 ft when *naturally* extended.

Five-foot-long giant earthworms dug up by a bulldozer near Toonumbar, New South Wales, Australia in 1957. (Associated Press.)

The longest accurately measured Megascolides on record was one collected before 1930 in southern Gippsland which measured 7 ft 2 inches in length and over 13 ft when naturally extended. Barrett (1931) says another huge individual measured by his friend L. C. Cook on his farm at Holbrook, southern Gippsland in the 1920s was 6 ft long and 11 ft when naturally extended. Lengths up to 15 ft have been quoted for specimens collected near Loch, but Barrett says these measurements were probably obtained by "stretching" the worm to its utmost limit ("*Megascolides* is liable to break under such barbarous treatment, despite a generous allowance of rings and its surprising elasticity").

The only known enemy of this worm, apart from man who uses it as fish bait, appears to be the Kookaburra (*Dacelo gigas*), which often engages in a tug-of-war with one of these monstrosities.

"The bird uses strategy to gain its meal," writes Barrett (1931). "Darting from its observation perch, it seizes the protruding head of a worm. The giant immediately contracts, having its tail anchored perhaps several feet down in the burrow. The kookaburra, without loosening the grip of his beak, yields a little length.

"A few moments' waiting, then the bird suddenly tugs again, his victim having lowered resistance. Another violent contraction follows, but the worm now has some inches of its body in the open. Thus the tussle continues, until the luckless annelid breaks under the strain or is hauled clear from its burrow."

In November 1967 a specimen of the African giant earthworm *Microchaetus rappi* (= *M. microchaetus*) measuring 11 ft in length and 21 ft when naturally extended was found on the road between Alice and King William's Town, Eastern Cape Province, South Africa by two scientists working at Potchefstroom University. The average length of this species is 3 ft 6 in and 6–7 ft when naturally extended.

In 1961 Mrs. Marte Latham, an American explorer and collector, discovered a new genus of giant earthworm in the Colombian Andes at a height of 15,000 ft. In June the same year she presented one specimen (*Martiodrilus* sp.) measuring 5 ft 6 in when naturally extended to the London Zoological Society. Unfortunately it died ten days later, and the worm is now preserved in the British Museum of Natural History, London.

Other giant earthworms found round the world include *Drawida grandis* of India, which has been measured up to 42·5 in; *Spenceriella gigantea* of New Zealand up to 4 ft 6 in (naturally extended); and *Glossoscolex giganteus* of Brazil up to 4 ft 1·5 in (Stephenson, 1930).

The heaviest giant earthworm is probably *Rhinodrilus fafner* of Brazil, which exceeds 1 lb in weight. This species has been measured up to 2·1 m (6 ft 10·75 in) in length and nearly 3 cm (1·18 in) in diameter (Kukenthal, 1928–34).

Another Giant earthworm (?*Digaster* sp.) discovered by forestry workers in the Toonumbar State Forest, near Kyogle, northern New South Wales in 1939 is equally as bulky. The largest of the forty-four specimens collected by a scientific expedition from the Australian Museum in May 1957 measured 5 ft 5 inches in length when naturally extended and over 1 inch in diameter, but it contracted to 3 ft 6 in on being preserved in alcohol (Pope, 1958).

The longest segmented worm found in Britain is the earthworm *Lumbricus terristris*, which has been reliably measured up to 350 mm (13·78 in) when naturally extended. Measurements up to 20 in have been claimed for this species, but in each case the body was probably macerated first.

The smallest known segmented worm is *Chaetogaster annandalei*, which measures less than 0·5 mm (0·0019 in) in length.

Some species of segmented worm are relatively long-lived. According to Wilson (1949) the Marine worm *Sabella pavonia* is not sexually mature until it reaches ten years of age, and he also quotes a figure of ten years for *Allolobophora longa*. Nothing is known about the longevity of giant earthworms like *Megascolides*, but they probably live at least eight years.

The longest-lived segmented worm found in Britain is *L. terrestris* with a life-span of five to six years.

SECTION XIII

Molluscs

(phylum *Mollusca*)

A mollusc is a soft-bodied unsegmented invertebrate which lives on land or in water, and breathes by means of a mantle cavity folded to form a lung or by gills. The body, which does not have a standard shape, is divided into four sections: a well-developed head with tentacles (missing in bivalves); a muscular foot or "arms" which serve for locomotion or are modified to perform other functions; a rounded visceral mass in which the internal organs are housed; and a protective shell or mantle which grows with the body and is not shed periodically. It also has a highly complex nervous and circulatory system, and young are usually hatched from eggs.

The earliest known mollusc was Neophilina galathea, which lived about 500,000,000 years ago. Its remains were first discovered off Costa Rica in 1952.

There are about 45,000 living species of mollusc, and the phylum is divided into six classes. These are: the Monoplacophora (monoplacophs); the Chitons (chitons); the Gastropoda (slugs, snails and limpets); the Scaphopoda (tusk shells); the Lamellibranchia (bivalve molluscs); and the Cephalopoda (squids, cuttlefish and octopods). The largest class is Gastropoda, which contains about 35,000 species or 77 per cent of the total number.

The heaviest—but not the longest—of all invertebrates is the Giant squid (*Architeuthis* sp.), the animal which gave rise to the Scandinavian legends of the Middle Ages about the dreaded kraken . . . a colossal sea monster said to have a body measuring 1·5 miles in circumference and mast-like arms capable of dragging the largest ship down to the bottom.

Although some of the great museums of Europe had physical evidence of this creature in the shape of preserved fragments of arms or bodily remains from as early as the sixteenth century, the scientific world remained sceptical of the existence of the giant squid right up to the middle of the nineteenth century.

Then, in December 1853, a gigantic cephalopod was washed up on Aalbaek Beach in Jutland (Denmark). Unfortunately the body of this specimen, which "represented a full cart load", was cut up for fish bait before it could be secured for scientific examination, but the horny jaws measuring 4·5 in × 3·25 in and the attached muscles came into the hands of Professor Japetus Steenstrup, the eminent Danish zoologist, who described the specimen under the name *Architeuthis monachus* in 1857.

In 1856 parts of another giant squid found floating in the sea near the Bahama Islands by a Captain Hygom the previous autumn were brought back to Copenhagen and described by Steenstrup under the name *Architeuthis dux*. This animal had a 6 ft 2·5 in long head and body and arms the same length (the two long tentacles were missing).

Four years later a Giant squid (*A. monachus*) was stranded between Hillswick and Scalloway on the west coast of Shetland. This one had a 7 ft long head and body and measured 23 ft in total length.

The scientific sceptics were knocked back even further on their heels in 1861.

On 30th November that year the French steam dispatch boat *Alecton* was 40 leagues (about 120 miles) north-east of Teneriffe in the Canary Islands when a large squirming mass was sighted on the surface. The commander of the vessel, Lieutenant Frederick-Marie Bouyer, immediately recognised it as the semi-fabulous kraken of ancient tradition and decided to capture the great beast.

Musket-fire, however, had little or no effect on the squid, and none of the harpoons thrust into its soft flesh stayed embedded for long. Eventually, after a three-hour-long battle, the sailors succeeded in passing

A giant cranchid removed from the stomach of a sperm whale captured in the Antarctic. The huge eye can be seen slightly left of centre in the picture. (Malcolm Clarke.)

a slip noose along the cephalopod's body until it was held fast over the junction of the broad caudal fin.

They then attempted to hoist the repulsive-looking squid on deck, but its weight—estimated at more than 2,000 kg or 4,400 lb—was so enormous that the rope cut through the caudal fin like a knife through butter and the rest of the body crashed back into the sea.

By this time the officers and men were in a state of high excitement and wanted to launch a boat to continue the struggle with the brick-red monster, but Lieutenant Bouyer refused to hazard the lives of his crew against such a formidable adversary and reluctantly ordered them to abandon the mutilated animal.

The head and body of this squid was estimated to have measured 15–18 ft in length, and its eight arms 5–6 ft (the two tentacles were missing).

The section of the caudal fin sliced off by the rope weighed about 40 lb, and when the *Alecton* arrived at Teneriffe ten days later Lieutenant Bouyer showed it to M. Sabin Berthelot, the French Consul there, who sent a full report to the French Academy of Sciences in Paris, together with a drawing of the squid sketched by one of the ship's officers.

The animal was subsequently named *Architeuthis bouyeri* (Cross & Fischer, 1862).

If any doubts still lingered in the minds of man after that incident that there was such a creature as the giant squid, they were finally put to rest in 1873 when two herring fishermen and a twelve-year-old boy were attacked by a huge individual off the coast of Newfoundland.

The men, Theophilus Piccot and Daniel Squires, and Piccot's son Tom, were fishing in a dory off Portugal Cove, Conception Bay, about 9 miles from St. John's, on 26th October when they saw a dark mass floating in the water.

Thinking it was the debris of a wreck they decided to investigate, and one of the men prodded it with a boating hook. Suddenly the "mass" opened out like a gigantic umbrella to reveal two huge green eyes and a parrot-like beak "as big as a six-gallon keg", and the fishermen saw to their horror that they had accidentally disturbed a kraken.

The monster immediately launched an attack and hit the gunwale with its horny beak. Then it wrapped one arm and a tentacle round the flimsy craft and threatened to drag it, occupants and all, below the surface.

The two men were terrified and sat there virtually paralysed as water began pouring into the boat, but fortunately young Tom was made of sterner stuff. With great presence of mind for a person of such tender years he snatched up a small axe and cut through the two appendages; whereupon the injured cephalopod ejected a huge amount of ink into the surrounding water and slowly sunk from view.

When the badly shaken trio returned to shore the severed arm was thrown on the ground and eaten by dogs. But the long, thin tentacle was kept by Tom Piccot, who later sold it to the Rev. Moses Harvey, a local amateur naturalist interested in kraken lore, after whom the Squid (*Architeuthis harveyi*) was named.

According to Harvey (1879), who had the pale pink appendage preserved in strong brine, the tentacle measured 19 ft in length and 3.5 inches in maximum circumference, but the fishermen told him that 6 ft had already been destroyed and there had been a further 6–10 ft still attached to the creature.

From this data—and the diameter of the suckers—it was possible to estimate the size of this squid: head and body length 12 ft; tentacles 32 ft; total length 44 ft.

Three weeks later another large Squid (*A. dux*) was caught in the net of four herring fishermen in near-by Logie Bay and dispatched after a fierce struggle. This time Harvey was able to purchase the animal intact, but his attempts to preserve it in brine were not very successful, and in the end he had to make do with preserving parts of the squid in strong alcohol. He said the total length of this specimen was 32 ft, the head and body measuring 7 ft 9 in and the tentacles 24 ft 3 in.

There was also a stranding in Coomb's Cove, Fortune Bay. This squid had a total length of 52 ft (head and body 10 ft, tentacles 42 ft). Another very large example washed up at West St. Modent, in the Strait of Belle Isle, Labrador, also measured 52 ft in total length (head and body 15 ft, tentacles 37 ft) and was probably heavier (Verrill, 1874).

The giant squid was now official, and in the next decade there were numerous sightings and strandings in Newfoundland waters. In October 1875 alone more than thirty dead specimens were found on the Grand Banks, most of them measuring over 30 ft in length (Verrill, 1882).

In 1878 the largest giant squid ever recorded was captured in Thimble Tickle Bay. The capture of this monster (*A. princeps*) was described by Harvey in a letter to the *Boston Traveller* (30th January 1879):

"On the 2d day of November last, Stephen Sherring, a fisherman residing in Thimble Tickle . . . was out in a boat with two other men; not far from the shore they observed some bulky object, and, supposing it might be part of a wreck, they rowed toward it, and, to their horror, found themselves close to a huge fish, having large glassy eyes, which was making desperate efforts to escape, and churning the water into foam by the motion of its immense arms and tail. It was aground and the tide was ebbing. From the funnel at the back of its head it was ejecting large volumes of water, this being its method of moving backward, the force of the stream, by the reaction of the surrounding medium, driving it in the required direction. At times the water from the siphon was black as ink.

"Finding the monster partially disabled, the fishermen plucked up courage and ventured near enough to throw the grapnel of their boat, the sharp flukes of which, having barbed points, sunk into the soft body. To the grapnel they had attached a stout rope which they had carried ashore and tied to a tree, so as to prevent the fish from going out with the tide. It was a happy thought, for the devil-fish found himself effectually moored to the shore. His struggles were terrific as he flung his ten arms about in dying agony. The fishermen took care to keep a respectful distance from the long tentacles, which ever and anon darted out like great tongues from the central mass. At length it became exhausted, and as the water receded it expired.

"The fishermen, alas! knowing no better, proceeded to convert it into dog's meat. It was a splendid specimen—the largest yet taken—the body measuring 20 feet from the beak to the extremity of the tail. . . . The circumference of the body is not stated, but one of the arms measured 35 feet. This must have been a tentacle."

According to the calculations of Dr. Bernard Heuvelmans (1968) this giant squid would have tipped the scales at 27·126 metric tons if it had been "very thickset", but this weight is *impossibly high* for an animal of this head and body length.

What Heuvelmans is saying, in effect, is that a giant squid with a head and body length of 20 ft and a maximum bodily circumference of about 15 ft (if that) is *twice as heavy* as a Whale shark (*Rhineodon typus*) with a body length of 38 ft and a maximum bodily circumference of 20 ft, and *nearly eight times as heavy* as a Southern elephant seal (*Mirounga leonina*) with a body length of 20 ft and a maximum bodily circumference of 16 ft. This, of course, is absurd.

Earlier MacGinitie and MacGinitie (1949), basing their calculations on a maximum bodily circumference of 12 ft, had come up with a weight of 29·25 tons, or 30 tons including the arms and tentacles, for this monster, but in 1968 they admitted that these calculations were wrong and corrected the weight to a more reasonable 16,827 lb (7·5 tons). This poundage, however, is still excessive.

Dr. Igor Akimushkin (1965), the Russian teuthologist, says a 12 m (39 ft 3 in) long squid will weigh *1 ton* if the head, body and arms combined make up half the total length. If we base our calculations on these figures, then the Thimble Tickle specimen must have scaled about 2·84 tons, which is the weight of a large hippopotamus, but 4,000 lb (1·78 tons) is probably a more realistic figure.

Another squid washed up on the beach at Arnaraesvick, northern Iceland in November or December 1790 and cut up for cod bait may have been even heavier. Svein Paulsson (1792), the Icelandic naturalist, says it had a head and body length of 3·5 fathoms (21 ft 7·5 in) and *four* tentacles measuring 3 fathoms (18 ft 6 in), making a total length of 40 ft 1·5 in. These figures, however, have been questioned by Steenstrup (1857), who says the description of the animal fits an elongated version of *Todarodes sagittatus* (=*Loligo todarus*), a squid commonly found in Icelandic waters.

In Steenstrup's opinion the measurements given by Paulsson were not due to exaggeration but to "an error in writing", and should have read: head and body 3·5 ells (7 ft 3 in); tentacles 3 ells (6 ft 2 in); total length 13 ft 5 in.

Giant squids are also found in other parts of the world, but the lengths they attain outside the North Atlantic are generally less spectacular than those reached by species like *Architeuthis harveyi* and *A. princeps*. This has prompted some teuthologists to query the accuracy of the Newfoundland measurements already quoted, but although some of them may have been taken roughly (i.e. paced out) there is no real reason to suspect that any of the lengths were deliberately exaggerated.

Dr. F. Hilgendorf (quoted by Lee, 1884) says a large Squid (*A. martensii*) measuring 12 ft 7·5 inches in total length but missing the "tongs" of its tentacles, was exhibited at Yedo (now Tokyo), Japan in 1873, and he saw another one of similar size for sale in Yedo fish market.

In 1895 a "young giant squid" (*A. mouchezi*) was caught by fishermen in the Bay of Tateyami near Tokyo. It measured 3·8 m (12 ft 5·5 in) in total length (Mitsukuri & Ikeda, 1895).

On 16th April 1930 a large squid was washed ashore on the Miura Peninsula, Japan. Its head and body measured 11 ft 9·75 inches in length and its tentacles 11 ft 9·75 in, making a total length of 23 ft 7·5 in (Tomilin, 1967).

In June 1958 a squid with 24 ft long tentacles was reportedly caught off Tobata on northern Kyushu Island, Japan, but further information is lacking.

On 2nd November 1874 a French expedition to the uninhabited island of St. Paul in the southern Indian Ocean found "a great calamary" (*A. sancti-pauli*) cast up on the northern shore which had a head and body length of 7 ft and tentacles measuring 16 ft, making a total length of 23 ft (Velain, 1875).

In June 1911 fishermen found a dead giant squid floating in Monterey Bay, California, U.S.A. The animal was towed to shore and dragged up on the wharf where it was measured before being thrown back in the sea. It had a total length of over 30 ft (Berry, 1911).

There are also several records from New Zealand. In September 1870 a squid with 5 ft 6 in long arms (the tentacles were missing) and a head and body measuring 10 ft 5 in was washed ashore at Waimarama, North Island. Another specimen (*A. kirkii*) discovered alive among the rocks at Cape Campbell in the early 1870s measured 28 ft 10 inches in total length (head and body 10 ft, tentacles 18 ft 10 in) (Robson, 1886), and three boys found a squid (*A. stockii*) on the beach in Lyall Bay, Cook Strait on 3rd May 1879 which had a head and body length of 11 ft 1 in and arms measuring 4 ft 3 in (the mutilated tentacles of this specimen measured 6 ft 2 inches in length, but they were probably over 12 ft long when intact) (Kirk, 1881).

On 6th June 1880 another large squid stranded in Island Bay, Cook Strait. It had a head and body length of 9 ft 1 in and measured 34 ft 1 inch in total length when intact (half of the tentacles were later torn off and carried out to sea) (Kirk, 1881).

Seven years later a giant squid with exceptionally long tentacles was washed up in Lyall Bay. This bizarre specimen was described by T. W. Kirk of the Dominion Museum, Wellington who wrote:

"Early last month, October 1887, Mr. Smith, a local fisherman, brought to the Museum the beak and buccal-mass of a cuttle which had that morning been found lying on the 'Big Beach' (Lyall Bay), and he assured us that the creature measured sixty-two feet in total length. I that afternoon proceeded to the spot and made a careful examination, took notes, measurements, and also obtained a sketch.

"Measurements showed that, although Mr. Smith was over the mark in giving the total length as 62 feet (probably, not having a measure with him, he only stepped the distance), those figures were not so vary far out; for, although the body was in all ways smaller than any of the hitherto-described New Zealand species, the enormous development of the very slight tentacular arms brought the total length up to 55 feet 2 inches, or more than half as long again as the largest species yet recorded from these seas."

It should be pointed out here that the tentacles of *Architeuthis* are highly elastic and can be extended or retracted at will by the animal; so it is quite possible that the length of 62 ft paced out by the fisherman may have been correct at the time he found the squid.

This probably also explains the discrepancy in Kirk's figures, because in the table of measurements for this individual he gives the total length as 57 ft (head and body 7 ft 9 in, tentacles 49 ft 3 in).

Architeuthis longimanus, as it was named, is the longest squid so far recorded. Unfortunately it is known only from the type specimen; this means that teuthologists have yet to establish whether the exceptional tentacular development is normal in this species or merely an aberration of nature.

Nothing more was heard of *Architeuthis* in Oceania until September 1948 when the mutilated body of a specimen of *A. kirkii* was washed ashore at Wingan Inlet, Victoria, the first giant squid ever recorded in Australian waters. According to Allan (1948) this one had a head and body length of 9 ft 2 in and measured about 28 ft in total length when intact (the arms and tentacles had been torn off at a length of 4 ft).

In June 1955 scientists at Wellington University reported that giant squids with eyes as big as dinner-plates and tentacles 25 ft long had been discovered in a 6,000 ft deep canyon in Cook Strait, the 30-mile-wide channel separating North and South Islands, and that they were building a huge steel "mousetrap" device with which they hoped to catch one of these monsters alive. Nothing appears to have come of this project, however, because no more information was published.

Eleven months later the remains of a 30 ft long squid were washed ashore on a beach near Wellington.

Although Norway is closely associated with kraken lore, surprisingly few giant squids have been stranded on her coasts in the past 100 years. The largest recorded specimen appears to have been one found on a beach at Kyrksaeterora (formerly Heven), 40 miles south-west of Trondheim, in 1896 which measured about 37 ft in total length (Heuvelmans, 1968). Another one stranded at Ranheim on Trondheim Fjord in October 1964 measured just under 30 ft in total length and was estimated to weigh between 200 and 300 kg (between 440 and 660 lb).

On 8th June 1935 a large Squid (*A. nawaji*) was caught in the Gulf of Gascogne in the Bay of Biscay. It measured only 4 ft 6 inches in head and body length, but the total length was 25 ft 2 in (Cadenet, 1936).

In 1966 a 47 ft long squid, **the largest recorded this century,** was captured by a U.S. Coast Guard vessel near the Tongue of the Ocean on the Great Bahamas Bank after it had been involved in a fight with a sperm whale, and the carcass was later deposited with the Institute of Marine Sciences at the University of Miami, Florida.

In a letter to the author dated 29th October 1971, Dr. Gilbert L. Voss, Chairman of the Division of Biology at Miami University, said: "Unfortunately much of this specimen was destroyed through the actions of a graduate student who attempted to preserve a couple of shark heads in the same formalin tank, with the result that most of the contents spoiled. One arm is on deposit in the Natural History Museum at Vienna, and the head is still in our possession."

On 12th July 1968 two doctors fishing off the resort of Luanco, on the north-western coast of Spain, found a dead giant squid floating on the surface and towed it to shore where it was weighed and measured before being cut up for fish bait. It scaled 256 kg (563·2 lb) and measured 9·5 m (31 ft 3 in) in total length.

Very few giant squids have been stranded on British shores. The largest recorded specimen was probably one found at the head of Whalefirth Voe, Shetland on 2nd October 1949 which had a 4 ft long head and body and a total length of 24 ft. It was identified as *A. monachus* (Stephen, 1950).

Another squid identified as *A. harveyi* washed ashore at Skateraw, Haddingtonshire, Scotland on 2nd November 1917 had a total length of 19 ft 9 in (head and body 5 ft 9 in, tentacles 14 ft) (Ritchie, 1921).

Clarke (1933) examined a Squid (*A. clarkei*) stranded near Scarborough, Yorkshire on 14th January 1933 which had a head and body length of 5 ft 8·5 in and a total length of 17 ft 5 in, but he says 2–3 ft of the tentacles were missing.

On 30th November 1949 a giant squid was washed up in the Bay of Nigg, Aberdeenshire, Scotland. It had a head and body length of 1·45 m (4 ft 9 in) and a total length of 5·87 m (19 ft 3 in). The weight of this animal was estimated to be over 1 cwt (112 lb) (Rae, 1950).

On 1st February 1957 the Aberdeen trawler *Viking Prestige* caught an *Architeuthis* sp. off Rattray Head which measured 23 ft 11 inches in total length (Stephen *et al.*, 1957).

In August 1971 a squid measuring 22 ft 2 inches in total length was caught in Scottish waters (McCall, *in litt.* 10.10.71).

Giant squid caught in Scottish waters in August 1971. It had an overall length of 22 ft 2 in. (Crown copyright.)

Nearly a century ago a colossal squid was killed off the west coast of Ireland. An account of its capture was given in the *Zoologist* (June 1875) by Sergeant Thomas O'Connor, of the Royal Irish Constabulary:

"On the 26th of April, 1875, a very large calamary was met with on the north-west of Boffin Island, Connemara. The crew of a curragh . . . observed to seaward a large floating mass, surrounded by gulls. They pulled out to it, believing it to be a wreck, but to their astonishment found it was an enormous cuttle-fish, lying perfectly still, as if basking on the surface of the water. Paddling up with caution, they lopped off one of its arms. The animal immediately set out to sea, rushing through the water at a tremendous pace.

"The men gave chase, and, after a hard pull in their frail canvas craft, came up with it, five miles out in the open Atlantic, and severed another of its arms and the head. These portions are now in the Dublin Museum. The shorter arms measure, each, eight feet in length, and fifteen inches round the base; the tentacular arms are said to have been thirty feet long. The body sank."

This squid must have had a total length of over 40 ft when alive, **which makes it one of the largest specimens on record, and the largest ever recorded in Irish or British waters.**

At the moment no one really knows how large squids can grow, but it would be foolish to suppose that the monstrous Thimble Tickle specimen represents the absolute limit of size for this animal.

Captain A. Kean claims he found a huge individual stranded in Flowers Cove, Newfoundland, which measured 72 ft in total length (Frost, 1934). Another one washed up on the same coast in *c.* 1882 was credited with a length of 88 ft (head and body 30 ft, tentacles 58 ft), and Murray (1874) says two gigantic squids stranded on the coast of Labrador before 1870 measured 80 and 90 ft respectively. None of these measurements, however, have been verified, and they could be tentacular spreads in disguise (*A. longimanus* measured in this fashion would have a "length" of about 100 ft 6 in).

Lengths up to 90 and even 130 ft have been conjectured for squids from the size of sucker marks found on the skins of captured sperm whales, but these measurements should be treated with considerable reserve.

Verrill (1879) says the largest suckers on the arms of a 32 ft long squid with a head and body length of 7 ft 9 in measured 1·25 inches in diameter, and those on a 52-footer about 2 in; but sucker marks up to 5 in across have reportedly been found on sperm whales caught in the North Atlantic! Ring marks this size, however, are probably caused by large parasitic creatures.

According to Sanderson (1956) sucker marks "over 18 in [*sic*]" in diameter have been found on the heads of cachalots, but he doesn't explain how the poor whales managed to escape from the clutches of such monsters!

Huge fragments of squids' arms (not tentacles) said to have been recovered or vomited up from the stomachs of sperm whales have also been cited as *evidence* of outsized giant squids. Heuvelmans, for instance, gives records of arms measuring 27, 35 and even 45 ft in length and "as thick as a ship's mast". But, as none of these appendages have ever found their way into museums or research institutes, measurements like this must be considered suspect.

Although the North Atlantic appears to have a monopoly on exceptionally large squids, one or two of the species found in the rich feeding-grounds of the Antarctic Ocean probably rival their northern counterparts in size and weight. The largest squid so far discovered in these waters is the gelatinous cranchid *Mesonychoteuthis hamiltoni*. According to Dr. Malcolm Clarke (1966) of the National Institute of Oceanography, Wormley, Surrey, the largest measured example (taken from the stomach of a sperm whale) had a length of 350 cm (11 ft 6 in) excluding the tentacles, but he says even larger specimens were collected by the British research vessel *Southern Harvester* in the Bellingshausen Sea in 1955–56.

On 16th December 1924 the badly mutilated carcass of what was alleged to be a giant squid was washed up on a beach near Port Shepstone, Natal, South Africa. All of its arms and tentacles had been bitten off, leaving just stumps, but the former were estimated to have measured 30 ft in length when intact. This presupposes a total length of more than 100 ft, but as the 9 ft thick mound of flesh was stated to have resisted all attempts to cut it up—squid flesh is very soft and pliable—the "body" must have been a piece of tough whale blubber.

In September 1971 Dr. Ann Bidder, a former Curator of the Zoology Department at Cambridge University and a noted authority on squids, told a meeting of the British Association for the Advancement of Science in Swansea that she personally believed giant squids 200 ft long existed among deep-sea life. As an illustration she quoted the story of a ship's officer who used to hang a bulb cluster over the side at night to observe the marine life.

"One night the light was suddenly obscured and he realised an enormous eye was looking at him," said Dr. Bidder. "He walked along to the forecastle and saw the ends of tentacles. He went to the stern and there were the other ends of the tentacles. The ship was 175 ft long. A squid with tentacles as long as that would have a body at least 25 feet long" (*The Times*, 7th September 1971).

A full account of this sighting, which occurred off one of the Maldive Islands in the Indian Ocean during the Second World War, was originally published in the 21st November 1963 issue of *Animals* magazine.

The writer, A. G. Starkey, who was serving aboard an Admiralty trawler at the time, says he was leaning over the stern one morning gazing at the teeming marine life below attracted by the light when suddenly the bulk of something huge came into view.

"As I gazed, fascinated, a circle of green light glowed in my area of illumination. This green unwinking orb I suddenly realised was an eye. The surface of the water undulated with some strange disturbance. Gradually, I realised that I was gazing at almost point blank range at a huge squid.

"I say 'huge'—the word should be 'colossal', as so far all I could see was the body, and that alone filled my view as far as my sight could penetrate. I am not squeamish, but that cold, malevolent, unblinking eye seemed to be looking directly at me. I don't think I have ever seen anything so coldly hypnotic and intelligent before or since.

"I took my quartermaster's torch and shining it into the water I walked forward. I climbed the ladder to the fo'c'sle and shone the torch downwards. There, in the pool of light, were its tentacles . . . these were at least 24 in thick. The suction discs could clearly be seen. The ends of the arms appeared to be twitching slightly, but this may have been a trick of the light.

"My heart was going like a sledge hammer. Remember, I was alone on the deck, everyone else turned in. I was not so much afraid as excited, as if this were some opportunity to see something but rarely seen by man.

"I walked aft keeping the squid in view. This was not difficult as it was lying alongside the ship, quite still except for a pulsing movement. As I approached the stern where my bulb cluster was hanging, there was the body. Every detail was visible—the valve through which the creature appeared to breathe, and the parrot-like beak.

"Gradually the truth dawned: I had walked the length of the ship, 175 feet plus. Here at the stern was the head or body and at the bows the tentacles were plainly visible. . . . The giant lay, all its arms stretched alongside gazing up, first with one then both eyes as it gently rolled. After 15 minutes it seemed to swell as its valve opened fully and without any visible effort it 'zoomed', if I may use the expression, into the night."

This story has been dismissed by some people as no more than a seaman's yarn because they said the officer would not have been able to see the animal's parrot-like beak from his position, but Dr. Malcolm Clarke tells me the beak of a giant squid can easily be distinguished if the arms and tentacles are reasonably spread out.

A much more reasonable explanation, however, is that two giant squids were involved in this sighting: one lying flat on the surface at the stern; the other lying below the surface near the bow in a perpendicular position with its arms and tentacles spread out above it. But even if this is the answer, they would still be awfully big squids.

The Common octopus
(Octopus vulgaris) is the
largest octopus found in British
waters. An average-sized
specimen has a radial spread
of 4–5 ft. (L. Perkins/F. Lane.)

The venomous Giant
scolopenders (Scolopendra
sp.) of Central and South
America and South-East Asia
are the longest known
centipedes. Specimens have been
measured up to 11 in.
(J. Burton/B. Coleman Ltd.)

The only known enemy of *Architeuthis* in its natural habitat is the bull sperm whale, which sometimes swallows its victims whole. On 4th July 1955 Robert Clark (1955) found an intact giant squid in the stomach of a 47 ft long cachalot brought into the whaling station on Fayal Island in the Azores. It measured 34 ft 5 inches in total length and weighed 405 lb. Another one taken *alive* from the stomach of a sperm whale caught by a Soviet whaling fleet in the North Pacific on 31st December 1964 weighed 204·5 kg (450 lb). With the possible exception of the cranchid *Mesonychoteuthis hamiltoni*, this latter squid represents the largest "swallow" for any living carnivore.

Although there are no authentic records of *Architeuthis* sp. attacking and seizing a man in the water, **there is one unique case of a large squid attacking a human being on land.**

This amazing encounter took place in Broadford Bay, on the Isle of Skye, on 12th January 1952. Police-constable John Morrisey was walking along the beach early one morning after a heavy storm when he saw a strange, fleshy-looking object lying half-buried in the sand. He gave it a hefty kick, and the next moment a long tentacle whipped out and seized him by the foot.

A vigorous tug-of-war followed, and in the end the policeman had to leave his wellington boot in the animal's clutches before he could make good his escape. Later he managed to kill the squid with a pair of garden shears borrowed from a near-by house (Morrisey, *in litt.* 5.10.71).

The cephalopod, which had a total length of nearly 9 ft, was later identified as a specimen of *Stenoteuthiis caroli* by Dr. A. C. Stephen of the Royal Scottish Museum, Edinburgh.

In October 1966 a life-and-death struggle between what was believed to have been a giant squid and a right whale calf was reported from South Africa.

The fight was observed by two lighthouse-keepers at Danger Point, near Cape Town, who said the whale's mother circled helplessly as the squid slowly drowned her calf, its tentacles clamped round its head.

For ninety minutes the two men watched the little whale battle on, gradually weakening under the squid's pressure and surfacing less and less frequently for air.

Afterwards, one of the lighthouse-keepers said: "We watched the fight through binoculars. The little whale could stay down for 10 to 12 minutes, then come up. It would just have enough time to spout—only two or three seconds—and then down again.

"We saw it lashing with its tail in the water and the squid's tentacles wrapped around its head. Each time the baby came up to breathe the mother whale surfaced with it, and then went down with her infant.

"The little whale was only just able to reach the surface and spout. The squid never moved. Finally we saw it come up for a second, blow then go down. We never saw it again" (Associated Press 9th October 1966).

If this story is true it is quite remarkable because *Architeuthis* is normally a deep-sea creature. When it is found on or near the surface it is usually dying or very sick. The lighthouse-keepers could have been mistaken and seen a very large octopus, but if this had been the case the shorter arms of this cephalopod would have prevented the whale calf from reaching the surface to breathe.

The giant squid has the largest eye of any living or extinct animal, the ocular diameter in massive species like *A. princeps* measuring up to 15 in (cf. 8·5 in for a football). An eyeball this size would weigh several pounds. The eyes of the largest

Blue whales (*Balaenoptera musculus*) have an ocular diameter of 10–12 cm (3·93 to 4·71 in) (Akimushkin, 1965).

The smallest of the 350 species of squid so far recorded is *Parateuthis tunicata* of the Antarctic Ocean, which is known from only two specimens. The largest of these had a body length of 0·31 in and a total length of just over 0·5 in (Clarke, 1966).

The smallest squid found in British waters is *Alloteuthis media*, which has a total length of 7 in.

The most dangerous of all squids is *Dosidicus gigas* (= *Ommastrephes gigas*) of the Humboldt Current, which may reach 12 ft in total length and a weight of 350 lb. This extremely aggressive and cannibalistic animal is greatly feared by native fishermen, and Frank Lane (1957) says anyone unfortunate enough to fall overboard in the vicinity of these demons would be torn to pieces in less than half a minute. So far, however, no human fatalities have been reported.

Nearly all squids are rapid swimmers, and some of the smaller surface-dwelling species like *Stenoteuthis bartrami* and *Onychoteuthis banksii* are among the swiftest animals in the sea. It has been calculated from their flight trajectory that flying squids of these genera leave the water at speeds up to 55 km (34·35 mile/h) when escaping from fast enemies like tunny (Akimushkin, 1965).

When Commander Arne Groenninsaeter (quoted by Lane, 1957) was serving aboard the 15,000-ton tanker *Brunswick* in the South Pacific during the early 1930s the ship was attacked three times by giant squids. On each occasion the animal rapidly overtook the tanker while it was travelling at 12 knots, which means that the squid must have been moving at more than 20 mile/h.

Fast-swimming squids are very popular with neurological researchers because they have **the largest nerve fibres of any known animal**. According to Akimushkin (1965) those of *Dosidicus gigas* have been measured up to 18 mm (0·7 in) in diameter, which means they are about 1,000 times thicker than human nerves. Impulses from the brain can be transmitted along fibres this size at speeds up to 50 mile/h (Young, 1938; 1944).

Very little research has been done on the longevity of squids, but most species probably live less than four years. Akimushkin says it must take "several decades" for squids like the one caught in Thimble Tickle Bay to attain their enormous size, but in marine animals there is no real relationship between size and age.

The largest of the 150 known species of octopod is the Common Pacific octopus (*Octopus apollyon*).

One huge specimen trapped in a fisherman's net in Monterey Bay, California, U.S.A. had a radial spread of over 20 ft and scaled 110 lb (MacGinitie & MacGinitie, 1949), and a weight of 125 lb has been reported for another individual (Wood, 1971). In Puget Sound, Washington, U.S.A., where large octopods are regularly "wrestled" to the surface by skin-divers for sport, radial spreads up to 28 ft and weights up to 360 lb have been claimed, but these figures must be considered exaggerated.

In 1874 William H. Dall, the Curator of Molluscs at the U.S. National Museum in Washington, D.C., speared an octopus of the North Pacific species *O. hongkongensis* in Illiuliuk Harbour, Unalaska Island, Alaska which had a radial spread of 32 ft, but the body of this cephalopod

*The most feared of all siphonophores is the Portuguese man-of-war (*Physalia physalis*), although its sting is seldom fatal to man. (F. Lane.)*

*The Giant clam (*Tridacna derasa*) of the Indo-Pacific coral reefs is the largest existing bivalve mollusc. One specimen collected from the Great Barrier Reef in 1917 and now preserved in the American Museum of Natural History measures 43 × 29 in and weighs 579·5 lb. (D. Hughes/B. Coleman Ltd.)*

only measured 12 in × 6 in, and the animal probably weighed less than 20 lb (parts of this specimen are preserved in the U.S. National Museum).

Professor B. G. Wilder (quoted by Verrill, 1879) says an octopus (species not identified) with 5 ft long arms and estimated to weigh "between two hundred and three hundred pounds" was found dead on a beach near Nassau, in the Bahamas, but further details are lacking.

Pliny the Elder (c. AD 23–79), quoting Trebius Niger, tells of a gigantic octopus which used to crawl out of the sea at Carteia (now known as Rocadillo), a Roman colony near Gibraltar, every evening after dusk and devour the salted tunnies in the pickling-tubs at the curing depot there.

"At last by its repeated thefts and immoderate depredations it drew down upon itself the wrath of the keepers of the works. Palisades were placed before them, but these the polypus managed to get over by the aid of a tree [?], and it was only caught at last by calling in the assistance of trained dogs, which surrounded it at night as it was returning to its prey; upon which the keepers, awakened by the noise, were struck with alarm at the novelty of the sight presented.

"First of all, the size of the polypus was enormous beyond all conception; and then it was covered all over with dried brine and exhaled a most dreadful stench. Who could have expected to find a polypus there or could have recognised it as such under these circumstances? They really thought that they were joining battle with some monster, for at one instant it would drive off the dogs by its horrible fumes and lash at them with the extremities of its feelers, while at another it would strike them with its stronger arms, giving blows with so many clubs, as it were; and it was only with the greatest difficulty that it could be dispatched with the aid of a considerable number of three-pronged fish spears.

"The head [body] of this animal was shewn to Lucullus; it was in size as large as a cask of 135 gallons and had a beard [tentacles], to use the expression of Trebius himself, which could hardly be encircled with both arms, full of knots, like those upon a club, and 30 feet in length; the suckers, or caliculus, as large as an urn, resembled a basin in shape, while the *teeth* [author's italics] again were of a corresponding largeness; its remains, which were carefully preserved as a curiosity, weighed 700 pounds."

The size and weight quoted for this animal by Pliny, and his statement that it had "feelers" and arms, suggest the polypus was a giant squid, but as these creatures are unable to crawl on land, let alone climb trees, the story must be considered largely apocryphal.

At the end of November 1896 the remains of a large marine animal were found by two boys on a beach 12 miles south of St. Augustine, Florida, U.S.A. At first the fleshy mass was thought to be part of a large whale, but after a careful examination Dr. DeWitt Webb, president of the local scientific society, pronounced it to be a gigantic octopus of a type unknown to science.

On 3rd January 1897 the *New York Herald* devoted considerable space to the story, the following being an extract:

"It had evidently been dead some days and was much mutilated. Its head was nearly destroyed, and only the stumps of two arms were visible. Its gigantic proportions, however, were astounding. The body, as it lies somewhat imbedded in the sand, is 18 feet long and about 7 feet wide, while it rises 3½ feet above the sand. This indicates that when living its diameter must have been at least 5½ feet. The weight of the body and head would have been at least four or five tons [U.S. short tons of 2,000 lb]. If the eight arms held the proportions usually seen in smaller species of the octopus, they would have been at least 75 to 100 feet in length and about 18 inches in diameter at the base.''

"The form of the body and its proportions show that it is an eight-armed cuttlefish, or octopus, and not a giant ten-armed squid like the devil fishes of other regions.

"No such gigantic octopus has been heretofore discovered.''

Full details of the monster, together with photographs taken by Dr. Webb, were sent to Professor A. E. Verrill of Yale University, the noted authority on giant squids and other cephalopods, who later wrote in the *American Journal of Science*:

"These photographs show that it is an eight-armed cephalopod, and probably a true octopus, of colossal size. Its body is pear-shaped. . . . The head is scarcely recognizable, owing to mutilation and decay. Dr. Webb writes that a few days after the photographs were taken . . . excavations were made in the sand and the stumps of an arm was found, still attached, 36 feet long and 10 inches in diameter where it was broken off. . . . This probably represents less than half of their original length. . . . The length, given as 18 feet, includes the mutilated head region. . . . The parts cast ashore probably weighed at least 6 or 7 tons, and this is doubtless less than half of its total mass when living . . . this species is evidently distinct from all known forms, and I therefore propose to name it *Octopus giganteus*.''

Soon afterwards, however, Verrill had second thoughts about the true identity of this animal and made a retraction in a later issue of the same journal.

"Additional facts have been ascertained and specimens received, that render it quite certain that this remarkable structure is not the body of a Cephalopod. It was described by me . . . as the body of an Octopus, from the examination of a number of photographs, and the statement made to me that, when it was first cast ashore, stumps of arms were found adherent to one end, one of which was said to have been 36 feet long. Subsequently, when it was excavated and moved, this statement proved to be erroneous. Apparently nothing that can be called stumps of arms, or any other appendages, were present.''

Verrill also said that the tissue samples Dr. Webb had sent him were not from a cephalopod, and in another journal called *Science*, he wrote:

"The extreme firmness and toughness of the thick elastic masses of integument [skin] show that the structure must have been intended for resistance to blows and to great pressure, and could not have pertained to any part of an animal where mobility is necessary. They are composed of a complex of strong elastic connective tissue fibres, like those of cetaceans. There are no muscular fibres present in any of the parts sent. This lack of muscular tissue and the resistant nature of the integument are sufficient to show that the creature could not have been a cephalopod, for in that group a highly contractive muscular tissue is essential.''

He suggested that the great mass might be part of the head of a creature like a sperm whale, although he admitted that it was decidedly unlike the head of any ordinary cachalot.

Dr. F. A. Lucas, Curator of Comparative Anatomy at the U.S. National Museum, also had an opportunity to examine some of the preserved tissues which Dr. Webb had sent to W. H. Dall, and he supported Verrill's view that they showed whale affinities. Writing in the same issue of *Science*, he said: "The substance looks like blubber, and smells like blubber and it is blubber, nothing more or less.''

Interest in the mysterious carcass rapidly waned after that, and within a few years the St. Augustine monster had been forgotten.

The story, however, didn't quite end there. . . .

In 1970 Joseph Gennaro, Jr., Associate Professor of Biology at New York University, carried out some microscopic tests on one of the tissue samples of "Octopus giganteus" preserved in the Department of Molluscs at the U.S. National Museum and his findings, along with a detailed article on the strange creature by F. G. Wood, former Curator of the Marineland Research Laboratory at St. Augustine, were published in the March 1971 issue of *Natural History*, the journal of the American Museum of Natural History.

Professor Gennaro writes: "Viewing section after section of the St. Augustine sample, we decided at once, and beyond any doubt, that the sample was not whale blubber . . . the connective tissue pattern was . . . similar, if not identical with, that in my octopus sample. The evidence appears unmistakable that the St. Augustine sea monster was in fact an octopus."

The largest octopus found in British waters is the Common octopus (*Octopus vulgaris*), which is confined mainly to the English Channel. A specimen with a radial spread of just over 6 ft and weighing 7·5 lb was caught near the Palace Pier, Brighton, Sussex in September 1960.

This specimen attains a much greater size in the warmer waters of the Mediterranean. Verany (1851) speaks of an octopus with a radial spread of 3 m (9 ft 10·75 in) which tipped the scales at 11 kg (24·2 lb), and other specimens weighing up to 25 kg (55 lb) have been reliably reported.

According to Heuvelmans (1968) octopods have been taken in the Mediterranean measuring up to 25 ft in radial spread and 130 lb in weight, but these figures must be considered excessive.

The smallest known octopus is *O. arborescens* of Ceylon which has a radial spread of less than 2 in.

The smallest octopus found in British waters is the Curled octopus (*Eledone cirrhosa*), which is widely distributed. It has a maximum radial spread of less than 2 ft.

Although a lot of blood-curdling stories have been written about octopods, they are normally shy, inoffensive creatures and rarely (if ever) attack man deliberately.

They are curious, however, and will sometimes investigate the arm or leg of a diver simply because it is a moving object, but if the person is experienced and remains motionless, the octopus soon loses interest and withdraws its exploratory arm. The diver is only in danger if he struggles and the octopus is firmly anchored to a rock, because the beast then gets excited and holds on tightly to the limb it has seized.

In 1962 a large octopus seized and drowned a diver in an undersea grotto in the Azores.

The total adhesive power of an octopod's suckers is tremendous. According to Lane (1957) a 14-stone man can be held under water by a pull of only 10 lb if he doesn't struggle, and Parker (1921) says the 2,000 suckers of an average-sized octopus (5 ft radial spread) can theoretically exert a pulling force of over 700 lb!

The most dangerous octopus in the world, and one of the deadliest creatures known to man, is the Blue-ringed octopus (*O. maculosus*) of the Indo-Pacific region. The neurotoxic venom carried by this small cephalopod (radial spread 4–6 in) is so potent that scientists at the Commonwealth Serum Laboratories in Melbourne, Victoria, Australia say the amount ejected through the horny beak in one bite is sufficient to kill seven people.

The venom acts so quickly that even if an antidote is developed—in January 1969 scientists at the University of Queensland announced that they had discovered the chemical properties of the venom, and that it was just a matter of time before an antidote was developed—it could only rarely, if ever, be used in time to save a life.

The bite of the blue-ringed octopus causes immediate pain, and within five to ten minutes the victim starts to stagger about as though inebriated. Breathing becomes increasingly laboured, and this rapidly progresses to a state of total paralysis—and death.

In September 1954 a twenty-one-year-old skin-diver was bitten on the shoulder by one of these creatures off East Point, near Darwin, Northern Territory, Australia and died less than two hours later (Lane, 1957), and in 1968 there were two more fatalities in Australian waters, including a twenty-three-year-old soldier who was bitten on the hand while paddling in a rock pool near Sydney and died ninety minutes later.

It is believed that many apparent drownings in tropical waters are caused by this octopus.

The only person known to have survived a bite from this animal is a young school-teacher who was bitten at Cowes, Victoria in December 1962. The man was immediately given oxygen and artificial respiration, and pulled through after five hours.

A pecularity of this octopus is that when it gets angry the normal dark brown and ochre bands on its body and arms change to the iridescent peacock blue that gives this species its name, making it dangerously attractive to curious beachcombers.

Octopods have the largest brains of all invertebrates in proportion to their size and are good learners. The most "intelligent" species tested so far at the Zoological Station at Naples is the Common octopus (*O. vulgaris*), which can be taught to recognise different shapes (including letters) and associate them with food, lack of food or electric shocks until a gradual memory is built up (Boycott & Young, 1955; 1956). There are even reports of octopods using stones or pieces of coral as "tools" to force open the valves of shellfish, but these have been discounted by most marine biologists.

Octopods are remarkably insensitive to pain when they are emotionally upset. This is perhaps as well, because when things get really on top of them some species have a gruesome habit of eating their own arms as a prelude to death.

In 1965 a case of self-cannibalism was reported from West Berlin Aquarium when a common octopus named "Otto" with a radial spread of more than 4 ft suddenly gave up his normal diet of mussels, fish and crayfish and started nibbling on himself instead. After ten days he had eaten half-way through his eight arms, and he continued feeding upon himself until only the stumps were left, at which time the poor creature expired. A similar case of self-cannibalism was reported from the aquarium at Leipzig Zoological Gardens in 1901.

The greatest depth at which an octopus has been recovered is 8,100 m (26,574 ft) for a specimen taken in a trawl by the Russian research vessel *Vityaz* in *c*. 1950, but the animal was unfortunately lost before it could be identified (Zenkovich *et al.*, 1955).

Very little is known about the longevity of octopods. The average life-span of a Common octopus (*O. vulgaris*) is probably two to three years (Rees & Lumby, 1954), but MacGinitie and MacGinitie (1949) believe some of the large species like *O. apollyon* may live for many years.

Octopods are extremely fertile animals and lay enormous numbers of eggs. The record is held by a common octopus kept in an aquarium at Salambo, northern Tunisia which deposited 192 batches containing 150,000 eggs! (Heldt, 1948).

The largest of all existing bivalve molluscs is the Giant clam (*Tridacna derasa*), which is found on the Indo-Pacific coral reefs.

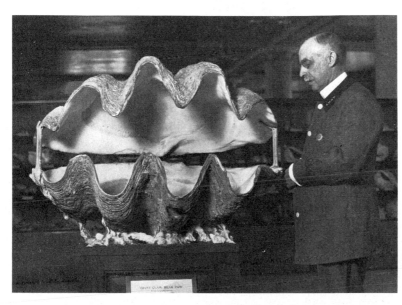

The 579·5 lb giant clam preserved in the American Museum of Natural History, New York. (American Museum of Natural History.)

The largest giant clam ever recorded is one preserved in the American Museum of Natural History, New York City, N.Y., U.S.A. which measures 43 in × 29 in and weighs 579·5 lb. It was collected from the Great Barrier Reef in 1917 and probably weighed 600 lb when alive. Another huge specimen collected at Tapanoeli (Tapanula) on the north-west coast of Sumatra before 1817 and now preserved at Arno's Vale, Northern Ireland, measures 4 ft 6 inches in length and weighs 507 lb (Rosewater, 1966), and the Australian Museum in Sydney, New South Wales has a giant clam weighing 500 lb (Allan, 1959).

The large white adductor muscle which connects the two valves of the clam and closes it like a vice tastes a bit like lobster and is considered a great delicacy by the natives of the Indo-Pacific region, although it is difficult to digest. Captain James Cook (1773) says that those taken from the giant clams found on the Great Barrier Reef where his ship was nearly wrecked in 1771 were so enormous "that one of them was more than two men could eat".

During the Renaissance (fourteenth to sixteenth centuries) sailors often brought giant clams back to Europe with them. The Venetian Republic presented one particularly fine specimen to Francis I of France, which later found its way to the Church of St. Sulpice in Paris where it was converted into two holy-water basins.

The churches of Rome boasted even larger examples. In China the wealthy mandarins frequently used them as baths, and they were also used as water-troughs for cattle.

Although the giant clam is popularly believed to be a man-killer, and there have been many stories of pearl divers and others drowning after getting their foot or leg caught in the steel-trap jaws of one of these molluscs, not one single case has ever been authenticated. Caras (1964) says the purple mantle of this clam is so conspicuous that only a fool or someone very unobservant would tread on it; he also points out that even if a person did accidentally put his foot between the giant teeth he would still have plenty of time to withdraw it because the valves do not *snap* shut as many people imagine (the speed is governed by the size of the clam; small specimens close much more rapidly than large ones).

This doesn't mean though that the giant clam is not dangerous. On the contrary, if a large specimen did trap a limb and the man was unarmed and unable to sever the great adductor muscle with a knife, then he would surely drown.

In 1963 Dr. Joseph Rosewater, Curator of Molluscs at the U.S. National Museum, Washington, D.C., received a personal communication from a Malaysian named Johnny Johnson who attributed the loss of one of his legs to a giant clam.

M. Vaillant, the French naturalist, once put the strength of the giant clam to the test by fastening a huge specimen weighing 560 lb to a post and then hooking buckets of water to the lip of one of the valves until the weight forced it to open.

By this method he found that the clam yielded to a pressure of 1,960 lb or three and a half times its own weight, which means it would be impossible for a trapped man to wrench open the two valves of a clam this size with his bare hands.

The largest bivalve mollusc found in British waters is the Fan mussel (*Pinna fragilis*), which is most abundant off the south coasts. One specimen found at Tor Bay, Devon measured 37 cm (14·56 in) in length and 20 cm (7·87 in) in breadth at the hind end.

The smallest bivalve mollusc found in British waters is *Neolepton skyesi*, which measures less than 16 mm (0·629 in) in length. This species is only known from a few species collected off Guernsey in the Channel Islands in 1894 (Tebble, 1966).

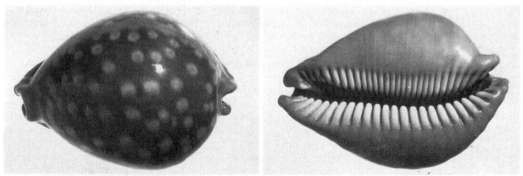

Two views of a white-tooth cowrie, one of only three examples known to exist in the world. (British Museum of Natural History, London.)

The most highly prized of all molluscan shells in the hands of conchologists is the White-tooth cowrie (*Cypraea leucodon*), which is found in the Philippines. Up to 1960 says Dance (1971) this shell was known only from the type specimen preserved in the British Museum of Natural History, London (included in the Broderip Shell Collection purchased by the Trustees of the British Museum in 1837 for £1,575), but that year a second specimen was "re-discovered" in the Shell Collection of the Boston Society of Natural History (now preserved in the Museum of Comparative Zoology at Harvard University, Cambridge, Massachusetts). In 1965 another example was found in the stomach of a fish caught in the Sulu Sea, a large inter-island sea of the Philippine Islands, bringing the number of known specimens up to three.

Other highly prized shells are *Aurinia kieneri* of the Gulf of Mexico, and *Conus milneedwardsi* of the Indian Ocean (Dance, 1971).

The rarest highly prized shell is *C. dusaveli*, which is known only from the type specimen recovered from the stomach of a fish caught off Mauritius in the Indian Ocean.

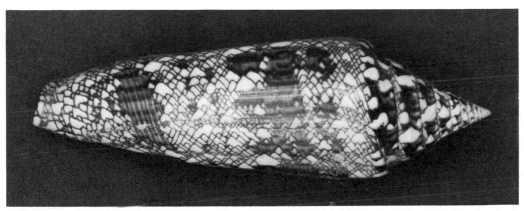

Conus bengalensis, *one of the most valuable shells in the world. This specimen was sold at Sotheby's, London in March 1971 for £1,350.*

The highest price ever paid for a sea shell is £1,350, which was the sum given on 4th March 1971 in a sale held by Messrs. Sotheby and Co., London for one of the four known examples of *C. bengalensis*. The 4 in long shell was trawled by fisher-men off north-western Thailand in December 1970. It has been described as "one of the most beautiful cone shells in the world".

The previous highest price paid for a single shell was 2,000 dollars (now £781) by a collector in New York in 1964 for one of the forty-four known specimens of the "Glory of the Sea" shell (*C. gloria-maris*), which he later presented to the Academy of Natural Sciences in Philadelphia, Pennsylvania, U.S.A.

In December 1965 a technician at the Johannesburg School of Medicine was offered £1,000 by an American collector for four *C. milneedwardsi* shells he had found on a Mozambique beach.

In theory, the most valuable shells in the world should be some of the unique specimens collected in deep-sea trawls, but these shells are always dull and unattractive and hold very little interest for the collector.

The greatest shell collector of all time was the Englishman Hugh Cummings (1791–1865) who, during his lifetime, accumulated nearly 100,000 specimens. His collection, the most valuable ever owned by a private individual, was purchased by the Trustees of the British Museum of Natural History, London for £6,000 in 1866 (Dance, 1966).

Pearls are protective secretory bodies produced by molluscs. Gem pearls come chiefly from the western Pacific oyster (family Pinctada) and the freshwater mussel (family Quadrula).

The largest known natural pearl is a milk-white opaque necreous mass known as the "Pearl of Allah" which measures 9·5 inches in length, 5·5 inches in diameter and weighs 127,374 grains (18 lb 5 oz). It was found by native fishermen in a giant clam (*Tridacna derasa*) collected off the coast of Palawan, one of the Philippine Islands, on 7th May 1934. In 1936 the chief of the fishing village presented the pearl to Wilburn D. Cobb of San Francisco, California, U.S.A. after he had saved the life of his sick son with an anti-malaria injection. In April 1969 the pearl was offered for sale in London at £1,458,333, but there were no buyers.

If we exclude this misshapen freak, then the largest pearl in the world is the poorly formed "Hope Pearl" of 1,800 grains or over 4 oz. It is fractionally over 3 inches in length and has a circumference at its globular end of 4·5 in.

The largest known pearl of regular shape is a specimen known as "La Peregrina" (The Wanderer), which was found by a Negro slave in the Gulf of Panama in the early sixteenth century. This specimen was taken to Europe, and Philip II of Spain gave it to Princess Mary Tudor (later Mary I) of England when he married her in 1554. Later it came into the possession of the Bonaparte family. Napoleon's brother Joseph, King of Spain from 1808 to 1813, is said to have taken La Peregrina when he abdicated, and the Duke of Abercorn's family acquired it from Napoleon III, who spent his last years in exile at Chislehurst, Kent and died there in 1873.

In January 1969 the pearl was sold in New York to Welsh actor Richard Burton for £15,400. He wanted it as a present for his wife, Elizabeth Taylor.

The largest known British pearl is a specimen found in a Freshwater mussel (*Margaritan margaritifera*) collected in the River Tay, Perthshire, Scotland in August 1967. It measures 0·5 inch in length and weighs 44·5 grain (0·101 oz).

Two months later scientists working on the Teiritzberg in the Vienna Basin, Austria found a gigantic petrified pearl weighing 41·45 g (0·095 oz). This specimen, measuring 2 inches in length and 1·5 inches in diameter, had been produced by a salt-water mussel (family Mytilus) about 30,000,000 years ago.

The greatest number of pearls found in a single oyster is 1,716 for a specimen caught by two Chinese fishermen off the south coast of Kwantung in September 1958.

The longest lived of all molluscs is probably the Freshwater mussel (*M. margaritifera*). Rubbel (1913) says it lives seventy to eighty years under natural conditions, and Israel (1913) credits it with a potential maximum longevity of 100 years. The only other bivalve known to exceed fifty years is *Megalonaias gigantea*, specimens of which have lived for fifty-four and fifty-three years under natural conditions (Chamberlain, 1931; Haas, 1941). Rosewater (1966) says a 3 ft long giant clam is twenty years old, and a 4 ft 6 in specimen about thirty years.

In 1858 Professor Eaton of New York reported in *Silliman's Journal* (now the *American Journal of Science*) that several hundred *live* clams had been unearthed at a depth of 42 ft by workmen digging the Erie Canal. These creatures, he said, must have come from diluvial deposits more than 3,000 years old [*sic*].

The largest known species of snail is the seaweed-eating Sea hare *Tethys californicus*, also known as the "Sea slug", which is found in the waters off the coast of California, U.S.A. The average weight is 7 to 8 lb, but one specimen tipped the scales at 15 lb 13 oz (MacGinitie & MacGinitie, 1949). The only other snails which remotely approach this species in weight are the Queen conch (*Strombus gigas*) and the Horse conch (*Fasciolaria gigantea*) of the Caribbean, and the Trumpet or Baler conch (*Syrinx auranus*) of Australia, all of which weigh up to 5 lb and have a shell measuring 1–2 ft in length.

The African giant snail, the world's largest land snail. (Fox Photos.)

The largest known land snail is *Achatina fulica* of East Africa and some Pacific islands (introduced by the Japanese during the Second World War). One huge individual measured 10·75 inches in overall length and weighed 1 lb 2 oz.

In March 1964 a specimen with a shell length of 6 in and measuring 9 in overall was found at London Airport after a plane had landed from Africa. It was later presented to London Zoo.

The largest land snail found in Britain is the Roman or Edible snail (*Helex pomatia*), which measures up to 4 inches in overall length (shell 1·77 in × 1·77 in) and weighs up to 3 oz.

(In August 1971 a Roman snail weighing 4 oz was discovered at Cuiseaux, France. Its shell was "as big as a 10-year-old child's fist".)

The Common snail (*H. aspersa*) has a shell measuring 1·37 in × 1·37 in (Ellis, 1969).

The smallest land snail found in Britain is *Punctum pygmaeum*, which has a shell measuring 0·023–0·035 in × 0·047–0·059 in (Ellis, 1969).

The fastest-moving species of land snail is probably the Common snail (*H. aspersa*). In May 1970 a specimen named "Colly" covered a distance of 2 ft across glass in three minutes flat, giving him a speed of 132 hours per mile. Another example named "Mickey" covered a distance of 4 ft 5 in across glass in seven minutes at Hove, Sussex in September 1969.

At the Snails Olympic Games at Saint-Sebastien-sur-Loire, eastern France in 1967 a common snail dragged a load of 2 lb for 2 in.

The average life-span of large snails like *H. pomatia* and *H. aspersa* is two to three years, but they can live much longer under favourable conditions. Ellis says the common snail has been known to live for ten years, and he quotes a figure of eight years for the Roman snail. Timbs (1858) mentions a record of a common snail which recovered after an uninterrupted torpidity of "at least fifteen years", but this figure needs confirming.

The most fertile of all gastropods is the Sea hare *Tethys californicus*. MacGinitie and MacGinitie (1949) gives a record of a 5 lb 12 oz female which laid 478 million eggs in 4 months 1 week (41,000 eggs per minute), but they say larger females lay considerably more. At the other end of the scale, some species of gastropod lay less than 1,000 eggs a year, and there is a record of a Black slug (*Arion ater*) laying only 477 eggs in 480 days (Bartsch, 1934).

The Dwarf cerion (*Cerion nana*), a species of land snail found only on Little Cayman Island in the Caribbean, probably has the most restricted range of any known animal. According to Bartsch (1934) this species inhabits an area of land only 5–6 yd wide by 20 yd long.

The most dangerous of all snails are the tiny water species of Africa (genus *Bulinus*), the Far East (genus *Onconelania*) and South America (genus *Biomphalaria*) which carry the amoebic parasitic worms responsible for the terrible wasting disease, bilharzia.

The process works as follows: the eggs or ova of the schistosomes, as the worms are called, enter the water-snail, where they undergo a vital period of development. They then take to the water in an immature state. Human infection occurs by wading or swimming in water containing these schistosomes. The microscopic creatures burrow through the skin on the soles of the feet or the palms of the hand and get into the bloodstream of their involuntary host. Eventually they lodge in the small veins that carry blood away from the intestines.

In mild infections there is general weakness and lassitude in the person. In stronger infections, however, the pathological effects are much more pronounced, leading in some cases to cancer of the bladder or cirrhosis of the liver.

Today there are over 80,000,000 people round the world with the disease, traces of which have been found in mummies in ancient Egyptian tombs. Egypt and Nigeria alone have 30,000,000 sufferers, and there are 5,000,000 in Brazil.

Bilharzia is the only major tropical disease actually on the increase at the present time. This is mainly due to the spread of irrigation and hydroelectric schemes which create new breeding-grounds for the water-snails.

The most venomous snails are probably the marine Cone shells (*Conus geographus* and *C. textile*) of the Indo-Pacific region. Their neurotoxic venom is similar to that of the stonefish. Kohn (1958) says at least five shell-collectors have died after handling these species.

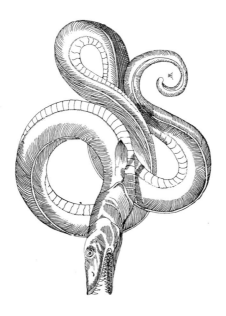

SECTION XIV

Roundworms

(class *Nematoda*)

A roundworm is a partially or wholly parasitic soft-bodied invertebrate which lives on land or in water and breathes through the skin or by means of gills. It has a cylindrical, elongated body covered by a thick layer of horny skin, and during growth this skin or cuticle is shed four times. Young are hatched from eggs deposited on land or shed in water.

The earliest known roundworms lived about 370,000,000 years ago.

There are about 10,000 living species of roundworm and the class is divided into seventeen orders. These are: the Enoploidea; the Dorylaimoidea; the Mermithoidea; the Chromadoroidea; the Araeolaimoidea; the Monhysteroidea; the Desmoscolecoidea; the Rhabditoidea; the Rhabdiasoidea; the Oxyuroidea; the Ascaroidea; the Strongloidea; the Spiruroidea; the Dracunculoidea; the Filaroidea; the Trichuroidea; and the Dioctophymoidea.

The largest known roundworm or nematode is *Dioctophyme renale*, a species found in the kidneys and liver of dogs and other mammals. Females have been measured up to 100 cm (39·37 in) in length and 1 cm (0·39 in) in diameter (Cox, 1967), with a weight of 43·3 g (von Brand, 1957).

The longest known roundworm is the very slender *Dracunculus medinensis*, which has been measured up to 4 m (13 ft 1·44 in) (Lapage, 1937).

The smallest known parasitic nematode is *Ollulanthus tricuspis*, which lives in the stomach wall of cats. Females measure 1 mm (0·039 in) in length (Rauther, 1925).

Nematodes are long-lived animals. *Wuchereria bancrofti* and *Loa loa* in man have been known to live seventeen and fifteen years respectively (Coutelen, 1935), and Taylor (1933) says *Ancylostoma duodenale* may live sixteen years and the hookworm *Necator americanus* fifteen years. There is also a record of a specimen of *Anguina tritici* living in a dried state for twenty-eight years, and thirty-nine years has been reported for a plant parasite (*Tylenchus polyhyprus*) living in a herbarium in Kansas, U.S.A. (Crofton, 1966).

SECTION XV

Ribbon Worms

(phylum *Nemertina* or *Rhynchocoela*)

A ribbon worm or nemertine is a carnivorous, soft-bodied marine invertebrate which breathes air through gills. Its most distinctive feature is the proboscis, a long muscular tube which can be thrown out to grasp prey and draw it back towards the mouth. Young are hatched from eggs or develop within the parent.

Fossil nemertines are unknown, but the earliest forms probably evolved about 350,000,000 years ago.

There are 750 living species of ribbon worm, and the phylum is divided into two classes. These are: the Anopla (proboscis unarmed); and the Enopla (proboscis armed).

The majority of ribbon worms or nemertines measure less than 8 inches in length, but some measure over 10 ft.

The longest known species is the "Boot-lace worm" (*Lineus longissimus*), which is found in the shallow waters of the North Sea. A specimen washed ashore at St. Andrews, Fifeshire, Scotland in 1864 after a storm and described by Professor W. C. McIntosh measured more than 180 ft in length (90 ft of the worm was actually measured before it ruptured, but this was less than half its total length), making it easily the longest recorded worm of any variety.

When food is scarce some nemertines absorb themselves, and Henry (1958) says there is a record of a ribbon worm digesting 95 per cent of its own body in a few months without apparently suffering any ill effects. As soon as food became available again, however, the lost tissues were restored.

SECTION XVI

Tapeworms

(class *Cestoda*)

A tapeworm is a ribbon-like invertebrate which lives as an adult in the intestine of a vertebrate animal. Its body is divided into three parts: a minute head with four suckers or hooks for maintaining its place in the intestine; a short neck or growing region; and a long series of body sections which are produced by a budding process of the neck region. Young are hatched from eggs after leaving the parent.

Fossil tapeworms are unknown, but they probably evolved later than the nematode and nemertine worms.

There are 3,000 living species of tapeworm and the class is divided into two subclasses. These are: the Cestodaria and the Eucestoda.

The longest species of tapeworm is the Beef tapeworm (*Taenia saginata*) of man which has been measured up to 25 m (82 ft) in length (Olsen, 1962). The Broad or Fish tapeworm (*Diphyllobothrium latum*) of man also attains a considerable length. Tarassov tells of a Russian woman who served as intermediate host to six specimens measuring 290 ft in total length, and a measurement of 60 ft has been reported for a single specimen. In 1957 a tapeworm (species not identified) with an alleged length of 100 ft was removed from the intestine of a whale captured off Santa Catalina Island, California, U.S.A., but this measurement has not yet been substantiated. Another Tapeworm (*Multiductus physeteris*) found in the bile duct of a sperm whale caught in the Bellingshausen Sea, in Antarctica, during the 1957–58 whaling season and described by Clarke (1962) measured 21 m (68 ft 11 in) in length.

The shortest known tapeworm is probably *Echinococcus oligarthrus*, which measures only 1·7–2·5 mm (0·066–0·098 in) in length (Wardle & McLeod, 1952). This diminutiveness may be matched by *E. minimus*.

The tapeworm in man has a long life-span. According to Penfold *et al.* (1937) eighty-three persons in Australia harboured a beef tapeworm for an average period of thirteen years, and one specimen infected a man for thirty-five years. Riley (1919) gives a record of a fish tapeworm which lived inside its human host for twenty-nine years, and Lawson (1939) quotes a figure of fifty-six years for an enormous *Echinococcus* cyst.

The shortest-lived tapeworm is probably *Ligula intestinalis*, found in water-birds, which lives only a few days (Joyeux and Baer, 1929).

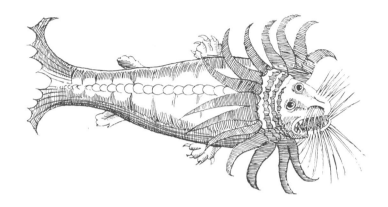

SECTION XVII

Coelenterates
(phylum *Coelenterata*)

A coelenterate is a soft-bodied marine invertebrate with a radially symmetrical body which is little more than a stomach. It occurs in two forms: the cylindrical polyp which attaches itself to rocks, and the gelatinous umbrella-shaped medusa which is free-swimming. Both types, however, have a mouth fringed by delicate tentacles which can sting and paralyse prey or act as defensive weapons. Young are reproduced from eggs discharged into the sea where they are fertilised (medusa), or from larva buds which detach from the parent and grow directly into adults (polyp).

The earliest known coelenterates lived about 570,000,000 years ago.

There are about 9,400 living species of coelenterate, and the phylum is divided into three classes. These are: the Hydrozoa (hydroids); the Scyphozoa (jellyfish); and the Anthozoa (sea-anemones and corals). The largest class is Anthozoa which contains about 6,500 species or nearly 70 per cent of the total number.

The largest true jellyfish, and the longest animal ever recorded, is *Cyanea arctica*, which is found in the north-western Atlantic Ocean from Greenland to North Carolina, U.S.A. One specimen examined by Professor Alexander Agassiz (1865) in Massachusetts Bay had a bell measuring 7 ft 6 inches in diameter and tentacles stretching for 120 ft, thus giving a theoretical tentacular spread of some 245 ft. Buchsbaum (1948) says another huge individual had a bell measuring 12 ft in diameter and tentacles over 100 ft long.

The largest coelenterate found in British waters is the rare "Lion's mane" jellyfish (*C. capillata*), which is also known as the common sea blubber. One specimen measured by Professor W. T. McIntosh (1885) at St. Andrews Marine Laboratory, Fifeshire, Scotland had a bell diameter 910 mm (35·82 in) and tentacles stretching over 45 ft, and Russell (1970) says he saw the impression of another one in the sand at Newton-by-the-Sea, Northumberland in September 1967 which must have had a bell diameter of at least 910 mm (35·43 in). This species reaches a greater size in northern seas where bell diameters up to 4 ft 6 in have been recorded.

Some true jellyfish have a bell diameter of less than 20 mm (0·78 in).

The most dangerous of all coelenterates are the sea-wasps or box jellies of the genera *Chiropsalmus* and *Chironex* of the Indo-Pacific region, which carry a neurotoxic venom similar in strength to that found in the Asiatic cobra. These jellyfish, which are very similar in appearance, have caused the deaths of sixty people off the coast of Queensland, Australia in the past twenty-five years, and at least forty others have died in the waters of Malaysia, Borneo and the Philippines during the same period.

Clarke (1969) quotes a case of a man stung by a Box jelly (*Chironex fleckeri*) off a Queensland beach who died in agonizing pain *within thirty seconds* of being stung, and Caras (1964) says a twelve-year-old boy died a few minutes after being stung by a specimen of *Chiropsalmus quadragatus* off a Darwin beach. Another fatality was reported in May 1953 when a man was stung by a box jelly of the same genus (*C. salmus*) while in shallow water with his eleven-year-old son at Townsville, Queensland. Pope (1953) writes:

"The boy . . . and his father waded out with a box to reset their fish-trap. They were about 10 yards out from the shore in water that was knee-deep. They took a rest and were about to lift the box up again and proceed when . . . father stooped down, placing his hands between his legs. As he stood up the boy noticed thick cobweb-like-looking stings on his father's arms and legs. His father went pale immediately and said, 'Get out of the water quick, Ken.' The boy climbed upon the top of the trap and so got out of the water. His father staggered ashore and said, 'I copped the lot.' He died within a matter of from three to four minutes."

The symptoms of box jelly stings are profuse sweating, convulsions and blindness, followed by respiratory paralysis, and Dr. Bruce Halstead (1956) says death usually occurs in three to ten minutes. This means an antidote would be useless against such a fast-working venom, which has been classified by some marine biologists as the most deadly manufactured by any living creature.

The most dangerous jellyfish found in British waters is the Portuguese man-of-war (*Physalia physalis*) which, strictly speaking, is not a jellyfish but a closely related siphonophore. Most people stung by this highly coloured float experience a burning pain, followed by a large weal which may last for perhaps a week, but persons who are allergic to the venom may become seriously ill.

In August 1955 a six-year-old boy drowned at Camber Sands, Sussex after coming into contact with a Portuguese man-of-war.

According to Idyll (1964) the Octopus *Tremoctopus violaceus* uses the stinging cells of the Portuguese man-of-war as a defensive weapon. Apparently the cephalopod carefully removes pieces of the siphonophore's tentacles and then arranges them in orderly fashion along its four dorsal arms. The octopus appears to be immune to the stings.

Not a lot is known about the life-spans of jellyfish, but most small species probably live less than one year. There are exceptions, however. In July 1928 a small number of freshwater medusae suddenly reappeared in the great water-lily tank at the Botanic Gardens in Regent's Park, London after an absence of forty-five years. They were first observed in the tank in 1880, but "disappeared" three years later.

On 3rd October 1956 Reuter reported that a few days previously jellyfish had forced the British submarine H.M.S. *Thorough* to surface in the Tasman Sea. The crew of the submarine described how the jellyfish had blinded the periscope of the vessel and clogged the speed-recording apparatus situated underneath the boat. A full-speed spurt under water failed to dislodge the jellyfish, so the submarine had to surface.

The largest known sea-anemone is *Discoma* sp. of the Great Barrier Reef, Queensland, Australia, which has an oral disc measuring up to 2 ft in diameter.

Sea-anemones are the longest lived of all invertebrates. According to Comfort (1963) *Actinia mesembryanthemum* and *Cereus pedunculatus* have lived under artificial conditions for sixty-five to seventy and eighty-five to ninety years respectively, and Stephenson (1928) believes they "live for hundreds of years under suitable conditions".

SECTION XVIII

Sponges
(phylum *Parazoa*)

A sponge is a multi-celled invertebrate which is found in both fresh and marine water and at all depths. It is held together by an elaborate skeleton of horny fibres, silica or carbonate of lime which takes the form of minute wheels, darts, etc., strongly linked together. Internally it consists of thousands of minute canals which run down through the tissues from the tiny pores on the surface to spherical chambers containing lash-bearing cells (flagella). These draw in the water through the pores, dredge it of tiny food particles and then sweep the waste matter out through a complex system of galleries to the round surface openings known as vents. Reproduction is either from fertilised eggs which develop into free-swimming larvae or from budding like plants.

The earliest known sponges lived about 600,000,000 years ago.

There are about 2,500 living species of sponge, and the phylum is divided into three classes. These are: the Calcarea (calcareous sponges); the Hexactinellida (glass sponges); and the Demospongiae (horny sponges).

The largest known sponge is the barrel-shaped Loggerhead sponge (*Spheciospongia vesparia*) of the West Indies and Florida, U.S.A., *single* individuals measuring up to 3 ft 6 inches in height and 3 ft in diameter. Neptune's cup or goblet (*Poterion patera*) of Indonesia grows up to 4 ft in height, but it is not such a bulky creature as *S. vesparia*.

In 1909 an enormous Wool sponge (*Hippospongia canaliculatta*) was collected off the Bahama Islands and brought to Nassau. Perfectly formed and arched like an immense fruit cake, it measured 6 ft in circumference and 2 ft in diameter in every direction. When first taken from the water it weighed between 80 and 90 lb, but after it had been dried and relieved of all excrescences it scaled 12 lb. This sponge is now preserved in the U.S. National Museum, Washington, D.C., U.S.A.

The smallest known sponge is the widely distributed *Leucosolenia blanca* which measures 3 mm (0·11 in) in height when fully grown.

Sponges have been recovered from depths of up to 18,500 ft (3·5 miles).

The rarest coloration among sponges is blue, which is usually the result of blue-green algae or bacteria.

Sponges have been used by man since early times. Homer in the *Iliad* describes Hephaestus as washing the grime of the smithy off his body with a sponge, and in the *Odyssey* we read that the household servants of Penelope and Odysseus used sponges to swab down the tables in the dining-hall. Aristotle gives the name "Achilleion" to a kind of sponge used for padding helmets and greaves, and describes it as "very fine, very dense and very tough"; this sponge would be of the horny "elephant's ear" variety (Demospongiae).

According to Pliny the Elder, the Romans used sponges on wooden handles for mops and for paintbrushes. The reference in St. Mark's Gospel (Chapter 15, verse 36) shows that sponges were in common use in Roman Palestine. In the Middle Ages pulverised sponges were used as a cure for wounds.

Before 1938 about half the world's supply of natural sponges came from the Bahamas, Florida and the West Indies, but most of these sponge beds were killed off by a mysterious fungus disease. Today practically all the natural sponges come from the Mediterranean, and Greece is now the centre of the sponge-fishing trade.

Diving for sponges is a hazardous occupation, and each year eight to ten divers die from accidents in the Mediterranean, while two dozen or so others are crippled by the bends or caisson disease. This disease (nitrogen bubbles in the blood) is caused by rising to the surface too quickly from a great depth. If the diver is put into a decompression chamber straight away he can be cured, but only a few sponge boats can afford to be equipped with one.

SECTION XIX

Extinct Animals

An extinct animal is a creature which no longer exists on the face of the earth in a living state, although at one time it flourished. It is only known from fossil remains, and these consist either of organic material or the impression of organic objects like feet. The word "fossil" is derived from the Latin verb "fodere" meaning "to dig" and originally applied to almost anything of interest that was dug up out of the ground. For a living thing to become a fossil it must be buried soon after death so that it cannot be eaten by scavengers or destroyed by oxygen-breathing bacteria. The exact age at which an animal becomes a fossil is not known, but it is probably at least 25,000 years, and the science dedicated to their study is called palaeontology.

The first dinosaur to be scientifically described was *Megalosaurus* ("large lizard") in 1824. A lower jaw and other bones of this animal had been found before 1818 in a slate quarry at Stonesfield, near Woodstock, Oxon., and placed in the University Museum, Oxford where they were examined by Dean William Buckland. This 20 ft long bipedal theropod (carnivore) stalked across what is now southern England about 130,000,000 years ago. In March 1822 Dr. Gideon Mantell of Lewes, Sussex discovered the remains of another bipedal dinosaur of the same period (Lower Cretaceous) in the near-by district of Cuckfield and described them in 1825 under the name *Iguanodon* ("iguana-tooth"). Unlike *Megalosaurus*, however, this 30 ft long dinosaur was herbivorous. Seven years later Mantell found fragmentary remains of a 30 ft long armoured dinosaur in the Tilside Forest, Sussex and called it *Hylaeosaurus* ("toad lizard"). It was not until 1842, however, that the name *Dinosauria* ("fearfully great lizards") was given to these reptiles by Professor Richard Owen, the great English anatomist and vertebrate palaeontologist.

Diplodocus carnegii, *the longest known dinosaur, reached a length of 87 ft. (Smithsonian Institution, Washington, D.C.)*

The longest dinosaur so far recorded is *Diplodocus* ("double-beam"), an attenuated sauropod which ranged over western North America about 150,000,000 years ago. A composite skeleton of three individuals excavated near Split Mountain, Utah between 1909 and 1922 for the Carnegie Museum of the Natural Sciences in Pittsburgh, Pennsylvania and subsequently named *Diplodocus carnegii*, measures 87 ft 6 inches in total length (neck 22 ft, body 15 ft, tail 50 ft 6 in)—nearly the length of three London double-decker buses—and has a mounted height of 11 ft 9 in at the pelvis (the highest point on the body). This animal weighed an estimated 10.56 metric tons in life.

Andrew Carnegie, the steel tycoon, was so impressed by his namesake that he ordered five plaster replicas of the sauropod to be made which he donated to various foreign museums (one of the replicas is on display in the British Museum of Natural History, London).

In October 1949 a 14 ft section of a spinal column believed to be part of a fossilised skeleton of a 100 ft long dinosaur was found near Roma, Queensland, Australia, but further information is lacking.

The remains of another dinosaur measuring 99 ft in length were reportedly found near the village of Cofradia, in the State of Sinaloa, Mexico in August 1956 and examined by scientists from the University of Sinaloa, but this measurement has not been authenticated.

Britain's longest dinosaur was the sauropod *Cetiosaurus* ("whale lizard") which lived in what is now England about 165,000,000 years ago. It measured up to 60 ft in length and weighed over 15 tons. This reptile was originally described by Owen in 1841 who—on the evidence of a few fragmentary remains—thought it was a crocodile. In May 1898, however, a partial skeleton was found in the No. 1 Brickyard of the New Peterborough Brick Co., Peterborough, Northamptonshire and other remains were later discovered in the quarries of Oxfordshire.

The heaviest of all prehistoric animals, and the heaviest land vertebrate of all time, was *Brachiosaurus* ("arm lizard") which lived in East Africa (Rhodesia and Tanzania) and Colorado and Oklahoma, U.S.A. between 135,000,000 and 165,000,000 years ago. A complete skeleton excavated near Tendaguru Hill, southern Tanganyika (Tanzania) in 1909 and mounted in the Museum für Naturkunde in East Berlin, Germany measures 74 ft 6 inches in length and 21 ft at the shoulder (the raised head of this exhibit reaches 39 ft into the air).

In 1930 the British Museum East African Expedition discovered 20 ft of the vertebrae of another *Brachiosaurus* near Tendaguru Hill which must have measured well over 70 ft when alive.

Until quite recently *Brachiosaurus* was estimated by palaeontologists to have weighed 40–50 tons when alive, which is a staggering weight for a land vertebrate. Then, in 1962, Dr. Edwin Colbert, Curator of the Department of Vertebrate Paleontology at the American Museum of Natural History, New York, carried out a series of experiments to determine *more accurately* the tonnage of this gigantic sauropod and other dinosaurs. His calculations were based on miniature models carefully scaled at 0·041–0·037 natural size. First of all, he worked out the volume of each restoration in cubic centimetres. Then he multiplied the result by the cube of the linear scale of the model to give the volume of the dinosaur when it was alive. It was now possible to calculate the weight fairly easily by multiplying the metric volume by the *assumed specific gravity* of the extinct animal. An acceptable value was obtained by checking the specific gravity of a young alligator, a living reptile closely related taxonomically to the dinosaurs.

Most of the calculated dinosaur weights ran very close to earlier estimates, but the biggest surprise of all was the tonnage worked out for *Brachiosaurus*. This was 78·26 metric tons or double the weight of an average-sized bull sperm whale! Even Dr. Colbert was startled by this finding.

"It has been generally supposed", he says, "that 40 to 50 avoirdupois tons constitute about the upper limit for the weight of a land-living vertebrate, the assumption being that greater weights would exceed the limitations of the supporting strength of bone, ligament and muscle. Yet here is a dinosaur that, on the basis of the calculations, weighed as much as a large whale. Extra volumetric measurements of the model were made, and linear measurements of the model . . . checked several times. After all possible checks of method and measurements had been made, the figure still held. Therefore, unless one is prepared to reject the . . . model of *Brachiosaurus* as being completely inaccurate, a proposition that I for one cannot accept, it appears that *Brachiosaurus* was indeed a gigantic sauropod, in weight almost two and a half times the size of *Brontosaurus* [32·42 metric tons]. . . . Certainly no other land-living vertebrate ever approached it in massiveness and weight."

Dr. Colbert's model for his *Brachiosaurus* was the specimen in the Museum für Naturkunde in East Berlin. This skeleton, however, does not represent the maximum size for this dinosaur. Fragmentary remains have

The skeleton of Brachiosaurus, *the largest of all the dinosaurs. (Museum fur Naturkunde, Berlin.)*

The skeleton of Tyrannosaurus rex, *one of the largest of the carnivorous dinosaurs. (American Museum of Natural History.)*

since been discovered in East Africa which indicate that some individuals may have weighed as much as 100 tons and measured over 90 ft in length, which would also have made it the longest of all dinosaurs.

Although it is described as a land animal, *Brachiosaurus* probably spent most of its life in lakes or estuaries where its enormous weight would be buoyed up by the water. This is evidenced by the nostrils which are placed high up on the skull. But females still had to come ashore to lay their eggs.

Until quite recently it was widely believed that the largest theropod or carnosaur was *Tyrannosaurus rex* ("tyrant lizard") which lived about 75,000,000 years ago in what are now the states of Montana and Wyoming in the U.S.A. and Mongolia. This dinosaur measured up to 47 ft in overall length, had a bipedal height of up to 18 ft 6 in, a stride of 13 ft and weighed a calculated 6·78 metric tons (Colbert, 1962). It also had a 4 ft long skull containing serrated teeth measuring up to 7·25 inches in length (Kerr, *in litt.* 11.1.71). It is now known, however, that some other carnosaurs were just as large or even larger than *Tyrannosaurus*.

In 1934 labourers working on Highway 64 near Kenton in Cimarron

County, Oklahoma accidentally unearthed a huge rib 7 ft long and 1 ft
in circumference. Dr. J. W. Stovall, palaentologist at Norman University,
was hurriedly called to the site of the discovery and over the next few
months he and a special crew of men unearthed the bones of a *Brontosaurus*,
a *Ceratosaurus*, a *Camptosaurus*, a *Stegosaurus* and a huge carnosaur new to
science. This specimen, which measured 42 ft in overall length and had a
bipedal height of 16 ft, was much more massive in proportion to its height
than *Tyrannosaurus* and had arms more than twice as long (Ray, 1941).
Stovell named the carnosaur *Saurophagus maximus* ("lizard-eater"), but
after his death the bones were re-examined and found to be those of a very
large *Allosaurus*. Since then the remains of other allosaurs of comparable
size have been found in Utah (De Camp & De Camp, 1968).

In 1930 the British Museum Expedition to East Africa dug up the
pelvic bones and part of the vertebrae of another huge carnosaur at
Tendaguru Hill which must have measured about 54 ft in overall length
when alive.

During the summers of 1963–65 a Polish-Mongolian expedition led
by Dr. Zofia Kielan-Jaworowska, the Polish woman palaentologist,
discovered the remains of a carnosaur in the Gobi Desert which had
8 ft 6 in long forelimbs! (De Camp & De Camp, 1968). It is not yet known,
however, whether the rest of this animal was built on the same gigantic
scale.

In the Museum of Palaeontology at the Academy of Sciences of the
U.S.S.R. in Moscow there is preserved a dinosaur claw which measures a
staggering 70 cm (27·55 in) in length! (Louis, *in litt.* 1.6.71). Unfortunately
no other information is available about this fossil, but it must have
belonged to a dinosaur of truly nightmarish proportions (cf. the 11 in
long claws of the large *Allosaurus* found in Oklahoma).

Stegosaurus ("plated reptile"), which roamed across the Northern
Hemisphere about 150,000,000 years ago, had been credited with being
the most brainless of all the dinosaurs. It had a walnut-sized brain
weighing only 2·5 oz, which represented 0·004 of 1 per cent of its body
weight, compared with 0·074 of 1 per cent for an elephant and 1·88 per
cent for a human. Despite this "handicap" however the stegosaurs were a
very successful form of life and flourished for millions of years.

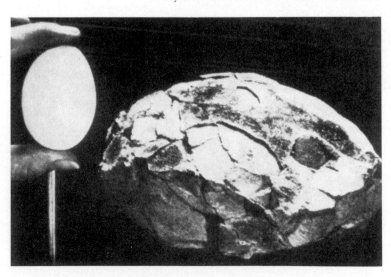

*The largest known
reptilian egg, that of
Hypselosaurus priscus,
compared to that of a hen.*

The largest known dinosaur eggs are those of *Hypselosaurus priscus*, a 30 ft long sauropod which lived about 80,000,000 years ago. Some specimens found in the valley of the Durance near Aix-en-Provence, southern France in October 1961 would have had, uncrushed, a length of 12 in and a diameter of 10 in.

The earliest known flying reptile was *Dimorphodon*, the remains of which were first discovered by Mary Anning at Lyme Regis in Dorset in 1828. It lived about 150,000,000 years ago and had a wing-span of 4 ft.

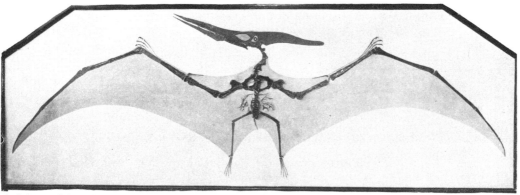

A skeleton of the extinct winged reptile Pteranodon, *whose wing-span of 27 ft is the largest of any known flying creature. (American Museum of Natural History.)*

The largest known flying reptile was probably *Pteranodon ingens*, a dynamic soarer which glided over what is now the State of Kansas, U.S.A. about 80,000,000 years ago. It had a wing-span of up to 27 ft and weighed an estimated 40 lb. This creature probably launched itself from cliff-tops, and Swinton (1966) says it could stay aloft like the albatross for days on end. Sometimes, however, it must have crashed accidentally into the sea when snatching at fish. When this happened the reptile had to wait for a reasonably strong wind (i.e. over 15 mile/h) before it could become airborne again.

Fragments of an even larger pterosaur which lived about 100,000,000 years ago have reportedly been found in Jordan, but further information is lacking.

Britain's largest known flying reptile was *Ornithocheirus*, with a wing-span of 10 ft, which flew over what is now the Weald about 100,000,000 years ago.

The largest marine reptile ever recorded was probably *Kronosaurus queenslandicus*, a short-necked pliosaur which swam in the seas round what is now Australia about 100,000,000 years ago. In 1931 an expedition from the Harvard Museum of Comparative Zoology found a nearly complete skeleton in Queensland. It measured 42 ft in length and had a 9 ft long skull. The fossil remains of another specimen found at Hughenden, Queensland and consisting of a 12 ft long mandible containing six very large teeth must have come from a *Kronosaurus* measuring at least 55 ft in length (Fletcher, 1958).

The Long-necked plesiosaur *Elasmosaurus*, which swam in the seas over what is now the State of Kansas, U.S.A. about 130,000,000 years ago measured up to 47 ft, of which the neck accounted for 25 ft.

Most of the ichthyosaurs measured less than 30 ft in length, but *Leptophtergius acutirostris*, which lived about 140,000,000 years ago, had a

The jaws of Kronosaurus queenslandicus, *the largest marine reptile ever recorded. (Museum of Comparative Zoology, Harvard University, Cambridge, Massachusetts, U.S.A.)*

7 ft skull and measured about 40 ft in length (the largest known vertebrae, 8 inches in diameter, indicate a length of 65 ft).

In September 1966 the fossilised head of a 40 ft long *Ichthyosaurus* was found by a thirteen-year-old girl at Charmouth, Dorset.

Tylosaurus, the largest of the mosasaurs, which swam in the seas over what is now North America, about 135,000,000 years ago, measured up to 40 ft.

The largest known crocodile was *Phobosuchus* ("horror crocodile") which lived in the lakes and swamps of what are now the States of Montana and Texas, U.S.A. about 75,000,000 years ago. It measured up to 50 ft in length and had a 6 ft long skull. The gavial *Rhamphosuchus*, which lived in what is now northern India about 7,000,000 years ago, also reached a length of 50 ft.

A skeleton of the largest recorded turtle, Archelon ischyros, *with an overall length of 11 ft. (Peabody Museum of Natural History, Yale University, New Haven, Connecticut, U.S.A.)*

The largest prehistoric marine turtle was probably *Archelon ischyros*, which lived in the shallow seas over what are now the states of North Dakota and Kansas, U.S.A. about 80,000 years ago. An almost complete skeleton with a carapace (shell) 6 ft 6 in long was discovered in August 1895 near the south fork of the Cheyenne River in Custer County, South Dakota. The skeleton, which has an overall length of 11 ft 4 in (20 ft across the outstretched fore flippers) is now preserved in the Peabody Museum of Natural History at Yale University, New Haven, Connecticut, U.S.A. This turtle, which has its right hind flipper bitten off, was estimated to have weighed 6,000 lb (2·7 tons) when it was alive, but this poundage is probably too high.

A skeleton of Colossochelys atlas, *the largest pre-historic tortoise, which weighed about a ton when alive. (American Museum of Natural History.)*

The largest prehistoric tortoise was *Colossochelys atlas* which lived in northern India between 7,000,000 and 12,000,000 years ago The remains of a specimen with a carapace 5 ft 5 in long (7 ft 4 in over the curve) and 2 ft 11 in high were discovered by Barnum Brown (1931), Curator of Fossil Reptiles at the American Museum of Natural History, near Chandigarh in the Siwalik Hills in 1923.

"In order to compute its weight when alive," he writes, "an exact model was made to scale and the weight determined by displacement. By this method it was estimated that it weighed during life approximately 2,100 pounds."

The remains of other prehistoric tortoises of about the same size have since been discovered in North America.

The longest prehistoric snake was the python-like *Gigantophis garstini*, which inhabited what is now Egypt about 50,000,000 years ago. Parts of a spinal column and a small piece of jaw discovered at El Faiyum indicate a length of about 42 ft (some authorities say 60 ft), which puts it on a par with the anaconda (maximum length about 45 ft) for size.

The largest amphibian ever recorded was the alligator-like *Eogyrinus* which lived between 280,000,000 and 345,000,000 years ago. It measured nearly 15 ft in length. *Mastodonsaurus*, which lived about 200,000,000 years ago in what is now Germany, had a 3–4 ft long head and measured up to 12 ft in total length.

The largest fish ever recorded was the Great shark (*Carcharodon megalodon*), an ancestor of the present-day Great white shark (*C. carcharias*). In 1909 the American Museum of Natural History undertook a restoration of the jaws of this giant shark basing the size on 4 in long fossil teeth and found that the jaws measured 9 ft across and had a gape of 6 ft. The length of this fish was estimated at 80 ft. Other fossil teeth measuring up to 6 inches in length and weighing 12 oz have since been discovered near Bakersfield, California, U.S.A. (McCormick *et al.*, 1963).

A reconstruction of the jaws of the extinct great shark which reached a length of 80 ft. (American Museum of Natural History.)

The largest arthropod ever recorded was the carnivorous *Ptergotus buffaloensis*, a huge eurypterid (sea-scorpion) which lived in estuaries or coastal waters about 400,000,000 years ago. It grew to a length of 9 ft.

The largest shell mollusc ever recorded was the Ammonite *Pachydiscus seppenradensis* which lived about 75,000,000 years ago. It had a shell measuring up to 8 ft 5 inches in diameter. Some of the nautiloids of the Ordovician era (440,000,000 to 500,000,000 years ago) had straight shells measuring over 15 ft in length, but they were not such bulky animals.

The largest prehistoric insect was the Dragon-fly *Meganeura monyi* which lived between 280,000,000 and 325,000,000 years ago. Fossil remains (i.e. impressions of wings) discovered at Commentry, central France indicate that it had a wing-span reaching up to 70 cm (27·5 in).

The earliest known bird was *Archaeopteryx lithographica*, which was described by Professor Hermann von Meyer in 1861 from a feather impression found in lithographic stone in a quarry near Pappenheim, Bavaria, Germany. The same year a skeleton was discovered in the Ottmann Quarry near Pappenheim and was purchased in 1862 by the Trustees of the British Museum of Natural History, London. *Archaeopteryx* lived about 140,000,000 years ago.

A fossilised egg of the elephant bird compared with that of a hen. (Sotheby & Co. Ltd.)

A model of the flightless moa of New Zealand, which reached a height of over 13 ft.

The largest prehistoric bird was the Elephant bird (*Aepyornis maximus*), also known as the "Roc bird", which lived in southern Madagascar. It was a flightless bird standing 9–10 ft in height and weighing nearly 1,000 lb.

Aepyornis also had the largest eggs of any known animal. One example preserved in the British Museum of Natural History, London measures 33·75 in round the long axis with a circumference of 28·5 in, giving a capacity of 2·35 gal—seven times that of an ostrich egg.

A more cylindrical egg preserved in the Academie des Sciences, Paris, France measures 12·875 in × 15·375 in and probably weighed about 27 lb with the contents.

According to Dr. Josef Augusta (1966) an American collector once paid $10,000 for an *Aepyornis* egg measuring 12 in × 10 in.

This bird may have survived until *c.* 1660.

The flightless Moa (*Dinornis giganteus*) of North Island, New Zealand was taller, attaining a height of over 13 ft, but it only weighed about 500 lb.

In May 1962 a single fossilised ankle joint of an enormous flightless bird was found at Gainsville, Florida, U.S.A.

The largest prehistoric bird actually to fly was probably the condor-like *Teratornis incredibilis*, which lived in what is now North America about 125,000,000 years ago. The remains of one of this species, discovered in Smith Creek Cave, Nevada, in 1952 indicate a wing-span of 5 m (16 ft 4 in), and the bird must have weighed nearly 50 lb (Howard, 1952). Another gigantic flying bird named *Osteodontornis orri*, which lived in what is now the State of California, U.S.A. about 20,000,000 years ago, had a wing-span of 16 ft and was probably even heavier. It was related to the pelicans and storks. The albatross-like *Gigantornis eaglesomei*, which flew over what is now Nigeria between 34,000,000 and 58,000,000 years ago, has been credited with a wing-span of 20 ft on the evidence of a single fossilised breastbone.

The largest prehistoric mammal, and the largest land mammal ever recorded, was *Baluchitherium* (= *Indricotherium, Paraceratherium, Aceratherium, Thaumastotherium, Aralotherium* and *Benaratherium*), a long-necked hornless rhinoceros which lived in Europe and central and western Asia between 20,000,000 and 40,000,000 years ago. It stood up to 17 ft 9 in to the top of the shoulder hump (27 ft to the crown of the head), measured 27–28 ft in length and probably weighed at least 20 tons. The bones of this gigantic browser were first discovered in 1907–8 in the Bugti Hills in East Baluchistan (Augusta, 1966).

The largest sirenian ever recorded was Steller's sea-cow (*Hydrodamalis gigas* = *H. stelleri*), first discovered in the waters around Bering Island and other small islands in the Komandorskie group in the Bering Sea in 1741. An adult female killed by Georg Steller, the famous German naturalist, measured 7·52 m (24 ft 8 in) from the tip of the nose to the tip of the tail and weighed an estimated 4,000 kg (3·97 tons), but some males may have reached 30 ft and a weight of over 7 tons. This species became extinct about twenty-seven years after its discovery.

The longest tusks of any prehistoric animal were those of the Straight-tusked elephant (*Hesperoloxodon antiquus germanicus*), which lived in what is now northern Germany about 2,000,000 years ago. The average length in adult bulls was 5 m (16 ft 4·75 in). A single tusk of a woolly mammoth (*Mammonteus primigenius*) preserved in the Franzens Museum at Brno, Czechoslovakia measures 5·02 m (16 ft 5·5 in) along the outside curve (Osborne 1936–42).

In c. August 1933 a single tusk of an Imperial mammoth (*Archidiskodon imperator*) measuring 16+˙ ft (anterior end missing) was found by Mr. George B. Doughty in Gorza County near Post, Texas, U.S.A. The following year Doughty presented this tusk, which measured 2 ft in maximum circumference, together with two molars to the American Museum of Natural History, New York (Holsinger, *in litt.* 28.4.66).

The heaviest single tusk on record is one weighing 330 lb with a maximum circumference of 35 in now preserved in the Museo Archeologico, Milan, Italy. It measures 11 ft 9 inches in length (Osborne, 1936–42). The heaviest recorded mammoth tusks are a pair in the Peabody Museum of Archaeology and Ethnology at Harvard University, Cambridge, Massachusettsetts, U.S.A. which have a combined weight of 498 lb and measure 13 ft 9 in and 13 ft 7 in respectively.

The tallest extinct elephant was the Mammoth *Parelephas trogontherii* which lived about 1,000,000 years ago in central Europe and North America. A fragmentary skeleton found in Mosbach, Germany indicates a height of 4·5 m (14 ft 9 in) at the shoulder, but measurements up to 15 ft have been reported elsewhere. In February 1970 the skeleton of an unidentified extinct elephant reputedly measuring 16 ft at the shoulder was put on display at a museum in Azov, U.S.S.R. The specimen was believed to be 500,000 years old.

The prehistoric giant deer which had greatly palmated antlers measuring up to 14 ft across. (Photo-Reportage Ltd.)

The prehistoric Giant deer (*Megaceros giganteus*), which lived in northern Europe and northern Asia as recently as 50,000 B.C. had the longest horns of any known animal. One specimen found in Ireland had greatly palmated antlers measuring 14 ft across (Whitehead, 1964).

The largest extinct whale was the serpentine *Basilosaurus* (formerly called *Zeuglodon*) which swam in the Eocene seas (38,000,000 to 54,000,000 years ago). It measured up to 70 ft in length.

List of Correspondents

Professor Frederick A. Aldrich
William J. Allen, Jr.
Dr. Dean Amadon
Svend Andersen
E. N. Arnold
Isaac Asimov
David Attenborough

H. W. Ball
Mrs. Eiselle Banks
Howard Baron
K. A. Beattie
Harry Berry
Roy W. Bird
Gordon Blower
James Bond
Professor Osmond P. Breland
David H. Brown
Dr. A. M. Bruner
Frank Burton

Roger Caras
James Carney
The Carpenter
Richard Carrington
Denis Charlesworth
Dr. Vre Guy Chauvier
P. A. Clancey
D. J. Clark
Dr. Malcolm Clarke
Dr. John Cloudsley-Thompson
Dr. Doris M. Cochran
B. H. Cogan
H. G. Cogger
Dr. Edwin H. Colbert
William Conway
Mrs. P. B. Coward
Lee S. Crandall
Michael J. Crotty
W. P. Crowcroft
Dr. K. Curry-Lindahl

Robert A. Dahne
Miss Grace Davall
Bruce Dawson
J. F. Dawson
Dr. A. B. van Deinse

Myvanwy M. Dick
H. J. de S. Disney
Herndon G. Dowling

Malcolm Edwards
Tom Ewing

Dr. R. Faust
I. J. Ferguson-Lees
James Fisher
Lester E. Fisher
John A. Fletcher
Dr. F. C. Fraser
W. C. Fripp

Professor V. G. Geptner
Dr. Willis J. Gertsch
Professor Perry W. Gilbert
Dr. Raymond M. Gilmore
Dr. Coleman J. Goin
S. Gordon
Miss A. G. Grandison
G. R. Greed
Lawrence G. Green
Dr. Bernhard Grzimek

W. D. Haacke
Carl-Heinrich Hagenbeck
P. A. Halley
Sir Edward Hallstrom
Charles O. Handley, Jr.
Professor H. Hediger
Dr. D. Hellenius
Dr. John R. Hendrickson
David Heppell
Gerald E. Holsinger
F. W. Hooper
T. G. Howarth
Dr. L. Howell-Rivero
H. G. Hurrell
Professor Victor H. Hutchison

J. M. Ingles
M. P. Irwin

S. N. A. Jacobs
Robert Jarvis
David Jay

Dr. A. P. Kapur
Robert L. Kendell
Smith P. Kerr
D. King
Dr. F. Wayne King
Miss Judith E. King
J. R. Kinghorn
Dr. S. E. Kleinenberg
Dr. Heinz-Georg Klos
Karl F. Koopman

Ernest A. Lachner
Frank Lane
Dr. Ernst M. Lang
P. N. Lawrence
Donald Levin
F. Lexster
J. H. Lockett
Victor Louis
Arthur Loveridge
Dr. V. Lukin
Richard Lund

H. McCall
D. McFarland
Dr. G. R. McLachlan
J. McNally
V. J. A. Manton
Stanley Marcus
B. J. Marlow
Hymen Marx
Lord Massereene and Ferrard
Miss Judith Meadows
William E. Meeker
Burt J. Monroe, Jr.
Thomas A. Moody, Jr.
J. Moreland
Mrs. Rosemary Morley
J. Morrison
G. S. Mottershead
Professor George S. Myers

Dr. Murray A. Newman
Dr. Masaharu Nishiwaki
L. D. Nuckles
Adrian Nyoka

Peter Ommundsen
Dr. Hideo Omura
Dr. Fairfield Osborn

Dr. H. W. Parker
R. Marlin Perkins
Dr. Jorge Sabater Pi
Ian Player
R. D. Pope
K. M. Poulton
Dr. J. C. Poynton
J. W. Provan

Dr. G. Sundara Rajulu
Dr. G. Ramakrishna
Professor Edward C. Raney
Miss Jean Rankin
Dr. G. Raun
D. B. Redway
A. C. Reid
Miss Betty I. Roots

David E. Sale
Ivan T. Sanderson
Charles R. Schroeder
Dr. William C. Schroeder
Dr. Albert Schwartz
Miss Sheelagh Seale
Miss Elspeth Sellar
Charles E. Shaw
Mrs. R. Simon
Dr. E. J. Slijper
M. C. Small
William F. Smith-Veniz
George E. Sneath
George Speidel
Dr. Stewart Springer
J. F. Stephenson
Dr. Margaret M. Stewart
Miss S. M. K. Stone

Mrs. Walter F. Toerge
Dr. Frederick B. Turner
J. N. Tweedie

Frederick A. Ulmer, Jr.

Dr. Z. Veselovsky
Dr. Gilbert L. Voss
A. E. Vyse

Dr. H. Wackernagel
H. J. Wady
Peter Ward
Dr. Ernest E. Williams
Professor J. M. Winterbottom
Dr. Bernhard Witkop
Dr. Torben Wolff
W. J. Woods
Dr. C. E. Wright

Dr. D. W. Yalden
I. H. H. Yarrow
Henry Young

Dr. Richard L. Zusi
Richard G. Zweifel

Bibliography

Abramov, V. K. (1969). Area and abundance of the Amur tiger (*Panthera tigris amurensis*) in the Far East. Abstracts of Symposium Papers. *Increasing of Productivity of Game Management. Int. Cong. Game Biologists* (Moscow), pp. 92–94.

Akeley, Carl E. (1912). Elephant hunting in equatorial Africa with rifle and camera. *Nat. Geogr. Mag.* (Washington, D.C.), vol. 23, pp. 779–810.

Akeley, Carl E. (1923). Gorillas—real and mythical. *Nat. Hist.* (New York), vol. 23 (5), pp. 29–47.

Akimushkin, I. I. (1965). *Cephalopods of the seas of the U.S.S.R.* Jerusalem (Israel Program for Scientific Translations), 223 pp.

Alexander, W. B. (1955). *Birds of the ocean: a handbook for voyagers*. London, 282 pp.

Allan, J. (1948). A rare giant squid. *Aust. Mus. Mag.* (Sydney), vol. 9, pp. 306–308.

Allen, Glover M. (1916). The whalebone whales of New England. *Mem. Boston Soc. Nat. Hist.*, vol. 8, No. 2, pp. 108–322.

Allen, Glover M. (1936). Zoological results of the George Vanderbilt African Expedition of 1934. Part 2. The Forest elephant of Africa. *Proc. Acad. Nat. Sci. Phila.*, vol. 88, pp. 15–44.

Allen, Glover M. (1942). *Extinct and vanishing mammals of the Western Hemisphere with marine species of all oceans*. Am. Comm. Inter. Wildl. Protection, Spec. Publ. 11, 620 pp.

Allen, J. A. (1880). *History of North American pinnipeds, a monograph of the walruses, sea-lions, sea-bears and seals of North America*. U.S. Geol. and Geogr. Surv. Terr., Misc. Publ. (Washington, D.C.), No. 12, pp. 16–785.

Amadon, Dean (1943). Bird weights and egg weights. *Auk*, vol. 60, pp. 221–234.

Amaral, Afranio do (1948). Serpentes gigantes. *Boletim do Museu Paraense*. E. Goeldi (Belem), vol. 10, pp. 211–237.

Anderson, Sydney and Jones, J. Knox (1967). *Recent mammals of the world. A synopsis of families*. New York, 452 pp.

Andrews, C. W. (1904). On the evolution of the Proboscidea. *Phil. Trans. Roy. Soc.*, vol. 196, pp. 99–118.

Andrews, Roy Chapman (1916). *Whale hunting with gun and camera*. London.

Andrews, Roy Chapman (1924). Living animals of the Gobi Desert. *Nat. Hist.* (New York), vol. 24, pp. 150–159.

Angot, Michel (1954). Notes sur quelques oiseaux de l'Archipel de Kerguelen. *Rev. Fr. Orn.* (Paris), vol. 24, pp. 123–127.

Anon. (1935). Fourth list of fishes in the Newfoundland fishing area. *Ann. Rep. Newfoundland Fish. Res. Lab. for 1934*, vol. 2 (3), p. 79.

Anon. (1935). Record proboscidean tusk. *Nat. Hist.* (New York), vol. 35, (4), p. 357.

Anon. (1942). Mbongo—mountain gorilla. *San Diego Zoonooz*, vol. 15, No. 4, pp. 3–4.

Anon. (1954). 152-year-old sturgeon caught in Ontario. *Comm. Fish. Rev.*, vol. 16, No. 9, p. 28.

Ash, Edward C. (1927). *Dogs: their history and development*. 2 vols. London, 778 pp.

Augusta, Josef and Burian, Zdenek (1966). *The age of monsters*. London, 79 pp.

Aymar, Gordon C. (1936). *Bird flight*. London, 234 pp.

Baerg, William J. (1958). *The tarantula*. Lawrence, Kansas, 88 pp.

Baikov, N. A. (1936). *Big game hunting in Manchuria*. London, 281 pp.

Bainbridge, R. (1958). The speed of swimming of fish as related to size and to the frequency and amplitude of tail beat. *J. Exp. Biol.*, vol. 35, pp. 109–133.

Baker, A. B. (1912). Notes on animals now, or recently living, in the National Zoological Park. *Smithson. Misc. Collections* (Washington D.C.), vol. 59, No. 9, 3 pp.

Baker, Samuel W. (1874). *Eight years in Ceylon*. London, 376 pp.

Baldwin, William C. (1863). *African hunting from Natal to the Zambesi, etc.* London, 451 pp.

Bandini, Ralph (1933). Swordfishing. *Calif. Fish and Game*, vol. 19, pp. 241–248.

Barabash-Nikiforov, I. I. (1938). Mammals of the Commander Islands and the surrounding seas. *J. Mamm.*, vol. 19, pp. 423–429.

Barabash-Nikiforov, I. I. (1962). *The sea otter*. Jerusalem (Israel Program for Scientific Translations).

Barbour, Roger W. (1950). Notes on banded bats. *J. Mamm.*, vol. 31, p. 350.

Barbour, Thomas (1926). *Reptiles and amphibians: their habits and adaptations*. Boston, 129 pp.

Barnes, T. Alexander (1923). *Across the great craterland to the Congo*. London.

Barrett, Charles (1931). Megascolides, the world's biggest earthworm. *Aust. Mus. Mag.* (Sydney), vol. 4, No. 7, pp. 227–230.

Barrett, J. H. and Yonge, C. M. (1965). *Collins pocket book to the seashore.* London 272 pp.

Bartlett, A. D. (1890). *Wild animals in captivity.* London, 371 pp.

Bartsch, P. (1917). Pirates of the deep—stories of the squid and octopus. *Rept. Smithson. Instn.* (Washington, D.C.), pp. 347–375.

Bates, Henry Walter (1863). *The naturalist on the River Amazon, etc.* London, 395 pp.

Baughman, J. L. (1955). The oviparity of the Whale shark, *Rhineodon typus etc. Copeia,* No. 1, pp. 54–55.

Beale, Thomas (1839). *The natural history of the sperm whale, to which is added a sketch of a South-Sea whaling voyage.* London.

Beatty, Clyde and Anthony, Edward (1965). *Facing the big cats.* London, 306 pp.

Beebe, William (1923). The leisurely sloth. *Bull. New York Zool. Soc.,* vol. 26, No. 1, pp. 12–16.

Beebe, William (1927). The vampire's bite. *Bull. New York Zool. Soc.,* vol. 30, pp. 113–115.

Beebe, William (1938). *Zaca venture.* London, 316 pp.

Belkin, D. A. (1961). The running speeds of the lizards *Dipsosaurus dorsalis* and *Callisaurus draconoides. Copeia,* No. 2, pp. 223–224.

Bell, W. D. M. (1923). *The wanderings of an elephant hunter.* London.

Benchley, Belle J. (1930). Experiences with elephant seals. *Parks and Recreation,* vol. 13, No. 5, pp. 317–320.

Benchley, Belle J. (1942a). Mbongo—1926–1942. *Parks and Recreation,* vol. 25, No. 9, pp. 377–380.

Benchley, Belle J. (1942b). *My friends the apes.* Boston.

Beneden, Pierre Joseph van (1889). *Histoire naturelle des cetaces des mers d'Europe.* Bruxelles.

Benedict, Francis G. (1936). *The physiology of the elephant.* Carnegie Instit., Washington, D.C. Pub. No. 474.

Benedict, Francis G. and Lee, Robert C. (1938). Further observations on the physiology of the elephant. *J. Mamm.,* vol. 19, No. 2, pp. 175–194.

Bere, Rennie (1966). *The African elephant.* London and New York, 96 pp.

Berg, Leo S. (1962–65). *The freshwater fishes of the U.S.S.R. and adjacent countries.* 3 vols. Jerusalem (Israel Program for Scientific Translations) 1,520 pp.

Berry, S. Stillman (1912a). A review of the cephalopods of western North America. *Bull. Bur of Fish.* (Washington, D.C.), vol. 30, pp. 263–336.

Berry, S. Stillman (1912b). *Notes on the occurrence of a giant squid off the California coast. Nautilus,* vol. 25, pp. 117–118.

Bertram, G. C. and Bertram, C. K. R. (1964). Manatees in the Guianas. *Zoologica* (New York), Issue 2, pp. 216–217.

Bigelow, Henry B. and Schroeder, William C. (1948). Fishes of the Western North Atlantic. *Mem. Sears Found. Mar. Res. Yale Univ.* (New Haven, Conn.) No. 1, pt. 1, 552 pp.

Bigourdain, Jacques and Prunier, Roger (1937). *Les mammifères sauvages de l'Ouest Africain et leur milieu.* Paris, 367 pp.

Bishoop, F. C. and Laake, E. W. (1919). The dispersion of flies in flight. *J. Econ. Ent.,* vol. 12, pp. 210–211.

Bishop, Sherman C. (1943). *Handbook of salamanders.* Ithaca, New York, 555 pp.

Blackmore, M. (1956). An occurrence of the mouse-eared bat, *Myotis myotis* Borkhausen, in England. *Proc. Zool. Soc. London,* vol. 127, pp. 201–203.

Blake, Charles H. (1947). *Wing flapping rates of birds. Auk,* vol. 64, pp. 619–620.

Blunt, David Enderby (1933). *Elephant.* London, 260 pp.

Bond, James (1929). The distribution and habits of the birds of the Republic of Haiti. *Proc. Acad. Nat. Sci. Phila.,* vol. 80, pp. 483–521.

Bond, James (1960). *Birds of the West Indies.* London, 256 pp.

Boulenger, E. G. (1936). *Apes and monkeys.* London, 235 pp.

Boulenger, George Albert (1897–98). *The tailless batrachians of Europe.* 2 vols. London, 376 pp.

Boulenger, George Albert (1912). *A vertebrate fauna of the Malay Peninsula.* Vol. 1 *Reptilia and Batrachia.* London, 294 pp.

Bourliere, François (1955). *The natural history of mammals.* London, 363 pp.

Bourlière, Francis and Verschueren, J. (1960). *Introduction a l'écologie des ongules du Parc National Albert.* Institut. des Parcs Nationaux du Congo Belge, Bruxelles.

Boyle, David (1929). Height in elephants. *J. Bomb. Nat. Hist. Soc.,* vol. 33, No. 2, p. 437.

Brander, A. Dunbar (1923). *Wild animals in central India.* London, 296 pp.

Brander, A. Dunbar (1931). An enormous estuarine crocodile (*C. porosus*). *J. Bomb. Nat. Hist. Soc.,* vol. 34, p. 584.

Brazenor, C. W. (1940). Locomotion in mammals. *Vic. Nat.,* vol. 57, No. 8, pp. 143–146.

Brazenor, C. W. (1962). Rediscovery of a rare Australian possum. *Proc. Zool. Soc. London,* vol. 139, p. 529.

Breland, Osmond P. (1963). *Animal life and lore.* New York and London, 388 pp.

Bridges, William (1946). The Belgian Congo's gift to the New York Zoological Society. *Animal Kingdom,* vol. 49, No. 5, pp. 158–164.

Brink, F. H. van den (1967). *A field guide to the mammals of Britain and Europe.* London, 221 pp.

Bristowe, William S. (1939–41). *The comity of spiders.* 2 vols. London, 560 pp.

Bristowe, William S. (1958). *The world of spiders.* London, 304 pp.

Brown, Barnum (1931). The largest known land tortoise. *Nat. Hist.* (New York), vol. 31, No. 2, pp. 186–188.

Brown, Joe David (1962). The monster fish of American rivers. *Sports Illus.*, vol. 17, No. 12, pp. 21–24.

Brown, Leslie (1970). *Eagles.* London and New York, 96 pp.

Brown, Leslie and Amadon, Dean (1968). *Eagles, hawks and falcons of the world.* 2 vols. London, 945 pp.

Brunn, Anton F. et al. (1956). *The Galathea deep sea expedition 1950–1952.* London, 296 pp.

Bryden, Henry Anderson (1936). *Wild life in South Africa.* London, 281 pp.

Buchanan, J. B. (1964). A comparative study of some features of the biology of *Amphiura filiformis* and *Amphiura chiajei* (Ophiuroidea) considered in relation to their distribution. *J. Mar. Biol. Ass. U.K.*, vol. 44, pp. 565–576.

Buchsbaum, Ralph (1955). *Animals without backbones. An introduction to the invertebrates.* Chicago, 405 pp.

Buchsbaum, Ralph and Milne, L. Y. (1960). *Living invertebrates of the world.* London, 303 pp.

Buckland, Francis T. (1900). *Curiosities of natural history* (3rd series). London, 353 pp.

Buckley, E. E. and Porges, N. (ed.) (1956). *Venoms.* Pub. No. 44 of American Association for the advancement of Science (Washington, D.C.), 467 pp.

Budker, Paul (1958). *Whales and whaling.* London, 182 pp.

Budker, Paul (1971). *The life of sharks.* London, 222 pp.

Burbridge, Ben (1928). *Gorilla. Tracking and capturing the ape-man of Africa.* London, 285 pp.

Burden, W. Douglas (1927). *Dragon lizards of Komodo.* New York and London, 221 pp.

Burne, E. C. (1943). A record of gestation periods and growth of trained elephant calves in the southern Shan States, Burma. *Proc. Zool. Soc. London*, vol. 133, p. 27.

Burr, Malcolm (1954). *The insect legion.* London, 336 pp.

Burton, Maurice (1965). *Systematic dictionary of mammals of the world.* London, 307 pp.

Burton, R. G. (1928). *Sport and wild life in the Deccan.* London, 282 pp.

Burton, R. G. (1953). The record Indian crocodile. *J. Bomb. Nat. Hist. Soc.*, vol. 34, pp. 1086–1088.

Butler, L. S. G. (1932). Studies in Australian spiders. *Proc. Roy. Soc. Vic.*, vol. 44, No. 2, pp. 103–117.

Cadenat, Jean (1936). Notes sur un céphalopode géant (*Architeuthis harveyi Verrill*) capturé dans le Golfe de Gascogne. *Bull. Mus. Hist. Nat.* (Paris), vol. 2, No. 8, pp. 277–285.

Caldwell, Norman (1937). *Fangs of the Sea.* London, 282 pp.

Camp, Sprague L. de and Camp, Catherine C. de (1968). *The day of the dinosaur.* New York, 286 pp.

Campbell, Dugald (1837). *Wanderings in wildest Africa.* London.

Cansdale, George W. (1955). *Reptiles of West Africa.* London, 104 pp.

Caras, Roger (1964). *Dangerous to man.* Philadelphia, 433 pp.

Carr, Archie (1952). *Handbook of turtles. The turtles of the United States, Canada and Baja California.* Ithaca, N.Y. and London, 542 pp.

Carr, Carlyle (1927). The speed of pronghorn antelope. *J. Mamm.*, vol. 8, No. 33, pp. 249–250.

Carrington, Richard (1958). *Elephants. A short account of their natural history, evolution and influence on mankind.* London, 272 pp.

Cavendish, Alfred E. J. (1894). *Korea and the sacred white mountain, being a brief account of a journey in Korea in 1891, etc.* London.

Chalmers, P. Mitchell (1911). On longevity and relative viability in mammals and birds; with a note on the theory of longevity. *Proc. Zool. Soc. London*, pp. 425–548.

Chapman, Abel (1908). *On safari. Big game hunting in British East Africa.* London, 340 pp.

Chasen, Frederick Nutter (1940). A handlist of Malaysian animals. A systematic list of the Malay Peninsula, Sumatra, Borneo and Java, including the adjacent small islands. *Bull. Raffles. Mus.* (Singapore), vol. 15, pp. 1–209.

Christy, Cuthbert (1924). *Big game and pygmies.* London, 325 pp.

Clark, Aisla M. (1962). *Starfishes and their relations.* Pub. British Natural History Museum, London, 119 pp.

Clarke, James (1969). *Man is the prey.* London, 272 pp.

Clarke, Malcolm R. (1962). *Multiductus physeteris* gen. et sp. nov.—a new *diphyllobothriid cestode* from a sperm whale. *J. Helminthology*, vol. 36, Nos. 1/2, pp. 1–10.

Clarke, Malcolm R. (1966). A review of the systematics and ecology of oceanic squids. *Adv. Mar. Bio.*, vol. 4, pp. 91–300.

Clarke, Robert (1955). A giant squid swallowed by a sperm whale. *Norsk. Hvalfangst-Tidende*, vol. 44, No. 10, pp. 589–593.

Clarke, Robert (1956). Sperm whales of the Azores. *Disc. Rept.* (London), vol. 28, pp. 237–298.

Clarke, W. J. and Robson, G. C. (1929). Notes on the stranding of giant squids on the north-east coast of England. *Proc. Malac. Soc. London*, vol. 18, pp. 154–158.

Clarke, W. J. (1933). Giant squid (new to science) at Scarborough. *Nat. Hull*, pp. 157–158.

Clausen, H. and Ipsen, E. J. (1970). *Farm animals.* London, 181 pp.

Clay, C. I. (1911). Some diving notes on cormorants. *Condor,* vol. 13, p. 138.

Cloudsley-Thompson, J. L. (1958). *Spiders, scorpions, centipedes and mites.* London, 226 pp.

Coates, C. W. et al. (1937). The electric discharge of the electric eel *Electrophorus electricus* (Linnaeus). *Zoologica* (New York), vol. 22, No. 1, pp. 1–31.

Cochran, Doris M. (1961). *Living amphibians of the world.* New York, 199 pp.

Colbert, Edwin H. (1962a). The weights of dinosaurs. *Amer. Mus. Novitates,* No. 2076, pp. 1–16.

Colbert, Edwin H. (1962b). *Dinosaurs: their discovery and their world.* London, 288 pp.

Comfort, Alex (1964). *Ageing: the biology of senescence.* London, 365 pp.

Conant, Roger and Hudson, Robert G. (1949). Longevity records for reptiles and amphibians in the Philadelphia Zoological Garden. *Herpetologica,* vol. 5, pp. 1–8.

Condry, R. (1954). The polecat in Wales. *Oryx,* vol. 2, pp. 238–240.

Conley, Clare (1956). Record giant in the Snake River. *Field & Stream,* vol. 61, No. 3, pp. 16–17.

Cooch Behar, Maharajah of (1908). *Thirty-seven years' big game shooting.* Bombay, 461 pp.

Coolidge, Harold J. (1936). Zoological results of the George Vanderbilt African Expedition of 1934. Part 4. Notes on four gorillas from the Sanga River region. *Proc. Acad. Nat. Sci. Phila.,* vol. 88, pp. 479–501.

Corbett, Jim (1948). *The man-eating leopard of Rudra-prayag.* New York and Bombay

Corse, J. (1799). Observations on the manners, habits and natural history of the elephant. *Phil. Trans. Roy. Soc. London,* vol. 89, pt. 1, pp. 31–328.

Cotts, H. B. (1961). Scientific results of an inquiry into the ecology and economic status of the Nile crocodile (*Crocodilus niloticus*) in Uganda and Northern Rhodesia. *Trans. Zool. Soc. London,* vol. 29, No. 4, pp. 211–336.

Court, Alfred (1954). *Wild circus animals.* London, 192 pp.

Cousteau, Jacques-Y. and Dumas, Frederick (1953). *The silent world.* London.

Couturier, Marcel A. J. (1954). *L'ours brun,* Ursus arctos L. Grenoble, 904 pp.

Crandall, Lee S. (1964). *Management of wild mammals in captivity.* Chicago and London, 761 pp.

Crile, George (1941). *Intelligence, power and personality.* New York, 342 pp.

Crofton, H. D. (1966). *Nematodes.* London, 160 pp.

Cronwright-Schreiner, S. C. (1925). *The migrating springbucks of South Africa.* London, 140 pp.

Cross, H. and Fischer, P. (1862). Nouveaux documents sur les céphalopodes. *J. Conch* (Paris), vol. 10, pp. 124–140.

Crowcroft, Peter (1956). On the life span of the Common shrew (*Sorex araneus* L.). *Proc. Zool. Soc. London,* vol. 127, pp. 285–292.

Cumming, Roualeyn G. (1850). *Five years of a hunter's life in the interior of South Africa.* 2 vols. London, 756 pp.

Curran, C. H. (1945). *Insects of the Pacific world.* New York, 317 pp.

Dakin, William John (1934) *Whalemen adventurers.* Sydney.

Dance, S. Peter (1966). *Shell collection: an illustrated history.* London, 346 pp.

Dance, S. Peter (1969). *Rare shells.* London, 128 pp.

Daniel, William B. (1812). *Rural sports.* 4 vols. London.

David, Armand (1875). *Journal de mon troisieme voyage d'exploration dans l'empire Chinois.* 2 vols. Paris.

Davies, David H. (1964). *About sharks and shark attack.* Pietermaritzburg, 237 pp.

Davis, Malcolm (1950). Hybrids of the polar and Kodiak bears. *J. Mamm.,* vol. 31, No. 4, pp. 449–450.

Day, Francis (1880–84). *The fishes of Great Britain and Ireland.* 2 vols. London, 724 pp.

Dementev, J. et al. (1966–69). *The birds of the Soviet Union.* 4 vols. Jerusalem (Israel Program for Scientific Translations).

Denis, Armand (1964). *Cats of the world.* London, 118 pp.

Deraniyagala, P. E. P. (1939). *The tetrapod reptiles of Ceylon. Vol. 1. Testudinates and crocodilians.* Colombo Nat. Mus., Ceylon, 161 pp.

Deraniyagala, P. E. P. (1951). *Elephas maximus, the elephant of Ceylon.* Colombo Nat. Mus., Ceylon, vol. 1, pp. 1–48.

Deraniyagala, P. E. P. (1955). *Some extinct elephants, their relatives and the two living species.* Colombo Nat. Mus., Ceylon, 161 pp.

Devoe, Alan (1954). *This fascinating animal world.* London, 303 pp.

Dewar, John M. (1924). *The bird as a diver.* London, 173 pp.

Dice, Lee R. (1945). Minimum intensities of illumination under which owls find dead prey by sight. *Amer. Nat.,* vol. 70, pp. 385–416.

Dinsdale, T. (1966). *The leviathans.* London, 219 pp.

Ditmars, Raymond (1960). *Snakes of the world.* New York, 207 pp.

Donisthorpe, H. (1927). *British ants: their life-history and classification.* London, 379 pp.

Donisthorpe, H. (1936). The oldest insect on record. *Mammalia* (Paris), vol. 18, pp. 231–236.

Dorst, Jean (1962). *The migration of birds.* London, 476 pp.

Dorst, Jean and Dandelot, Pierre (1970). *A field guide to the larger mammals of Africa*. London, 287 pp.

Dowling, Herndon G. (1961). How old are they and how big do they grow? *Animal Kingdom*, vol. 64. No. 6, pp. 171–175.

Droscher, Vitus B. (1965). *The mysterious sense of animals*. London, 255 pp.

Droscher, Vitus B. (1969). *The magic of the senses*. London, 298 pp.

Dubar, J. (1828). *Osteographie de la baleine echouée à l'est du port d'Ostende, le 4 Novembre 1827; procédée d'une notice sur la découverte et la dissection du cétacé*. Bruxelles, 61 pp.

Du Chaillu, Paul P. (1861). *Exploration and adventures in equatorial Africa*. London, 479 pp.

Dukes, H. H. (1955). *The physiology of domestic animals*. London, 721 pp.

Dunn, Emmett R. (1944). *Los generos de anfibios y reptiles de Colombia*. Pt. III. *Caldasia*, pp. 155–224.

D'Yakonov, A. M. (1968). *Sea stars (asteroids) of the U.S.S.R. seas*. Jerusalem (Israel Program for Scientific Translations), 183 pp.

Eason, E. H. (1964). *Centipedes of the British Isles*. London, 294 pp.

Eaton, E. S. (1910). Birds of New York. *Mem. New York State Mus.*, No. 12, pt. 1.

Einarsen, Arthur S. (1948). *The pronghorn antelope and its management*. Wildl. Management Instit. (Washington, D.C.), 238 pp.

Ellis, Arthur E. (1925). *British snails: a guide to the non-marine gastropods of Great Britain and Ireland, Pleistocene to recent*. London, 298 pp.

Endean, R. (1964). Venomous cones. *Aust. Mus. Mag.* (Sydney), vol. 14, No. 12, pp. 400–403.

Evans, G. H. (1910). *Elephants and their diseases*. Rangoon, 343 pp.

Faber, F. (1826). *Ueber das leben hochnordischen Vogel*. Leipzig.

Fairley, N. H. and Splatt, B. Venom yields in Australian poisonous snakes. *Med. J. Aust.* (16th March 1929), pp. 1–10.

Fawcett, Percy Herbert (1953). *Exploration Fawcett*. London, 312 pp.

Feder, Howard M. and Christensen, Aage Moller (1966). Aspects of asteroid biology. In: *Physiology of Echinodermata* (ed. Boolootian, Richard A.). New York, London and Syndey, pp. 87–128.

Fell, H. Barraclough (1966). The ecology of Ophiuroids. In: *Physiology of Echinodermata*. New York, London and Sydney, pp. 129–144.

Figuier, Louis (1892). *Mammalia: their various form and habits*. Paris, London and Melbourne, 605 pp.

Filipek, Karl (1934). Aus der wildschatzkammer des fernen ostens. In: *Deutsches weidwerk und jagd in uberseeischen landern* (ed. Kaiser-Verlag B. Leipa). Prague, Vienna and Leipzig.

Firth, Frank E. (1940). Giant lobsters. *New Eng. Nat.*, No. 9, pp. 84–87.

Fischer, P. (1881). Cetacés du sud-ouest de la France. *Actes Soc. Linn. Bordeaux*, vol. 35 (Ser. No. 5).

Fisher, Edna M. (1939). Habits of the southern sea otter. *J. Mamm.*, vol. 20, No. 1, pp. 21–36.

Fisher, James and Petersen, Roger (1964). *The world of birds: a comprehensive guide to general ornithology*. London, 288 pp.

Fisher, James et al. (1969). *The red book*. London, 368 pp.

Fitter, Richard (1968). *Vanishing wild animals of the world*. London.

Fletcher, H. O. (1958). Marine giants past and present. *Aust. Mus. Mag.* (Sydney), vol. 12, No. 9, pp. 300–305.

Fletcher, H. O. (1959). A giant marine reptile from the Cretaceous rocks of Queensland. *Aust. Mus. Mag.* (Sydney), vol. 13, No. 2, pp. 47–49.

Fletcher, H. O. (1960). Turtles of the past. *Aust. Mus. Mag.* (Sydney), vol. 13, No. 6, pp. 191–195.

Flower, Stanley S. (1925). Contributions to our knowledge of the duration of life in vertebrate animals. Pt. I Fishes, p. 247; Pt. II Batrachians, p. 269; Pt. III Reptiles, p. 911; Pt. IV Birds, p. 1365. *Proc. Zool. Soc. London*.

Flower, Stanley S. (1931). Contributions to our knowledge of the duration of life in vertebrate animals. Pt. V Mammals, p. 145. *Proc. Zool. Soc. London*.

Flower, Stanley S. (1935). Further notes on the duration of life in animals. Pt. I Fishes, p. 265. *Proc. Zool. Soc. London*.

Flower, Stanley S. (1936). Further notes on the duration of life in animals. Pt. II Amphibians, p. 369. *Proc. Zool. Soc. London*.

Flower, Stanley S. (1937). Further notes on the duration of life in animals. Pt. III Reptiles, p. 1. *Proc. Zool. Soc. London*.

Flower, Stanley S. (1938). Further notes on the duration of life in animals. Pt. IV Birds, p. 195. *Proc. Zool. Soc. London*.

Flower, Stanley S. (1947–48). Further notes on the duration of life in animals. Pt. V The alleged and actual ages to which elephants live, p. 680. *Proc. Zool. Soc. London*.

Foa, Edouard (1899). *After big game in Central Africa, etc*. London, 330 pp.

Foran, W. Robert (1958). *A breath of the wilds*. London, 206 pp.

Forbush, E. H. (1922). Some underwater activities of certain waterfowl. *Bull. Mass. Agr.*, No. 8, p. 49.

Ford, E. B. (1951). *British butterflies*. London, 32 pp.

Ford, E. B. (1955). *Moths*. London, 266 pp.

François, Donald D. (1960). Freshwater crayfishes. *Aust. Mus. Mag.*, vol. 13, No. 7, pp. 217–221.

Fraser, Francis C. (1934). *Report on cetacea stranded on* the British coasts from 1927 to 1932. Pub. British Natural History Museum, London, No. 11, 41 pp.

Fraser, Francis C. (1946). *Report on cetacea stranded on the British coasts from 1933 to 1937.* Pub. British Natural History Museum, London, No. 12, 56 pp.

Fraser, Francis C. (1953). *Report on cetacea stranded on the British coasts from 1938 to 1947.* Pub. British Natural History Museum, London, No. 13, 56 pp.

Frost, Nancy (1934). Notes on a giant squid (*Architeuthis* sp.) captured at Dildo, Newfoundland in December 1933. *Rept. Newfoundland Fish. Comm.*, vol. 22, pp. 100–114.

Gaetke, H. (1895). *Heligoland: an ornithological observatory.* Edinburgh.

Gandar Dower, K. C. (1938). Racing cheetahs: the greyhounds of the East. *Indian wild life* (Lucknow), vol. 3, No. 2, pp. 62–65.

Garretson, Martin S. (1938). *The American bison, etc.* Pub. New York Zool. Soc., 254 pp.

Gatti, Attilio (1938). *Great mother forest.* London, 319 pp.

Gawn, R. W. L. (1948). Aspects of the locomotion of whales. *Nature, London*, vol. 161, No. 4080, pp. 44–46.

Gerard, Jules (1856). *Lion hunting and sporting life in Algeria.* London.

Gilliard, E. T. (1958). *Living birds of the world.* London, 400 pp.

Gironière, Paul de la (1854). *Twenty years in the Philippine Islands.* London.

Goetsch, W. (1940). *Vergleichende biologie de insektenstadten.* Leipzig.

Gosse, Philip Henry (1862). *The romance of natural history* (1st series). London, 361 pp.

Gosse, Philip Henry (1886). *The romance of natural history* (2nd series). London, 353 pp.

Gould, Rupert T. (1930). *The case for the sea-serpent.* London, 291 pp.

Gray, James (1968). *Animal locomotion.* London, 479 pp.

Gray, John Edward (1866). *Catalogue of the seals and whales in the British Museum.* Pub. British Natural History Museum, London, 402 pp.

Green, Lawrence (1958). *South African beachcomber.* Cape Town, 244 pp.

Greenewalt, Crawford H. (1960). *Dimensional relationships for flying animals.* Delaware.

Greenewalt, Crawford H. (1960b). *Hummingbirds.* Pub. Amer. Mus. Nat. Hist. New York, 250 pp.

Greenway, James C. (1967). *Extinct and vanishing birds of the world.* New York, 518 pp.

Grinnell, J. et al. (1937). *Fur-bearing mammals of California.* 2 vols. Berkeley, 777 pp.

Grogan, E. S. and Sharp, A. S. (1900). *From the Cape to Cairo, etc.* London, 377 pp.

Grzimek, Bernhard (1963). *Twenty animals, one man.* London, 197 pp.

Grzimek, Bernhard (1970). *Among animals of Africa.* 368 pp.

Gromier, E. (1936). *La vie des animaux sauvages d'Afrique.* Paris, 343 pp.

Gudger, E. W. (1915). On the occurence in the Southern Hemisphere of the basking or bone shark, *Cetorhinus maximus. Sci.*, N.S., vol. 42, No. 1088, pp. 653–656.

Gudger, E. W. (1934a). The geographical distribution of the whale-shark (*Rhineodontypus*). *Proc. Zool. Soc. London*, pp. 863–893.

Gudger, E. W. (1934b). The largest freshwater fishes—the giant sturgeons of the world. *Nat. Hist.* (New York), vol. 34, pp. 282–286.

Gudger, E. W. (1936). From atom to colossus. *Nat. Hist.* (New York), vol. 36, pp. 27–30.

Gudger, E. W. (1938). Tales of attacks by the ocean gladiator (*Xiphias gladius*) on dories. *Nat. Hist.* (New York), vol. 41, pp. 128–137.

Gudger, E. W. (1940a). Whale sharks rammed by ocean vessels. *New Eng. Nat.*, vol. 7.

Gudger, E. W. (1940b). The alleged pugnacity of the swordfish and the spearfishes as shown by their attacks on vessels. *Mem. Roy. Asiatic Soc. Bengal*, vol. 12, No. 2, pp. 215–315.

Gudger, E. W. (1941). The quest for the smallest fish. *Nat. Hist.* (New York), vol. 43, No. 4, pp. 216–223.

Gudger, E. W. (1942). The giant fishes of North America. *Sci. Mon.*, vol. 49, pp. 115–121.

Gudger, E. W. (1943). The giant freshwater fishes of South America. *Sci. Mon.*, vol. 57, pp. 500–513.

Gudger, E. W. (1944). The giant freshwater perch of Africa. *Sci. Mon.*, vol. 58, pp. 269–272.

Gudger, E. W. (1945a). Giant freshwater fish of Europe. *Field* (Aug.).

Gudger, E. W. (1945b). The giant freshwater fishes of Asia. *J. Bomb. Nat. Hist. Soc.*, vol. 45, No. 3, pp. 1–17.

Gudger, E. W. (1948). The basking shark, *Cetorhinus maximus*, on the North Carolina coast. *J. Elisha Mitchell Sci. Soc.*, vol. 64, No. 1.

Gudger, E. W. (1953). What ultimately terminates the life span of the whale shark *Rhineodon typus? J. Bomb. Nat. Hist. Soc.*, vol. 51, pp. 879–881.

Guggisberg, C. A. W. (1961). *Simba: the life of the lion.* London, 309 pp.

Guggisberg, C. A. W. (1966). *S.O.S. Rhino.* London, 174 pp.

Gurney, J. H. (1899). Comparative ages to which birds live. *Ibid.*, pp. 19–42 (Jan.).

Gurney, Robert (1950). The lobster. *Illus. Lond. News* (30th Sept.), p. 14.

Hagenbeck, Carl (1910). *Beasts and men.* London, 299 pp.

Haldane, R. C. (1907). Whaling in Scotland. *Ann. Scott. Nat. Hist.*, No. 59, pp. 130–137; No. 61, pp. 10–15.

Halstead, Bruce W. (1959). *Dangerous marine animals.* Cambridge (Maryland), 146 pp.

Hamilton, H. E. (1949). Weight, etc. of elephant seal. *Nature, London*, vol. 163, No. 4144, p. 536.

Harmer, Sidney F. (1927). *Report on cetacea stranded on the British coasts from 1913 to 1926.* Pub. British Natural History Museum, London, No. 10, 91 pp.

Harper, Francis (1945). *Extinct and vanishing mammals of the world.* Spec. Pub. 12 Amer. Comm. Int. Wild Life Protection. New York, 850 pp.

Harris, C. J. (1968). *Otters: a study of the recent Lutrinae.* London, 397 pp.

Harris, W. Victor (1961). *Termites, their recognition and control.* London, 187 pp.

Harvey, M. (1874). Gigantic cuttlefishes in Newfoundland. *Ann. Mag. Nat. Hist.*, Ser. 4, vol. 13, pp. 67–70.

Heck, L. (1929). Merkwurdige todesuraache eines straubes. *Zoolog. garten* (N.F.) (Leipzig), vol. 1, p. 335.

Hediger, Heini (1970). *Man and animal in the zoo.* London, 303 pp.

Heezen, Bruce C. (1957). Whales entangled in deep-sea cables. *Deep-Sea Res.* (London), vol. 4, pp. 105–115.

Heldt, J. H. (1948). Observations sur un ponte d'*Octopus vulgaris* Limk. *Bull. Soc. Sci. Nat. Tunisie*, vol. 1, pp. 87–90.

Helm, Thomas (1962). *Shark! Killer of the sea.* London, 190 pp.

Henry, Thomas R. (1958). *The strangest things in the world.* Washington, D.C., 223 pp.

Herrick, F. H. (1911). Natural history of the American lobster. *Bull. Bur. Fish.* (Washington, D.C.), vol. 29, pp. 149–408.

Herre, A. W. (1927). *Gobies of the Philippines and the China Sea.* New York.

Hertel, Heinrich (1966). *Structure, form, movement.* New York, 251 pp.

Heuvelmans, Bernard (1958). *On the track of unknown animals.* London, 558 pp.

Heuvelmans, Bernard (1968). *In the wake of the sea-serpents.* New York, 645 pp.

Hevery, G. F. and Hems, J. (1948). *The goldfish.* London.

Hewett, John Prescott (1938). *Jungle trails in northern India.* London.

Hildebrand, Milton (1959). Motions of the running cheetah and horse. *J. Mamm.*, vol. 40, pp. 481–495.

Hill, W. C. Osman et al. (1953). *The elephant in east Central Africa.* London and Nairobi, 150 pp.

Hittell, T. H. (1860). *The adventures of James Capen Adams, mountaineer and grizzly bear hunter of California.* Boston, 378 pp.

Holder, Charles Frederick (1886). *Marvels of animal life.* London, 240 pp.

Home, Everard (1809). An anatomical account of the *Squalus maximus*, etc. *Phil. Trans. Roy. Soc. London*, vol. 98, pp. 206–220.

Hooper, J. H. D. and Hooper, W. M. (1965). Longevity of horseshoe bats in Britain. *Proc. Zool. Soc. London*, vol. 145, pp. 146–147.

Hooton, Ernest Albert (1942). *Man's poor relations.* New York, 412 pp.

Hornaday, William T. (1889). The extermination of the American bison, with a sketch of its discovery and life history. *Ann. Rept. U.S. Nat. Mus.* (Washington, D.C.) for 1887, pp. 367–548.

Hornaday, William T. (1923). The real height of Jumbo. *Bull. New York Zool. Soc.*, vol. 26, No. 1, pp. 3–4.

Horring, R. (1919). Fugle. l. Andefugle og honsefugle. *Danmarks Fauna* (København), Nr. 23.

Howard, E. (1952). The prehistoric avifauna of Smith Creek Cave, Nevada with a description of a new gigantic raptor. *Bull. Southern Calif. Acad. Sci.*, vol. 51, pp. 50–54.

Howarth, T. H. (1967). Expensive butterflies. *Animals* (July).

Howell, A. Brazier (1944). *Speed in animals, etc.* Chicago, 270 pp.

Hoyt, J. S. Y. (1941). High speed attained by *Cnemidophorus sexlineatus. Copeia*, No. 3, p. 280.

Hundley, Gordon (1934). Statistics of height increments of Indian calf elephants. *Proc. Zool. Soc. London*, pp. 697–698.

Hurrell, H. G. (1968). *Pine martens.* Forestry Comm.: Forest Record No. 64, H.M. Stationery Office, 23 pp.

Ichihara, T. (1961). Blue whales in the waters around Kerguelen Island. *Norwegian Whal. Gaz.* (Oslo), vol. 50, No. 1, pp. 1–22.

Idriess, Ion L. (1946). *In crocodile land.* Sydney and London, 241 pp.

Idyll, C. P. (1965). *Abyss.* London, 396 pp.

International whaling statistics (1930–   ). Ed. by Comm. Whal. Stat. appointed by Norwegian Gov. Oslo.

Jackson, Frederick G. (1899). *A thousand days in the Arctic, etc.* 2 vols. London and New York.

Jenkins, J. Travis (1942). *The fishes of the British Isles, both freshwater and salt.* London, 408 pp.

Johnson, O. W. and Buss, I. O. (1967). Molariform teeth of male African elephants in relation to age, body dimensions and growth. *J. Mamm.*, vol. 46, pp. 373–384.

Jones, C. J. (1899). *Buffalo Jones' forty years of adventure.* London.

Jones, Marvin L. (1968). Longevity of primates in captivity. *Intl. Zoo Year Book No. 8*, pp. 183–192. Pub. Zool. Soc. London.

Jordan, David Starr and Evermann, Barton W. (1896). *The fishes of North and Middle America.* Washington, D.C.

Kaestner, Alfred (1968). *Invertebrate zoology.* New York, London and Sydney.

Kerr, Alex (1957). *No bars between.* London, 215 pp.

King, Judith (1964). *Seals of the world*. Pub. British Natural History Museum, London, 154 pp.

King, W. Ross (1866). *The sportsman and naturalist in Canada, etc.* London, 334 pp.

Kinghorn, J. R. (1930). What is the life span of a bird? *Aust. Mus. Mag.* (Sydney), vol. 4, No. 2, pp. 43–46.

Kirby, F. Vaughan (1895). *In haunts of wild game. A hunter-naturalist's wanderings from Kahlamba to Libombo.* London, 576 pp.

Kirk, T. W. (1880). On the occurrence of giant cuttlefish on the New Zealand coast. *Trans. N.Z. Inst.*, vol. 12, pp. 310–313.

Kirk, T. W. (1888). Brief description of a new species of large decapod (*Architeuthis longimanus*). *Trans. N.Z. Inst.*, vol. 20. pp. 34–39.

Klauber, Laurence M. (1956). *Rattlesnakes, their habits, life histories and influence on mankind.* 2 vols. Berkeley and Los Angeles, 1476 pp.

Klots, A. B. and Klots, E. B. (1959). *Living insects of the world.* London, 304 pp.

Knobel, Peter (1962). Blombergkroten im terrarium. *Die Aquarien-und-Terrarien-Zeitschrift* (Stuttgart), vol. 15, No. 8, pp. 247–249.

Kohn, Alan J. (1963). Venomous marine snails of the genus Conus. In: *Venomous and poisonous animals and noxious plants of the Pacific region* (ed. Keegan, H. L. and MacFarlane, W. V.). London, pp. 83–98.

Kojima, Tokuzo (1951). On the brain of the sperm whale (*Physeter catadon*). *Sci. Repts. Whales Res. Inst., Tokyo*, No. 6, pp. 49–72.

Kopstein, Felex (1927). Over het verslinden van menschen door *Python recticulatus. Tropische Natuur*, vol. 4, pp. 65–67.

Kurten, Bjorn (1968). *The age of the dinosaurs.* London, 255 pp.

Labitte, A. (1916) Longévité de quelques insectes en captivité. *Bull. Mus. Hist. Nat. Paris*, vol. 22, p. 105.

Lack, David (1960). The height of bird migration. *Brit. Birds*, vol. 53, pp. 5–10.

Lamont, James (1876). *Yachting in Arctic seas, or notes of five voyages of sport and discovery in the neighbourhood of Spitzbergen and Novaya Zemlya.* London.

Landsborough, A. (ed.) (1964). *A new dictionary of birds.* London, 927 pp.

Lane, Frank W. (1955). *Nature Parade.* London, 288 pp.

Lane, Frank W. (1957). *Kingdom of the octopus.* London, 287 pp.

Lankester, E. Ray (1870). *On comparative longevity in man and the lower animals.* London.

Lapage, Geoffrey (1951). *Parasitic animals.* Cambridge, 351 pp.

Laurie, A. H. (1933). Some aspects of respiration in blue and fin whales. *Disc. Repts.*, No. 7, pp. 363–406.

Laurie, E. M. O. (1946). The Coypu (*Myocastor coypus*) in Great Britain. *J. Animal Ecol.*, vol. 15, No. 1, pp. 22–34.

Laws, R. M. (1953). Elephant seal (*Mirounga leonina lin.*). 1. Growth and age. *Sci. Repts. Falkland Is. Dep. Surv.* (London), No. 8, 62 pp.

Laws, R. M. (1966). Age criteria for the African elephant, *Loxodonta a. africana. E. Afri. Wildl. J.*, vol. 4, p. 1.

Laws, R. M. et al. (1967). Estimating live weights of elephants from hind leg weights. *E. Afr. Wildl. J.*, vol. 5, pp. 105–106.

Lederer, Gustav (1944). Nahrungserwerb, Entwicklung, Paarung und Brutfursorge von *Python reticulatus* (Schneider). *Zool. Jahrbucher* (*Anatomie*) (Jena), vol. 68, pp. 363–398 (Leipzig).

Lee, Henry (1884). *Sea monsters unmasked.* London, 121 pp.

Leim, A. R. and Day, L. R. (1959). Records of uncommon and unusual fishes from eastern Canadian waters 1950–1958. *J. Fish. Res. Bd. Canada*, vol. 16, No. 4, pp. 503–514.

Lesueur, C. A. (1822). Description of a squalus, of very large size which was taken on the coast of New Jersey. *J. Acad. Nat. Sci. Phila.*, vol. 2, No. 2, pp. 343–352.

Leveson, H. S. (1877). *Sport in many lands.* 2 vols. London, 628 pp.

Lineaweaver, Thomas H. and Backus, Richard H. (1970). *The natural history of sharks.* London, 253 pp.

Locket, G. H. and Millidge, A. F. (1951–53). *British spiders.* 2 vols. London, 759 pp.

Lockley, R. M. (1970). The most aerial bird in the world. *Animals*, vol. 13, No. 1, pp. 4–7.

Longfield, Cynthia (1937). *The dragonflies of the British Isles.* London, 206 pp.

Loomis, H. F. (1964). *The millipedes of Panama* (*Diplopoda*). Fieldiana: *Zoology* (Chicago), vol. 47, No. 1, pp. 1–136.

Loveridge, Arthur (1945). *Reptiles of the Pacific world.* New York, 259 pp.

Lydekker, Richard (ed.) (1893–96). *The royal natural history.* 6 vols. London.

Lydekker, Richard (1907a). *The game animals of India, Burma, Malaya and Tibet, etc.* London, 409 pp.

Lydekker, Richard (1907b). The ears as a race character in the African elephant. *Proc. Zool. Soc. London*, pp. 380–403.

Lyell, Denis D. (1924). *The African elephant and its hunters.* London, 221 pp.

Lyon, George Francis (1884). *The private journal of Capt. G. F. Lyon of H.M.S. "Hecla" during the recent voyage of discovery under Capt. Parry.* London.

MacAskie, I. B. and Forrester, C. R. (1962). Pacific leatherback turtles (*Dermochelys*) off the coast of British Columbia. *Copeia*, No. 3, p. 646.

MacGinitie, G. E. and MacGinitie, N. (1949). *Natural history of marine animals.* New York, London and Toronto.

MacGinitie, G. E. and MacGinitie, N. (1968). *Natural history of marine animals* (2nd ed.). New York, London and Toronto.

Mackintosh, N. A. (1942). *The southern stocks of whalebone whales Disc. Repts.* (London), vol. 22, pp. 197–300.

Mani, S. B. (1960). Occurrence of the sea cow *Halicore dugong* (*erxl*) off the Saurashtra coast. *J. Bomb. Nat. Hist. Soc.*, vol. 57, pp. 216–217.

Marki, F. and Witkop, B. (1963). The venom of the Colombian arrow poison frog *Phyllobates bicolor. Separatum Experientia* (Basel), vol. 19, p. 329.

Marshall, N. B. (1954). *Aspects of deep sea biology.* London, 380 pp.

Matheson, C. (1950). *Longevity in the grey seal. Nature,* London, No. 166, pp. 73–74.

Matthews, Leonard Harrison (ed.) (1968). *The whale.* London, 287 pp.

Mayard, N. (1950). *Traité de zoologie.* Vol. 15 *Oiseaux.* Paris.

Maxwell, Gavin (1952). *Harpoon at a venture.* London, 272 pp.

Mayer, Charles (1922). *Trapping wild animals in Malay jungles.* London.

Mazak, Vratislav (1965). *Der tiger.* Wittenberg Lutherstadt, 162 pp.

McCormick, Leandor, J. (1949). The Pirarucu, or Arapaima, of the South American tropics. In: *Game fish of the world* (ed. Vesey-Fitzgerald, B. and LaMonte, F.). London, pp. 225–236.

McCoy, F. (1878–90). *Prodromus of the zoology of Victoria, etc.* Melbourne.

McCracken, Harold (1955). *The beast that walks like man.* New York, 224 pp.

McKeown, K. C. (1936). *Spider wonders of Australia.* Sydney, 270 pp.

Mead, Tom (1962). *The killers of Eden.* London and Sydney, 222 pp.

Meinertzhagen, Richard (1938). Some weights and measurements of large mammals. *Proc. Zool. Soc. London,* vol. 108, pp. 433–439.

Meinertzhagen, Richard (1955). The speed and altitude of bird flight (with notes on other animals). *Ibis,* vol. 97, No. 1, pp. 81–117.

Meise, W. (1954). Über Zucht Eintritt der Geschlechts reife zwischenmund weiterzug der Wachtel (*C. corturnix*). *Die Vogelwarte,* vol. 17, pp. 211–215.

Melland, Frank (1938). *Elephants in Africa.* London, 186 pp.

Mellen, I. (1940). *The science and mystery of the cat, etc.* New York and London, 275 pp.

Merriam, C. Hart (1918). Review of the grizzly and big brown bears of North America (genus *Ursus*) with description of a new genus *Vetularctos. N. Amer. Fauna,* vol. 41, pp. 1–36. Bur. Biol. Survey, U.S. Dept. Agric., (Washington, D.C.).

Millais, John G. (1906). *The mammals of Great Britain and Ireland.* 3 vols. London, 1047 pp.

Moore, Hilary B. (1966). Ecology of Echinoids. In: *Physiology of Echinodermata* (ed. Boolootian, R.A.). New York, London and Sydney, pp. 73–86.

Morris, R. C. (1940). Measurements and weights of elephant tusks. *J. Bomb. Nat. Hist. Soc.,* vol. 41, No. 3, p. 660.

Morrison-Scott, T. C. S. (1946). *Suncus etruscus* (Savi) in Africa. *Mammalia* (Paris), vol. 10, Nos. 3–4, p. 145.

Mortensen, T. (1927). *Handbook of the Echinoderms of the British Isles.* London, 471 pp.

Morton, J. E. (1967). *Molluscs.* London, 244 pp.

Mosauer, Walter (1935). How fast can snakes travel? *Copeia,* No. 1, pp. 6–9.

Murphy, Robert Cushman (1914). Notes on the sea elephant *Mirounga leonina* (Linne). *Bull. Amer. Mus. Nat. Hist.,* vol. 33, pp. 63–79.

Murphy, Robert Cushman (1936). *Oceanic birds of South America.* 2 vols. Pub. Amer. Mus. Nat. His., 1245 pp.

Murphy, Robert Cushman and Amadon, Dean (1953). *Land birds of America.* New York, Toronto and London, 230 pp.

Murray, Alexander (1874). *Capture of a gigantic squid at Newfoundland. Am. Nat.,* Salem 8, No. 2, p. 140.

Nelson, E. W. (1930). *Wild animals of North America.* Nat. Geogr. Soc. (Washington, D.C.) 254 pp.

Neumann, A. H. (1898). *Elephant hunting in east equatorial Africa, etc.* London, 455 pp.

Newman, L. Hugh (1965). *Hawk-moths of Great Britain and Europe.* London, 148 pp.

Newmark, Harris (1926). *Sixty years in southern California, 1853–1913, etc.* New York, 732 pp.

Nice, Margaret Morse (1954). Problems of incubation periods in North American birds *Condor,* vol. 56, pp. 173–197.

Nigrelli, R. F. (1959). Longevity of fishes in captivity with special reference to those kept in the New York Aquarium. In: *C.I.B.A. Found. Colloquia on Ageing.* Vol. 5: *The lifespan of animals* (ed. Wolstenholme, G. E. W. and O'Connor, Maeve) London pp. 212–226.

Nishiwaki, Masaharu (1950). On the body weight of whales. *Sci. Repts. Whales Res. Inst., Tokyo,* No. 4, pp. 184–209.

Noack, T. (1906). Eine zwergform des Afrikanischen elefanten. *Zool. Anz., Leipzig,* vol. 29, pp. 631–633.

Noback, Charles V. (1932). Report of the veterinarian. *36th Annual Rept., N.Y. Zool. Spc.,* pp. 40–42.

Norman, J. R. and Fraser, F. C. (1948). *Giant fishes, whales and dolphins.* London, 279 pp.

Norris, K.S. (ed.) (1966). *Whales, dolphins and porpoises.* Los Angeles, 789 pp.

Norwood, Victor (1964). *Jungle life in Guiana.* London, 180 pp.

Nuttall, Thomas (1832). *A manual of the ornithology of the United States and of Canada.* Cambridge, Mass.

Novikov, G. A. (1962). *Carnivorous mammals of the fauna of the U.S.S.R.* Jerusalem (Israel Program for Scientific Translations), 284 pp.

O'Connor, Thomas (1875). Capture of an enormous cuttle-fish off Boffin Island, on the coast of Connemara. *Zoologist* (2) vol. 10, pp. 4502–4503.

Offermann, P. P. (1953). *The elephant in the Belgian Congo.* In: *The elephant in East Central Africa.* A monograph (ed. Hill, W. C. Osman) pp. 114–125.

Ognev, S. I. (1962). *Mammals of the U.S.S.R. and adjacent countries.* Vol. III. *Carnivora.* Jerusalem (Israel Program for Scientific Translations) 641 pp.

Oldroyd, Harold (1964). *The natural history of flies.* London 324 pp.

Oliver, James A. (1963). *Snakes in fact and fiction.* New York 214 pp.

Oliver, James A. (1955). *The natural history of North American amphibians and reptiles.* Princeton, N.J., 359 pp.

Oliver, R. B. (1937). *Tasmacetus shepherdi:* a new genus and species of beaked whale from New Zealand. *Proc. Zool. Soc. London,* vol. 107, pp. 371–381.

Omura, Hideo (1950). On the body weight of sperm and sei whales located in the adjacent waters of Japan. *Sci. Repts. Whales Res. Instit., Tokyo,* No. 4, pp. 1–13.

Osborn, Henry Fairfield (1936–42). *Proboscidea. A monograph of the discovery, evolution, migration and extinction of the mastodonts and elephants of the world.* Amer. Mus. Nat. Hist., New York, 2 vols., 1675 pp.

Osgood, W. H. (1943). The mammals of Chile. Publ. *Field Mus. Zoo.,* Ser. 30, pp. 1–268.

Oswell, W. Cotton (1894). *South Africa fifty years ago.* Badminton Library of Sports and Pastimes (Big Game Shooting). London.

Ouwens, H. (1912). On a large *Varanus* species from the island of Komodo. *Bull. Jardin Botan. Buitenzorg* (2) vol. 6, p. 1.

Owen, Richard (1861). *Paleontology, or a systematic summary of extinct animals and their geological relations.* Edinburgh, 420 pp.

Owen, T. R. H. (1960). *Hunting big game with gun and camera in Africa.*

Packard, A. S. (1873). Colossal cuttlefishes. *Amer. Nat.,* vol. 7, pp. 87–94.

Parker, Eric (1943). *Oddities of natural history.* London, 228 pp.

Parker, H. W. (1946). *The dragon of Komodo. Zoo Life No. 3,* pp. 86–87 Bull Zool. Soc. of London.

Parkinson, John (1930). *The dinosaur in East Africa, etc.* London, 192 pp.

Patten, Robert A. (1940). Jessie joins her ancestors. *Parks and Recreations,* vol. 23 (5), pp. 200–202.

Pawson, David L. (1966). Ecology of Holuthurians. In: *Physiology of Echinodermata* (ed. Boolootian, R. A.). New York, London and Sydney.

Peacock, E. H. (1933). *A game book for Burma and adjacent territories.* London, 292 pp.

Pearson, Oliver T. (1953). Metabolism of hummingbirds. *Sci. Amer.* vol. 188, pp. 69–72.

Pennant, Thomas (1781). *History of quadrupeds.* 2 vols. London.

Peron, Francoise (1824). *Voyage de découvertes aux terres Australes sur les corvettes "Geographe", "Naturaliste" et la guelette "Casuarina" pendant les années 1800–1804, etc.* 4 vols. Paris.

Perry, Richard (1964). *The world of the tiger.* London, 263 pp.

Perry, Richard (1966). *The world of the polar bear.* London, 195 pp.

Perry, Richard (1967). *The world of the walrus.* London, 162 pp.

Perry, Richard (1970). *The world of the jaguar.* London.

Perry, J. S. (1952). The growth and reproduction of elephants in Uganda. *Uganda J.,* vol. 16, p. 51.

Perry, Gilbert P. (ed.) (1963). *Sharks and survival.* Boston 578 pp.

Pesson, P. (1959). *The world of insects.* London and New York, 204 pp.

Peterson, Roger T. and Editors of 'Life' (1964). *The Birds.* New York, 192 pp.

Peterson, Russell (1964). *Silent by night.* London, 227 pp.

Pi, Jorge Sabater (1965). La mayor rana del mundo, vive en nuestra provincia Africana de Rio Muni. *Iber. Rev. Sci. News* (Barcelona), vol. 43, No. 32, pp. 69–71.

Piccard, Jacques (1960). Man's deepest dive. *Nat. Georg. Mag.* (Washington, D.C.), vol. 118, No. 2, pp. 224–239.

Piers, Harry (1934). Accidental occurrence of the man-eater or Great white shark, *Carcharodon carcharias* (Linn.) in Nova Scotian waters. *Proc. Nova Scotian Inst. Sci.,* vol. 18, No. 3, pp. 192–203.

Pillai, N. G. (1941). On the height and age of an elephant. *J. Bomb. Nat. Hist. Soc.,* vol. 42, No. 4, pp. 927–928.

Pitman, C. R. S. (1925). The length attained by and the habits of the Gahrial (*G. gangeticus*). *J. Bomb. Nat. Hist. Soc.,* vol. 30, p. 703.

Pitman, C. R. S. (1931). *A game warden among his charges.* London.

Pitman, C. R. S. (1938). *A guide to the snakes of Uganda.* Kampala, 362 pp.

Pitman, C. R. S. (1942). *A game warden takes stock.* London, 287 pp.

Pitman, C. R. S. (1953). The elephant in Uganda. In: *The elephant in East Central Africa.* A monograph (Hill, W. C. Osman *et al.*), pp. 99–113.

Pixell-Goodrich, H. (1920). Determination of age in honey bees. *Quart. J. Micr. Sci.,* vol. 64, p. 191.

Pollock, F. T. and Thom, W. S. (1900). *Wild sports of Burma and Assam.* London.

Pollock, F. T. (1903). *Sporting days in Southern India.* London.

Poole, Trevor B. (1970). *Polecats* Forestry Comm.: Forest Record No. 76, H.M. Stationery Office.

Pooley, A. C. (1962). The Nile crocodile. *Lammergeyer*, vol. 2, pp. 1–55.

Pope, Clifford H. (1930). *Snakes alive and how they live.* New York, 238 pp.

Pope, Clifford H. (1939). *Turtles of the United States and Canada.* New York, 343 pp.

Pope, Clifford H. (1956). *The reptile world, etc.* New York, 325 pp.

Pope, Clifford H. (1961). *The giant snakes.* London, 290 pp.

Pope, Elizabeth C. (1958). Giant earthworms. *Aust. Mus. Mag.* (Sydney), vol. 12, No. 10, pp. 309–311.

Poynton, J. C. (1964). Amphibia of southern Africa. *Ann. Natal Mus.*, vol. 17, pp. 67–73.

Pretorius, P. J. (1947). *Jungle man.* London, 232 pp.

Pritchard, Peter (1967) *Living turtles of the world.* N.J., 208 pp.

Probst, R. T. and Cooper, E. L. (1954). Age, growth and productions of the Lake sturgeon (*Acipenser fulvescens*) in the Lake Winnebago region, Wisconsin. *Trans. Amer. Fish. Soc.*, vol. 84, pp. 207–227.

Proske, Roman (1957). *My turn next.* London, 208 pp.

Quoy, J. R. C. and Gaimard, J. P. (1832). *Zoologie du voyage d l'astrolabe sous les ordres du Capitaine Dumont d'Urville, pendant les années 1826–29.* Paris.

Rae, B. B. (1950). Description of a giant squid stranded near Aberdeen. *Proc. Malac. Soc. London*, vol. 28, pp. 163–167.

Rae, B. B. et al. (1957). Rare marine invertebrates recently found in the Scottish area. *Scott. Nat.*, vol. 69, pp. 1–4.

Rand, A. Stanley (1952). Jumping ability of certain anurans, with notes on endurance. *Copeia*, No. 1, pp. 15–20.

Raven, Henry C. (1931). Gorilla: the greatest of all apes. *Nat. Hist.* (New York), vol. 31, No. 3, pp. 231–242.

Raven, Henry C. (1946). Adventures in python country. *Nat. Hist.* (New York), vol. 55, pp. 38–41.

Ray, Carlton (1966). Stalking seals under Antarctic ice. *Nat. Geogr. Mag.* (Washington, D.C.), vol. 129, No. 1, pp. 54–65.

Ray, Grace Ernestine (1941). Big for his day. *Nat. Hist.* (New York), vol. 48, pp. 36–39.

Rees, W. J. and Lumbay, J. R. (1954). The abundance of octopus in the English Channel. *J. Mar. Biol. Ass. U.K.*, vol. 33, pp. 515–536.

Regan, Charles Tate (1911). *The freshwater fishes of the British Isles.* London, 287 pp.

Reid, G. K. (1957). External morphology of an embryo whale shark, *Rhineodon typus. Copeia*, No. 2, pp. 157–158.

Remington, C. L. (1950). The bite and habits of a giant centipede (*Scolopendra subspinipes*) in the Philippine Is. *Amer. J. Trop. Med.*, vol. 30, pp. 453–455.

Rensch, Bernhard and Harde, K. W. (1955). Growth-gradient of Indian elephants. *J. Bomb. Nat. Hist. Soc.*, vol. 52, pp. 841–851.

Reynolds, Vernon (1967). *The apes: the gorilla, chimpanzee, orangutan and gibbon—their history and their world.* London, 296 pp.

Rice, W. (1857). *Tiger shooting in India.* London.

Riedman, Sarah R. and Gustafson, Elton T. (1969). *Focus on sharks.* New York, London and Toronto, 256 pp.

Riess, B. H. et al. (1949). The behaviour of two captive specimens of the lowland gorilla, *Gorilla gorilla gorilla* (Savage and Wyman). *Zoologica* (New York), vol. 34, No. 13, pp. 111–117.

Riley, W. A. and Johannsen, O. A. (1932). *Medical entomology.* New York, 476 pp.

Ring, T. P. A. (1923). Elephant seals of Kerguelen land. *Proc. Zool. Soc. London*, pp. 431–443.

Risting, S. (1928). Whales and whale foetuses. Statistics of catch and measurements collected from the Norwegian Whalers' Association 1922–1925. *Rapp. Cons. Explor. Mer.*, vol. 50, pp. 1–122.

Ritchie, J. (1918). Occurrence of a giant squid (*Architeuthis*) on the Scottish coast. *Scott. Nat.*, vol. 32, pp. 133–139.

Ritchie, J. (1922). Giant squids on the Scottish coast. *Rept. Br. Ass. Advmt. Sci. 1921*, p. 423.

Rivière, B. B. (1930). *A history of the birds of Norfolk.* London, 296 pp.

Roberts, Austin (1951). *The mammals of South Africa.* Cape Town, 700 pp.

Robertson-Bullock, W. (1962). The weight of the African elephant, *Loxodonta africana. Proc. Zool. Soc. London*, vol. 138, pp. 133–135.

Robson, C. W. (1887). On a new species of giant cuttlefish stranded at Cape Campbell, June 30th 1886 (*Architeuthis kirkii*). "*Trans. Proc.*" *N.Z. Inst.*, vol. 19, pp. 155–157.

Rockstein (1959). The biology of ageing in insects. In: *C.I.B.A. Found. Colloquia on Ageing.* Vol. 5: *The lifespan of animals* (ed. Wolstenholme, G. E. W. and O'Connor, Maeve) London.

Roe, Frank Gilbert (1951). *The North American buffalo.* Toronto, 955 pp.

Roe, H. S. J. (1967). Seasonal formation of laminae in the fin whale. *Disc. Repts.*, vol. 35, pp. 1–30.

Romer, Alfred S. (1964). *Vertebrate paleontology.* Chicago and Toronto, 687 pp.

Roosevelt, Theodore (1914). *Through the Brazilian wilderness.* London 374 pp.

Roosevelt, Theodore and Heller, Edmund (1915). *Life histories of African game animals.* 2 vols. London, 798 pp.

Rooij, Nelly de (1915). *The reptiles of the Indo-Australian archipelago.* Vol. 1, Leiden.

Rose, Walter (1950). *The reptiles and amphibians of southern Africa.*

Rothschild, Lord (1962). *A classification of living animals.* London, 106 pp.

Roughley, T. C. (1937). *Wonders of the Great Barrier Reef.* Sydney, 279 pp.

Russell, F. S. (1970). *The Medusae of the British Isles.* 2 vols. London, 814 pp.

Ruud, Johan T. (1945). The surface structure of the baleen plates as a possible clue to age in whales. Hvalradets skrifter, *Sci. Res. Marine Biol. Res.,* Oslo, No. 23, pp. 460–463.

Rydzewski, W. (1962). Longevity list for birds. *The Ring* vol. 3 (33), pp. 147–152.

Savory, Theodore H. (1928). *The biology of spiders.* London, 376 pp.

Savory, Theodore H. (1945). *The spiders and allied orders of the British Isles.* London, 224 pp.

Savory, Theodore H. (1952). *The spider's web.* London, 154 pp.

Savory, Theodore (1966). Britain's most elusive spider. *Animals,* vol. 13, No. 1, pp. 500–501.

Sanderson, G. P. (1882). *Thirteen years among the wild beasts of India, etc.* London, 387 pp.

Sanderson, Ivan T. (1937). *Animal Treasure.* London, 325 pp.

Sanderson, Ivan T. (1958). *Follow the whale.* London, 423 pp.

Scammon, Charles M. (1874). *The marine mammals of the north-western coast of North America, etc.* San Francisco and New York, 319 pp.

Schaller, George B. (1963). *The mountain gorilla.* Chicago, 431 pp.

Schaller, George B. (1967). *The deer and the tiger.* Chicago and London, 370 pp.

Schaller, George B. (1968). Hunting behaviour of the cheetah in the Serengeti National Park, Tanzania. *E. Afr. Wildl. J.,* vol. 6, p. 95.

Scheffer, Victor B. (1958). *Seals, sea lions and walruses.* Oxford, 179 pp.

Scheffer, Victor B. and Rice, D. W. (1963). A list of the marine mammals of the world. *U.S. Fish. and Wildl. Ser. Spec. Sci. Rept.—Fish,* No. 431.

Scheithauer, Walter (1967). *Hummingbirds, flying jewels.* London, 176 pp.

Schmidt-Hoensdorf, F. (1930). *Tod eines Straubenhahnes durch eine verschluckte Modelliernadel. Zoolog. Garten (N.F.),* (Leipzig), vol. 24, pp. 104–105.

Schomburgk, Robert et al. (1847–48). *Reisen in British Guiana den Zahren 1840–44.* 3 vols. Leipzig.

Schroeder, William C. (1939). The Provincetown "sea serpent". *New Eng. Nat.,* No. 7, 2, pp. 1–2.

Schorger, A. W. (1955). *The passenger pigeon: its natural history and extinction.* Madison, Wisconsin 424 pp.

Schultz, Leonard and Stern, Edith (1948). *The ways of fishes.* New York, Toronto and London, 264 pp.

Scoresby, William (1820). *An account of the Arctic regions, with a history and description of the northern whale-fishery.* Edinburgh, 2 vols.

Seeley, H. G. (1886). *The freshwater fishes of Europe.* London 444 pp.

Serventy, D. L. (1957). The recovery of a South Australian shearwater in the Bering Sea. *South Aust. Ornith.,* vol. 22, No. 4, p. 56.

Shaw, Charles E. (1969). Longevity of snakes in North American collections as of 1 January, 1968. *Zoolog. Garten (N.F.),* (Leipzig), vol. 37, pt. 4/5.

Shields, G. O. (ed.) (1890). *The big game of North America.* Chicago, 575 pp.

Shortridge, G. C. (1934). *The mammals of South West Africa.* 2 vols. London, 779 pp.

Shufeldt, Robert W. (1915). Anatomical and other notes on the passenger pigeon (*Ectopistes migratorius*) lately living in the Cincinnati Zoological Gardens. *Auk,* vol. 32, pp. 29–41.

Sikes, Sylvia K. (1971). *The natural history of the African elephant.* London, 397 pp.

Simon, E. S. (1943). Life span of some wild animals in captivity. *J. Bom. Nat. Hist. Soc.,* vol. 44, pp. 117–118.

Simon, Noel and Geroudet, Paul (1970). *Last survivors.* London, 275 pp.

Sivertsen, Erling (1954). Blekksprut. *K. norske vidensk. Selsk. Arbok.*

Slijper, E. J. (1962). *Whales.* London, 475 pp.

Smith, Andrew (1829). Contributions to the natural history of South Africa, etc. *Zool. J. London,* pp. 442–448.

Smith, Jerome van C. (1843). *Natural history of the fishes of Massachusetts, etc.* Boston.

Smith, Malcolm (1964). *The British amphibians and reptiles.* London, 318 pp.

Smith, N. S. and Ledger, H. P. (1965). A method of predicting live weight from dissected leg weight. *J. Wildl. Mgmt.,* vol. 29, p. 504.

Smythies, E. A. (1942). *Big game shooting in Nepal.* London.

Sody, J. J. V. (1959). Das javanische Nashorn *Rhinoceros sondaicus,* historisch und biologisch. *Zeitschr. f. Saeugetierkunde,* vol. 24.

Sorell, George (1928). *The man before the mast.* London.

Soule, Gardner (1965). *The mystery monsters.* New York, 191 pp.

Sowerby, Arthur (1925). *A naturalist's note-book in China.* Shanghai, 270 pp.

Spinage, C. A. (1968). *The book of the giraffe.* London, 191 pp.

Sotavalta, Olavi (1947). *The flight tone of insects,* Helsinki.

Southern H. N. (ed.) (1964). *Handbook of British mammals.* Oxford, 465 pp.

Stanek, V. J. (1969). *The pictorial encyclopedia of insects.* London.

Stead, David G. (1964) *Sharks and rays of Australian seas.* London, Toronto, Melbourne and Sydney, 364 pp.

Steenstrup, Japettus (1962). *The cephalopod papers of Japettus Steenstrup* (ed. Volsoe *et al.*). Copenhagen, 333 pp.

Steinmetz, H. (1954). *Beitrage zur Geschichte unserer Kenntnisse vom See-elefanten* (*N.F.*), vol. 21, pt. 1/2, pp. 24–43.

Stenuit, R. (1968). *The dolphin, cousin to man.* London, 176 pp.

Step, Edward (1901). *Shell life, an introduction to the British mollusca.* London.

Step, Edward (1924). *Go to the ant, etc.* London, 276 pp.

Step, Edward (1932). *Bees, wasps, ants and allied insects of the British Isles.* London, 238 pp.

Stephen, A. C. (1950). Giant squid *Architeuthis* in Shetland. *Scott. Nat.* vol. 62, pp. 52–53.

Stephenson, J. (1930). *The Oligochaeta.* Oxford, 978 pp.

Sterndale, Robert A. (1884). *Natural history of the mammalia of India and Ceylon.* London, 540 pp.

Stevenson-Hamilton, J. (1947). *Wild life in South Africa.* London, 364 pp.

Stigand, Chauncy H. (1913). *Hunting the elephant in Africa.* London 364 pp.

Stokes, C. W. (1953). *Sanctuary.* Cape Town, 457 pp.

Storer, Douglas (1963). *Amazing but true animals.* Greenwich, Conn., 144 pp.

Stracey, P. D. (1963). *Elephant gold.* London, 223 pp.

Swaroop, S. and Grab, B. (1956). The snakebite mortality problem in the world. *Venoms* (ed. Buckley, E. E. and Porges, N.). Washington, D.C.

Swinton, W. E. (1965). *Fossil amphibians and reptiles.* Publ. British Natural History Museum, London, 133 pp.

Talbot, Lee Merrian (1959). *A look at threatened species: a report on some animals of the Middle East and South Asia which are threatened with extermination.* Fauna Preservation Society.

Tao, L. (1930). Notes on the ecology and the physiology of *Caudina chilensis* (Muller) in Mutsu Bay. *Proc. 4th Pacif. Sci. Cong.*, vol. 3, pp. 7–11.

Taylor, R. (1964). Giant cray, *Animals*, vol. 4, No. 5.

Taylor, W. L. (1952). The Polecat (*Mustela putorius*) in Wales. *J. Anim. Ecol.*, vol. 21, pp. 272–274.

Teare, S. P. (1936). Weights of lions. *Field*, London, vol. 167, No. 4355, p. 1444.

Tebble, Norman (1966). *British bivalve seashells.* Publ. British Natural History Museum, London, 212 pp.

Templeman, Wilfred (1963). Distribution of sharks in the Canadian Atlantic (with special reference to Newfoundland waters). *Fish. Res. Bd. Canada, Ottawa Bull. No. 140*, 77 pp.

Tennent, J. E. (1867). *The wild elephant and the method of capturing and taming it in Ceylon.* London.

Thomas, Richard (1965a). A new gecko from the Virgin Islands. *Quart. J. Florida Acad. Sci.*, vol. 28, No. 1, pp. 117–122.

Thomas, Richard (1965b). The genus *Leptotyphlops*

in the West Indies, etc. *Breviora*, No. 222. Mus. Comp. Zool. Harv. Univ., Cambridge, Mass.

Thomas, Richard (1966). A new Hispaniolan gecko. *Breviora*, No. 253, pp. 1–5. Mus. Comp. Zool. Harv. Univ., Cambridge, Mass.

Thompson, D'Arcy W. (1928). On whales landed at the Scottish whaling stations during the years 1908–1914 and 1920–1927. *Scot. Fish. Board Sci. Invest.*, No. 3, pp. 3–39.

Tillyard, R. J. (1917). *The biology of dragonflies.* Cambridge, 396 pp.

Timbs, John (1858). *Strange stories of the animal world.* London, 368 pp.

Tomilin, A. G. (1967). *Mammals of the U.S.S.R. and adjacent countries.* Vol. 9: *Cetacea.* Jerusalem (Israel Program for Scientific Translations).

Townsend, C. H. (1906). West Indian seal at the aquarium. *Science* (Lancaster), vol. 30, No. 763, p. 212.

Townsend, C. H. (1924). Northern elephant seal and the Guadalupe fur seal. *Nat. Hist.* (New York), vol. 24, pp. 566–577.

Travis, William (1961). *Shark for sale.* London, 181 pp.

Treus, V. D. and Lobanov, G. (1971). Acclimatisation and domestication of the Eland (*Taurotragus oryx*) at Askanya Nova Zoo. In: *Int. Zoo Year Book*, vol. 2, pp. 147–156.

Troughton, E. (1946). *The furred animals of Australia.* Sydney and London, 376 pp.

True, Frederick W. (1904). The whalebone whales of the western north Atlantic compared with those occurring in European waters, etc. *Smithson. Contrib. to Knowledge* (Washington, D.C.), vol. 33, 332 pp.

Tschudi, Johann Jacob von (1847). *Travels in Peru during the years 1838–42, etc.* London.

Ulmer, Frederick J. (1953). The greatest beast on earth. *America's First Zoo*, vol. 5, No. 3, pp. 3–6.

Verany, J. B. (1851). *Mollusques Mediterranéens. l. Cephalopodes.* Geneva, 132 pp.

Verrill, A. E. (1872). Marine fauna of Eastport, Me. *Bull. Essex Inst.*, vol. 3, No. 1, pp. 2–6.

Verrill, A. E. (1879–81). The cephalopods of the northeastern coast of America. *Trans. Conn. Acad. Arts. Sci.*, vol. 5, pp. 177–446.

Verrill, A. E. (1897a). A gigantic cephalopod on the Florida coast. *Am. J. Sci.*, Ser. 4, pp. 3, 79, 162–3 and 355–6.

Verrill, A. E. (1897b). The Florida monster. *Science*, (New York), vol. 5, pp. 393 and 476.

Verrill, A. H. (1937). *Strange reptiles and their stories.* London, Bombay and Sydney, 195 pp.

Verrill, A. H. (1938) *Strange fish and their stories.* London, 220 pp.

Vesey-Fitzgerald, B. and LaMonte, F. (1949). *Game fishes of the world.* London and Brussels, 446 pp.

Vladykov, V. D. and McKenzie, R. A. (1935). The marine fishes of Nova Scotia. *Proc. Nova. Scotian Inst. Sci.*, vol. 19, No. 1, pp. 17–113.

Waldon, C. W. (1950). The largest whale ever weighed. *Nat. Hist.* (New York), vol. 59, No. 9, pp. 393–399.

Walker, Ernest P. (1954). *The monkey book.* New York.

Walker, Ernest P. (1964). *Mammals of the world.* 3 vols. Baltimore, 2269 pp.

Wall, F. (1921). *The snakes of Ceylon.* Colombo, 581 pp.

Wall, F. (1926). The reticulated python. *J. Bomb. Nat. Hist. Soc.*, vol. 31, p. 558.

Ward, Rowland (1907). *Records of big game (Africa and Asia).* London, 326 pp.

Ward, Rowland (1928). *Records of big game (Africa and Asia).* London, 523 pp.

Ward, Rowland (1935). *Records of big game (Africa and Asia).* London, 408 pp.

Ward, Rowland (1962). *Records of big game (Africa).* London, 438 pp.

Wardle, R. A. and McLeod, J. A. (1952). *The zoology of tape worms.* Minnesota, 708 pp.

Wetmore, Alexander (1921). A study of body temperature of birds. *Smithson. Misc. Collections,* vol. 72, No. 12, Washington, D.C.

Wetmore, Alexander (1936). The number of contour feathers in Passeriform and related birds. *Auk,* vol. 53, pp. 159–169.

Wood, F. G. and Gennero, J. F. (1971). *An octopus trilogy.* Nat. Hist. New York (March), pp. 14–23, 24, 84–87.

Yerkes, Robert M. and Yerkes Ada W. (1929). *The great apes: a study of anthropoid life.* New Haven, Conn., 652 pp.

Young, J. (1944). Giant nerve-fibres. *Endeavour,* vol. 3, pp. 108–113.

Young, Stanley P. and Goldman, Edward A. (1946). *The Puma, mysterious American cat.* N. Amer. Wildl. Inst., Washington D.C., 2 vols.

Zahl, Paul A. (1959). Giant insects of the Amazon. *Nat. Geogr. Mag.,* vol. 115, No. 5, pp. 632–669.

TABLE 1—ANIMAL YOUNG

antelope—calf
bear—cub
beaver—kit
birds—fledgeling, nestling
bull—bullock
cat—kit, kitten, catling, puss
cattle—calf
chicken—chick
codfish—codling, sprag
cow—heifer
deer—fawn
dog—pup, whelp
duck—duckling
eagle—eaglet
eel—elver
elephant—calf
fish—fingerling or fry

fowl (domestic)—chick
fowl (wild)—flapper
frog—polliwog, tadpole
goat—kid
goose—gosling
grouse—cheeper
hare—leveret
hawk—eyas
hen—pullet
horse—foal, colt, filly
hippopotamus—calf
kangaroo—joey
lion—cub
mackerel—spike, blinker, tinker
owl—owlet
partridge—cheeper

pidgeon—squeaker, squab
pig—piglet, shoat, farrow, suckling
quail—cheeper
rabbit—bunny
rhinoceros—calf
rooster—cockerel
salmon—parr, smolt, grilse
shark—cub
sheep—lamb, lambkin
swan—cygnet
tiger—whelp
turkey—poult
whale—calf
younglet, youngling—animals generally
zebra—foal

TABLE 2—ANIMALS COLLECTIVELY

band of gorillas
bed of clams, oysters
bevy of quails, swans
brace of ducks
brood of chicks
cast of hawks
cete of badgers
charm of goldfinches
chattering of choughs
cloud of gnats
clowder of cats
clutch of chicks
clutter of cats
colony of rabbits, ants
company of widgeon
congregation of plovers
covert of coots
covey of quail, partridge
cry of hounds
down of hares
draft of fish
drift of swine
drove of cattle, sheep, pigs
exaltation of larks
flight of birds

flock of sheep, geese, ducks
gaggle of geese
gam of whales
gang of elks
grist of bees
head of curlews, elephants, horses, etc.
hive of bees
horde of gnats
husk of hares
kindle or kendle of kittens
knot of toads
labor of moles
leap of leopards
leash of greyhounds, foxes
litter of pigs
murder of crows
murmuration of starlings
muster of peacocks
mute of hounds
nest of vipers
nest, nide or nye of pheasants
pack of hounds, wolves, mules
pair of horses
plump of wildfowl

pod of whales, seals
pride of lions
rafter of turkeys
school of fish
sedge or siege of cranes, bitterns, herons
shoal of fish
skein of geese
skulk of foxes
sloth or sleuth of bears
sounder or singular of boars, swine
span of mules
spring of teals
stud of mares
swarm of bees
team of ducks, horses
tribe of goats
trip of goats
troup of kangaroos, monkeys
volery of birds
walk of snipe
watch of nightingales
wing of plovers
yoke of oxen

Index